D1499674

The History of Feudalism

A volume
in
THE DOCUMENTARY HISTORY
of
WESTERN CIVILIZATION

THE HISTORY
OF
FEUDALISM

edited by
DAVID HERLIHY

WALKER AND COMPANY
New York

THE HISTORY OF FEUDALISM

Copyright © 1970 by David Herlihy

First published in the United States of America in 1971
by the Walker Publishing Company, Inc.

Published simultaneously in Canada
by The Ryerson Press, Toronto.

Library of Congress Catalog Card Number: 71-126284
ISBN: 0-8027-2024-2

Printed in the United States of America

Volumes in this series are published in association
with Harper & Row, Publishers, Inc., from
whom paperback editions are available in Harper
Torchbooks.

Printed in the United States of America.

Contents

PART THREE: THE FEUDAL PRINCIPALITY

PART FOUR: CHIVALRY

Preface

In the concluding books of his *Spirit of the Laws* (1748), Charles
Louis de Secondat, sieur de Montesquieu, commented on the vast
numbers of records which had survived to illustrate the feudal
institutions of his native France. He compared them to "an immense expanse, a boundless ocean," and applied to them a quota-
tion from Ovid: "There were also no shores to this sea." Rapidly
shifting metaphors, he further affirmed that "all these frigid, dry,
insipid and hard writings must be read and devoured in the same
manner as Saturn is fabled to have devoured stones."

In contrast to Montesquieu, the modern editor of feudal documents may well pretend to find some jewels among the stones. But
there is no doubt that the sea is there. To keep this anthology
within a reasonable length, we have concentrated upon that period
which most historians consider to be the classic age of Western
feudalism. This is the early and central Middle Ages, from roughly
750 to about 1300, and especially the twelfth and thirteenth
centuries. We have not included documents from the long period
between the fourteenth and eighteenth centuries, during which
feudal institutions declined or were transformed. To do so would
have required illustrations of the complex social history of the late
medieval and early modern age. This would be a formidable task
for a single collection of sources, and these later changes are at all
events already illustrated in other volumes of this series. So also, we
have not included records directly bearing on the peasantry, the
towns, or the clergy, for the reason that the design of the series
gives abundant space to these groups in other volumes.

In Part One the documents chosen are meant to illustrate the
social and intellectual milieu of the feudal age or ages. Section II
provides illustrations of the basic institutions of feudalism—vassalage, the fief, and what has traditionally been called "private justice." In Part Three, on the feudal principality, the documents

illustrate the uses made of these institutions in at least some of the states of Europe, again especially in the twelfth and thirteenth centuries. The fourth and final part examines the self-image and the values of the warrior class through documents showing the character of chivalry.

In all these sections, the editor has attempted to give examples of the principal types of records which historians now use in their investigations of feudal society. He has therefore included not only laws and legal commentaries, private charters and administrative records, but also selections from chronicles, saints' lives, sermons, liturgical works, and imaginative literature. His hope is that they may together illustrate in concrete and human terms the relationships between men and men, and men and governments, which were at the heart of the feudal system. Some of the documents will be familiar to readers already acquainted with medieval history; the excuse for presenting them here is that they are so important in themselves, or so concise and clear in illustrating certain aspects of feudal society, that their presence is indispensable in a fairly rounded anthology. Most documents, familiar or not, have been given fresh translations. Many of them, to this editor's knowledge, have not before been rendered into English.

The editor would like to thank his wife, Patricia, who helped in many of the translations and generously gave him the benefit of her comments and criticisms concerning the selections and the introductory sections. Several of his former students—especially Stephen Weinberger, Jane Tibbits Schulenberg, and Jane Beitscher —pointed out to him some of the documents presented in this anthology. To them too he expresses his gratitude.

Madison, Wisconsin
August, 1969

General Introduction

Meanings

"Feudal" is a word which, over the centuries, has borne many shades of meaning and has been used in many ways by different writers. The term, or its immediate ancestor, seems first to have appeared in Burgundian charters from about 881, in the form *feos* or *feus*. There it conveys the sense of a kind of movable property, probably cattle, in which payments could be made. Philologists are not agreed concerning its origins, but a reputable opinion sets as its root a Frankish word (*fehu*), signifying possession or property. Also according to reputable opinion, the word is cognate with the modern German *Vieh*, or cattle.

The years in which the word first appeared, and still more the generations which followed, were for most areas of western Europe a time of profound disturbances. Northmen, Saracens, and Magyars struck at Europe from abroad, and at home lords great and small battled one another incessantly. It was also a period of flux, in which the terminology of the written sources, and the institutions and life they depicted, were subject to constant change. These shifts can be followed with particular detail in the abundant Latin charters of France and Spain. *Feos*, in the sense of movable property, disappears from the charters after the first decades of the tenth century. At the same time the term was acquiring different forms and a different meaning. The forms are *fevum, fevo, feo*, and others. The new meaning was a grant of land, still a form of payment but, as we shall see, much different from an unrestricted conveyance. It was used in this sense, in the form *fevum*, apparently for the first time in a charter from Maguelone in southern France, in 899. But such usage remained rare for the next hundred years.

From the eleventh century, Europe began to recover from the tumult of the tenth, and gradually achieved a new stability in its institutions. References to the land grant become far more frequent in the charters. From the end of the eleventh century, one of its variant forms, *feodum* or *feudum*, began to prevail over the others and eventually became the standard Latin term for what today we call the fief. At the same time, the records show a proliferation of other terms associated with feudalism—*vassus*, or vassal; *hominium* or *hommagium* for homage; *miles* in the unmistakable sense of knight; even titles such as *dominus*, lord, in reference to members of the knightly order and the new feudal nobility. Many of these terms were of course known before, but it remains accurate to say that the developed terminology of feudalism is primarily a product of the eleventh and twelfth centuries.

The word *feudum*, fief, was thus initially called to life to connote a concrete object—a piece of land, conveyed not absolutely but with conditions attached, the nature of which we shall later examine. The term hardly designated a full system of law, or of government, or of social relationships. The Middle Ages never knew that its society or its governments deserved to be called "feudal."

From the late eleventh century, western Europe further witnessed a true cultural and intellectual renaissance. Men seem obsessed with a passion for order, and in the Middle Ages they sought it not only in their religious beliefs and philosophical assumptions, but also in the laws and customs by which they were living. Jurists and lawyers, for example, assiduously studied the legal monuments of the ancient Roman world. Their new consciousness and skill helped the Church develop its own great system of canon law, and Roman legal concepts similarly influenced conceptions of lay authority.

The new jurisprudence affected feudal customs too. Practical problems of adjudication were making it abundantly clear that the written laws of antiquity or the decrees of princes did not comprehend all fundamental social institutions and practices. Beyond the written laws existed a great body of customs, and of those customs a significant part concerned personal relations, land tenures, vassalage, and the fief. In the twelfth and still more in the thirteenth century, lawyers, judges, and administrators, practical men more than scholars, set about codifying these regional customs; this anthology will later give several examples of their work. These codes, and the new desire for clarity and order which they represented, invited reflection and comment on the nature of customary law and its relationships with the laws of the ancient emperors or modern rulers. It also invited a consideration of the relationship of custom to custom. Were there, for example, customs common to an entire region or an entire kingdom? If there was a common customary law, what was its nature and how could it be discerned? In England, an example of this interest is the twelfth-century treatise traditionally attributed to Glanville and entitled "On the Laws and Customs of the Realm of England"; in the thirteenth century, another tract, attributed to Henry of Bratton (Bracton), who died in 1268, offered a still more comprehensive commentary on the common law of England.

This further question could be posed: Was there a common customary law for the whole of Europe? Or were there at least certain common principles evident in the regional collection of customs? One of the first scholars to pose this question and to attempt an answer to it was a jurist of Padua, Giacomo Alvarotto (1385–1453), who sought in a tract, called in short title *De feudis,* to describe basic principles governing the law of the fief. Although Italy itself remained the land par excellence of written law, nonetheless its lawyers were accustomed through their training in Roman jurisprudence to think in terms of the universality of law and were confident in their ability to reconcile apparently diverse customs. Alvarotto himself used the term *feudalis scientia,* "feudal science," implying that the customary law of the fief was logically consistent and entirely amenable to scientific investigation. His work was widely read in the subsequent centuries, several times printed, and frequently imitated by jurists even beyond the frontiers of Italy.

Alvarotto and other jurists of the late Middle Ages thus assumed that the aggregate of feudal customs was more than a formless mass of regional idiosyncrasies; rather, the customs shared common principles and therefore did constitute a true legal system. But the jurists fully recognized that these customs still constituted only one part of the total body of laws by which society was governed. They did not conceive that there then existed, or ever had existed, an authentic "feudal government" or "feudal society."

From a kind of conditional tenure to the designation of an important body of customs and traditions common, at least in basic principles, to all Europe—this was the manner in which the meaning of "feudal" evolved in the late Middle Ages. In the sixteenth century, the word seems to have experienced no great changes, nor even to have enjoyed much popularity beyond the writings of the professional jurists. Jean Bodin (1530–1596), for example, who is generally considered the architect of the modern conception of sovereignty, referred in his *Six Books on the Republic* to the "law of fiefs," and makes use of the term *feudataire*, or feudatory. The latter term means for him only "tributory," and he cites it only to show that dependent princes cannot be considered sovereign in his sense of the term. He is obviously concerned with the nature of power and those who exercised it at the highest levels of society. But there is evident in his writings no conception of a distinctively feudal order or a feudal state and society.

A broader meaning for the word, and more frequent usage, had to await the European Enlightenment of the eighteenth century and the searching examination it inspired of the fundamental institutions of the *ancien régime*. Men came to question the value of Europe's ancient traditions and compared them unfavorably with the supposed good sense of the simple savage or the wisdom of exotic foreign civilizations, such as the Persian or Chinese. The critics needed a term which could conveniently identify the body of practices inherited from the past which seemed to them largely irrational and obnoxious. Thus, in English, apparently the first use of the term "feudal system" is found in Adam Smith's *Wealth of Nations* (1776). Smith meant by it not really a system of law but of production. Under the "feudal system," workers were moved to their labors not by the incentives naturally generated by a free market but by force and coercion, by the power of the lord and the state which stood behind him. Such a system, he believed, so obstructed incentive and so weakened the natural and beneficent operation of economic laws that it inevitably led to grudging effort, low production, and general misery for all but the very rich. "Feudal" thus identified an economy and a society marked by wide contrasts between rich and poor; a miserable and exploited peasantry; and an unresponsive, unproductive economy. These overtones of poverty, stupidity, and injustice have ever since hovered over the word "feudal," at least in popular usage.

For the continental reformers too, feudalism in its most fundamental and precise sense meant the aggregate of seigneurial prerogatives, which established the rule of the privileged few over the many, and which could be justified neither by reason nor by justice. Lords could demand rents from the land, such as the *cens* (quitrent) or tithe, for which they offered nothing in return, either in the form of improvements on the land or in help extended to make it more productive. Lords could further, through inheritance taxes or other charges imposed upon their human dependents, take from them payments for which they performed no service in return. These dues, whether collected from persons or from lands, were "feudal rents," in the sense of uncompensated payments extracted not by contract or by recognition of mutual services and benefits, but by force. The scholars and commentators of the age, including Montesquieu, Voltaire, and other leaders of the Enlightenment, discussed with considerable spirit the origins of this deplorable regime. Some attributed it to the Romans, who supposedly made such concessions to the invading Germans; still more held the Germans, who allegedly reduced to servitude the peoples they conquered, responsible; still others attributed it to the constant wars, constant defeats, and consequent enslavements of peoples characteristic of the Middle Ages. But all agreed that feudalism and its furnishings—an aristocracy which offered nothing in return for its privileges, an oppressed and impoverished peasantry forced to work without reward, an encumbered market powerless to rationalize through its influence the forms of production—represented survivals of a former bondage. All this, men of reason should reject. Thus, in August, 1789, the National Constituent Assembly, in one of its first acts intended for the reform of France, abolished entirely and forever the feudal regime. Only later decades and generations would reveal that the ogre, whose death was so cleanly decreed by the Assembly, was hard to identify in all its members.

With the Enlightenment and the French Revolution, a certain bifurcation becomes evident in the meaning and uses of the word "feudal," and this variance has persisted to the present, to the frequent confusion of students and the annoyance of scholars. To some historians, then and now, feudalism retains its late-medieval, early-modern, essentially juridic sense as the aggregate of those institutions connected with the support and service of knights. To investigate feudalism therefore requires a consideration of the relationships, personal and proprietary, between the ruler or the chief and the warriors who attended and served him. Feudalism in this reconstruction is a system of law, of government, and of military organization, but not of economic production. "Manorialism" is the term usually used to connote the system of large estates which frequently, although not always, accompanied the "feudalism" of the aristocracy. This concept of feudalism thus exclusively describes the political and social relations within the free, ruling, and preeminently fighting classes. Serfs, who were not free and thus could not enter into the feudal contract, should therefore be excluded from consideration under the feudal rubric. To write "feudal" is necessarily to think of an aristocracy.

But there remains a second, quite different use of the word; it was later in emerging but was already established in the writings of Adam Smith and the reformers of the eighteenth century. Tautologically defined, feudalism is a system of economic production founded upon "feudal rent," which means in turn reliance on force and not on incentives to secure labor and support from the workers. It is not exactly slavery, as the peasant was not chattel and could not be moved about at the lord's will; there were, moreover, traditional limits set upon the services and payments the lord could demand. But it was a survival of bondage, and of course it contrasted greatly with the wage system and the "cash nexus" of the capitalistic economy, which stimulated and disciplined the worker not by direct power but by the incentive of monetary payments.

In the nineteenth century, the socialists borrowed this conception of feudalism (as they did much else) from the liberal economists. Marx and Engels in particular made it a part of their sweeping characterization of the stages of human development. In the beginning there was primitive communism, poor and unproductive; there followed slavery, which allowed greater wealth at the cost of human degradation; feudalism came next, and then capitalism; finally, communism returned, now wealthy and triumphant. The word "feudal" is scattered through the Communist Manifesto of 1848 ("feudal society," "feudal property," "feudal system of industry," and the like). It is viewed of course with opprobrium, but often favorably compared with the subsequent, still crueler exploitations of the bourgeois state.

This understanding of feudalism has remained canonical for Marxists and has retained considerable appeal to some other, especially economic historians, who find the concept of feudal rent a valid one and a cornerstone in the social and economic structure of medieval society. Disagreement over the meaning of this basic term has produced a major anomaly in the historical literature concerning feudalism. Marxist scholars have professed that they were investigating feudalism and have written extensively on tenures, rents, and the methods by which the peasants were allegedly exploited. Many non-Marxists have professed the same intent and have not gone beyond a consideration of the services owed by knights and the means used to support them.

Today, many historians, anxious to avoid battles over terminology which soon become idle, prefer not to offer rigorous definitions of feudalism, but rather to describe feudal society, in the sense of listing those characteristics which seem central to it. This descriptive approach avoids the implication that one factor— whether the practices of the aristocracy or the organization of production—necessarily determined all others.

As summarized by Marc Bloch, one of the great historians of the medieval world, whose work we shall subsequently consider, the following characteristics may justifiably earn for a society the name "feudal":

> A subject peasantry; widespread use of the service tenement (i.e. the fief) instead of salary; supremacy of a class of specialized warriors; ties of obedience and protection which bind man to man; fragmentation of authority; and, in the midst of all this, survival of other forms of association, family and State.

Bloch's large and loose definition of the essential characteristics of feudal society effectively combines much of what both Marxists and non-Marxists alike have said about it or have written concerning it. Although his words may be criticized as lacking both conceptual and methodological rigor, they offer a good working description, to which most scholars would readily give assent. In stressing the importance of investigating not feudalism alone, or feudal institutions, but feudal society, Bloch also laid great stress on the importance of comparative history. It was his hope and expectation that a careful comparison of western Europe in the Middle Ages with, for example, the lands of east Asia, Japan especially, would deepen our understanding of feudal institutions and our appreciation of the place a "feudal stage" might hold in human development. Although the results of a comparative history of feudal societies have not so far been spectacular, it remains fair to say that the quest is only now beginning and that with time Marc Bloch's great faith in its potential may prove justified.

Historians, over the centuries, have differed not only in their interpretations of the word "feudalism," but also in the methods they have used to investigate the feudal centuries. An appreciation of those methods is similarly needed to understand the nature of feudal society, or at least what historians have discovered concerning it.

Methodologies

The lawyers who made the earliest efforts to find dimension and order in the array of feudal customs were not primarily concerned with the historic origins of the practices they studied. Much in contrast, the social commentators and reformers who continued the effort were vitally concerned, as they wished to know when and why their society had adopted the institutions which most of them regarded as deplorable. We have already mentioned that the writers in the age of the Enlightenment concluded variously that feudalism was the product either of Roman decadence, German arrogance, or medieval brutality. In the course of the nineteenth century, the methods of historical research changed drastically, but the interest remained. This age marked the birth and development of scientific history, in the sense of a discipline which was rigorously exact, ingeniously critical, and powerful enough to uncover knowledge about the past which even contemporaries had not realized or recognized. This development of historical science has continued to the present, and in the course of its growth historians have made use of various approaches to their documents and to the realities behind them. Specifically in regard to feudal society, it is possible to discern in modern analysis three distinct methods, each with its own purposes and advantages.

THE GENEALOGY OF TRADITIONS

One of the oldest and still today one of the most cultivated of the scholarly approaches to feudalism is to establish the lines along which the basic institutions, customs, and traditions associated with it grew and changed. Historians, for example, have for long carefully investigated the changes in military institutions between the ancient and medieval worlds, and especially the replacement of the foot soldier of antiquity by the mounted warrior or knight as the main support of armies. They have studied with equal care the character and the history of the personal tie between warriors and their chiefs known as vassalage, and of the distinctive sort of land grant known as the fief. For both institutions, they have succeeded in finding antecedents in the Roman and barbarian worlds. So also, for a later period, scholars have investigated, and still investigate, the influences upon the legal systems and governments of Europe which the revived knowledge of Roman law or new philosophical ideas concerning nature or society may have exerted. On a more restricted scale, the question of origins has long posed one of the great problems of medieval English history: what impact did the Norman conquest and Norman policies have upon the growth of English government?

History conceived and pursued as a genealogy of institutions or of traditions offers several advantages to the scholar. The problems are usually well defined, and the method—chiefly the careful collation of documents—is proven and reliable. Moreover, the principal institutions of society are usually well illuminated, even in medieval sources. A strong documentary record, clearly delineated problems, and precise methods thus enable the historian of institutions to proceed with a rigor that is often the envy of scholars working in other areas of human culture. As a result of generations of research, we today possess a rather good idea concerning the development of the chief institutions of feudalism; we can date with some accuracy the major changes in them and observe with some detail how these institutions functioned.

But institutional history also possesses some limitations, as even its most accomplished practitioners have recognized. Institutions rarely explain themselves. Often the very sources which illuminate them appear only after the institutions have acquired a certain stability and maturity; law, someone has remarked, is born late. To investigate their formation, the historian must also consider why these institutions acquired certain characteristics rather than others, or developed in one direction rather than in another. At this point, the kind of history he is pursuing becomes less a consideration of the lines of institutional development and more an analysis of the causes and factors which explain social change.

THE SKEIN OF CAUSES

A second, major interest of historians concerned with feudalism has therefore been this: Why, at a certain point in time, did there occur changes in the social and political institutions of western Europe? If feudalism by definition consisted of those institutions concerned with the service and support of knights, to know its origin was primarily to determine when and why knights came to play so decisive a role in Western warfare, and hence in Western society and government. The armies of the ancient world—the Macedonian phalanxes or the Roman legions—had relied primarily upon foot soldiers to wage and win the wars. Medieval armies relied on the heavily armed, mounted warrior. When and why did the change occur?

In 1887, a German historian of law, Heinrich Brunner, advanced one of the most ingenious and still one of the most influential explanations for this shift in military tactics. Brunner argued that this fundamental change to cavalry occurred in the eighth century. In 755, King Pepin the Short ordered that the Frankish army be mustered in May instead of March. May offered more fodder, and this must have meant that more Frankish soldiers were coming on horseback. Shortly afterward, in 758, he changed the tribute imposed on the subject Saxons from cattle to horses, for which the Frankish army had an apparently greater need. Why was this happening? Brunner himself pointed to the penetration of the horse-riding Arabs through Spain and across the Pyrenees in the early eighth century; the Carolingian mayor of the palace, Charles Martel, repulsed them at the battle of Poitiers (732), but even afterward their menace continued. To resist the invaders required that the Franks adopt their tactics, and particularly enlarge and strengthen their cavalry. This military reform necessarily brought about a number of profound political, social, and economic changes. Horses were expensive engines of war, and the Carolingians had to find economic support for them and for the men who rode them. Charles Martel seized part of the possessions of the churches, or ordered ecclesiastical institutions to provide his soldiers with land, by grants known as *precaria* or *beneficia* (see following section). This was the origin of the fief, and the Carolingians further insisted that the mounted fighters assume toward their superiors and toward themselves the obligations of vassals.

The military change further made fighting an enterprise of the aristocracy, even its monopoly. The few freemen who had the means to afford the expensive horses and armor, or were favored with grants of land by the rulers, became the new feudal nobility. To fight was the great mark of freedom in early medieval society, and the poor who could no longer afford to fight sank into the ranks of full-time peasants and serfs. As the direct result of these ninth-century military reforms, medieval society thus acquired the basic feudal traits: a dependent peasantry and a warrior aristocracy tied to its chief or king, and he to them, by bonds created by the fief and by vassalage.

Scholars have since mounted a barrage of objections against Brunner's theory of the origins of the military fief, and hence of feudalism, in the West. It now appears that the Muslim cavalry was not nearly so important as Brunner maintained, and probably could not have served as so powerful an incentive for Frankish military reform. Rather, mounted horsemen seem to have been growing in numbers on both sides of the religious frontier in the eighth century at an almost equal pace.

But if this interpretation would tend to excise the prime mover from Brunner's link of causes, his views are by no means dead, and have recently been given a new breath of life by the researches of a historian of technology, Lynn White, Jr. In his *Medieval Technology and Social Change*, White has replaced the Saracen challenge with the introduction of a new tool, the stirrup, but he has otherwise left largely intact the sequence of causes leading to the formation of the feudal system. This stirrup, White maintains, was adopted for the Frankish army by Charles Martel, who learned of it from the East. For the first time, this deceptively simple device permitted a man on horseback to deliver a powerful blow without the danger of unseating himself. Feudalism was thus created by the Franks, "presumably led by the genius of Charles Martel," who recognized the military potential of the new tool and reorganized the Frankish army, and indirectly government and society, to take advantage of it.

Both Brunner and White thus offer an interpretation of feudalism which attributes its fundamental institutions to specific causes and links them together in a rational pattern. Martel (in White's reconstruction) adopted the stirrup, revolutionized warfare, and gave supremacy to the mounted horseman or knight. To support

the new warrior class, fiefs were introduced and personal obligations imposed upon the persons who held them. The nobility had
to train its sons from an early age in the difficult skills of mounted
shock combat, and this educational and professional experience
produced among the warrior class a kind of subculture, chivalry, a
name appropriately deriving from the late Latin word for horse
(*caballus*). Western society was thus transformed militarily, socially, and culturally, all because of the introduction of a small iron
implement supporting the feet of horsemen.

There are other, comparable attempts to explain feudalism in the
West through a reputed sequence of causes. One of the most
famous was that advanced between the two world wars by a
Belgian historian, Henri Pirenne. Pirenne's contention was that the
classical world had been founded on the unity of the Mediterranean Sea and the vigorous trade which this unity made possible.
Commerce provided the Roman state with an abundance of
money, with which it supported the two chief pillars of the empire,
a paid bureaucracy and a professional army. That unity and that
trade survived the barbarian invasions of the fourth and fifth
centuries. But in the seventh century, the Arab followers of
Muhammad broke into the Mediterranean, built a fleet, and turned
an avenue of peaceful trade into a battlefield. The West was cut off
from the East and from its life-giving trade. It was therefore
thrown back upon its own, exclusively agrarian resources. Charlemagne (king of the Franks, 768–814) recognized the realities of
the new situation and reorganized his army and his state in con-
formity with them. Without money revenues, he took to supporting his soldiers through granting them pieces of land in fief. Thus
he created the new feudal state and society, and with these changes
the Middle Ages was born. In a famous phrase, Pirenne affirmed
that without Muhammad, Charlemagne would have been incon-
ceivable. He meant that the economic and social order of the
Middle Ages—the feudal order, in sum—was unthinkable without
the intervention of the Saracen expansion and the destruction of
the Mediterranean unity. By a series of brilliantly linked arguments, the dazzled reader is led from cause to cause, until he finds
himself confronting the unlikely, nearly incredible conclusion that
the prime cause of feudalism in the West was the Koran.

These reconstructions offer the student numerous insights into
the origins of feudalism. Their validity has been endlessly but fruit-

fully discussed, and we shall content ourselves here with some comment on their methodological implications and some of the difficulties implicit in them. In locating the causes of feudalism in the Saracen horse, or the Asian stirrup, or the Arabian prophet, these arguments assume an answer to the most fundamental question of all the social sciences: What really causes or explains human behavior? For example, even if the recognized value of the stirrup prompted Charles Martel to reorganize the Frankish army and distribute land among his soldiers, the explanation remains evidently incomplete. Why did he place so much importance on a military decision? Was he influenced by a present and pressing military need or a traditional cultural value? Why could he not have supported the army by other means? His response to the problems which confronted him was clearly conditioned by many factors, by the economic, administrative, and cultural resources at his disposal, and further by the fundamental character of his own society. To understand human decisions and human behavior requires something more than an appreciation of immediate stimuli. It requires, too, a consideration of the totality of forces, material and spiritual, which condition, influence, or direct human responses. And because we are dealing with human beings, the forces which helped shape their actions must be recognized as multiple, subtle, and infinitely complex.

Thus, efforts to explain feudalism through single and simple causes, whether through horses or tools or prophets, are open to the criticism that they are founded on too simple a conception of human behavior. To explain what happened (at least according to some critics), the historian should function as does the social scientist. He should not try to isolate apparent causes, as these will often prove specious. Rather, he should seek to combine them, thus reconstructing the total social milieu, the total life situation, in which the events occurred. Only then will the actions of past generations become not explained but understandable.

In France, between the two world wars, a group of historians associated with a journal which today bears the name *Annales-Economies-Sociétés-Civilisations* took issue with the traditional methods of history which then dominated the schools. They called for a new historical method which would make use of the other social sciences and the insights they offer. They argued that the academic historians, for all their admitted power in establishing what happened in the past, were still guilty of self-deception. They pretended to write "definitive" works, in the sense of exploring, once and for all, given historical topics; they claimed that they could explain not only what happened but the causal relations among events. Definitive history, for these critics, was dehumanized history, as it pretended to a knowledge of the past and a mastery of human behavior which not even the most advanced social sciences possessed.

THE ANALYSIS OF A SITUATION

One of the prominent figures among these critics was also one of the great historians of feudalism. This was Marc Bloch, who died a hero's death in 1944 as a member of the French resistance in World War II. His great work, *Feudal Society*, characteristically begins with an extended treatment of the feudal environment. To understand how men act, one must know how they live, not only economically or politically, but culturally, intellectually, and religiously. Every human action is a product of many causes and many influences, and it would be naïve for a historian to rank them by supposed importance. Rather, he should seek to reconstruct the entire social milieu, the total life situation of the period he is studying.

Bloch's book on feudal society is one of the most influential historical works to have been written in this century, and its influence is by no means confined to medieval history. Many historians of many periods have sought to follow Bloch's advice, to reconstruct the "total social environment" of a past society. To be sure, this approach is itself not without some weaknesses. To reconstruct the total life situation, the tone and style of a past epoch, the historian must frequently propose conclusions beyond the power of traditional historical methods to prove or disprove; he must, in other words, resort to impressions. Bloch himself, in describing characteristics of the feudal period, frequently cited examples or evidence well beyond the chronological limits of the age he was examining. Because specific causes are all but lost in the total milieu, so specific events and specific personalities lose their importance. A kind of chronological vagueness hovers over the analysis. Bloch, as we shall see, distinguishes two fundamentally different feudal ages, but he shifts the division between them, according to his context, backwards and forwards, over a century or more. Finally, Bloch's approach has also developed a rhetoric of its own. The rhetorical question, suggesting a conclusion, frequently replaces the confident affirmation of the older academic historian. Historians inspired by the spirit of the *Annales*, anxious to avoid the pretense of writing definitive studies, now often parade an exaggerated modesty. Like the medieval authors who announced in excellent Latin their inability to write excellent Latin, they often claim that their chief purpose in writing is only to pose questions and to inspire others to carry the work a little further.

But in spite of some weaknesses, it is probably fair to say that this effort to reconstruct and to understand a total human situation has proved its merit in the past generation, and scholars are far from exhausting its potential. More rigorous use of the sources and a better exploitation of the other social sciences promise abundant harvests in the future.

The history of feudal society, illuminated by this and other methods, should attract not only those interested in the Western past but all who are concerned with the dynamics of human change. If the feudal society of the Middle Ages has left us comparatively few sources, its history has one advantage which the history of the modern age cannot duplicate. It has time; it permits the study of human change over centuries, amounting to a millennium. The legal issues involving the fief, the moral and social need for reform, which first brought men to the study of feudal society, have all but faded in our modern world. But the fascination of this lengthy chapter in Western history, and in human history, remains.

RECOMMENDED READINGS

MARC BLOCH, *Feudal Society*, trans. by L. A. Manyon, Foreword by M. M. Postan (Chicago: University of Chicago Press, 1961).

FREDRIC L. CHEYETTE (ed.), *Lordship and Community in Medieval Europe: Selected Readings* (New York: Holt, Rinehart and Winston, 1968).

RUSHTON COULBOURN (ed.), *Feudalism in History* (Princeton: Princeton University Press, 1956).

F. L. GANSHOF, *Feudalism*, trans. Philip Grierson (New York: Harper & Row, 1964).

R. S. HOYT, *Feudal Institutions: Cause or Consequence of Decen-*

tralization? (Source Problems in World Civilization; New York: Holt, Rinehart and Winston, 1963).

Henri Pirenne, *Mohammed and Charlemagne* (New York: W. W. Norton and Co., 1939).

Gaines Post, *Studies in Medieval Legal Thought: Public Law and the State* (Princeton: Princeton University Press, 1964).

Carl Stephenson, *Medieval Feudalism* (Ithaca: Cornell University Press, 1942).

Joseph R. Strayer, *Feudalism* (Anvil Original, 86; Princeton, New Jersey: Van Nostrand, 1965).

Lynn White, Jr., *Medieval Technology and Social Change* (Oxford: Clarendon Press, 1962).

Part One

The Feudal Milieu

Introduction

⎿⎾⎿⎿⎿⎾

Nearly all historians today agree that feudal society cannot be considered fixed and unchanging over all the centuries of its history. Rather, an accurate appreciation of the nature of the feudal order requires that historians recognize at least two feudal ages. The division between them falls approximately in the period 1050 to 1100, but it comes at various times in various parts of Europe.

The first feudal age
The "first feudal age" (the term is Marc Bloch's) witnessed the spontaneous formation of the basic institutions and practices of feudalism: the personal bond between man and man known as "vassalage"; the property bond created by the granting of fiefs; and the distribution of governmental powers among numerous petty lords. These institutions were not created by the conscious design of any lawgiver but resulted from spontaneous growth. They were rooted in the folk practices and folk culture of the peoples of the early medieval West.

To understand the nature and development of these institutions, and the function they assumed within early medieval society, it is necessary again to recall the conditions of life prevailing in the early Middle Ages. What, for example, were the numbers of the people living in western Europe in this first feudal age, and how did they occupy the land? We have of course no exact figures with which to respond to the first query, but the population was undoubtedly very small, whether in comparison with later periods or even with the age of the Roman Empire. The population, if small, does not seem to have been evenly distributed across the countryside. On the contrary, the pattern of settlement seems to have taken the form of numerous concentrations of peoples into densely settled communities, which were in turn cut off from one another by extensive areas of forests and virtually uninhabited wastelands. In the first quarter of the ninth century, for example, an abbot named Irminon of the monastery of St. Germain des Prés near Paris took an inventory and a census of the manors and villages then subject to the abbey. The population of these villages near Paris was as great in the ninth century as it was to be in the early eighteenth. There are even signs in these packed communities of an excessive partitioning of holdings and of relative overpopulation, in spite of the extent of surrounding forests. The peoples of the early Middle Ages, huddled together in the midst of emptiness, were never far removed from famine and starvation.

This pattern of fairly large, even densely populated settlements in a sea of nearly empty forests in turn had repercussions upon the economic life of the age. Trade, of course, never entirely disappeared. Wines for the liturgical services, salt for preserving food, iron for tools—these were permanent needs which usually could be satisfied only through trade. Moreover, the great lords and prelates never lost a taste for spices and other exotic products brought from distant lands. Perhaps the chief characteristic of commerce in the early Middle Ages was that it was inconstant and unreliable. Local communities could not depend upon a regular commerce to supply a substantial part of their essential needs. In this situation of a sporadic trade, self-sufficiency in an economic sense was sound policy for the isolated communities, even if complete economic autarchy could never be achieved. So also, because of few exchanges, money remained relatively rare within the economy, and the governments in turn could not expect to collect large monetary revenues or to use money payments to hire soldiers and support a bureaucracy. In such circumstances, retainers were best supported through grants of land, which brought consumers and producers close together and dispensed with the need for money. The peculiarities of settlement and commercial exchange affected also the exchange of information. The monastic scribe often shows a familiarity with happenings in areas far distant from his home—at Rome, for example, or the imperial court—but a defective knowledge of events occurring in his immediate neighborhood. Again, the exchange of information was not reliable, but often in this kind of human vacuum news could travel far. Early medieval society thus presents a peculiar balance of intense localism, coupled with a consciousness of membership in the universal communities of Church and empire.

Moreover, the settlements of the early Middle Ages faced a nearly continuous problem of insecurity and violence. The Carolingian state for about a hundred years maintained a semblance of unity and security in Europe, but from the middle ninth century its own unity and strength were destroyed both by internecine strife and by renewed invasions. The invaders—Vikings from the north, Magyars or Hungarians from the east, and Saracens from the south—were especially active in the last decades of the ninth century and opening decades of the tenth. Again, the persons concentrated within these communities had to meet this problem primarily with their own resources, as they could not rely upon the quick reactions and effective protection of a central government. Feudal institutions were not only spontaneous in development but were also in some sense "domestic," as they initially concerned not the king and the great men of the realm but the humbler freemen, who within the vacuum of governmental authority had to arrange for their own protection, security, and support. Part Two will examine the character of the institutions which grew up within this milieu in response to these pressing problems.

The second feudal age

From the late eleventh century or perhaps even earlier, the circumstances we have just described began to change and to ameliorate over wide areas of western Europe. To begin with, there are indications that the population of the West had begun to grow substantially. Men were passing out of their harassed and isolated communities and filling up the great empty spaces which had formerly separated their settlements. Forests and wastelands were cleared, marshes drained, and even the sea pushed back in regions such as Flanders. Similarly, these pioneers were pushing across

Europe's former frontiers both to the east and to the south. The lands beyond the Elbe and along the Danube welcomed German settlers in such numbers that by about 1350 the area of German settlement was virtually tripled over what it had been in Carolingian times. In the movement called the *reconquista*, the Christian states of Iberia pushed hard and successfully against the Spanish Saracens. Normans, knights more than colonists, simultaneously claimed southern Italy and Sicily for themselves and for Latin Christendom and were chief participants in the great expeditions, the Crusades, which from 1095 marched to the east.

The economy was also changing. As isolation diminished, so trade became possible on a regional basis, and it grew slowly but continuously. To serve the fledgling but vigorous exchange economy, money became more plentiful, largely through the simple device of ruthlessly debasing the old coinage. The dimensions of these economic changes ought not to be exaggerated, but it remains accurate to say that Europe by the late twelfth century was a different sort of community, founded upon a different sort of economy, than it had been two hundred years before.

The growing vigor of trade, the increasing availability of money, and the new importance of towns and town classes—all placed new resources at the disposal of the prince. He could hope to take advantage of the expanded trade, gain monetary revenues, hire mercenaries, support a bureaucracy, and emancipate himself partially from land grants tied to service. The towns offered him a new resource in the form of a pool of trained men, from whom he could select reliable and efficient administrators. The kind of government which these new conditions allowed was itself much different from the arrangements possible, for example, to the Carolingian rulers.

The transformations of the second feudal age were not limited to population or to economic production. They were also, and critically, mental or psychological. In particular, the age witnessed the emergence of a new sense of the autonomy and order of nature, and a new confidence in man's ability to bend it to his needs.

The men of the early Middle Ages (or at least the monks whose psychology is made most apparent to us through their writings) discerned two forces at work in the world—nature as made by original creation but impaired by sin; and grace, the special interventions of divine power, through which God was bringing the elect to salvation. The monastic writers tended to view fallen nature as the abode of chaos, and to organize their experiences primarily around the supposed interventions of grace. This explains the extraordinary taste for the miraculous and the wondrous in such writers as the monk of Cluny, Raoul Glaber (Document 4). History too was conceived not as the record of natural events causally related and distributed over time but primarily as the story of salvation. Many monastic writers began their chronicles with an account of creation, the Fall, and the Incarnation, so that the events of their neighborhood might be related to God's grand design for human salvation. The natural world and natural phenomena were conceded little inherent order; they were often treated as a great parade of symbolic events which cast indirect light on the supersensory world of the spirit, which primarily mattered.

The monastic writers and presumably their lay contemporaries show a lack of interest in and a defective sense of natural causation and of profane time. Charters are frequently left without dates, as if the time of their redaction had no special significance. Often, the monks believed that an event had occurred—a donation of land, for example, or a privilege from a king—for which they had no record. They seem to have felt no qualms in forging a charter, thus correcting the unfortunate omissions of the past. That they could do this in apparent good faith seems to mean that for them the past was not, as it is for us, a book entirely closed. However, the man who considers that profane nature has no inherent structure is not likely to reflect upon it in relation to his own needs, and not likely to develop much confidence in his ability to order the chaos to his own purposes.

In the second feudal age, as part of the intellectual renaissance of the West, there is evident a growing awareness of nature as a complex of largely autonomous forces, set in motion at the act of creation but from that moment freed by God to operate according to their own inherent character. It is of course largely among the intellectuals, which is to say within the cathedral schools and the universities which flourished from the eleventh and twelfth centuries, that this new mentality is most apparent. Gilbert de la Porrée, for example, a teacher at the cathedral school of Chartres in the early twelfth century, posed the question as to whether "cheese and shoes and other such things are made by God." He concluded

that they were made only remotely, and in the course of his specu-
lations he emphasized the importance both of nature and of man as
artisan in altering the raw materials provided by the original
creation. His contemporaries at Chartres and elsewhere were simultaneously advancing the concept that nature had an order which
could be observed, understood, and used. The world as he viewed
it was partially the result of the *opus creatoris*, the work of the
Creator. But the Creator had left it largely in chaos. Then followed
the *opus naturae*, the work of nature. Nature, the sum of the
potentialities and the powers God had placed in all things, ordered
and decorated the original chaos and did this without the immediate and unpredictable promptings of God. Man in turn could
imitate nature through working upon it as an artisan, and further
add to the decoration of the cosmos. While we discern this new
mentality primarily through the learned writers, we have reason to
believe that it represents an attitude widely shared in twelfth-
century society. Indeed, the men of this age—the colonists, merchants, crusaders, and thinkers—were fundamentally entrepreneurs
and innovators, and all entrepreneurs must have confidence in their
own abilities to reach their determined goals.

The new mentality also affected governments. The traditional
institutions of feudalism developed, as we mentioned, without
conscious direction, really the products of the folk culture of the
early medieval West. But the princes who were intent on
strengthening their own authority could, like good artisans, adopt
the materials the past had given them, manipulating and utilizing
them in their own interests. In the new wealth and skills growing in
their societies, the princes possessed resources not available to their
predecessors. They and their advisers were also gaining a new self-
consciousness, an awareness of their own situation, and a willingness to use traditional institutions in the interest of achieving a
higher level of social order. A heightened consciousness and a new
confidence are thus among the most salient contrasts which distinguish the two feudal ages.

RECOMMENDED READINGS

MARC BLOCH, *French Rural History: An Essay on Its Basic Char-
    acteristics* (Berkeley: University of California Press, 1966).
Cambridge Economic History of Europe (3 vols.; Cambridge:
    Cambridge University Press, 1941–67).

MARSHALL CLAGETT, GAINES POST, and ROBERT REYNOLDS (eds.), *Twelfth-Century Europe and the Foundations of Modern Society* (Madison: University of Wisconsin Press, 1961).

GEORGES DUBY. *The Making of the Christian West, 980–1140* (Cleveland: World Publishing Co., 1967).

———, *Rural Economy and Country Life in the Medieval West* (Columbia: University of South Carolina Press, 1968).

C. H. HASKINS, *The Renaissance of the Twelfth Century* (Cambridge: Harvard University Press, 1927).

J. C. RUSSELL, *British Medieval Population* (Albuquerque: University of New Mexico Press, 1948).

———, *Late Ancient and Medieval Population* (Philadelphia: American Philosophical Society, 1958).

B. H. SLICHER VAN BATH, *The Agrarian History of Western Europe*, A.D. *500–1850* (New York: St. Martin's Press, 1963).

I. *The First Feudal Age*

⎍⎍⎍⎍⎍⎍⎍⎍⎍⎍⎍⎍⎍⎍⎍⎍⎍⎍⎍⎍⎍⎍

1. The wandering relics of St. Philibert, described by the Monk Ermentarius

One of the most remarkable incidents of the ninth century, which illustrates both the havoc wrought by the Viking incursions and the instability of the population, is the wanderings of a community of monks who sought a refuge not only for themselves but for the holy body of their patron, St. Philibert. In the opening decades of the ninth century, the monks were established on the island of Noirmoutier at the mouth of the Loire River in France, near Nantes. But the ever more destructive raids of the Vikings led them in 836 to seek a safer home in the hinterland and to initiate a long trek which would take them through the heartland of France. From Noirmoutier they fled up the Loire Valley to Saumur, then to a place called Cunauld still farther inland, then south to Poitou, then to the Massif Central, and after another intervening stop to a refuge near Tournus, more than 300 miles from their original home. The following description of the first phases only of their travels and tribulations was written in 863 by a monk named Ermentarius, who included in his account an older description of miracles written in 837 and 839. The source is *Ex Ermentarii miraculis sancti Filiberti*, ed. O. Holder-Egger (Monumenta Germaniae Historica, Scriptores XV; Hanover, 1888), pp. 298–303. The translation is by D. Herlihy. The descriptions of miracles not directly relevant to the wanderings of the commmunity have been omitted.

From the first book of miracles
We wish to describe the miracles which the most mighty and gracious God deigned to display when the body of the most blessed Philibert was taken from the ocean island known as Herius

[Noirmoutier] to the place which used to be called Deé [St. Philbert de Grandlieu]. We want also to describe those deeds of heaven done in the same place, which we were present to see, or which we know to have been truthfully reported by the faithful. First, with all my strength I pray to the most powerful and gracious Lord, that He Who deigned to display so many miracles by the merits of His confessor should grant also to me the eloquence to describe them.

But before I broach these things, I thought it valuable to explain the reason why [the saint] had to be taken from that place which he loved more than anywhere else and which also had seen him deliver his soul to God and his body to the earth. Although this may be well known to almost everyone alive, nevertheless, for the benefit of those to come, I shall state that in this affair the difficulty was the sudden and unforeseen attacks of the Northmen. When these men so often converged on the island's port and, being a fierce people, savagely devastated it, the inhabitants followed the example of their leader and sought help in flight rather than in waiting for their own extermination. The inhabitants moved back and forth in accord with the seasons. For in the summer, when the weather favored navigation, they sought the monastery of Deé, which had been built for this purpose, and only during the winter did they return to the island of Noirmoutier. Even as the monks and their dependents who inhabited the island were struggling in so desperate a situation, dangers began to multiply, and for reason of the frequent raids of the Northmen, the people of the island began not only to be terrorized but to suffer the loss of their possessions and to be afflicted by extreme tribulations. But in truth this is what they feared most: that the faithless men would dig up the grave of the blessed Philibert and scatter whatever they found in it hither and yon, or rather throw it into the sea. This was known to have happened in the region of Brittany to the remains of certain holy men; this we were told by those who had seen it and had fled before the most oppressive rule of these men. Peace, however, will usually follow persecution; for the Lord does not abandon those who place their hopes in Him, as He says to His disciples: "Behold I am with you all days, even to the consummation of the world" (Matthew 28.20). Still, we must spend some time in explaining for what purpose and when the island was deprived of so great a patron and abandoned by the entire community of monks. Do not, however, wonder that I should have said that peace follows persecution. For in our mind no little peace was obtained when the most holy body was removed to a place where his servants, secure from barbarian attack, were allowed day and night to worship the Lord.

It was the year of the incarnation of the Lord and Redeemer Jesus Christ, 836, the fourteenth indiction, the twenty-third year in which the glorious emperor Louis was happily reigning under the protection of divine mercy, and his son Lothair ruled in Italy, Pepin in Aquitaine, and Louis in Norica. The venerable abbot Hilbodus was governing, with the favor of the Lord, the flock of the confessor of Christ, Philibert, according to the rule of the holy Benedict. At his command I, the most miserable of all his monks— not only in deeds, but also in words—assumed the task of telling these things. The frequent and unfortunate attacks of the Northmen, as has been said, were in no wise abating, and Abbot Hilbodus had built a castle on the island for protection against that faithless people. Together with the council of his brothers, he came to King Pepin and asked His Highness what he intended to do about this problem. Then the glorious king and the great men of the realm—a general assembly of the kingdom was then being held—deliberated concerning the problem with gracious concern and found themselves unable to help through mounting a vigorous assault. Because of the extremely dangerous tides, the island was not always readily accessible to our forces, while all knew that it was quite accessible to the Northmen whenever the sea was peaceful. The king and the great men chose what they believed to be the more advantageous policy. With the agreement of the most serene king Pepin, almost all the bishops of the province of Aquitaine, and the abbots, counts, and other faithful men who were present, and many others besides who had learned about the situation, unanimously advised that the body of the blessed Philibert ought to be taken from the island and no longer allowed to remain there. This decision was taken in the year of the Incarnation of our Lord Jesus Christ as was written above. But enough! Now we shall turn our pen to describing his miracles . . .

From the second book of miracles

In the preceding book I wrote, although less worthily than I should have, concerning the miracles of blessed Philibert. Insofar as I had the time, I set forth the signs of his powers and described his splendid wonders. I had promised that I would in the following book recount those miracles omitted, or which divine power might further grant. Alas! I am forced to describe not miracles but the distressing troubles of nearly all the kingdoms of the West. In order that my tale possess a logical order, I must explain the delays in time. This account was written for Hildoinus, who died some time back [842] and, as I had promised, for whoever might be interested in them. During the year of the Incarnation of Christ the Redeemer of all men 836, a little peace smiled forth under the reign of Louis, and amid the boundless joy of the people, as has been described, the body of the confessor was moved with solemn and universal honor, veneration, and glory. Not long thereafter, that is, four years later, the emperor died [840]. After a similar extent of time had passed, 67 ships of the Northmen suddenly attacked the valley of the Loire and captured the city of Nantes [843]. They put to the sword the bishop and his clergy together with a large multitude of the people; those who escaped death were delivered into slavery. The successor of Emperor Louis was Charles, who had been raised in the royal palace. The brothers mentioned above—Lothair and Louis, for Pepin had died before his father— each possessed his own kingdom. But since concise language is to be sought in such matters (for I did not begin this work to record deeds which were better left in silence, or better lamented, but to describe the miracles of the holy confessor), there first arose strife among the brothers, and finally among the chief persons of the realm. The younger brothers, Louis and Charles, rebelled against their older brother, Lothair. Wars, horrible as an intestinal disease, were heaped on wars. A sad and miserable victory fell to the younger brothers.

But their strife gave encouragement to the foreigners. Justice was abandoned, and evil advanced. No guards were mounted on the ocean beaches. Wars against foreign enemies ceased, and internal wars raged on. The number of ships grew larger, and the Northmen were beyond counting. Everywhere there were massacres of Christians, raids, devastations, and burnings. For as long as the world shall last, this will remain evident by manifest signs. Whatever cities the Northmen attacked, they captured without resistance: Bordeaux, Périgueux, Saintes, Limoges, Angoulême, and Toulouse; then Angers, Tours, and Orléans were destroyed. The remains of numerous saints were carried off. What the Lord warns through the prophet came close to fulfillment: "From the north shall an evil break forth upon all the inhabitants of the land" (Jeremias 1.14). We also fled to a place which is called Cunauld, in the territory of Anjou, on the banks of the Loire, which the glorious king Charles had given us for the sake of refuge, because of the imminent peril, before Angers was taken. The body of the blessed Philibert still remained in the monastery which is called Deé, although the place had been burned by the Northmen. For it was not permitted that the banks of the Herbauge River should have been deprived of so great a patron, as long as some few of the monks were able to remain there.

Then, a few years later, an almost immeasurable fleet of Norse ships sailed up the Seine River. The evil done in those regions was no less than that perpetrated elsewhere. The Northmen attacked the city of Rouen and devastated and burned it. They then captured Paris, Beauvais, and Meaux, and they also leveled the castle of Melun. Chartres was also taken. They struck into the cities of Evreux, Bayeux, and other neighboring towns. Almost no place, and no monastery, remained unscathed. Everyone gave himself over to flight; rare was the man who said: "Stay, stay, resist, fight for the fatherland, for children and relatives." Thus, losing heart and feuding among themselves, they purchased by tribute what they should have defended with arms, and the kingdom of the Christians succumbed.

The Northmen attacked Spain besides; they entered the Rhône River, and they devastated Italy. While everywhere so many domestic and foreign wars were raging, the year of the Incarnation of Christ 857 passed. As long as there had been in us some hope of returning to our own possessions (which, however, proved to be fruitless), the body of the blessed Philibert, as has been said, was left in his own soil. With evils surrounding us, we had not been able to obtain a definite place of security. But since a refuge was nowhere to be found, we did not permit the most holy body to be carried with us hither and yon. Now, it was more truly smuggled away from the grasp of the Northmen than carried with festive praises, and it was taken to the place we have mentioned, which is called Cunauld. This was done in such a way that, when necessity required, it might be moved elsewhere. The year of the Lord's Incarnation was 862 when the body was carried from

Cunauld to Messay. It will later be evident how many miracles shown forth in that place through his glorious merits. But first we shall describe those wonders which we omitted at the end of the preceding book. For just as the persecution of the pagans has not ceased, neither does time know how to stay its course; since the days menace me with their quick passing, already the hour and the circumstances require that I declare the miracles. . . .

⊓⎍r

2. Saracen raids, in two charters from Provence

Chronicles and other narrative sources have left us rich and colorful pictures of the tumult of the first feudal age, but they are often defective and suspect on two counts. They almost certainly exaggerate the troubles of the times, and they consistently report only the deeds of the powerful. Private acts or charters, which principally record transactions in land and were never intended for historians to see, offer one of our best means of judging the accuracy of narrative accounts and of penetrating levels of society largely ignored by the chroniclers. The first of the following two charters is a donation to the cathedral chapter of the small town of Apt in France; it is one of the few charters which specifically refer to the Saracen raids. The donor has apparently lost all his children to slavery in Spain, which at least suggests that one type of booty sought by the raiders was children. Interestingly, too, this authentic charter served as the basis for a much more elaborate version of the same events, recorded in a second charter probably dating from the late twelfth century. This fabrication illustrates the capacity of the medieval mind to embellish past events according to its taste. The source is the *Cartulaire de l'église d'Apt (835–1130?)*, eds. N. Didier, H. Dubled, and J. Barruol (Paris, 1967), Nos. 10 and 11. The translation is by D. Herlihy.

Authentic charter of July, 906

In the name of the holy and undivided Trinity. While the spirit of the flesh labors in this world, it should remember its eternal fatherland, as the Lord says, "Ask and you shall receive, seek and you shall find, knock and there will be opened to you the gate of the heavenly kingdom." Thus, in order that I may merit to hear in the fearful judgment the glorious voice, "Come, blessed of my Father," therefore in the name of God, I, George, in consideration of my own possible death and the burden of my sins, cede, give and convey all my possessions, which are in the district of Apt, in the village called Cocticus, to the use of holy Mary and St. Castor, with houses, courts, vineyards, fields, meadows, woods, clearings, trees both which bear fruit and those which do not, waters and waterways, with their entrances and exits, with their boundaries and ditches, all and everything whatsoever in the same village I hold or possess, as much as came to us from our parents or from purchase. We convey and grant all these things to holy Mary and St. Castor, with this stipulation, that one-half should belong to the canons of holy Mary and the other to those serving St. Castor. And while we live, we reserve for ourselves the use and the fruit of these possessions. And if God should command that our sons and daughters return from the frontier or from slavery, we shall give to them compensation, so that there may be none of my heirs who should ask to break our donation or extinguish the lights illuminated for our soul. And after our death let these houses of God, of holy Mary and St. Castor, both acquire possession and both have the right of giving, selling, ceding, donating, exchanging, or granting benefices. Certainly, if there is anyone or if anyone should appear and any other of my heirs should come who should want to break or remove the donation to holy Mary or St. Castor or also to the canons of holy Mary and St. Castor, let him not be allowed to attain what he seeks, but let him pay to the use of holy Mary and her canons and also St. Castor and his guardians two pounds of gold, and afterward this our present donation should remain firm, undisturbed and inviolable for all time, with all additional firmness. This donation was done in the month of July, the sixteenth year of the rule of King Louis son of Boso now deceased, on Thursday, which was the fourth of the nones of July. Done in the city of Apt. Signed by George, who requested that this cession or donation be written and signed in his presence, with his signature. The mark of Odoinus witness. The mark of Ansegno witness. The mark of Gauldus witness. The mark of Ainardus witness. The mark of Ledus witness.

Fabrication, probably from late twelfth century

[Preface omitted.]

And I, George, so much the sinner, and my wife, Deda, together, through the will of the omnipotent God and all His saints, because I know that He is merciful and propitious, have determined to give part of our possessions to God our Lord and holy Mary the mother of our Lord Jesus Christ, and to St. Auspice, bishop and martyr, and to the excellent bishop and most noble confessor Castor. And what we offer is in the district of Apt: a certain castle, famous and noble, which is located above the city on the east, by the name of Saignon. This castle we give to the See mentioned above, and to St. Castor, who sleeps there, and to the uncounted relics of the saints, whose names the mercy of God alone knows. This castle and its land, with fields cultivated and uncultivated, with vineyards and meadows and all appurtenances and, beyond the Caulon River, in the place which is called Sablonnet, and in Olivet, all pertaining to the said castle, now and in eternity. We at one time had a single heir of the masculine sex by name of Sisinnius. We lost him at the hands of the pagans. He was taken to Spain, and there remained for the space of seven years. We his parents, however, in the meantime did not cease to pray amid fasts and charities for our son, and every week we held a vigil on Saturdays before the altar of holy Mary and St. Castor. But the power and mercy of the Lord has made itself manifest after the end of those years. We were keeping our vigil before the altar of the Lord God the Savior and the tomb of St. Castor, and suddenly, without warning, in the early vigil of the night, their son came, and stood before them, still bearing the [chain] with which he had been bound for so great a span of years. He said to them: "Behold, father, the son whom you conceived, and you, mother, the one whom you suckled for three years. Behold I am here, with health of mind and body." At his appearance, his parents had great joy, as did all the people and citizens. And all of them together gave thanks to God. Amen. The castle, as it had been given, they dedicated together with their son, and they confirmed the act by charter and by witnesses. Done at the time of Charles.

ⅬⅬⅬⅬⅬⅬⅬⅬⅬⅬⅬⅬⅬⅬⅬⅬⅬⅬⅬⅬⅬⅬⅬⅬⅬⅬⅬⅬ

3. The savage environment, from the *Life* of St. Maieul of Cluny

Hagiography, the lives of saints, offers us the most vivid, if perhaps not the most precise, picture of European life in the first feudal age. In the following life of Abbot Maieul (d. 994) of the great monastery of Cluny in Burgundy, the author first alludes to the establishment by Saracen pirates of a base at Fréjus in what is now the French Riviera (*ca.* 890). They held it for nearly a century, and in 972 audaciously kidnapped Maieul himself, who was returning from a pilgrimage to Rome. This outrage finally prompted the Christians to expel the pirates. Reversing his chronology, the author then compares the battle waged by Maieul's father against wolves with Maieul's own against the devil. Caught among hostile raiders, wild animals, and the devil, the men of this age had reason for an acute sense of insecurity. The source is the Vita sancti Maioli abbatis cluniacensis, *Acta Sanctorum, Maii Tomus II* (Paris and Rome, 1866), p. 688. The translation is by D. Herlihy.

At that time, a gigantic, savage, and most cruel multitude of Saracens sailed from the territories of Spain to the frontiers of Italy and Provence. In both kingdoms they dealt out slaughter to persons of both clerical and lay status, of both sexes and of all ages. They destroyed monasteries and laid waste cities, villages and estates. In quick raids they struck across the Julian Alps as far as the Apennines. There, giving free reign to their impiety, they long afflicted the people of the Christian name with raids and punishments. Killing some, enslaving others, despoiling still others of all they owned, they sated the desires of their impiety by their criminal acts. Among the other foul deeds which this most accursed people perpetrated, they captured by deceit and ambush the most blessed Abbot Maieul, who was returning from the Apostolic See [972]. After robbing him of all his possessions, they bound him with chains and tortured him with hunger and thirst. He, however, freed by divine aid and finally ransomed by the moneys of his monastery, escaped uninjured from their hands, with the help of the Lord. And his criminal capture was the occasion of their own expulsion and perpetual ruin. Just as after the passion of Christ the Jews were exiled from their home, so after the capture of His slave and most faithful servant Maieul, the Saracens were expelled from the territory of the Christians. And just as through the Roman emperors Titus and Vespasian the Lord exacted vengeance from the Jews, so He also did through William [duke of Aquitaine], the most illustrious and Christian prince. By the merits of the blessed Maieul, he cast off the yoke of the Saracens from the backs of the Christians, and by his powerful virtue seized the wide expanses of land, which had been possessed by them, from their criminal control. But having said this, we must return to our theme.

But what was the theme which we had proposed to discuss? An unforgettable portent, which foretold the events which were to come in the times of the blessed Maieul. What were those predicted events? The unforeseen attack of the Saracens, the sufferings of the Christian peoples, the destruction of monasteries and cities, the capture of blessed Maieul himself, his ransom and liberation, and the expulsion of the same ferocious people from Christian territory, with the help of Christ. What was the unforgettable portent which predicted these things? The most cruel attacks of the Saracens were foreshadowed [at the time of Maieul's father] by the unprecedented ferocity of wolves, especially in those regions which the Saracens would later attack by sea. We related a little while back how the masses of the faithful were freed from the persecutions of the Saracens. Let us now tell according to our powers how it was that the land was saved from the invasion of wolves. There was at that time in those regions a certain knight by the name of Folcher. He was strong in arms and very wealthy in inherited property and other goods and riches. If we may mention his most distinguished ancestry, he shone with the twin nobility of both parents. He was a man of great counsel and of prudent and most wise intellect. He was, that is, the father of our most holy Abbot Maieul, of whom we are speaking.

In his lands and neighborhood, the attacks of the wolves which we have just mentioned were more savage than anywhere else. Among their pack (that is, of the wolves), one was seen to surpass the others in strength of body, speed of foot, viciousness in biting, and zeal in devouring, so much so that in his ferocity he swallowed whole the limbs of human bodies. Then this man, hearing and seeing how the great plague and ruin daily grew greater, took to considering not only his own needs but those of others. He began to plan most intensively how he might free himself and his dependents from this pressing danger. Finally, encouraged by divine approval and strengthened by divine counsel, he ordered fences to be erected and pens to be formed, and the goats, sheep, and lambs to be placed in them. Because of the ferocity of the wolves, no one before had dared to do this. Then, putting on his armor, cuirass, and helmet, and covering himself entirely with sheepskins, he began to pass the nights next to the sheepfolds. On one of the nights, the wolves attacked the pens. With the permission of God it came about that the wolf who was crueler than the others threw himself upon the waiting man. He leaped upon the knight's back and put both paws on his shoulders. He began to seek everywhere how he might quickly finish off the ram who was not a ram. He found the throat and neck protected by the cuirass, and the head covered by the helmet, and the body defended by armor fit for a king. At once the knight stretched out both his hands and seized both feet of the wolf. The equal of the wolf in strength, he powerfully grasped the limbs of the wolf with his own limbs, and with rapid pace returned to his companions. They had been waiting a long time and were fearful of the outcome of this struggle. He placed before their eyes as a great gift to them the huge wolf, which was kept alive until the following day and displayed to the men, to whom he had always been so evil. Then he was killed and cut open, and in his bowels were found whole limbs of human beings. The dead animal was hanged on a tree, and when this one wolf was killed, all the others fled from the land.

If anyone wishes to meditate prudently upon these things, he can discern spiritual meaning in them. In the violence of the wolves there was predicted, I believe, the ferocity of the Saracens. In that man, in lay clothing, praiseworthy in many things, who tricked the wolf and in tricking killed him, I think that his son was foretold. By him and by his example, learning, and merit, many souls of the faithful were rescued from the invisible wolf, that is, the ancient enemy [the devil]. Through his powers they were brought to the path of salvation, life, truth, and justice. Through him the ancient enemy was overcome by the power of Christ, rebuffed with all his vices and deceptions, and defeated by heavenly might and spiritual arms. And with Maieul there served as leader, companion, and follower the one who is the way, the truth, and the life, that is, the Lord Jesus Christ, who lives and reigns with God, forever and forever. Amen.

ⅬⅬⅬⅬⅬⅬⅬⅬⅬⅬⅬⅬⅬⅬⅬⅬⅬⅬⅬⅬⅬⅬⅬⅬⅬⅬⅬⅬⅬ

4. Miracles and mental attitudes in the *Histories* of Raoul Glaber

Raoul Glaber (the "bald" or the "beardless") was a monk who lived at Cluny and other Burgundian monasteries in the first half of the eleventh century. His *Historiarum libri quinque*, finished probably by 1048, rambles geographically and chronologically and overflows with visions and wonders. But it would be hard to find a more colorful introduction to the tumultuous social and mental world of the first feudal age. The first part of the following selections illustrates the characteristic monastic effort to structure reality according to its allegorical or symbolic significance. The selections also include Raoul's account of several of the great events of his times: the appalling famines of the period 1030–33; the movements known as the Truce of God and the Peace of God in southern France; and the mass pilgrimages to the Holy Land, the immediate prelude to the Crusades. The Latin text may be found in the *Patrologia Latina*, ed. J. P. Migne (Vol. 142, Paris, 1853); the translation is by D. Herlihy.

Raoul Glaber, to Odilo, the most illustrious of men, abbot of the monastery of Cluny.

I am responding to the just complaints which I have often heard expressed by my fellow scholars and which at times I have expressed myself. No one these days is concerned with transmitting to those who will come after us an account of the many deeds which we are witnessing both in the churches of God and among the peoples. Moreover, the Savior has declared that with the co-operation of the Holy Spirit in union with His Father, He would up to the last hour of the last day cause extraordinary events to happen in the world. For nearly two hundred years, since the time of Bede,[1] priest of Britain, and Paul of Italy, there has been no one who, inspired with such an intent, has left to posterity the slightest historical account. Even these two wrote nothing but the history of their own people and their own fatherland. It is, however, clear that both in the Roman world and in the lands beyond the sea or among the barbarians many things have happened which would be most profitable to men if memory of them could be preserved. Most especially, they would encourage the cultivation of prudence. I speak above all concerning the events which occurred with unaccustomed frequency about one thousand years after Christ became man. I have, therefore, according to my power, heeded your request and bowed to the wishes of my brothers. I shall first of all say briefly that although the chronology since the beginning of the world found in the histories of the Hebrews is not the same as in the translation of the seventy [the Septuagint], at least we can affirm certainly that the year 1002 of the Incarnation of the Word is the first of the reign of Henry, king of the Saxons. The year 1000 of our Savior was the thirteenth of the reign of Robert, king of the Franks. On this side of the ocean these two princes were considered to be the most Christian and the most powerful. The first, moreover, Henry, subsequently attained the Roman Empire. We can use their dates in order to establish the passage of time. Moreover, as we wish to relate the events which occurred in the four parts of the world, it seems to us proper and desirable, since we are primarily addressing religious persons, that the value of the divine and abstract quaternity and its harmonious relationship with real things be first treated in this work, with the help of God.

[On the divine quaternity]

I, 1.   God, Creator of all things, made many differences of figure and form in His creatures. He wished to aid the soul of the wise man, through those things which his eyes discern or his spirit understands, to rise to a simple understanding of the divinity. The Catholic Greek fathers, by no means weak philosophers, were the first to shine forth in the study and profound knowledge of these

---

1. Bede (673–735) was the greatest of the Anglo-Saxon scholars. His *Ecclesiastical History of the English People* is one of the most important documents of Anglo-Saxon history.

things. By perspicaciously investigating many things, they reached an understanding of certain quaternities, by which the present lower world and the heavenly world which is to come are explained to the intelligence. Once we have clearly understood them, these quaternities and their interactions render more alert the minds and the intellects of those who study them. Thus, there are four Gospels which in our minds constitute the superior world. There are an equal number of elements, which make up the inferior world. Also, there are four virtues, which surpass all the others and, by our admiration of them, infuse us with all the others. In like manner, there are four senses, excepting touch, which is placed beneath the more subtle senses as a servant. Thus, just as ether is the element of fire in the visible world, so is prudence within the spiritual world, for it aspires to go up and it pants with the desire to come closer to God. Similarly, what air is in the material order, fortitude is in the spiritual world, supporting everything which lives and strengthening everyone in the acts he is doing. Just as water acts in the material world, temperance does in the intellectual. It nourishes the good, brings with it a multitude of virtues, and preserves the faith by a desire for the love of God. And earth in the lower world presents an image corresponding to justice in the spiritual world, which is the permanent and unbending law of just distribution. . . .

[*On the great famine and the incursion of the Saracens*]
II, 9. At the same time a terrible famine, lasting five years, spread over the entire Roman world to such an extent that one did not hear speak of a single region that was spared from misery and lack of bread. A large part of the population died of starvation. In many places the terrible hunger forced men to consume not only unclean animals and reptiles but even human beings, women and children. No affection even within the family called a halt. The intensity of this famine reached a point that grown sons ate their mothers, while the mothers themselves, forgetting all sentiment, did the same with their little babies.

Subsequently, under the command of their king, Al-Mansur, the Saracen people poured out of the African lands and occupied almost the entire territory of Spain up to the southern borders of Gaul and perpetrated great massacres of Christians. Despite the inferiority of his forces, William, duke of Navarre, called the

Holy, several times attacked and joined battle with them. Lack of soldiers forced even the monks of the land to take up arms. Both sides suffered heavy losses. Finally, the Christians gained the victory, and with great loss of their numbers, the surviving Saracens fled back to Africa. But in this long series of battles certainly death also came to many Christians who wished to fight not out of fraternal love but rather for some sort of ambitious desire for glory.

In these days a brother named Vulferius, of sweet and loving morals, lived in the monastery of Réome in the Tardenais. One Sunday he had a divine vision worthy of belief. After the celebration of matins he withdrew to pray in the holy place while the other brothers were taking a little rest. Suddenly the entire church was filled with men dressed in white robes and adorned with purple stoles. Their grave faces told much of their quality to the one who saw them. At their head marched a man with a cross in his hand. He said he was the bishop of many peoples and asserted that he had to celebrate Holy Mass in this place on that very day. He and the others declared that they had been present that night at the celebration of matins with the brothers of the monastery. They added that the office of lauds which they had heard was perfectly suitable to this day. This was the Sunday within the octave of Pentecost, the day on which in celebration of the Lord's resurrection and ascension and the coming of the Holy Spirit, a custom exists in many lands to sing responses, composed in truly sublime words and set to a pleasing melody, as worthy of the Holy Trinity as a work of human ingenuity can be. The bishop drew near to the altar of the martyr St. Maurice and, chanting the anthem of the Trinity, began to celebrate Holy Mass. Our brother, nonetheless, asked who they were, whence they came, and the purpose of this visit. They responded politely.

"We exercise," they said, "the profession of Christianity, but in the protection of our fatherland and in the defense of the Christian people, the sword in the Saracen war has separated us from the habitation of our bodies. This is the reason why God summons us all together to share the inheritance of the blessed. But it has been necessary for us to pass through this province since there are many who in a brief time are going to join our company."

The one who celebrated the office of the Mass at the end of the Lord's Prayer gave peace to all and sent one of them to give also the kiss of peace to our brother. Having received a kiss, this one saw that the other made a sign for him to follow. As he started to accompany him, the vision ended and they disappeared. And the brother understood that within a short time he would depart this world—which also came about. Five months after having this vision, that is, in the following December, he went at the request of the abbot to Auxerre to take care of several brothers of the monastery of St. Germain who were sick, for he was well trained in the medical arts. From the time of his arrival he began to exhort the brothers for whom he had come to take care to do as rapidly as possible what was needed for their cure. He knew in truth that his own death was close. They answered him, "Take some rest today because of the exertion of your journey, in order that you might be stronger tomorrow."

He replied, "If I do not finish today what remains to be done as far as I am able, you shall see that tomorrow I shall do none of it."

They thought he was joking, for he always had a cheerful personality, and they ignored his advice. But when the new day dawned, he was seized by a sharp pain. He reached as he could the altar of the Blessed Mary ever Virgin, there to celebrate Holy Mass. When he had said it, he returned to the infirmary and, already in the grip of intolerable pain, extended himself on the bed. As often happens in such cases, sleep weighed upon his eyelids in the midst of his pains. Suddenly, he saw the Virgin in her splendor, shining with a brilliant light. She asked him of what he was afraid. As he watched her, she added, "If it is the passage that you fear, you have nothing to give you fright. I shall serve you as a guardian."

Encouraged by this vision, he asked that the prior of the place, named Achard, a man of profound learning, come alongside him. Achard later became abbot of this monastery and told in detail this vision and also the preceding one.

The monk said to him, "Take heart, my brother, in the Lord. But as you have seen what is rarely given to men to see, so you must pay the tribute of all flesh so that you may share the lot of those who appeared to you."

And the other brothers, summoned, made him the visit usually made in such instances. At the end of the third day, as night was falling, he left his body. . . .

[*Concerning the rain of stones*]

II, 10. At the same time in Burgundy, at the castle of Joigny, a truly astonishing and memorable event occurred in the home of a noble named Arlebaudus. For nearly three consecutive years almost without interruption—it cannot be said whether from the sky or from the roof—there fell large and small rocks, so many that even today piles of the stones are easily seen around the house. But although this hail rained day and night through the entire house, nevertheless it did not injure anyone and did not break even the smallest vase. Many people found there the stones (called by some the *bornes*) which marked the limits of their fields. They also recognized that stones coming from the roads, the houses, and other buildings near or far had been carried to this place. Events were clearly to prove that this was the sign of a disaster about to strike the family inhabiting this house. The man mentioned above, and his wife as well, came from very noble and rich parents. Thus, there had developed among their children and grandchildren and surrounding neighbors much strife concerning the patrimonial possessions. Not long after, an estate known by the name of Aillants, located in the country of Sens, came into their possession by a donation of the priors of Saint Colombe. Knights inhabiting Auxerre seized and sacked it, but the family made every effort to regain it. The struggle lasted over many years. One day, during the wine harvest, the two parties joined combat within this estate. In this combat many died on both sides. Of the children and grandchildren of the family mentioned above, eleven died. Subsequently, the quarrel continued. The discord grew bitter, and many unhappy events continued to strike this family, of whom many were murdered over thirty and more years.

[*Concerning the most fierce famine which occurred in the world*]

IV, 4. At the approach of the year 1033 of the Incarnation of Christ, the millennium of the Passion of the Savior, several illustrious men died in the Roman world who were true representatives of holy religion: Benedict, the sovereign pontiff; and, as we have said, Robert, king of the Franks; also Fulbert, incomparable bishop of Chartres, a man full of wisdom; and finally, that father of monks and eminent founder of monasteries, William [da Volpiano], concerning whom many useful things might be said if, as is known, they had not already some time ago been stated in a little book which we have published concerning his life and his virtues. There remains, however, one deed which I have learned and which is not found in that book. This father departed our world for the rest of the blessed in the land of Neustria, at the monastery of Fécamp, located on the shores of the ocean, about forty miles from the town of Rouen. He was buried as was fitting for such a man in the place of honor in this sanctuary. Now, a few days later, it happened that a little child some ten years of age, struck by a serious illness, was brought to the tomb of the abbot to recover his health. His parents left him there, and he lay down all alone. Suddenly, lifting up his eyes, he saw that on the tomb was perched a little bird, showing the form of a dove. Looking at it for a long time, he fell asleep. Then, after a light sleep, upon awakening he found himself in perfect health, just as if he had never been sick. His parents took back with joy their child amid general rejoicing.

Subsequently, famine began to extend its ravages over the whole world. There was fear that nearly the entire human race would disappear. The climate of the air became so unfavorable that no place could be found suitable for any sowing; nor, because of floods, was it possible to collect the harvest. It was as if these hostile elements were battling one with the other, since beyond doubt they were taking vengeance on the insolence of humanity. Continuing rains soaked the entire earth, so that for three years no furrows could be found suitable to receive the seed. At the time of the harvest wild weeds and damaging tares covered all the surface of the fields. A *modius* of seed even on the best land gave at harvest a *sextarius* [between a sixth and a twenty-fourth of a *modius*], and this *sextarius* itself returned hardly a handful. This avenging sterility first began in the lands of the East. It laid waste Greece, arrived in Italy, and from there, having passed into Gaul, crossed this land to reach all the peoples of England. Since the lack of food struck the entire people, great men and those of the middle class shared with the poor the horrors of hunger. The brigandage of the powerful gave way before the universal want. If by accident some food was offered in sale, the seller could at his will demand an excessive price for it. In many places, a *modius* sold for sixty *solidi*, and elsewhere the *sextarius* for fifteen. Meanwhile, after the savage beasts and the birds had been eaten, men in the grasp of consuming hunger set about gathering all sorts of carrion and things horrible to relate, in order to consume them. Certain ones among them, in order to escape death, had recourse to the roots of trees and to river grasses. But uselessly: there is no escape from the vengeance of God unless one turns to Him. Finally, it is horrible to hear of the perversions which then came to the human race. Alas! O sorrow! Something rarely heard of in the course of the ages, a raging hunger led men to eat human flesh. Some travelers were killed by the stronger among them, their limbs cut off, cooked on a fire, and eaten. Many people who took themselves from one place to another to flee the hunger and who had found hospitality on the road were murdered during the night and served as food to those who had welcomed them. Many others, by showing an apple or an egg to children, enticed them to remote places, massacred them, and ate them. The bodies of the dead were in many places dug up from the earth and similarly served to appease hunger. This uncontrolled madness assumed such proportions that the animals which remained alone were less menaced by the ravages than were the men. Just as if it were an established custom to eat human flesh, there was a man who sold it already cooked at the market place of Tournus, as if it had been made from the flesh of some animal. Caught, he did not at all deny his shameful crime; he was bound and thrown to the flames. Another came by night to unearth the flesh that had been buried in the soil, ate it, and was similarly burned in his turn.

There was a church dedicated to St. John about three miles distant from the town of Mâcon. It was located in the forest of Chattenet and was alone and without surrounding structures. Near this church, a savage man had built his cabin. All those who passed by the place or who came to his house, he murdered and used for food at his abominable meals. One day it happened that a man came with his wife to ask hospitality and to rest a little at his home. Suddenly, while casting his eye in the corners of the cabin, the visitor perceived the decapitated heads of men, women, and children. At once he grew pale and sought to escape. But the wicked owner of the cabin opposed him and forced him to remain. Frightened by this mortal trap, our man nevertheless made his escape and in all haste reached the town with his wife. Upon arrival he reported what he had seen to Count Otto and to the other citizens of the town. Without delay many men were dispatched to inquire after the truth of the matter. They left in haste and found the bloody individual in his cabin with the heads of forty-eight victims whose flesh had already been swallowed in his bestial throat. They brought him to the town, where he was tied to a stake in a barn. Then, as we saw with our own eyes, he was delivered to the flames.

In the same region an event occurred which to our knowledge never happened before. Many persons took from the soil a white earth which resembles clay and mixed it with bran or whatever flour they had. They made of this mixture loaves with which they might escape death from famine. However, in this practice there was only a hope of escape, and it proved empty. Palor and emaciation marked the faces of all. Many showed a skin distended by stomach swelling. The human voice itself became shrill, similar to the little cries of dying birds. The bodies of the dead, which for reason of their number had to be left here and there without burial, served as food for wolves, which continued for long to search their prey among men. And since, as we were saying, not everybody could be separately buried because of the great number of the dead, in certain places God-fearing men dug what were commonly called charnel houses, in which the bodies of the dead were thrown, five hundred or more in number, just as they were, pell-mell, half-naked or without any shroud. The thoroughfares and the borders of fields also served as cemeteries. Many persons, hearing that they might do better to travel to other lands, died on the road from exhaustion.

The world, in punishment for the sins of men, was the victim of this disastrous scourge for three years. The ornaments of the churches were taken to be sold for the benefit of the poor. Treasures were dispersed which, as is seen in the instructions left by the ancient abbots, had been accumulated in other times for this purpose. But just as there still remained vengeance to be taken, so the needs of the poor were frequently greater than the treasures of the churches. Some hungry persons, too deeply wasted by the lack of nourishment, if by chance they found something upon which to feed, puffed up and died at once. Others, their hands trembling over the food, sought to carry it to their mouth but gave up, discouraged, not having the strength to accomplish what they wished. What sorrow, what affliction, what moans, what cries, what tears such sights produced, especially among the people of the Church, bishops and abbots, monks and nuns, and, in general, all those men or women, clerics or laymen, who had the fear of

God in their hearts. Written words can hardly give an idea. It was believed that the ordering of the seasons and the elements, which had prevailed in past centuries since the beginning, had returned forever to chaos, and that this was the end of the human race. And here is a fact more likely than the others to produce fearful astonishment. Under this mysterious scourge of divine vengeance, rarely were there found people who before so much horror knew how to assume a contrite heart, and a humble stance, and to raise as they should have their souls and their hands toward God to call Him to their aid. Thus did our times see the fulfillment of the words of Isaiah saying, "And the people are not returned to him who has struck them." In truth, there was among men a kind of hardening of the heart, joined to a weakness of the intelligence, even though the supreme Judge, the Author of all goodness, grants the desire to pray—He Who knows when He ought to have pity.

[*Concerning the peace and abundance of the one-thousandth
year of the passing of the Lord*]

IV, 5. In the year 1000 after the passion of the Lord, which came after this disastrous famine, the clouds ceased to pour down rain. In obedience to divine goodness and mercy, the smiling heavens began to clear, to blow favorable winds, and to proclaim by their peaceful serenity the generosity of the Creator. All the earth was covered with a pleasant verdure, and it began to produce abundant fruits which completely dissipated the famine. First in the regions of Aquitaine, bishops, abbots, and other men dedicated to holy religion began to gather the people in full assembly. To them were carried many bodies of the blessed and cases filled with holy relics. Through the province of Arles, then that of Lyons, then through all of Burgundy to the farthest reaches of France, it was announced in all the dioceses that in appointed places the prelates and the great men of the entire country would hold councils for the reestablishment of peace and the maintenance of the holy faith. When news of these assemblies was known through the entire population, great lords and people of the middle and the lower classes gathered there full of joy, unanimously disposed to do whatever the pastors of the church prescribed. A voice coming from heaven and speaking to men on the earth could not have accomplished more. For everyone remained under the effect of the terror of the calamities of the preceding period, and all were seized by the fear of seeing themselves deprived in the future of the pleasant abundance. A document was drawn up, divided into chapters, which contained the list of forbidden actions as well as those sacred obligations which they decreed should be assumed toward Almighty God. The most important of these obligations was to observe an inviolable peace. Both clerics and laymen henceforth were to go in peace and without arms, no matter what dangers had formerly weighed upon them. Thieves and those who invaded the land of another were subject to the rigor of the law and punished either by the confiscation of their property or by corporal punishment. The holy places of all the churches became the object of such veneration that if a man guilty of any crime fled into them, no evil could be done to him, provided only that he had not violated the agreement of peace. Then he was seized at the very foot of the altar and had to pay the prescribed penalty. No harm was to be done to monks and nuns or those who crossed a land in their company.

Many decisions were made in these assemblies which we wish to describe at length. One deed worth recalling is that all the world agreed to hold holy from that time forward the sixth day of each week by abstaining from wine and the seventh day by abstaining from meat, except in cases of grave illness or if a great feast fell on those days. If anyone by any circumstances relaxed this rule, he was then to feed three poor persons. Many sick people regained their health at these meetings, where the bodies of so many saints had been brought. And lest anyone take these miracles for illusions, many times it happened that at the moment when crippled arms or legs regained their former soundness, the skin was seen to be torn, the flesh to be exposed, and the blood to rush out in gushes. This shows the truth of the other instances concerning which doubt might remain. These miracles excited such enthusiasm that the bishops lifted their crosses toward heaven and all present stretched their hands to God, crying in a single voice: "Peace, peace, peace." They saw in such miracles the sign of a perpetual agreement and of the obligation which bound them with God. It was further understood that after five years had passed, everyone in the entire world would renew these manifestations with a marvelous splendor to consolidate the peace. Finally, in this very year wheat, wine, and the other produce of the earth were in such abundance that an equal quantity could not have been hoped for during the subsequent five years. All food good for man, saving only meats and dishes of special delicacy, was sold for a pittance. It was as in the ancient times of the great jubilee of Moses. In the second, third, and fourth years the harvest did not lessen.

But alas! O sorrow! The human race, forgetful from the start of the favors of God, inclined to evil, as the dog which returns to its vomit, like the hog wallowing in the filthy mud, many times violated its own obligations. And as it is written, "The beloved grew fat and wicked," the great nobles and the prelates, returning to their avarice, set about as much as, or even more than, in the past to satisfy their rapacious appetites through numerous pillagings. Then the persons of the middle and lower classes were brought by the example of the great into infamous vices. For who until this time had heard speak of so many acts of incest, adultery, illicit unions among kinsmen, shameful concubinage, and so much rivalry in doing evil? And to cap all these evils, there was not even to be found among the people a few just men to reprehend the others and reproach them for their conduct. Thus was fulfilled the words of the prophet, "And it shall be as with the people so with the priest." One remarkable event was that, at the example of the secular authority, within the Church the duties of the supreme head were assumed by a child. For the sins of the people, the words of Solomon were fulfilled: "Woe to thee, O land." For the Roman sovereign pontiff himself, nephew of the two Benedicts and of John, his predecessor, was a child of some ten years. The silver of his treasures gained him the election by the Romans, who then expelled him many times, restored him dishonestly, and left him with no authority. As we have already expressed our indignation above, all the other prelates at that time owed their election to gold and silver rather than to their merit. O shame! Concerning them, sacred Scripture clearly speaks, and for these princes of God it says, "They have been princes and I know them not."

[*On the confluence of the people of the entire world to the sepulcher of the Lord at Jerusalem*]
IV, 6.   At the same time an uncounted multitude from the entire world took to traveling toward the sepulcher of the Savior at Jerusalem. Never before had so many been seen. First, there went people from the lowest classes, then those of the middle ranks, then all the greatest kings, counts, marquises, and prelates. Finally, what

had never happened before, women of the high nobility were seen traveling to this place in the company of the most miserable people. Many wished to die before returning to their countries. A Burgundian named Lethbaldus from the region of Auxerre arrived one day with the others. After having viewed the holy places with the others, he came to pass by the Mount of Olives, from which the Savior was taken up to heaven in the view of so many trustworthy witnesses, and from where He promised to judge the living and the dead. Throwing himself forward in the manner of a cross, prostrate for his entire length, all in tears, the man felt himself exulting in the Lord through an indescribable inner joy. Every now and then he stood up, raised his hands toward the sky, stretched with all his power upward, and gave evidence by his word of the desire with which his heart was filled.

"Lord Jesus, Who for us deigned to descend from the seat of Your majesty upon the earth to save the human race, and Who, from this place which I see with my own eyes, returned with Your body to the heaven from which You came, I pray Your omnipotent goodness to allow that, if my soul is to pass this year from my body, I do not depart from this place, but that this should happen to me in sight of the place of Your ascension. I truly believe that as I have followed You with my body in coming here, thus my soul may enter safely, soundly, and joyously into Your company in paradise."

After this prayer, he returned with his companions to his hostel. Mealtime came, but while the others sat down at table, he went to his bed with a happy spirit, as if in a heavy drowsiness he was going to take some rest. He fell asleep at once, and it is not known what he saw; but in his sleep he cried, "Glory to You, God, glory to You, God." His companions heard him and sought to raise him and to have him eat with them. He refused and, turning on the other side, declared that he did not feel well. He remained in bed until the evening, summoned his traveling companions, and asked for and received the viaticum of the life-giving Eucharist. Then he saluted them with sweetness and gave up the spirit.

Certainly, this man was exempt from the feelings of vanity which inspire so many people to undertake the journey, those who are eager only to embellish themselves with the prestigious title of pilgrims to Jerusalem. With faith he had asked in the name of the Lord Jesus to draw near to the Father, and he was heard. His companions, upon their return, told us this tale when we were at the monastery of Bèze. At the same time Ulric, bishop of Orléans, made the same journey. That which he saw and told us seems to us a miracle which ought not to be left in silence.

On the day of Holy Saturday, when the entire people prayed for the fire to come through a miracle of divine power, this bishop was with them. It was already evening; toward the hour when the arrival of the fire was expected, a mischievous Saracen, full of impudence, rose from the large crowd which each year customarily mixed with the Christians. He cried, as is the practice of the faithful once the fire appears, *"Alios kyrie eleison."* He broke into a mocking smile, stretched his arm, then seized a candle from the hands of a Christian and tried to flee. But immediately he was the prey of the demon and began to feel unbearable torments. The Christian caught him and took back his candle. As for the Saracen, twisted by pain, he expired soon afterward in the arms of his fellows. The incident spread among the Saracens a general fear, while it inspired joy and happiness among the faithful of Christ. At the same time, as was usual, by divine power the fire leaped from one of the seven lamps which may be seen hanging in this place and, spreading rapidly, enkindled the others. The bishop purchased this lamp with its oil for the price of one pound of gold from Jordanus, then patriarch of Jerusalem. He brought it home and placed it in his episcopal church, where it worked many miracles for the sick. He also brought to King Robert a large piece of the venerable cross of Our Lord Savior from Constantine, emperor of the Greeks, who sent to the prince at the same time a quantity of silk cloth. On his part, the king had sent to the emperor by the same prelate a sword whose handle was gold and whose scabbard was gold inlaid with precious stones.

Also at this time Robert, duke of the Normans, among others set out for Jerusalem with an enormous crowd of his subjects, carrying with him a large number of presents in gold and silver for distribution. Upon his return he died in the city of Nice, where he was buried. His death spread among his subjects a great desolation, for he left no legitimate heir to assume the government of the province. As is known, he did indeed marry a sister of Canute, king of England, but he fell out with her and repudiated her. However, he did have by a concubine a son to whom he gave the name of his ancestor William. Before his departure he had all the nobles of his duchy swear upon their honor as warriors to choose this son for their chief in case he did not return. Without hesitation, with the consent of Henry, king of France, they then kept their promise. Besides, it was the custom of this nation from its first settlement in France, as is noted above, to have as its princes men born of illegitimate unions. To avoid excessive scandal, the example of the sons of the concubines of Jacob could be invoked. These were not, for that reason, deprived of paternal dignities, and are counted among the patriarchs with the same right as the other brothers. And much more recently, in the last years of the universal monarchy, history teaches us that the great initiator of the faith of Christ into the empire, Constantine, was the son of the concubine Helena.

Many persons most inclined to worry in this period went to consult certain seers concerning the significance of such a great movement of people to Jerusalem, to which no prior century had seen anything similar. Weighing their words, the seers replied that this signified nothing else but the coming of the dread Antichrist, who was necessarily expected to appear when the end of the world was approaching. With this understanding, all the peoples crowded the road to the Orient, where he was supposed to arrive, and the nations marched directly to meet him. And thus, in truth, was accomplished the prophecy of the Lord according to which even the elect, if possible, shall in the last days fall into temptation. We shall restrain ourselves further on this subject; at all events, we do not deny that the pious works of the faithful will allow them to receive from the just Judge their recompense and salary.

II. *The Second Feudal Age*

⎿⎾⎿⎾⎿⎾⎿⎾⎿⎾⎿⎾⎿⎾⎿⎾⎿⎾⎿⎾⎿⎾⎿⎾⎿⎿⎿

5. The growth of Arras, according to the Monk Guimann

Nearly all historians are agreed that an underlying phenomenon of the second feudal age was a substantial and continuing growth in population. But no historian can really measure it, and the reconstruction is based exclusively on indirect evidence, chiefly allusions in and inferences derived from reticent documents. The following records are examples of such documents; they are drawn from a chartulary of the abbey of St. Vaast in Arras in northwest France, written in 1175 by a monk named Guimann. The reader should be able to judge for himself what conclusions can, or cannot, be drawn from them. The source is *Cartulaire de l'abbaye de Saint-Vaast, rédigé au XII siècle par Guimann*, ed. E. Van Drival (Arras, 1875), pp. 239, 332. The translation is by D. Herlihy. The échevin was an elected official of the town; the cellerarius was a monastic official in charge of provisioning the monastery.

That the Entire City of Arras Is Located in the Domain of St. Vaast

You should note therefore, diligent reader, from the preceding description of the neighborhoods and squares, and hold as most certain that the entire city of Arras is in the domain of St. Vaast. There is nothing in the entire circuit of the city which can be constructed without the approval of the abbot and the church, saving only in the neighborhood or the part of the street which specifically belongs to the bishop. For this reason, it is much to be wondered at that some churches in this city do not belong to St. Vaast, since to one who diligently scrutinizes [the record] there can be no doubt that all the churches of this city ought to belong to St. Vaast, or to be dependent on it. But this we believe to have occurred because of the stupidity and negligence of the preceding abbots. They saw the extraordinary extent of land and the scarcity of inhabitants and could hardly have anticipated the present situation, the extreme shortage of habitations, and the copious flood of inhabitants. For in our days when the insolence both of powerful citizens and of the canons sought to erect churches in the domain of St. Vaast, at the protest of the abbot and the chapter and with the disapproval of the Apostolic See, this was not allowed, as in the earlier parts of this chartulary is made evident, in the privilege which is included concerning the parishes. . . .

Concerning the milling of the bakers [1115]

In the name of the Lord, Father, Son, and Holy Spirit. Amen. Balduin, son of Robert the count who is buried at Arras, count of Flanders, to all the faithful of God, greetings. It pleases me to inform those present and to come that as I, Count Balduin, was staying at Arras, and was sitting with my court in attendance in the room of the abbot Henry, behold the same abbot and his monks came to me and made in our hearing a great complaint against the bakers of this city, who daily were depriving them of sustenance. For the monks said that by ancient law and custom all the bakers of the city were supposed to bear their wheat to the mills of Mellens, and there and nowhere else to have it ground. Now by unlawful presumption they seek to free themselves of this obligation, to the injury and damage of the church. When I heard this, because it was my responsibility to protect the church, I consulted the échevin in office and the worthier and more creditable men of the city, so that they might bring the truth of the affair out into the open. I adjured them to inform me by the faith and oath which they had made to me. They replied that it was the truth that all the bakers were supposed to go to Mellens, and there and not elsewhere to grind their wheat. If the sergeant of the cellerarius should capture any baker carrying his wheat elsewhere, he should have the ass with the wheat brought to Mellens without any opposition. If he should catch someone returning from elsewhere, he should bring him to the court of the cellerarius, and [the wheat] should remain in his possession. At this report, with the urging of the entire court, and upon their request, I restored its right to the church, and I commanded and ordered that a decree be written to assure that those present and to come would remember it, and also that it be proclaimed in the market place in the name of the law that if any baker henceforth should go and be captured by the sergeant of the cellerarius, being in contempt of my edict he should incur penalty.

I, Count Balduin, promulgated this command, and the witnesses of the command are the following. . . .

Done at Arras, the year 1115, in the reign of King Louis.

[Guimann's comment:] This custom lasted a long time, but as the number of bakers grew great, permission was given them to go to the mills of St. Vaast, which are located from Anzin to Athies.

6. Monetary revenues and the bureaucratic spirit, in the *Dialogue concerning the Exchequer*

The *Dialogue concerning the Exchequer* was written by Richard Fitzneal, bishop of London, probably in 1177. It describes in detail the operation of the royal "exchequer," named for the use of a table covered with squares, resembling a checkerboard, which was used for accounting purposes. In fact there were two Exchequers, a lower one to which the sheriff made his payments to the royal treasury, and a higher Exchequer, which functioned as a court and settled disputes concerning financial matters. The *Dialogue* is a unique tract, as it elucidates not only the technical operation of the Exchequer but the new bureaucratic skills and spirit needed in its operation. There is manifest in its pages an unmistakable pride in what is explicitly called the "art" and the "mysteries" of royal finance. The account concerning the origins of the monetary rents paid the crown, given in Chapter 7, is considered generally accurate by most historians, even though simplified. The best edition of the *Dialogue* is *Dialogus de Scaccario*, eds. A. Hughes, C. G. Crump, and C. Johnson (Oxford, 1902). Complete English translations are available in *English Historical Documents, 1042–1189*, ed. D. C. Douglas and G. W. Greenway (English Historical Documents, 2; New York: Oxford University Press, 1955), pp. 490–569; and C. Johnson, *The Course of the Exchequer by Richard, Son of Nigel* (London: Thomas Nelson, 1950), with the Latin text. The translation here is by D. Herlihy.

Preface

It is necessary in all fear to be subject to and to honor the powers ordained by God. "For there is no power but from God" (Romans 13.1). Therefore, it does not appear foolish or inappropriate for ecclesiastical persons to preserve the rights of kings by serving them, as they are preeminent, and to serve other authorities, especially in those things which are not opposed to truth and good behavior. They should be served not only in regard to the offices which maintain them, through which the glory of the royal authority shows its splendor, but also in regard to the abundance of worldly wealth, which pertains to them by virtue of their status. For the former provides glory but the latter gives support. Therefore, copious or meager funds either raise or lower the powers of princes. Those deficient in this wealth fall prey to their enemies; to whom, however, this wealth is available, their enemies fall prey to them. To be sure, this wealth is frequently accumulated by kings not in strict justice, but sometimes by their regional laws and sometimes by the hidden counsels of their hearts or even by the decision of their own arbitrary power. Nonetheless, their deeds are not to be discussed or condemned by their subjects. For their hearts and the movements of their hearts are in the hands of God. Those whom God Himself has individually entrusted with the care of their subjects stand or fall by divine and not by human judgments. However, let no ruler, however rich, congratulate himself, as if he could count on his own impunity, since of this it is written, "A most severe punishment shall be for them that bear rule" (Wisdom 6.6). Therefore, whatever may be the purpose or the means of acquiring wealth, those who are appointed by their office to its administration may not be remiss in their duty. Rather, in collecting, saving, or spending that wealth they should fittingly show solicitous diligence, as if they were to render an account for the state of the realm, which through this wealth preserves its security. We know, of course, that chiefly by prudence, fortitude, temperance, or justice and by the other virtues kingdoms are ruled and rights upheld; therefore, these rulers of the world must insist on their cultivation with all their efforts. But it happens sometimes that that which healthy advice and outstanding intelligence may conceive is more quickly realized with the aid of money. And what appears to be difficult is easily implemented through money, as if it provided some special way of handling affairs. Money seems to be needed not only in times of war but also of peace. For funds are spent in strengthening cities, in paying salaries, and in many other areas according to the quality of the persons, in order to conserve the state of the realm. Although arms are quiet, devout princes with money build churches, feed and clothe Christ in the persons of the poor, and distribute the Mammon of this world through pursuing other works of charity. In both peace and war princes may take glory in vigorous actions, but glory excels in those princes when by their present expenditures they earn permanent rewards as happy recompense.

Therefore, O illustrious king, greatest of earthly princes, because I have often seen you, glorious in both peace and war, unsparing of the money of the treasury, and eager to meet legitimate expenses according to the place, the time, and the person, we dedicate this slight work to your excellency, written not concerning great affairs nor in brilliant language, but in the crude style concerning the necessary procedure of your Exchequer. Indeed, I have at times discerned that you have been worried about these things to the point that through discreet men, your personal emissaries, you took counsel concerning it with the then Lord Bishop of Ely. Nor was it foolish that a man of your outstanding intellect, a prince of such unique authority, should have taken an interest in this, among other important matters. Certainly the Exchequer functions with its own laws, not capriciously but under the supervision of important men. If its rules are respected in all things, the rights of individuals can be maintained, and you will enjoy a copious income from all that is due you. Under the impulse of your most noble mind, your hand may spend this wealth in opportune enterprise.

Prologue

In the twenty-third year of the reign of King Henry II [1176–77], when I was sitting at the window of a tower which stands next to the river Thames, I was assaulted by the words of a person who addressed me in the following fashion: "Master, have you not read that in a concealed science or in a buried treasure there is no profit?"

When I answered, "Yes, I've read that," he immediately pressed on: "Why then do you not instruct others in the science of the Exchequer which you possess so abundantly? Why do you not commit it to writing lest it perish with you?"

"Come now, brother," I answered, "you have sat at the Exchequer for a long time now, and nothing could have eluded you, since you are so observant. And this is probably true also of the others who are present."

But he replied: "Just as those who walk in darkness and grope with their hands frequently collide, even so, there are many who sit there who, seeing, do not see and, hearing, do not understand."

"You speak disrespectfully," I countered, "for the science is not that exalted nor does it concern great matters. Perhaps those persons who hunt great things have minds similar to the talons of the eagle, which cannot grasp small objects but from which great things cannot escape."

"So be it," he said, "but although eagles fly high, nonetheless they rest and are refreshed in low places, and for this reason we ask you to expound to us the humble facts from which we eagles may profit."

I said in answer: "I have feared to compose a book concerning matters which are observed by the bodily senses and which are cheapened by daily use. Nor is there nor could there be in them a description of subtleties or the pleasing discovery of novelties."

"Those who take pleasure in novelties," he answered, "or yearn for the pursuit of subtle matters have Aristotle and the books of Plato. Let them listen to them. You should write not of subtle but of useful things."

"I cannot," I said, "give you what you seek concerning these matters unless I use rustic speech and familiar words."

At this, as if provoked to wrath (as nothing moves quickly enough for the soul who wants it), he affirmed: "Writers on the liberal arts have compiled many books and have clothed them in inscrutable language, lest they be proved to know very little, and in order that their art should be the more difficult to master. You do not undertake the discussion of an academic subject but rather certain customs and laws of the Exchequer, which because they ought to be commonplace must necessarily be treated in familiar language. Thus, your words concerning the things of which we speak may be understood. Moreover, although it is often necessary to coin new words, still with your permission I request that you be not loathe to utilize the popular terms for those things which are used at court. By this means no new difficulties arising from unfamiliar language would further disturb us."

"I see that you are irritated," I told him, "but calm yourself. I shall do what you request. Get up therefore and sit across from me, and question me concerning those things which strike you. If you should bring up anything unknown to me, I shall not be ashamed to confess my ignorance. Then we may both consult more learned men."

"You fulfill my wishes," he said. "Although it may appear embarrassing and ridiculous for an old man to go to grammar school, nonetheless I'll start from scratch."

[*The origins of money rents*]

Student: By whom and for what reason was this examination [of the quality of the coins given as rent to the king] or assay first instituted?

Master: In order that it may be clear to you concerning these things, we must go back a little. As our fathers have told us, in the former state of the realm after the conquest the kings received from their estates not weights of gold or silver but only payments in kind. These payments provided what was necessary for the daily consumption of the royal household, and those servants who were responsible for this knew how much was paid by the individual estates. But for wages and gifts given to the knights and for other necessities, the needed coined money accrued from the profits of justice and from voluntary payments, and also from towns and castles where agriculture was not practiced. Therefore, through the entire reign of King William I, this practice continued, up until the time of King Henry his son. Even I knew individuals who had seen the payments in kind carried at the appropriate times from the royal estates to the court. The officials of the royal household had an accurate knowledge of those countries from which wheat was due, or various types of meat, or fodder for the horses, and other necessities. When these payments were made according to the accustomed measure for each commodity, the royal officials credited the sheriff by converting their value into monetary terms. Thus, for a measure of wheat suitable to make bread for one hundred men, they assigned one shilling; for one head of a pastured ox, one shilling; for a ram or for a sheep, four pennies; for fodder for twenty horses, similarly four pennies. Later, however, when the same king was struggling in lands beyond the sea away from home to suppress armed unrest, it became necessary for him to have coined money with which to execute his plans. Meanwhile, protesting mobs of peasants flocked to the king's court or, even more distressing to him, they frequently accosted him on the road, holding up their plowshares in symbol of their ruined agriculture. For they were oppressed by innumerable aggravations, since they had to transport the payments in kind from their own homes to many parts of the realm. The king heard their complaints, and upon the stated advice of his barons, he dispatched to the realm men whom he knew to be most prudent and discreet for this task. These men canvassed the individual estates and inspected them with their own eyes; they estimated the value of payments in kind which were paid for them, and they converted it into a sum of money. For the total of all the sums which derived from all the estates in a single county, they made the sheriff of that county responsible before the Exchequer, adding that he should pay according to scale, that is, six pennies over and above each pound of coined money. For they considered that with the passage of time it could easily happen that the good coin of those years might fall from its former excellence. They were not mistaken. Therefore, they were obligated to require that the rent [*firma*] of the manors be paid not only by scale but also by weight, which could not be done unless a great deal more was added. This regulation for making payments was followed for many years at the Exchequer; therefore, frequently in the old pipe rolls [treasury records] of the king you will find written, "in the treasury 100 pounds according to scale," or "in the treasury 100 pounds by weight."

Meanwhile, there appeared a prudent man [Roger of Salisbury, great-uncle of the author], foresighted in his counsels, learned in his speech, and by the grace of God greatly suited for important affairs. You might say that there was fulfilled in him that which is written, "The grace of the Holy Spirit knows no slow movements." Summoned by the same king to his court, this man of no reputation but by no means a contemptible one showed by his example "how fertile is utter poverty in raising men." As a result of his growing popularity with the king, clergy, and people, he was made bishop of Salisbury, attained the highest offices, and was accorded the greatest honors in the kingdom. He also gained a full understanding of the Exchequer. This cannot be doubted, since the very rolls make manifest how greatly it flourished under him. From his superabundant learning we also have inherited what little knowledge we have in us. But for now I will omit much comment, since he has left a reputation as living proof of his most noble mind, entirely worthy of his high rank.

After coming by order of the king to sit at the Exchequer, this man remained there for many years and perceived that the treasury did not receive its due through this manner of payment. Although it appeared to receive what was due it in number and weight of coins, it did not in regard to the substance of the money. For if a man paid, for one pound, twenty shillings by count, even when they corresponded to a pound by weight, it did not follow that he was consequently paying one pound in silver. For it could be that the metal was alloyed with copper, or some kind of bronze, since no assay was made. In order, therefore, that both the public and the royal interest be together served, after deliberation by the king's council, it was decreed that there should be an assay or an examination of the money paid as rent as described above.

Student: How was the public interest thereby served?

Master: As the sheriff now knows that he will be penalized through this testing of inferior money when he is to pay the rent, he applies great diligence that the moneyers established under him do not violate the limits set by law. When he apprehends any, they are punished so severely that their example discourages others.

Student: Ought then "blanch farm" ["white," or assayed rent in silver] to be paid from all the counties?

Master: No. But those which by ancient right are assigned to the crown pay it. Those, however, which by incidental ways came into the possession of the crown pay in counted coins only. The sheriff is free to pay his blanch farm in weight of assayed silver and thus escape the risk of an examination. This happens, however, only if the king's melter determines that the silver is to be accepted. You have therefore what you ask, by whom and for what reason the assay was instituted.

⎍⎍⎍⎍⎍⎍⎍⎍⎍⎍⎍⎍⎍⎍⎍⎍⎍⎍⎍⎍⎍⎍⎍⎍⎍⎍⎍⎍⎍⎍

7. Consciousness of class, in Andreas Capellanus, *The Art of Courtly Love*

In the second feudal age, rising trade and expanding commercial wealth brought into prominence a new class of townsmen who were able by the power of money to challenge the traditional dominance of the warriors. The warriors themselves seem to have reacted to the new competition by stressing their moral and cultural superiority over the crude money grubbers of the city. As we shall discuss in Part IV, they also sought to close their ranks to newcomers by insisting that birth and blood were prerequisites to knighthood and nobility. The new consciousness of class is admirably apparent in the following selections from a twelfth-century handbook for lovers. Its author was Andreas Capellanus, chaplain at the court of Champagne under the Countess Marie (1164–1198). Among the major obstacles to a successful love affair, as Andreas saw it, were class divisions. Here, he proposes model dialogues in which the man, in spite of class fences, can win the lady of his choice. The source is Andreas Capellanus, *The Art of Courtly Love*, trans. John J. Parry (Records of Civilization, Sources and Studies, 33; New York: Columbia University Press, 1941); it is reprinted by permission of the publisher.

Second Dialogue

A man of the middle class speaks with a woman of the nobility
If a man of the middle class should seek the love of a noblewoman, he may follow this plan. If he finds that the woman, although noble, is not sophisticated, all the things will serve which were given in the dialogue between the man and the woman of the middle class, except that here commendation of the nobility of her family may claim a place. But if the woman should be wise and shrewd, he ought to be careful not to overdo the praise of her beauty. For if he should praise a noble and prudent woman beyond all measure, she will think that he isn't very good at the art of

conversation or that he is making up all this flattery and thinks her a fool. So after he has begun the conversation in the usual way, let him come down to words of love in this manner. "If I could shut up my heart within the bounds of my will, I would, perhaps, pass over in silence many things which I am urgently driven to say. But my heart drives on my will with sharp spurs, diverting it from its natural path and causing it to wander and to seek things too great for me to express. So if love compels me to say anything aimless or foolish, I ask Your Nobility to endure it patiently and to reprove me gently. I know well that Love is not in the habit of differentiating men with titles of distinction, but that he obligates all equally to serve in his (that is, Love's) army, making no exceptions for beauty or birth and making no distinctions of sex or of inequality of family, considering only this, whether anybody is fit to bear Love's armor. Love is a thing that copies Nature herself, and so lovers ought to make no more distinction between classes of men than Love himself does. Just as love inflames men of all classes, so lovers should draw no distinctions of rank, but consider only whether the man who asks for love has been wounded by Love. Supported by this unanswerable argument, I may select for my beloved any woman I choose so long as I have no depravity of character to debase me.

"So if you will give me a patient hearing, I shall try to ask only what you can have no good reason for denying me, and if my remarks offend you in any way and you use harsh words in defending yourself, that will be an unbearable misfortune to me and the cause of all sorts of grief.

"You must know, then, that many days ago I was smitten with the arrow of your love, and that I have tried with all my might to conceal the wound, not because I consider myself an incompetent soldier of Love, but because I am afraid of Your Highness's wisdom. The sight of your face so terrifies my spirit and disturbs my mind that I completely forget even those things I have carefully thought out in my mind. With reason, therefore, I tried to hide my grief, but the more I sought to cover up my wound, the more the pain of it increased. Yet the wound did remain hidden so long as the pain of it was not too much for me; but after I was overcome by the strength of it, by its mighty power it forced me to ask for great things and to seek for a cure for my ever-present pain. You are the cause of my suffering and the cure for my mortal pain, for you hold both my life and my death shut up in your hand.[1] If you grant what I ask, you will give me back the life I have lost and much solace in living, but if you deny me, my life will be a torment to me, and that is worse than if I met with sudden death; for a quick death would be preferable to suffering continually such terrible torture. I cannot tell you all the things my soul thinks should be told, but God knows the words that the dumb man wishes to speak."

The woman says: "I am very much surprised—it is enough to surprise anyone—that in such a great upsetting of things the elements do not come to an end and the world itself fall into ruin. If I were not determined to ignore the shame you cast on my nobility, I would rebuke you very bitterly; but since it is too unladylike for a noblewoman to speak harsh and discourteous words to anyone, no matter who he is, my soul endures with patience your crazy remarks and gives you a soft answer. Who are you that you ask for such great gifts? I know well enough what you look like, and the family you come from is obvious. But where can one find greater effrontery than in a man who for the space of a whole week devotes all his efforts to the various gains of business and then on the seventh day, his day of rest, tries to enjoy the gifts of love and to dishonor Love's commands and confound the distinctions of classes established among men from of old? It is not without cause or reason that this distinction of rank has been found among men from the very beginning; it is so that every man will stay within the bounds of his own class and be content with all things therein and never presume to arrogate to himself the things that were naturally set aside as belonging to a higher class, but will leave them severely alone. Who are you, then, to try to defile such ancient statues and under the pretense of love to attempt to subvert the precepts of our ancestors and so presumptuously go beyond the limits of your own class? If I should so far forget my senses as to be induced to assent to what you say, your heart would not be able to endure such great things. Did a buzzard[2] ever overcome a

1. Compare Peter Alphonsus *Clerical Instruction*, Ex. ii.
2. What bird Andreas means by *lacertiva avis* is unknown; the translation is merely conjectural.

partridge or a pheasant by its courage? It is for falcons and hawks to capture this prey, which should not be annoyed by cowardly kites. Your folly needs to be sharply checked, because you seek a love from the upper class, although you are not worthy of her.

"Nor can what you have just said support your opinion. You said that Love makes no distinction of classes, but forces all to love who are found fit to bear his arms, and that lovers likewise should not distinguish beyond asking whether the man who seeks for love has been wounded by Love. Now without attempting to contradict you, I admit that Love forces everyone, without distinctions, to love, but that which follows (that a lover ought not to distinguish beyond asking whether he who seeks for love is in love) I do not accept, because it rests wholly on a falsehood. If it were true, it would rule out the saying that Love carries an unequal weight in his hand. When the conclusion of this assumption is disproved, you will be refuted; therefore you see my contention firmly established. And if you should try to say, what many have boldly said, that we should all call Love an unjust judge, since he carries unequal weights,[3] I shall refute you with this answer. Although Love does carry unequal weights, yet he may truly be called a just judge, for he does not use them except when compelled by the best of reasons. Although he sees that all men are by the natural desire of their passions drawn to anybody of the opposite sex, he considers it shameful for him to pitch his tents at once over against the other person, so that she whose love is sought must immediately be driven to love. If he did this, any rough, shaggy person who spent his time in farming or in begging his bread publicly in the streets might impel a queen to love him. But lest such an impropriety or absurdity happen, Love regularly leaves it to the choice of each woman either to love or not, as she may wish, the person who asks for her love. And if this rule you mention, that everyone who loves is always loved, were kept unbroken without any exceptions, it would in the natural course of events run foul of another rule. Any man would rather seek his love in a higher class than in his own or a lower one, and on the other hand the woman whose love is sought, because of the same rule and her natural inclination, would gladly have a lover from her own or a higher class, lest people think that she is unjustly

3. Lev. 19:36; Deut. 25:15.

excepted from the regular rule of love. From this it should be clear
that your efforts are worse than useless, and when you finish you
will see that you have spent your labor in vain."

The man says: "You show your great worth by giving me a kindly
and gentle answer, since you choose to act in accordance with your
character and to suit your words to your rank. Nothing is more
suited to the character of a well-born woman than to use gentle
words when she speaks, and nothing seems more contrary to a
noble character and more degrading to nobility of blood than to
use harsh, discourteous ones. But I marvel greatly at your remark
that the family I come from is as apparent as my face; I see that in
this Your Prudence is going wrong, since you seem to agree with
those mistaken people who reject worth of character if it is un-
accompanied by good birth or beauty, but who accept physical
beauty and noble blood without any character. How grave and
troublesome an assertion this is to make, how absurd to speak of, is
shown beyond all contradiction by the law which says that nobility came in the beginning only from good character and manly
worth and courtesy. If, then, it is only good character which can
give men the privileges of nobility and allow them to take the name
'well-born,' you must lay aside completely this error I have mentioned and let good character alone induce you to love.

"As for your objection that it is a disgrace for me to engage in
business, if you will listen attentively to what I say you will certainly see that this cannot justly be held against me. That I devote
myself to the honorable gains of business is, I contend, devotion to
my position in life; because I am trying to do those things that are
accordant with my nature and thereby to avoid the murmur of the
crowd, which is in the habit of saying, 'Everybody ought to do the
things suitable to his birth and his social position.'[4] I do not say
that I pile up these gains dishonestly for the future, but I give them
to others carefully and very liberally at the proper time and place,[5]
and in this I defend my nobility of manners and character. Furthermore, if I did not concern myself with honest and legitimate
gains, I would fall into obscure poverty, and so I could not do

---

4. "That which is most consistent with each man's nature is most seemly
for him." Cicero *Offices* i. xxxi. 113.
5. Aristotle *Nicomachean Ethics* iv. 1.

noble deeds, and my nobility of character would remain only an empty name, a kind of courtesy or nobility which men never put much faith in. Suppose a well-born man who was poor and needy should talk about generosity. The common people would say things like this about him, 'This man boasts of his generosity, because he has nothing he can give away; if he did have anything on earth, he ought to act toward men in accordance with his birth and nature. It comes naturally from the fact that he has nothing, that he pours out his generosity in lavish words.' If you[6] should object that I have enough money, I shall still defend honest gain for men of my class.

"The next thing you said—that every man should stay within the limits of his own class and not seek for love in a higher one—I cannot deny. But if I have cultivated a character excellent through and through, I think that puts me inside the walls of nobility and gives me the true virtue of rank, and so my character puts me among the nobles. It cannot be considered a presumption, therefore, if I seek a love from among the nobility, for any man's nobility is determined more by his character than by his birth. You said, too, that even if my words should win you over to stoop to my desire, my heart would not be able to endure such great things. A soldier is a fool who seeks to bear arms that his limbs are too weak to endure, and no one wants a horse that he is incapable of managing or guiding. Such people are laughing stocks for the crowd. Now I grant that the things I am asking for are very great, so if you consider that I am not competent to receive them, Your Grace should grant only what you can without having people know about it, and then, if you find me wholly unworthy, you may expose me to your own derision or that of anyone else. But I have complete confidence that the same greatness of heart that impels me to ask for such great things would, if Your Grace granted them to me, keep them as possessions for me forever.

"What you said about the kite and the buzzard is no objection, since it is their bravery alone that makes hawks, falcons, and merlins valuable. At times we see hawks of the lighter kind by their courage take great pheasants and partridges, for a boar is often held by a fairly small dog. On the other hand, we see many gerfalcons

6. The man here changes from the formal plural of address (the modern *vous*) to the more familiar singular (the modern *tu*).

and peregrine falcons terrified by the commonest sparrows and put to flight by a buzzard. So if the kite or the buzzard proves to be hardy and bold, different from his parents, he deserves to be honored with the perch of the falcon or the hawk and to be carried on a warrior's left fist. So, then, if you find that I am unlike my parents, you should not call me by the disgraceful name 'kite,' but by the honorable one 'tercel.' And do not look down on worth, no matter in whom you find it, since we gather roses from the sharp thorns amid which they grow, and gold which we find in a vessel of cheap material cannot lose any of its value.

"It is clear from your answer that you did not understand me correctly when I said that no one should ask more than whether the person who seeks for love has been wounded by Love; it is the indefiniteness of the word that caused you the confusion. You should take my remark that a lover ought not ask as meaning that she whose love is sought ought not ask whether the man who seeks it comes of a noble or an ignoble family; she should ask only whether he has good habits and a good character. Therefore you may well say, 'Love at times carries an inequitable weight in his hand.' But although it is true that Love does carry at times unequal[7] weights, you cannot attribute it to his injustice, for it is sufficient if he touches one of the lovers with his dewy breath and from the fountain of his abundance sets him loving. After he has struck one of the lovers with an arrow of love, he very properly leaves the other free to do as she chooses; so that if she does those things which Love finds pleasing, she may deserve to receive great rewards from him and to have her praise proclaimed among men, but if she goes counter to his desire, she may receive the contrary kind of rewards. Love therefore leaves it to the woman's choice, so that when she is loved she may love in return if she wishes to, but if she does not wish, she shall not be compelled to, since a person is thought to deserve greater rewards when he does well of his own accord than when he has done so under compulsion. And we believe that this is done after the example of the Heavenly King, who leaves each man to his own free choice after he has acquired knowledge of good and evil, promising unutterable rewards to

7. The play on the two meanings of the word *inaequalis* (translated here as "inequitable" and "unequal") is difficult to render in English. The same play is implied also by the Biblical passages, cited above.

those who do well, but threatening unbearable torments to those who do evil. Therefore a woman ought to inquire diligently whether the man who asks for her love is worthy of it, and if she finds that he is perfectly worthy, she ought by no means to refuse him her love unless she is obligated to love someone else. If, then, you are not obligated to anyone else, you have no reason not to love me."

The woman says: "You are trying to bolster up your errors with so much eloquence that it will not be easy for me to reply to your more-than-empty words, but I shall try by my argument to refute some of them. If, as you say, we find good character alone worthy of Love's rewards and that this makes people look upon a man as noble, then the order of nobility, discovered and set apart by such obvious marks of distinction, would long ago have been found to be useless, when it was clear that every man distinguished by character and worth would have to be called noble. And so we would have to say emphatically that those who founded the order of nobility wasted their efforts, and I shall not try to show you how absurd that is. Therefore I say firmly that no one should go beyond the bounds of his rank, but each worthy man should seek within it for the love of some worthy woman, and a man of the middle class should seek for the love of a woman of that same class, and then everybody's class would remain inviolate and each man would come away with a reward for his efforts. The fact that you engage in honorable business suitable to your station in life is no concern of mine, except for the fact that you are seeking a love from the noble class, while your mind is on business—an unseemly thing and one that will result in great bitterness and grief. As for the fact that you are generous in giving away what you make in business, this makes you very worthy of the love of a woman of your own class. But even if a falcon should sometimes be put to flight by a buzzard, still the falcon is classed with falcons, and the buzzard with buzzards—the one being called a worthless falcon, the other a very good buzzard. Similarly, your good character doesn't put you in the class with the nobles, but gets you the name of a good man of the middle class, worthy of the love of a good woman of that same class. That is perfectly clear and obvious, and even if I am not obligated to anyone else, I find you just as unworthy of my love as though I were a woman from another country."

The man says: "Although I would not like to dispute what you say, still I cannot see any reason why if a man of the middle class excels a nobleman in the excellence of his character he ought not receive a greater reward since we are both descended from a common ancestor, Adam."

The woman says: "Gold is more appropriate on the king's table than in the home of a poor man or the hut of a peasant, and it is far more honorable to ride a thin horse that trots than a fat ass with the finest and gentlest of gaits. Therefore turn your back on your errors, and leave me for others."

The man says: "Although I am repulsed by what you say, still as long as I live I shall not give up the idea of your love, because even if I am never to get the result I hope for, the mere hope I have gained from the greatness of my heart will cause my body to lead a tranquil life, and ultimately, perhaps, God will put into your mind a cure for my pain."

The woman says: "May God give you a reward suited to your effort."

The man says: "That word alone shows me that my hope is bearing fruit, and I pray to God that you may always be interested in the care of my health and that my sails may find a quiet haven."

Third Dialogue

A man of the middle class speaks with a woman of the higher nobility

If a man of the middle class seeks the love of a woman of the higher nobility, he ought to have a most excellent character, for in order that a man of this class may prove worthy of the love of a woman of the higher nobility he must be a man with innumerable good things to his credit, one whom uncounted good deeds extol. It would seem a very great shame and a cause of reproach for a noblewoman to pass over the upper and the intermediate ranks and take a lover from the lower class unless good character in overwhelming quantity makes up for the lack of nobility. For it would not seem reasonable to any sensible people that one could find in the lowest class good and excellent men, worthy of the love of a woman of such high rank, while in the two upper classes no worthy man could be found, but all had to be rejected as of inferior quality. This is what you are told by the general rule of the logicians, which says, "If what appears more present is not present, neither will that which is believed less be."[8] A man of the middle class must therefore greatly excel in character all the men of the two noble classes in order to deserve the love of a woman of the higher nobility, for no matter how worthy any commoner may be, it seems very much out of place if a countess or a marchioness or any woman of the same or a higher rank gives her love to a man of the middle class, and even the lower classes look upon it as a lowering and a demeaning of herself. The first thing people will think is that she does it out of too great an abundance of passion (a thing which I shall show later is wholly reprehensible), unless the man's character is so well known as to remove the suspicion of that. Well, then, isn't it proper that a woman of the higher nobility should give her love to a commoner if she finds him excellent in every way? I answer that if she finds anyone in the classes above him who is more worthy or as worthy, she ought to prefer the love of that man; but if she doesn't find any such person in these classes, then she should not reject the commoner. But she ought to test his constancy by many trials before he deserves to have the hope of her love granted him, for that which is not in keeping with anyone's character is usually blown away by a light breeze and lasts but a brief moment. It is said that at times some are born among the buzzards who capture partridges by their courage or ferocity, but since we know that this is not in accord with their natures, this ferocity, men say, does not last in them for more than a year after their birth. Therefore a man of the middle class may be chosen in love by a woman of the higher nobility if after long probation he is found to be worthy; in that case they may make use of all the

8. Aristotle *Topics* 11. x; Boethius *Interpretation of the Topics of Aristotle* 11. IV.

speeches that have already been given in the dialogue between the man of the middle class and the woman of the simple nobility, or the commoner may make use of this other speech.

"It doesn't seem at all profitable to dwell very much on the praise of your person, for your character and your beauty echo through widely separated parts of the world, and, furthermore, praise uttered in the presence of the person praised seems to have the appearance of clever flattery. For the present, then, it is my intention, and the principal object which brings me here to you, to offer you myself and my services and to beg earnestly that Your Grace may see fit to accept them. And I beseech God in heaven that of His grace He may grant me to do those things which are wholly pleasing to your desire. I have in my heart a firm and fixed desire, not only to offer you my services, but on your behalf to offer them to everybody and to serve with an humble and acceptable spirit, since I have a firm faith that my labor can never remain with you without the delightfulness of fruit. If my trouble should prove fruitless, I must, after many waves and tempests of death, suffer shipwreck unless my soul is guided by hope, even though it is a false one. For only a hope, even one granted with a deceitful mind, can keep the anchor of my support firmly fixed."

The woman says: "I have no intention of refusing your services or those of any other man or of not responding to gifts which I accept as suitable, for anyone who refuses to accept services when they are offered embarrasses the giver and shows that he himself is constrained by the vice of avarice. He, then, who freely gives his services to others receives from others fitting rewards. But you seem to be tending in another direction and hunting other game than you are worthy to take, for, as your remarks seem to indicate, you are asking to be loved by me. But I do not wish to love, particularly a man in a class two below my own, although you might under other circumstances be infinitely worthy. You say that if I will grant you only the hope of my love it will be enough to keep you from the perils of death. To this I answer that the mere fact that you accuse me of clever deceit and falsehood shows that you are infected with this same failing and that you keep one idea in your mind and speak another with your deceitful tongue. By rights, therefore, you should be repulsed from Love's bosom, because fickle and untruthful people ought not come under the sway of Love's court. Moreover, you appear to be urging me to neglect my good name, and this is a worse fault than the other, for nothing is more disgraceful for a noblewoman than not to keep her promises, to destroy a hope she has given, and to say things that belie her birth. This sort of thing seems more appropriate to those women who conduct themselves like harlots, who for the sake of money strive to subvert Love's mandates and to disgrace his service for the sake of gain. Your advice therefore seems unsound, since from it so many grave perils threaten."

The man says: "I admit that I ask to be loved, because to live in love is more pleasant than any other way of life in the world. But your remarks show clearly that you refuse to love me because of the humbleness of my inferior rank, although my character is of the very best. To these remarks I reply that my family, as represented by myself, is driven by its natural instincts and cannot be kept within the bounds of its own class. Since, then, nature did not wish me to remain fixed within the established bounds of my class and she did not wish to close to me the doors of the higher ones, on what grounds, since I have no bad qualities to bar me, do you presume to set up definite limits for me and impose upon me the yoke of a class? We find that from very ancient times this distinction of classes has been used only against those who prove themselves unworthy of the rank to which they have been assigned or those who keep to their own class but are not found at all worthy of a higher one. I say this because of the resemblance to that passage in Holy Writ which says that the law is not made for the just man, but for sinners.[9] This ancient distinction of classes does not forbid me to be enrolled in any of the higher ones or to ask the rewards of a higher class, provided, however, that no one may justly raise any objections to my character. Moreover, when I said that a hope, even though granted with the intent to deceive, was enough to keep me from death, I didn't say this with the desire of detracting from your glorious reputation or because I was conscious of any trace of fraud which would be to your disadvantage. I said it to give you a clear proof what affection I feel for you and how much I would prize the full grant of your love, so that when

9. I Tim. 1:9.

you recognized the immensity of my love for you, you in turn might the more easily incline your mind to me."

The woman says: "Although good character may ennoble a commoner, still it cannot change his rank to the extent of making him a lord or a vavasor unless this is done by the power of the prince, who may add nobility to the good character of any man he pleases, and so it is proper that you should be refused advancement to the love of a countess. Besides, the hope of attaining to her has deceived you too much, since you were not ashamed to utter falsehoods boldly in her presence. You contend that you are renowned among the warriors, yet in you I see many things that are harmful or opposed to such service. For although soldiers ought naturally to have long, slender calves and a moderate-sized foot,[10] longer than it is broad and looking as though formed with some skill, I see that your calves are fat and roundly turned, ending abruptly, and your feet are huge and immensely spread out so that they are as broad as they are long."

The man says: "If we find any commoner who because of his habits and his character deserves to be ennobled by the prince, I do not see why he is not worthy of a noble love. For since it is character alone that makes a man worthy to be ennobled and we find that only nobility deserves the love of a noblewoman, properly then only good character is worthy of the crown of a noblewoman's love. And that objection you raised about my large, flabby legs and my big feet doesn't show much intelligence. Men say that in the further parts of Italy there lives a man of a line of counts[11] who has slender legs and is descended from the best of parents who enjoyed great privileges in the sacred palace; he himself is famous for every kind of beauty and is said to have immense wealth, and yet, so they say, he has no character at all—all good habits fear to adorn him, and in him everything bad has found a home. On the other hand, there is a king in Hungary[12] who has

10. The mixture of singular and plural follows the Latin here.
11. Arpad Steiner suggests (*Speculum*, XIII, 304) that the reference is to Count William I ("The Bad") of Sicily. In 1176 or 1177 his son William II had married Joanna, daughter of Queen Eleanor and of Henry II.
12. Steiner suggests (in *Speculum*, IV, 92) that the verbs in this passage are historical presents and that the king referred to is King Coloman, who

very fat, round legs, and long, broad feet and who is almost wholly destitute of beauty; yet because the worth of his character shines so bright, he deserved to receive the glory of the royal crown, and proclamations of his praise resound throughout almost the whole world. You should not, therefore, inquire what my feet and legs are like, but what my character is like and what I have made of myself. When you receive gifts, you should not consider how beautiful the giver is, but how much he deserves because of his own merits. You should learn to base your objections on a man's character, not on his legs, because in objecting to legs you seem to be blaming divine nature."

The woman says: "You seem to have a reasonable defense, but what good deeds glorify you, what sort of character makes you worthy to obtain what you ask, I have never heard. For he who asks for the love of an honorable woman, especially one of the upper nobility, ought to be of great fame and of all courtliness; but of you lofty fame seems to be perfectly silent. First, therefore, you should strive to do such things as deserve the reward which you ask, so that your request may not be considered too impudent."

The man says: "The height of courtesy seems to be contained in your remarks, in which you are so clearly concerned that all my actions should be laudable. And so, since I see that you are thoroughly instructed in the art of love, I ask you to give me a lesson— that is, I ask that Your Grace may see fit to teach me those things that are specially demanded in love, those which make a man most worthy of being loved, because after I have been instructed I shall have no defense for any mistakes I make and no opportunity to excuse myself. Since all courtesy comes from the plentiful stream of Love and to this generous lord should be credited the beginning of all good deeds and the carrying out to the end of every good, and since I am still inexperienced in love and ignorant of the subject, it is no wonder that I know nothing of what he can do and that I urgently seek to be taught his precepts; because what anyone

---

reigned from 1095 to 1116 (Steiner says 1114); he was one of the greatest of the Hungarian kings, but is described by the chroniclers as flabby and very ugly. Béla III, who reigned from 1163 to 1198, was a tall, handsome man.

desires with all his mind he begs for vehemently and receives with eagerness."

The woman says: "You seem to be upsetting the natural order and course of things, since first you ask for love and then you show yourself in every way unworthy of it by asking like a raw recruit to be trained in the science of love. But since it would seem to set a shameful precedent, one prompted by avarice, if those who have experience were to deny their lessons to those who have not and ask to be taught, you will without a doubt obtain the grant of our instruction; and if you will pay careful attention to our words, before you leave you will be fully informed on the subjects you ask about.

"Well then, the man who would be considered worthy to serve in Love's army must not be in the least avaricious, but very generous; he must, in fact, give generously to as many people as he can. When he sees that money is needed, especially by noblemen and men of character, and when he thinks that his gifts would be helpful to anybody, he ought not wait to be urged, for a gift made in answer to a request seems dearly bought.[13] But if he cannot find a pressing opportunity of giving something under these circumstances, let him give something helpful to the man who does ask, and give it with such a spirit that it may seem more pleasing and acceptable to his feelings to give the thing to his friend than to keep possession of it himself. And also if he sees that the poor are hungry and gives them nourishment, that is considered very courteous and generous. And if he has a lord, he should offer him due respect. He should utter no word of blasphemy against God and His saints; he should show himself humble to all and should stand ready to serve everybody. He ought never speak a word in disparagement of any man, since those who speak evil may not remain within the threshold of courtesy. He ought not utter falsehood in praise of the wicked, but he should if possible make them better by secret reproofs. If he finds that they remain wholly incorrigible, he should consider them stiff-necked and banish them from his company lest he be considered, and rightly, a promoter and a sharer of

13. Seneca *Benefits* ii. i. Andreas may get the idea through the *Moral Philosophy* (i. 13) of Hildebert of Le Mans.

the error. He ought never mock anyone, especially the wretched, and he should not be quarrelsome or ready to take part in disputes; but he should be, so far as possible, a composer of differences. In the presence of women he should be moderate about his laughter, because, according to Solomon's saying,[14] too much laughter is a sign of foolishness; and clever women are in the habit of turning away fools and unwise men in contempt or of eluding them beautifully. Great prudence is necessary in the management of a love affair and diligence in all one does. He ought to frequent assemblies of great men and to visit great courts. He should be moderate about indulging in games of dice. He should gladly call to mind and take to heart the great deeds of the men of old. He ought to be courageous in battle and hardy against his enemies, wise, cautious, and clever. He should not be a lover of several women at the same time, but for the sake of one he should be a devoted servant of all. He should devote only a moderate amount of care to the adornment of his person and should show himself wise and tractable and pleasant to everybody, although some men have the idea that women like it very much if they utter foolish, almost crazy, remarks and act like madmen. He should be careful, too, not to utter falsehoods and should take care not to talk too much or to keep silent too much. He should not be too quick and sudden about making promises, because the man who is good-natured about making promises will be slow to keep them, and the man who is too ready to make them gets little credit. If any worthy man wants to give him some money, he should accept it with a look of joy and by no means refuse it unless the giver had the idea that he needed it, when he didn't. In that case he may decline it in this way: 'Since I have no need for this at present, I consider it as given to me, and I return it to you that you may make use of it in my name in any way you please.' He should never utter foul words and should avoid serious crimes, especially ones that are notorious. He should never cheat anyone with a false promise, because anybody can be rich in promises. If anybody has deceived him with a false promise or has been rude to him, he should never say anything to disparage the man, but on the contrary he should do good to him in return

14. Apparently the verse he has in mind is Ecclesiasticus 21.23, which some persons in the Middle Ages attributed to Solomon. See, for example, John of Salisbury *Policraticus* II. XXIX.

and serve him in every way, and thus prudently compel him to acknowledge his fault. He should offer hospitality freely to everybody. He should not utter harmful or shameful or mocking words against God's clergy or monks or any person connected with a religious house, but he should always and everywhere render them due honor with all his strength and with all his mind, for the sake of Him whose service they perform. He ought to go to church frequently and there listen gladly to those who are constantly celebrating the divine service, although some men very foolishly believe that the women like it if they despise everything connected with the Church. He ought to be truthful in everything he says and never envy any man's renown. I have presented to you briefly the main points. If you have listened attentively to them and will be careful to practice them, you will be found worthy to plead in the court of Love."

The man says: "I am impelled to give all sorts of thanks to Your Dignity for being willing to explain to me so industriously and so prudently the articles of love and to give me a conception of the subject. But still I shall not cease to ask continually that you may see fit to grant me the hope I seek, at least on condition that I try to do all those things that you have taught me. For the hope of the love I desire will always keep before my mind the determination to do good deeds, and what you said about mixing up the regular order will not raise any difficulties. For since love offers everybody in the world an incentive to do good, properly before everything else we ought to seek love as the root and principal cause of everything good."

The woman says: "It would be unseemly and discourteous to give anybody a hope of love in this fashion; one should wholly grant it or else wholly deny it, because even after it is granted the woman may draw back her hand and take away the hope that she has given. Strive, therefore, to do good deeds, that my words of instruction may seem to have been profitable to you."

The man says: "It was with good reason that the Heavenly Majesty put you in the class of the greater women, since you have been willing so prudently to respond to all men according to their deserts and to grant me more than I knew how to ask, and I pray

God that He may ever increase my determination to serve you and that He may incline your mind toward me, and ever keep it so, to reward me to the extent of my deserts."

Fourth Dialogue

A nobleman speaks with a woman of the middle class
If a nobleman prefers to select for his love a woman of the middle class, he should woo her with a speech of this kind. First let him greet her in his own fashion, and next he may, even without her permission, choose a seat at her side, by virtue of the privileges his higher rank gives him. For I tell you, Walter, it is the usual rule that when a man is considered to be of a more privileged rank than the woman, he may, if he wishes, sit down beside her without asking permission. If they are of the same rank he may ask permission to sit beside her, and if she grants it he may sit down by her side, but not unless she does. But where the man is of lower rank than the woman, he must not ask permission to sit beside her, but he may ask to sit in a lower place. If, however, she gives him permission to sit beside her, he may without fear oblige her. Then he should begin talking in this fashion.

"To tell you the truth, I am an ambassador sent to you from the court of Love to entrust to Your Prudence the solution of a certain doubt: In which woman does a good character deserve more praise—in a woman of noble blood, or in one who is known to have no nobility of family?"

The woman says: "It doesn't seem very appropriate to leave it to me to make a final decision in such a matter, since the subject concerns me and everybody is forbidden to pass judgment on his own case; still, because I cannot refuse a task laid upon me by Love, I shall try to define my feeling on the subject. But first I want you to tell me something about the case, so that I may get my information from an excellent presentation of the facts and may not make any mistake about them. At first sight it would seem that excellence of birth deserves the more praise, for those things we come by naturally seem more to be desired than those which are external and come from without. Now in the case of women, a color that is natural is more admired than one that is applied, and words spoken by a man are more pleasing than the same words spoken by a parrot. Likewise the color of the brilliant scarlet dye looks better in English wool than in the wool of lambs from Champagne or Italy. So I suppose good character is more suited to noble blood than to a person descended from the middle class."

The man says: "I wonder whether you think and feel what your tongue seems to pronounce, for what you say cannot properly be proved by the examples you give; in every one of them it is human skill that we commend, and men prefer natural qualities to accidents. But character in a plebeian woman arises only from the innate qualities of her soul and the admirable ordering of her mind, and so we may consider it natural. Therefore your illustrations cannot support your contention, and I believe we should properly say that good character deserves more praise in a plebeian than in a noblewoman. We value more highly a pheasant captured by a sparrow hawk than one taken by a falcon, and a man who pays more than he owes deserves greater credit than one who offers only what he is bound to. Again we think more of the skill of an artisan who is able to make a good boat out of poor timbers than of that of a man who builds it of very good, well-fitted ones. And is it not considered better and more laudable if a man acquires some admirable craft all by himself than if he learns it from some other craftsman? That, at any rate, is certainly true if you would but admit it. It is quite proper, then, that in this case we should give the decision against the woman who is of noble descent."

The woman says: "It seems to me there is a good deal of doubt of your good sense, since you are so clearly trying to speak against yourself. Although you are of noble blood and well-born, you are openly trying to belittle nobility and to plead against your own rights. And you make such a reasonable defense of your position that I am inclined to believe we should consider that good character deserves more credit in a plebeian than in a noblewoman, because no one has any doubt that the rarer any good thing is the more dearly is it prized."

The man says: "I consider your opinion very just and think it quite correct, and so of necessity I am forced to admit that one ought to seek the love of a plebeian woman with an excellent character rather than that of a noblewoman with a very good one. There-

fore, since in you the plebeian class has been exalted by reason of
your good character, I have quite properly chosen you, out of all
the women in the world, as my lady, and I have determined to do
all my good deeds for the sake of you alone. And therefore I pray
God unceasingly to keep always firmly fixed in your heart the idea
of accepting my services without delay, that my soul may daily
increase in well-doing and thereby I may worthily attain to the
rewards I desire."

The woman says: "It does not seem very appropriate to your
nobility to condescend to a woman of the plebeian class or to seek
for love from her, nor do you seem to have obtained the name
'nobleman' through your merits, because you have not been
worthy of the love of any woman of your own class. He who has
not proved himself a good soldier in his own class does not do well,
I believe, when he serves in some other one. Seek, therefore, a love
within your own class and do not try to attack a woman in another
one, lest you meet with a well-deserved rebuke for your presumption."

The man says: "You seem to have very little experience in the art
of love, since you show that you are ignorant of what is clear to
everybody else. For it seems to be 'known to all the half-blind and
the barbers'[15] that neither excellence of birth nor beauty of person
has much to do with the loosing of Love's arrow, but it is love
alone that impels men's hearts to love, and very often it strongly
compels lovers to claim the love of a stranger woman—that is, to
throw aside all equality of rank and beauty. For love often makes a
man think that a base and ugly woman is noble and beautiful and
makes him class her above all other women in nobility and beauty.
For when a man has seen fit to love a woman honorably, her
beauty is always very pleasing to him even though others find her
misshapen and spiritless. Compared to her, all other women seem to
him plain. Therefore you should not wonder that although you are
of humble birth I persist in loving you with all my might because
of your dazzling beauty and the fame of your excellent character. I
do not seek for these things like a man who has been rejected by
the women of his own class; but Love compels me to love as I do,

15. Horace *Satires* I. vii. 3.

and your worth and your nobility have pleased me more than those of any other women. From all these things it should be clear enough to Your Prudence that you should by no means reject my love if you find that my character corresponds with my birth."

The woman says: "Even if what you say rested upon clear truth, still I could derive from your own words another just reason for refusing you, since the opinion I advanced and you approved of a little while ago seems to imply that good character deserves more praise in a plebeian than in a noblewoman. From these words you have drawn the conclusion that any man should choose for his love an excellent plebeian rather than a noblewoman of great worth. Why, then, shouldn't I choose for my lover a plebeian of perfect character rather than a man of great nobility? Answer me that, if you please."

The man says: "Although I did say in so many words that the love of an excellent plebeian was more to be preferred than that of a suitable noblewoman, still you must not get the idea that the love of a noblewoman is not a praiseworthy thing and very desirable. In fact the love of the noblewoman is to be preferred if her character is better than that of the plebeian. When I used the word 'more' I meant that if we find a plebeian woman more worthy than the noblewoman she is to be preferred to her; if we see that in character they go along together side by side, one is free to choose either of them, according to the opinion of Queen Eleanor of England.[16] But I say that when they are equal in this respect the one of lower rank is preferable and should be chosen. But if the adverb 'more' should be interpreted otherwise than as I have tried to explain it to you, it would lead to great absurdity and great harm, for it seems that belonging to a good family would bring a man intolerable loss rather than any advantage if a more worthy noblewoman were placed below a less worthy plebeian. If, then, you should find a plebeian in whom you know there is a better character than there is in me, and if you give him your love, I will not urge that this idea of yours is improper, because, according to what we have already said, it seems that you are permitted to do this.

16. Eleanor of Aquitaine, divorced wife of King Louis VII of France, and mother of Countess Marie of Champagne, married Prince Henry, later King Henry II of England, in 1152.

Therefore let Your Prudence make a careful investigation and accept the love of the more worthy man."

The woman says: "In your remarks you seem to be going backward, the way a crab walks, because now you are trying to deny what you asserted so firmly and boldly when you were praising me. But it doesn't seem like a man of sense to go so shamelessly against his own opinion in order to agree with any sort of opinion that a prudent woman utters and to deny now what a little while ago he admitted so plainly. However, since it is right for anyone to depart from his error and come to his senses in a matter in which he now feels that he was wrong, if you want to correct your unconsidered and unqualified statement you will deserve a great deal of praise for this and you ought to be commended by the good sense of everyone. I am greatly pleased by the interpretation of your words by which you allow me to consider which lover I should select as preferable, because I guard that gate of Love's palace which neither refuses to let anybody into the palace nor permits everybody to enter who asks, but admits only the man who gets in on the strength of his own good character after we have consulted long and deliberated carefully. Therefore after I have thought the matter over and carefully weighed the considerations, I shall try to admit the better man."

The man says: "If there weren't a snake here hidden in the grass, and if you were not asking for a chance to think the matter over only as a clever pretext, such a deliberation would be very sweet and pleasant to me. But because I am very much afraid that this comes at bottom from a desire to put things off, it doesn't seem to me safe to give my assent to this deliberation. For to me the matter is a very serious one and it looks like the death of me if you let me go away without granting me the hope of your love. Such a capricious putting things off is usually a sign that love is departing, and with a little delay the chance of fortune usually changes. If, then, you send me away without the hope of your love, you will drive me to an early death, after which none of your remedies will do any good, and so you may be called a homicide."

The woman says: "I have no desire to commit a homicide, but you can have no reason to deny me a chance to deliberate, because according to the saying of a certain wise man whatever is done after deliberation does not need to be repented of in shame, but stands forever."

The man says: "I cannot refuse you the chance to deliberate, but I shall never cease to pray God earnestly to make you love the man you should."

The woman says: "If I should choose to devote myself to love, you may know of a certainty that I will try, so far as I can, to choose the solaces of the man who is preferable."

The man says: "There is no doubt that you have a free right to choose which one you will love, but I shall never cease to serve you, and on your account to offer to do everything I can for everybody."

The woman says: "If you really intend to do what you say you propose to, it can hardly be that you will not be abundantly rewarded, either by me or by some other woman."

The man says: "God grant that your words express what you really feel; I may seem to depart from you in the body, but in my heart I shall always be bound to you."

Part Two

Feudal Institutions

Introduction

⎏⎍⎏⎍⎏⎍⎏⎍⎏⎍⎏⎍⎏⎍⎏⎍⎏⎍⎏⎍⎏⎍⎏⎍⎏⎍⎏⎍⎏⎍⎏⎍⎏⎍⎏⎍⎏

Amid invasions from abroad and tumult at home, with the decay
and near-disappearance of effective government, the men of the
early Middle Ages faced a critical problem in supplying their basic
social needs—food, protection, companionship. Under such perilous conditions, the most immediate social unit which could offer
support and protection to harassed individuals was the family.
What was the nature of the family in early medieval society? This
is a question which must be asked in any consideration of the
feudal world, but it is surprisingly difficult to answer. Few and
uninformative records cast but dim light on this central institution;
they are enough to excite our interest but rarely sufficient to give
firm responses to our questions.

At one time the common view of historians was that the family
of the early Middle Ages was characteristically large, extended or
patriarchal. Married sons continued to live within their father's
house or with one another after their parents' deaths; they sought
security against external dangers primarily in their own large
numbers. There is, to be sure, much evidence of strong family
solidarity and sentiment in medieval society. A heavy moral obligation, everywhere evident, lay upon family members to avenge
the harm done to a kinsman. This is one of the principal themes of

the epic poem *Raoul of Cambrai* (Document 31), as it is of many medieval tales. The characters in it repeatedly assert that warriors who fail to seek vengeance are dastards and cowards, not worth a spur or a glove. In guaranteeing that injury to a relative would not go unnoticed and unpunished, this system of family vengeance, or vendetta, undoubtedly discouraged promiscuous violence. The barbarian legal codes, redacted between the sixth and ninth centuries (Document 8), similarly show a marked reliance upon the family in the punishment and deterrence of crime. Most forms of violence in society were considered offenses against the kinship group and not, as in later conceptions of law, against the community, sovereign, or state. The codes did set limits upon the vendetta, stipulating the monetary fines which might be reasonably demanded for the death of a kin (wergild) or for wounds inflicted upon him. But the barbarian rulers themselves assumed no responsibility in bringing criminals to justice. The family, or no one, enforced and protected the rights and security of its members.

Today, however, many historians and sociologists believe that both the size and solidarity of the kinship group in the early Middle Ages, and indeed in many presumably primitive societies, have been exaggerated. The family, based on the most powerful of human emotions, tends for that very reason to be unstable and unable to include large numbers of persons in its emotional universe. The love among siblings is obviously strong, and so also are their sensitivities and their hatreds. Few persons love, and fight, like brothers. Extended families have been of restricted importance in all communities in which studies have been carried out. A "small-family hypothesis" has thus been gaining credence among scholars. This view holds that even in those societies in which the extended family represented some kind of ideal, few families achieved it.

The glove fits early medieval society. From the eighth century on there have survived thousands of charters recording transactions in land which illustrate how the medieval family carried on its economic affairs, or at least managed its landed possessions. In their vast majority, the principals involved in such charters appear as individuals, and rarely is the permission or agreement of kinsmen sought or required. Whatever the strength of family sentiment or the moral weight of the obligation to demand vengeance, the extended kinship group had little visible importance as an economic administrator, at least in regard to the management of land. More-

over, family names begin to appear in those same documents only
in the late tenth century, and remain unusual for several centuries
thereafter. Apart from the high aristocracy, there seems little consciousness of membership in an identifiable kinship group, and little
memory of a common ancestry. In *Raoul of Cambrai* the hero,
Bernier, finds that his obligations toward his kin are counter-
manded and for a while overcome by other interests—by his duties
toward his lord and by the prospect of his own material advance
through the generous gifts which his lord offers him.

The family in the early Middle Ages of course served as the
kernel of society. Ties among brothers continued to be strong and
demanding. But this universe of high emotion remained, as we have
said, finite and fragile. The extended family or kinship group has
not left in the sources evidence of remarkable cohesion and solidarity. It rarely seems to have been capable of embracing large
numbers under an umbrella of support and protection. Members
scattered, and emotions cooled. Extended families or clans seem to
have functioned best and survived best in regions where extensive
agriculture, herding, and sheep raising had particular importance,
such as the predominantly upland, predominantly Celtic areas of
Brittany, Cornwall, Wales, Scotland, and Ireland. The management and defense of large herds invited and rewarded continuing
cooperation among heirs and relatives, and made those regions,
socially and perhaps culturally, among the most conservative of
Europe. On the other hand, systems of settled and intensive agriculture confronted the kinship group with difficult and disruptive
problems concerning inheritance, authority, marriage, and the distribution of functions and of benefits. For the settled peasant or
landlord, cooperation with a neighbor is likely to become more
vital than cooperation with a more distant kinsman, and ties formed
for reasons of self-interest are likely to rival and surpass in strength
the sentimental bonds among kin who do not inhabit a common
household.

The relative strength and endurance of kinship ties has a direct
relevance to the formation of the feudal bonds and to their character. Vassalage, for example, the personal link between man and
man, seems to emerge out of a relationship which bears many
similarities with the natural bonds between kinsmen, especially between father and son. This tie apparently first appeared, as several
of the following documents will illustrate, among men who fought

together, feasted together, lived together, and for all practical purposes formed part of a single household. This close personal and emotional relationship among warriors, apparently the direct ancestor of feudal vassalage, very much appears to modern observers to be an extension of the kinship bond and in some measure an effort to substitute for it. The solidarity of the feudal relationship between man and man, in other words, was comparable to, and frequently stronger than, the solidarity of the kinship group. It seems to have developed primarily in those areas of Europe where, because of economic and other pressures, the extended family could not offer its members adequate support and protection. Its members were therefore prone to seek and to create other associations, with nonkinsmen, which more effectively answered their needs. The feudal bond initially imposed moral and ethical rather than strictly legal obligations, and these were at first quite vaguely defined. The bond was not for that reason weaker; loyalty and love have often, and usually, proved stronger than law.

The personal relationship

The bond between man and man, the most characteristic feature of feudal society, seems to have been based initially on considerations of persons rather than of properties. Modern social historians, in the irresistible logic of their researches, have arrived at the paradoxical conclusion that there was at first little authentically "feudal" (that is, involving a particular type of land tenure) about feudal society. The personal bond united warriors, but of differing social status. One was senior by age, talent, experience, accomplishments, or wealth; he was the chief, or the lord. His partner was of lower social station but still a freeman, still with rights which had to be respected. Personal ties of this sort seem to have been common within both barbarian and Roman societies. The Roman historian Tacitus, writing A.D. 98, has left us a succinct but revealing description of a Gemanic battlefield association which he calls the *comitatus*, or "following" (Document 8). The young German warrior followed an older and more seasoned fighter into war. The young man's guiding ambition was to distinguish himself before his leader's eyes; gain from him honor, arms, food, and booty; and give to him in return his loyalty—even, if the tide of battle required, his life. "It is a lifelong infamy and shame if any of the followers survives his chief," writes Tacitus, and this measures the emotional content of the warrior bond. Roman patronage and Merovingian contracts of commendation (Documents 9 and 10) present similar if less colorful examples of the willing subservience of one freeman to a more powerful neighbor. The Slavic peoples of Europe knew an equivalent association among warriors, known as the *druzhina*, or "friendship." It seems in fact that any society in which military prowess is given an extremely high social value is likely to develop similar institutions. Young men will want to follow recognized heroes. They will want to serve them, imitate them, and perhaps attain, through faithful apprenticeship, the same levels of achievement.

In medieval social history, this warrior institution and ethos enjoyed a remarkably prolonged life. Nine centuries after Tacitus' account, a short epic poem, written in Anglo-Saxon, recounting a battle fought at Maldon in England in 991, describes the behavior of members of the retinue of a leader slain in the fray (Document 13). In judging their actions, the poet betrays values hardly to be distinguished from those attributed by Tacitus to Germanic followers and chiefs. This pact, agreement, contract, understanding, mutual commitment between generations of warriors, between the old successful survivors of a dangerous life and the young men zealous to imitate them and perhaps succeed them, seems to have been the direct antecedent, or at least the basic model, for the personal bond between lord and vassal in feudal society.

In the mature feudal system, which again does not certainly appear in our sources until the late eleventh century and is not fully illuminated until the twelfth and thirteenth, the senior warrior is called the lord, and his free follower the *vassus* (the term derives from a Celtic word for boy or servant) or simply his "man" (*homo*). The ceremony by which one man publicly declared that he wished to become the vassal of another, and was accepted by him, was called homage. It included, in its most elaborate form, at least three separate symbolic gestures. The vassal would place his hands within the hands of his lord (the *immixio manuum*); they would exchange a kiss of peace; and an oath would be taken by the vassal to abide by his commitment. Of these, the "mingling of hands" seems to have been the most common and the most important. It apparently set the model for the new posture of prayer which came to prevail in the Latin Church over the course of the Middle Ages. In the early Church, men had prayed with their arms outstretched, but in the feudal age they learned to pray with hands folded together. The image seems to have been that they were placing their hands within the hands of God. Thus, one who prays stands before God, much as a vassal before his lord; he recognizes that he owes Him love and fidelity, and hopes in turn for His protection and support.

As a personal tie freely created, vassalage imposed obligations upon both the lord and his vassal. The vassal owed his lord much what a son owes his father. Above all else, he owed him love and loyalty, which the technical language of the age identified as fealty. Initially, as far as we can judge, this remained an obligation more of sentiment than of law, and more of emotional commitment than of calculated consent to any precisely defined set of duties. In *Raoul of Cambrai*, as we have mentioned, the young Bernier had to reconcile the conflict between his duties as a nephew and his duties as a vassal; both obligations were equally vague, and equally pressing. So also, in the famous twelfth-century tale of the lovers Tristan and Iseult, the hero Tristan, in forming an adulterous union with Iseult, not only committed a crime against Christian marriage, but he also betrayed the love and fealty which he owed his lord, Mark of Cornwall, Iseult's deceived husband.

But not by love alone can households be managed and principalities maintained. As vassalage grew older, and particularly as it was utilized to define the relationship not just between a seasoned warrior and the admiring young men who followed him, but the equally seasoned barons and dukes of a realm, some precision was required to define precisely what love or fealty implied for both participants in the contract. In these circumstances, it was hard to preserve an authentic emotional content within the tie of vassalage, and all parties grew interested in precisely defined, even if emotionally vacant, definitions of what the relationship implied. The first feudal age was a period of warriors—bold, violent, emotional. The second feudal age was, in contrast, dominated by statesmen, administrators, and lawyers—rational, gifted, cool, eager to make sense of the confused traditions they had inherited, eager to put them together into systems supporting an ordered society.

The love and fealty which a vassal owed a lord were very early accepted as implying two derivative obligations. Clearly, the vassal, as a dutiful son, was bound to help his lord whenever help was required. That assistance might be of two types: material and moral—or, in the language of the epoch, *auxilium et concilium*, aid and counsel (Document 12).

Aid implied military help primarily. The vassal, when summoned, was to accompany his lord to battle, fight under his leadership, and if circumstances demanded, surrender for him his life upon the field. War, however, in the second feudal age was growing technically more complex and economically more expensive. Princes were understandably more interested in the arms and men their vassals might supply, and less in the depth of their love. Feudal custom came commonly to demand that the vassal appear for service with certain stipulated arms and serve for a prescribed period, usually forty days (Document 32). If his lord wished longer service, he had to pay the vassal, in fact to hire him as a mercenary. If the vassal was a baron with extensive lands, he would typically be required to bring to his lord's service a fixed number of knights. Well-run feudal states, such as Normandy and Norman England, kept precise records of the numbers of knights required from the baronial fiefs. Vassals might further be obligated to guard the lord's castle for stated periods, or in time of war to place their own castle at the lord's disposal. If they could not personally serve, they had to send an acceptable substitute or pay a special tax in commutation, which in England was called scutage.

Aid also implied financial help, and as we have already stated, money in the second feudal age was slowly but irrepressibly assuming its classical function as the *nervus belli*, the sinew or the muscle of war. But when did the lord truly need the vassal's financial help? A common feudal custom (Document 32) accepted that the vassals unquestionably owed the lord financial aid at three important "incidents" or events: the knighting of the lord's eldest son, the marriage of his eldest daughter, and the ransoming of his own person when he was captured in war. Some documents, such as the English Magna Carta of 1215, mention a fourth "feudal incident": the departure of the lord on crusade. The vassals still retained the obligation to help the lord on other occasions, but here they retained the right to consider and to discuss the request with their fellows and even to question the reality of the need. The right of the vassals, individually and collectively, to judge whether or not the lord truly needed the financial help he was asking is considered to be one distant but real root of the right of the English Parliament (in origin an assembly of vassals) to determine whether or not their lord the king needed financial aid, and thus to control the purse strings of the realm.

Aid also involved some lesser obligations. The vassal, like a dutiful son, was to welcome visits from his lord and be willing to feed him in his home. The lord's *droit de gîte*, or right to entertainment, similarly came to be defined rather precisely in the customs and law of the second feudal age; the lord could stay for a limited number of days, with a limited number of men in his party, and consume meals of a limited quality and substance.

Since aid included moral help, the vassal was obligated to give his lord his best advice, to keep his secrets, and to hide nothing from him which might be useful to him. If the vassal lived at a distance from the lord's court, he would be obligated to visit the court when summoned or on certain fixed days, as, for example, on the great feasts of Christmas, Easter, and Michaelmas (September 29). The obligation of counsel also required that the vassal participate in the lord's court when it sat as a judicial tribunal, in order to pass judgment on the cases brought before it. As those cases primarily involved other vassals, he found himself traditionally required to judge his own peers. This was originally an obligation, but it eventually came to be considered a right as well. In the constitution of Emperor Conrad II concerning the benefices of Italy (1037; Document 22), we have for the first time an explicit statement that vassals were not to be deprived of their fiefs without the judgment of their own peers. Essentially the same provision is included in the English Magna Carta. This tradition thus offered the vassal a guarantee against injury to his person or loss of his holdings on the basis of the lord's sole and arbitrary will and power.

This obligation, and the right which flowed out of it, has a further significance. It meant that the assembly of vassals was the highest court of the principality. The assembly of English vassals, for example, meeting in Parliament, constituted the "high court" of England. Some historians have found in this fact, established by feudal custom, one basis for Parliamentary supremacy in the English constitution. In most principalities of western Europe, the combined obligation and right to give counsel helped establish the tradition that rulers in reaching important decisions should consult the great men of their realms. This principle and practice exerted an important influence on the growth of constitutional government in the second feudal age.

The lord in turn had obligations toward his vassal, and these too became progressively clarified over time. Much as a father has obligations toward his son, the lord had to give his vassal protection and maintenance. The need for protection would usually have been, for the vassal, the strongest consideration in entering the feudal partnership. The lord's primary duty was therefore to defend his vassal against all enemies and dangers.

The lord's obligation to maintain or support his vassal could be met in several ways. He could feed him at his own table; he could regularly provide him with clothes, arms, and horses, as is depicted, for example, in *Raoul of Cambrai*. But the anemic economy of the first feudal age severely restricted the number of "house knights" which even the richest lord could maintain. The large quantities of food required to sate the appetites of hungry warriors could not easily be collected or transported. Nor could the lord readily support his men through gifts of money or regular salaries, at least before the fourteenth century. His own monetary revenues were for long insufficient, and salaries would at any rate have availed little in the absence of large markets in which they could be spent.

An evident solution to this problem of maintenance was to grant the vassal an estate, which he could manage for himself and from whose produce he could live. The lord could, and frequently did, convey such lands in full title. But unconditional gifts of land carried several disadvantages. The vassal might die, leaving no one in his family able to serve. Or the secure revenues he enjoyed might raise in him a spirit of independence or even defiance. Ideally, the lord wanted enjoyment of the tenure to be conditional upon the scrupulous fulfillment of the obligation to serve. An economic penalty would thus be added to the essentially moral force of vassalage, to ensure fidelity to the terms of the feudal contract.

The property relationship

Out of the lord's obligation to support his vassal, the bond between these men thus acquired a second aspect, one created by a distinctive sort of land tenure known as the benefice or fief. In a strict sense, the fief was a conditional, temporary, and nonhereditary form of land tenure. The tenant of a fief could enjoy its fruits only so long as he served the lord. At his death or incapacity to serve, the fief escheated to the lord, or it would be forfeited if he failed to meet his obligations, even though able. The fief was based on a conception of property quite different from that which had infused the law of classical Rome. The Romans tended to think in absolutes; a person owned a property or he did not, and therefore his right or *dominium* over it was absolute and indivisible. The men of the Middle Ages, on the other hand, readily admitted the possibility and the existence of gradations of ownership. In particular, one person might hold the "eminent domain" over land, and another own the right to enjoy its fruits. The definition of these rights and the relations between or among them constantly occupied the feudal lawyers.

Like homage, the property tie between lord and tenant was created by a special ceremony, investiture. The lord, usually after receiving the homage of the vassal, would hand him a branch or a clod of earth, symbol of the fief he was granting him for his support.

Historians do not know precisely the origins of this peculiar sort of land tenure, but over the decades they have constructed a rather convincing hypothesis concerning its development. They locate its distant origins in forms of land tenure associated with the Church, specifically the *beneficium* or *precarium* (Document 18). Canonical tradition prohibited churches from alienating land once acquired, even for ostensibly constructive purposes, such as more efficient management, reward to a faithful servant, or cultivation of a powerful friend. To circumvent this strict and sometimes awkward prohibition, the churches in the early Middle Ages took to granting the "favor" (the exact meaning of *beneficium*) of land, often in response to the prayers (*preces,* whence the term *precarium*) of the recipient. They would retain ownership in compliance with the canons, but grant use. Like the later fief, the benefice thus distinguished between right of ownership and right of use, which was itself conceived as a kind of ownership. In the eighth century the Carolingian rulers, hungry for lands to support their new cavalry, ordered churches and monasteries to make such grants to their soldiers, in what was known as the *"precarium* by order of the king" (Document 19). The *precarium,* or benefice, thus acquired a close association with military service, while remaining a conditional and temporary grant of land. By the ninth century, the Carolingian rulers were themselves making such precarial grants from their own property to their lay retainers (Document 20). This conditional form of land tenure, closely tied to military service, provided, in this plausible reconstruction, the juridical model for the fief, which does not fully appear in our records until the eleventh century.

The fief, as a conditional, temporary, and nonhereditary form of land tenure, was initially quite distinct from the allod, which resembled property in the Roman sense and was permanent, unconditional, and hereditary. But in the twelfth and especially the thirteenth centuries, the two forms of land tenure tended to become assimilated. To begin with, the principalities of many European areas, notably northern France, England, and Germany, accepted in their customary law the proposition of *nulle terre sans seigneur*, that all lands of the province or kingdom were in origin and in obligations fiefs held from the prince (see, for example, Document 33). Allodial property in these regions had no legal existence. In southern France and Spain the fief grew considerably in importance in the eleventh and twelfth centuries, but the allod never entirely disappeared. In Italy the allod remained the dominant form of land tenure through the Middle Ages.

But even as allods disappeared in some parts of Europe and declined in others, feudal tenure was acquiring some of the characteristics of allodial ownership. Almost from the first, the adult sons of tenants received their fathers' fiefs in inheritance; the lord, after all, wanted service, and grown sons could most readily and efficiently replace their deceased fathers. Moreover, the lord could not expect his vassals to fight zealously for him in war if they believed that death would bring the ruination of their families. Soon, too, feudal custom everywhere recognized the right of minor sons to inherit their fathers' fiefs. The lord retained a right of wardship over them (i.e., the right of naming their guardians) or could claim the revenues from the fiefs until the heirs were old enough to serve. A further problem was the "partibility" of the fief: could it be divided among many sons? The custom most commonly practiced admitted the partibility of smaller tenancies, but not that of knight's fiefs, baronies, counties, and the like, as division of the land might injure the fief's capacity to support service. However, even in regard to the great fiefs, a system known as "parage" was allowed in some parts of France (Document 33) and elsewhere. In it several relatives would divide a fief, but the senior among them was viewed as holding the totality of lands as a single fief from the lord, in return for a single homage.

Female heirs presented a still more difficult problem, as they could not of course fulfill military service. Still, the customs especially of southern France, Spain, and the crusading states of the Levant were favorable to them and very early admitted them to the inheritance of fiefs, at least in the absence of male issue. The lord, however, retained the right of choosing husbands for them, as their consorts would be responsible for fulfilling the obligation of service. Everywhere, when a fief passed in inheritance, the lord could claim a special payment known as "relief," since it "relieved" or freed the land from the lord's control and returned it to the heir. In the absence of any heir, the fief escheated permanently into the lord's possession.

In a strict sense also, the vassal had no right to donate, sell, or in any way alienate his fief, in whole or in part. However, in the thirteenth century exceptions here too were readily allowed. The lord's permission had always to be gained, and almost always purchased. The willingness of lords by the thirteenth century to allow trafficking in fiefs in return for monetary charges reflects the changing role of the fief in feudal society. As money became more important to princes, so they became more interested in fiefs as a source of revenue than as a support of service. At the same time, the property aspects of the feudal tie were coming to outweigh the personal aspects of vassalage. This process is what French scholars call the *réalisation* of the feudal bond, the growing dominance of "real" property and "real" rights in it over the considerations of sentiment and loyalty which had originally inspired the feudal relationship.

Justice and lordship

In considering the institutional basis of feudal society, it cannot be forgotten that institutions continued to function which were much older than the system of feudalism. Foremost of these institutions was kingship itself. The kings of Europe, as we shall see, were eager to make use of feudal institutions and feudal conceptions in strengthening their authority and in imposing precise obligations upon their subjects. But the medieval king was always something more than a feudal lord. The Church in particular held out a vision of kingship which made of it a sacred office (Document 30). This moral and spiritual prestige was to be a resource of immeasurable importance for the active kings of the second feudal age. So also, on the local level, the medieval courts continued to rely on procedures, such as ordeals and trial by combat (Documents 25 and 26), which had no direct relationship with feudal institutions but were rooted in much older juridical practices.

Perhaps the most distinctive feature of properly feudal justice was the exercise, by the lord who held the land, of some form of jurisdiction over the persons residing upon it. This has been traditionally called, not quite adequately, "private justice." Historians explain its origins in several ways. Through grants of immunity (Documents 28 and 29), Merovingian and Carolingian kings forbade their own officials from entering upon the lands of a church or monastery. These institutions were allowed to make their own arrangements for judging, taxing, and recruiting. But it is hardly likely that the Carolingians systematically established private justice by consciously and massively dismantling the powers of their own government. Further, all surviving charters of immunity concern ecclesiastical institutions, and they do not explain how laymen too gained these jurisdictional rights.

Still other scholars have interpreted private justice as the result of usurpation rather than of grant. Since the late Roman Empire, great landlords had been exercising jurisdiction over their dependents, and amid the chaos of the post-Carolingian epoch, the weakness of the government left no obstacle to the further assumption of such rights by local persons. Indeed, the vacuum of authority made it essential that someone assume the responsibilities of adjudication. In tenth-century Europe, the choice was between private justice and no justice at all.

Recently, however, some scholars have found the word "usurpation," and even the term "private justice," objectionable, as such terms suggest that jurisdiction exercised by local magnates, rather than by a central government, constitutes a deviation from some sort of absolute norm which nature has supposedly ordained that all states and societies should follow. Rather, these scholars argue that both in barbarian and in late Roman vulgar or popular law, *dominium*, the right of ownership over land, came necessarily to include some form of personal lordship over those settled upon it. In a primitive economy, the ownership of land alone would be valueless without settlers to work it and authority to require them to labor for the lord. So also, in granting fiefs, lords had to give all the rights needed to make the lands profitable to their vassals. In this interpretation, to ask how the central government lost its powers to private persons is to think anachronistically, and in fact to pose a meaningless question. Conceptions of ownership in the early Middle Ages, contrary to our own, seem necessarily to have included some notion of personal authority over those settled upon the land.

These then were the chief institutions which, in the second feudal age, the princes of Europe combined and manipulated in the interest of achieving a more ordered political life.

⎍⎍⎍⎍⎍⎍⎍⎍⎍⎍⎍⎍⎍⎍⎍⎍⎍⎍⎍⎍⎍

RECOMMENDED READINGS

J. M. W. BEAN, *The Decline of English Feudalism* (New York: Barnes and Noble, 1968).

MARION GIBBS, *Feudal Order: A Study of the Origins and Development of English Feudal Society* (New York: Schumann, 1953).

C. H. HASKINS, *Norman Institutions* (New York: F. Ungar, 1960).

C. WARREN HOLLISTER, *The Military Organization of Norman England* (Oxford: Clarendon Press, 1965).

F. KERN, *Kingship and Law in the Middle Ages* (Oxford: B. Blackwell, 1956).

ARCHIBALD LEWIS, *The Development of Southern French and Catalan Society, 718-1050* (Austin: University of Texas Press, 1965).

BRYCE LYON, *From Fief to Indenture: The Transition from Feudal to Non-Feudal Contract in Western Europe* (Cambridge: Harvard University Press, 1957).

F. W. MAITLAND, *Domesday Book and Beyond: Three Essays in the Early History of England* (New York: Norton, 1966).

C. E. ODEGAARD, *Vassi and Fideles in the Carolingian Empire* (Cambridge: Harvard University Press, 1942).

MICHAEL POWICKE, *Military Obligation in Medieval England: A Study in Liberty and Duty* (Oxford: Clarendon Press, 1962).

IVOR J. SANDERS, *Feudal Military Service in England* (London: Oxford University Press, 1956).

I. *Vassalage*

⌐⌐⌐⌐⌐⌐⌐⌐⌐⌐⌐⌐⌐⌐⌐⌐⌐⌐⌐⌐⌐⌐

8. The Germanic *Comitatus*, described by Tacitus

The following brief text from the *Germania* of the Roman historian Tacitus (written A.D. 98) has been one of the most intensively studied passages in the sources of ancient and medieval history. In it Tacitus describes the institution among the Germanic peoples which he calls the *comitatus*, "following." The bond among the warriors closely resembles and was undoubtedly an antecedent for the ties of vassalage under the later system of feudalism. The source is the thirteenth and fourteenth chapters of the *Germania*, in P. *Cornelli Taciti Libri qui supersunt* (Leipzig: Teubner, 1949), pp. 13–14. The translation is by D. Herlihy.

13. . . . Distinguished nobility or the great merits of their fathers secure even for young men the worthy status of a chief. Men cluster about others who are stronger than themselves and those who have already proved their valor. There is no shame in being reckoned among their followers. This retinue also has its different ranks, established by the judgment of its leader. There is great rivalry among the followers as to who shall hold the first place with the chief. There is rivalry also among the chiefs as to who shall have the largest band of followers and the most valorous. This is honor, this is strength, always to be surrounded by a great band of chosen youths. This confers distinction in peace and help in war. Each chief gains reputation and glory in proportion to the numbers and the courage of his following, not only among his own people but also among the neighboring communities. For then legations come seeking to enlist him; they shower him with gifts, and in many instances, his reputation alone decides the outcome of wars.

14. When they go into battle, it is shameful for the chief to be surpassed in feats of valor and for the followers not to strive to equal the courage of their chief. Moreover, it is a lifelong infamy and shame if any of the followers survives his chief and comes uninjured from the battle. Their sacred oath of loyalty requires them to defend and protect him and to attribute their bravest deeds to his fame. The chiefs fight for victory, the followers for their chief. If the community from which they come languishes in an extended peace and torpor, many of the noble young men seek those peoples which are waging war. Peace displeases the youths, and they gain glory more readily amid dangers. Nor can a great following be supported unless by violence and war. For the followers ask that war horse and that bloody and conquering spear from the generosity of the chief. The table of the chief with its plain but plentiful dishes is regarded as salary. The source of rich gifts is war and plunder. They could hardly be persuaded to work the soil and earn the yearly harvest; they are more easily moved to challenge an enemy and earn glorious wounds. They consider it dull and senseless to gain by their labor what they might obtain by their blood.

9. Dependency in late-Roman society, according to Salvian of Marseilles

Roman as well as Germanic society knew systems of patronage by which one man submitted himself to another. Even under the Republic, powerful men would maintain bands of *clientes* to support them in their rivalries and riots. In the period of the late empire, amid the disintegration of the Roman state, these systems of dependency gained a special prominence. In his *On the Governance of God* (written *ca.* 440), a priest of Marseilles named Salvian described and bitterly condemned two sorts of dependency. In the first, harassed freemen placed themselves and their possessions under the protection of a powerful neighbor; in the second, they surrendered their freedom also and assumed the status virtually of serfs. Salvian was committed to proving that the sins of the Romans accounted for all the ills of the world, and his strictures are doubtlessly exaggerated. Nevertheless, they excellently show how in a disintegrating society men were seeking their own protection and safety through spontaneously forming these associations. The source is *Salviani presbyteri massiliensis Opera omnia,* ed. F. Pauly (Corpus scriptorum ecclesiasticorum latinorum, 8; Vienna, 1883), pp. 114–15, Book V, Chapter 8, of the *Governance.* The translation is by D. Herlihy.

. . . I could well wonder why all our oppressed and miserable poor do not do this [flee to the barbarians], unless it be that they fail to act for this single reason: They are not able to move their poor possessions, miserable homes, and families. Since many of them desert their fields and huts to avoid the weight of taxes, why do they not wish to carry off with them, if they have the opportunity, that which they are compelled to abandon? This is the reason: They are not able to do what they themselves would much prefer. They have placed themselves under the eyes and protection of the powerful; they make themselves the dependents of the rich and pass all but completely under their control and authority. I would not consider this a grave or shameful act—rather, I would laud the generosity of the powerful to whom the poor commend themselves—if only the rich did not sell their protection, if only their professed intent of defending the poor were attributable to charity rather than to greed. Here is the grave and bitter fact: by the very law by which the poor are supposed to be protected, they are despoiled. The powerful defend the poor by a law which in the defense makes them still more miserable. For those who are supposedly gaining protection surrender all their property to their patrons before they are accepted into their patronage. Thus, in order that fathers may be defended, the sons lose their inheritance. The protection of parents is purchased by the poverty of their dependents.

See what the help and the patronage of the powerful mean! They give nothing to those they have accepted, but give only to themselves. By this arrangement something is temporarily given to parents so that in the future all may be taken from the sons. The great men sell, I say, all which they give. And when I say "sell," would that they did so in the usual and familiar manner! Perhaps something might then be left to the purchasers. But this is a new type of sale and purchase. The seller gives nothing and receives all. The purchaser receives nothing and loses almost all. Nearly all contracts have the characteristic that the purchasers have desire and the sellers have need—the purchaser sells to increase his property, and the seller to lessen it—but this is a kind of transaction never seen before. The wealth of the sellers grows, and to the purchasers nothing is left but mendicancy.

Then there is the monstrous fact, which I can hardly bear to mention, and at which the human mind boggles—I will not say to tolerate but even to hear—many of the poor and miserable people, deprived of their squalid possessions and driven from their fields, after they have lost their property, still must bear the taxes of what was lost. The possessions leave them, but the head assessment does not. They lack property and are destroyed by taxes! Who can measure this evil? Robbers press hard upon the property of the poor, and the poor pay taxes for the robbers. After the death of the father, the children, by submission to his will, do not possess the fields but are crushed by the charges on the fields. Amid such crimes, what further can be added, unless this: The one who is stripped by private theft dies by public persecution; taxes take the life of those whom robbery has deprived of their possessions.

Therefore, many of the persons of whom we are speaking, better advised, from the prudence necessity gives them do this: when they have lost homes and fields to the robbers or have fled, chased by the tax collectors, since they cannot retain their possessions, they seek the estates of the powerful and become the serfs [coloni] of the rich. They act similarly to those persons who, impelled by terror of enemies, seek out fortresses, or those who, losing the status of secure freedom, flee to any refuge. So also do they who are unable to defend further their home or the dignity of their children; they submit themselves to the yoke of servile dependency, forced to this necessary decision, since they are exiled not only from their wealth but also from their status, and are cast out not only from their belongings but also from themselves. Losing all their possessions together with their persons, they are deprived of property and also lose the right of freedom.

⎍⎍⎍⎍⎍⎍⎍⎍⎍⎍⎍⎍⎍⎍⎍⎍⎍⎍⎍⎍⎍⎍⎍⎍⎍⎍⎍

10. Merovingian dependency, illustrated by model charters

The early Middle Ages are desperately poor in sources. However, from the Merovingian kingdom of the Franks we do possess collections of formulas or model charters. These were designed to provide the scribe with the appropriate terms and formulas for the various transactions which might come before him. The oldest of these books of model charters date from the seventh century, and they provide us with one of our most important views of Frankish society and its principal institutions. The first of the following three charters illustrates a reception into the royal service; the second, a voluntary abandonment of free status in return for protection; and the third, an act of commendation. The first charter is the earliest known example of the symbolic use of hands to signify reception into service and protection. The last charter, in which the freedom of the dependent is maintained, most closely resembles in its terms later vassalage. The source is the *Formulae merovingici et karolini aevi*, ed. K. Zeumer (Monumenta Germaniae Historica, Legum Sectio V; Hanover, 1886), pp. 55, 140, 158. The translation is by D. Herlihy. The wergild mentioned was the characteristic fine imposed in compensation for the death of a man.

Marculfi formularum liber I.

No. 18. On royal protection [antrustione]

It is right that those who promise to us entire fidelity should be protected with our help. Since by the mercy of God our faithful man N. has come with his arms into our palace and publicly sworn in our hands trust and fidelity, we therefore decree and command through this present order that henceforth the same N. should be reckoned among the number of our retainers [*antruscioni*]. And if perchance anyone should presume to kill him, he should know that he will be held guilty for a wergild of 600 *solidi*.

Formulae turonenses
No. 10. A sale of one's own person, by which a free man sells himself

To my permanent lord N., I, N.: It has pleased me to bind my free status to your service. This I have done, and for this I have received from you payment, which pleases me, to the amount of so many *solidi*. Therefore, from this day forward you have free and most firm authority to do with me, your slave, in all things, what you may wish to do, as with your other slaves. And (which I do not believe will happen) if any persons should attempt to take action against or bring a complaint against this sale, which I have accomplished of my own free will and asked to be signed, let him not obtain what he seeks, and moreover let him pay to the person against whom he brought the complaint one pound of gold, and five pounds of silver, and this sale shall remain firm.

No. 43. Who places himself under the authority of another

To the magnificent lord N., I, N.: As it is evident to all that I have nothing wherewith I might feed and clothe myself, therefore I have appealed to your piety and you have willingly agreed that I should deliver or commend myself under your protection [*mundoburdum*]. This I have done in such a manner that you ought to help and console me both with food and with clothing, according to the degree that I serve you and merit from you. And for as long as I remain alive, I must provide you service and honor according to my free rank, and I shall not have the authority of releasing myself from your power and protection at any time in my life. Rather, I am to remain under your power and protection all the days of my life. Therefore, it is agreed that if one of us should wish to depart from these agreements, let him pay so many *solidi* to the other, and this agreement shall remain firm. Therefore, it is agreed that two charters identical in wording should be written and exchanged. This they have done.

⎍⎍⎍⎍⎍⎍⎍⎍⎍⎍⎍⎍⎍⎍⎍⎍⎍⎍⎍⎍⎍⎍⎍⎍⎍

11. The earliest known oath of vassalage, from the *Annales regni Francorum*

The following passage from a Carolingian chronicle of 757 is significant not only for its reference, the earliest known, to an oath taken by
a vassal to his Lord, but also because it represents an early effort to
define the obligations owed by a great man of the realm to the king in
terms of a vassal's duties. The source is the *Annales regni Francorum*,
ed. F. Kurze (Monumenta Germaniae Historica, Scriptores in usum
scholarum; Hanover, 1895), p. 14. The translation is by D. Herlihy.

[Year 757]. King Pepin held his assembly in Compiègne with the
Franks. Tassilo, the duke of the Bavarians, came there, and commended himself with his hands to vassalage. He swore many,
innumerable oaths, placing his hands upon the relics of the saints.
He promised fidelity to King Pepin and to his sons mentioned
above, the lord Charles and Carloman, as a vassal, with right mind
and firm devotion, ought in justice to do to his lords.

⎍⎍⎍⎍⎍⎍⎍⎍⎍⎍⎍⎍⎍⎍⎍⎍⎍⎍⎍⎍⎍⎍⎍⎍⎍

12. Vassalage and dependency in the Carolingian capitularies

The following excerpts from the laws of the Carolingian kings and
emperors, known as capitularies, cast light on the nature of vassalage
and also upon the efforts of the Carolingians to utilize the institutions
of vassalage as a foundation of the stability of their kingdom. The oath
taken to Charles the Bald in 858 contains the first reference to "aid and
counsel" in a feudal context. The passages, translated by D. Herlihy,
are taken from the *Capitularia regum francorum*, ed. A. Boretius and
V. Krause (Monumenta Germaniae Historica, Legum Section II;
Hanover, 1883–97).

No. 16, ca. 758–68

9. If anyone by necessity should flee into another duchy or province or should follow his lord, to whom he may not deny faith, and his wife, although she is able, should not wish to follow him for love of her relatives or possessions, she is to remain forever unmarried during the entire time that her husband, whom she did not wish to accompany, is alive. But her husband, who through necessity flees into another place, can with penitence take another wife, if he is unable to abstain.

No. 64, 810

17. Let every [lord] compel his dependents to obey better and better and consent to the imperial commands and orders.

No. 77, 802–3

16. Let no man abandon his lord after he has received from him the value of a single *solidus*, unless the lord wishes to kill him, or to beat him with a stick, or to violate his wife or daughter, or to deprive him of his inheritance.

No. 104, ca. 801–13

8. If any vassal should wish to abandon his lord, he may do so only if he can prove that the lord has committed one of these crimes: first, if the lord should have unjustly sought to enslave him; second, if the lord plotted against his life; third, if the lord committed adultery with the wife of his vassal; fourth, if the lord willingly attacked him with drawn sword in order to kill him; fifth, if after the vassal commended his hands into his, the lord failed to provide defense which he could have done. If the lord has committed any of these five offenses against his vassal, the vassal may abandon him.

No. 204, 847

2. We wish that every free man in our kingdom select the lord whom he prefers, us or one of our faithful subjects.

3. We also command that no man abandon his lord without just cause, nor should anyone receive him, unless according to the customs of our ancestors.

5. And we wish that the vassal of any one of us [Charles the Bald, Louis the German, and Lothar] should accompany his lord

into the army in order to fulfill his services, in no matter whose kindgom he should be. But if a general invasion of the kingdom should occur, called *Landwehr* (may it not happen!), then all the people of the realm should go together to repulse it.

No. 204, 847 [Oath taken to Charles the Bald]

1. Oath taken by the faithful: I shall be your faithful helper, as much as my knowledge and powers allow, with the help of God, without any deception or revolt, in counsel and in aid, according to my function and my person, so that you will be able to maintain and exercise that authority which God has given you, at His will and for your own salvation and that of your faithful subjects. . . .

⎍⎍⎍⎍⎍⎍⎍⎍⎍⎍⎍⎍⎍⎍⎍⎍⎍⎍⎍⎍⎍⎍

13. The Battle of Maldon

The strength of the bonds between man and man in the Germanic "following" is excellently illustrated in this short and unfortunately fragmented Anglo-Saxon poem, *The Battle of Maldon*. The battle, waged by the Saxons against Norse pirates, took place in 991 in Essex under King Aethelred the Redeless ("poorly advised"). The central event of the poem is the death of the Saxon chief Byrhtnoth, and the great interest it offers for historical purposes is the behavior of the members of his following. It helps show the full ethical and moral dimensions of this early form of vassalage. The poem, given here in its entirety, is taken from J. Duncan Spaeth, *Old English Poetry: Translations into Alliterative Verse with Introduction and Notes* (Princeton: Princeton University Press, 1922), pp. 165–74. Reprinted with the permission of the publishers.

> Byrhtnoth encouraged his comrades heartily;
> Rode through the ranks and roused their spirits;
> Marshalled his men to meet the onset;
> Showed them how they should hold their shields
> Firm in their grip, and fearless stand.
> When he had briskly whetted their courage,

He leaped from his steed and stood with his people,
His hearth-band beloved and household thanes.

Then strode to the strand a stalwart Northman,
The viking herald. They heard him shout,
Send o'er the tide the taunt of the pirates;
Hailing the earl, he hurled this challenge:
"Bold sea-rovers bade me tell thee
Straightway thou must send them tribute,
Rings for ransom, royal treasure;
Better with gifts ye buy us off,
Ere we deal hard blows and death in battle.
Why spill we blood when the bargain is easy?
Give us the pay and we grant ye peace.
If thou dost agree, who art greatest here,
To ransom thy folk with the fee we demand,
And give to the seamen the gold they ask,
Pay with tribute for treaty of peace,
We load the booty aboard our ships,
Haul to sea and hold the truce."
Byrhtnoth spake, he brandished his spear,
Lifted his shield and shouted aloud,
Grim was his wrath as he gave them his answer:
"Hearest thou, pirate, my people's reply?
Ancient swords they will send for ransom;
Poison-tipped points they will pay for tribute;
Treasure that scarce will serve you in battle
Go back, pirate, give them my answer;
Bring them this word of bitter defiance;
Tell them here standeth, stern and intrepid,
The earl with his folk, to defend his country,
Æthelred's realm, the rights of my lord,
His house and his home; the heathen shall fall,
Pirates and robbers. My people were shamed
If ye loaded our booty aboard your ships,
And floated them off unfought for, to sea,
Having sailed so far, to set foot on our soil.
Not all so easily earn ye our gold!
Sword-blades and spear-points we sell you first;
Battle-play grim, ere ye get our tribute!"

Forward he told his troop to come,
To step under shield and stand by the shore.
The breadth of the stream kept the bands asunder;
Strong came flowing the flood after ebb,
Filled the channel, and foamed between them.
Impatient stood by Panta stream,
East-Saxon host and horde of the pirates,
Longing to lock their lances in battle.
Neither could harass or harm the other,
Save that some fell by the flight of arrows.

Down went the tide, the Danes were ready;
Burned for battle the band of the Vikings;
On the bridge stood Wulfstan, and barred their way.
Byrhtnoth sent him, a seasoned warrior,
Ceola's son, with his kinsmen to hold it.
The first of the Vikings who ventured to set
Foot on the bridge, he felled with his spear.
Two sturdy warriors stood with Wulfstan,
Maccus and Ælfhere, mighty pair,
Kept the approach where the crossing was shallow;
Defended the bridge, and fought with the boldest,
As long as their hands could lift a sword.
When the strangers discovered and clearly saw
What bitter fighters the bridgewards proved,
They tried a trick, the treacherous robbers,
Begged they might cross, and bring their crews
Over the shallows, and up to the shore.
The earl was ready, in reckless daring,
To let them land too great a number.
Byrhthelm's son, while the seamen listened,
Called across, o'er the cold water:
"Come ye seamen, come and fight us!
We give you ground, but God alone knows
Who to-day shall hold the field."

Strode the battle-wolves bold through the water;
West over Panta waded the pirates;
Carried their shields o'er the shining waves;
Safely their lindenwoods landed the sailors.

Byrhtnoth awaited them, braced for the onslaught,
Haughty and bold at the head of his band.
Bade them build the bristling war-hedge,
Shield against shield, to shatter the enemy.
Near was the battle, now for the glory,
Now for the death of the doomed in the field.
Swelled the war-cry, circled the ravens,
Screamed the eagle, eager for prey;
Sped from the hand the hard-forged spear-head,
Straight went the lance, strong was the leader;
Sheer through the throat of the pirate he thrust it.
His dart meant death, so deadly his aim.
Swiftly he sent him a second javelin,
That crashed through the corslet and cleft his bosom,
Wounded him sore through his woven mail;
The poisonous spear-head stood in his heart.
Blithe was the leader, laughed in his breast,
Thanked his Lord for that day's work.

Now one of the pirates poised his weapon,
Sped from his hand a spear that wounded
Through and through the thane of Æthelred.
There stood at his side a stripling youth;
Brave was the boy; he bent o'er his lord,
Drew from his body the blood-dripping dart.
'Twas Wulfmær the youthful, Wulfstan's son;
Back he hurled the hard-forged spear.
In went the point, to earth fell the pirate
Who gave his master the mortal hurt.
A crafty seaman crept toward the earl,
Eager to rob him of armor and rings,
Bracelets and gear and graven sword.
Then Byrhtnoth drew his blade from the sheath,
Broad and blood-stained, struck at the breast-plate.
But one of the seamen stopped the warrior,
Beat down the arm of the earl with his lance.
Fell to the ground the gray-hilted sword;
No more he might grasp his goodly blade,
Wield his weapon; yet words he could utter;
The hoar-headed warrior heartened his men;

Bade them forward to fare and be brave.
Showers of darts, sharp from the grindstone.
Bows were busy, bolt stuck in buckler;
Bitter the battle-rush, brave men fell,
Heroes on either hand, hurt in the fray.
Wounded was Wulfmær, went to his battle-rest;
Cruelly mangled, kinsman of Byrhtnoth,
Son of his sister, slain on the field.

Pay of vengeance they paid the Vikings;
I heard of the deed of the doughty Edward:
He struck with his sword a stroke that was mighty,
Down fell the doomed man, dead at his feet.
For this the thane got the thanks of his leader,
Praise that was due for his prowess in fight.
Grimly they held their ground in the battle,
Strove with each other the stout-hearted heroes,
Strove with each other, eager to strike
First with their darts the foe that was doomed.
Warriors thronged, the wounded lay thick.
Stalwart and steady they stood about Byrhtnoth.
Bravely he heartened them, bade them to win
Glory in battle by beating the Danes.
Raising his shield, he rushed at the enemy;
Covered by buckler, he came at a Viking;
Charged him furious, earl against churl,
Each for the other had evil in store.
The sailorman sent from the south a javelin,
Sorely wounding the war-band's leader;
He shoved with his shield, the shaft snapped short;
The spear was splintered and sprang against him;
Wroth was Byrhtnoth, reached for his weapon;
Gored the Viking that gave him the wound.
When the stricken leader no longer could stand,
He looked to heaven and lifted his voice:
"I render Thee thanks O Ruler of men,
For the joys Thou hast given, that gladdened my life.
Merciful Maker, now most I need,
Thy goodness to grant me a gracious end,
That my soul may swiftly speed to Thee,

Come to Thy keeping, O King of angels,
Depart in peace. I pray Thee Lord
That the fiends of hell may not harm my spirit."
The heathen pirates then hewed him to pieces,
And both the brave men that by him stood;
Ælfnoth and Wulfmær, wounded to death,
Gave their lives for their lord in the fight.

Then quitted the field the cowards and faint-hearts;
The son of Odda started the flight.
Godric abandoned his good lord in battle,
Who many a steed had bestowed on his thane.
Leaped on the horse that belonged to his leader,
Not *his* were the trappings, *he* had no right to them.
Both of his brothers basely fled with him,
Godwin and Godwy, forgetful of honor,
Turned from the fight, and fled to the woods,
Seeking the cover, and saving their lives.
Those were with them, who would have remained,
Had they remembered how many favors
Their lord had done them in days of old.
Offa foretold it, what time he arose
To speak where they met to muster their forces.
Many, he said, were mighty in words
Whose courage would fail when it came to fighting.
There lay on the field the lord of the people,
Æthelred's earl; all of them saw him,
His hearth-companions beheld him dead.
Forward went fighting the fearless warriors,
Their courage was kindled, no cowards were they;
Their will was fixed on one or the other:
To lose their life, or avenge their leader
Ælfwiné spoke to them, son of Ælfric,
Youthful in years, but unyielding in battle;
Roused their courage, and called them to honor:
"Remember the time when we talked in the mead-hall,
When bold on our benches we boasted our valor,
Deeds of daring we'd do in the battle!
Now we may prove whose prowess is true.
My birth and my breeding I boldly proclaim:

I am sprung from a mighty Mercian line.
Aldhelm the alderman, honored and prosperous,
He was my grandsire, great was his fame:
My people who know me shall never reproach me,
Say I was ready to run from the battle,
Back to my home, and abandon my leader,
Slain on the field. My sorrow is double,
Both kinsman and lord I've lost in the fight."
Forward he threw himself, thirsting for vengeance;
Sent his javelin straight at a pirate.
Fell with a crash his foe to the earth,
His life-days ended. Then onward he strode,
Urging his comrades to keep in the thick of it.

Up spake Offa, with ashen spear lifted:
"Well hast thou counselled us, well hast encouraged;
Noble Ælfwiné, needs must we follow thee.
Now that our leader lies low on the field,
Needs must we steadfastly stand by each other,
Close in the conflict keeping together,
As long as our hands can hold a weapon,
Good blade wield. Godric the coward,
Son of Odda, deceived us all.
Too many believed 'twas our lord himself,
When they saw him astride the war-steed proud.
His run-away ride our ranks hath broken,
Shattered the shield-wall. Shame on the dastard,
Who caused his comrades like cowards to fly!"
Up spake Leofsunu, lifted his linden-wood,
Answered his comrades from under his shield:
"Here I stand, and here shall I stay!
Not a foot will I flinch, but forward I'll go!
Vengeance I've vowed for my valiant leader.
Now that my friend is fallen in battle,
My people shall never reproach me, in Stourmere;
Call me deserter, and say I returned,
Leaderless, lordless, alone from the fight.
Better is battle-death; boldly I welcome
The edge and the iron." Full angry he charged,
Daring all danger, disdaining to fly.

Up spake Dunheré, old and faithful,
Shook his lance and shouted aloud,
Bade them avenge the valiant Byrhtnoth:
"Wreak on the Danes the death of our lord!
Unfit is for vengeance who values his life."
Fell on the foe the faithful body-guard,
Battle-wroth spearmen, beseeching God
That they might avenge the thane of Æthelred,
Pay the heathen with havoc and slaughter.
The son of Ecglaf, Æscferth by name,
Sprung from a hardy North-humbrian race,
—He was their hostage,—helped them manfully.
Never he faltered or flinched in the war-play;
Lances a plenty he launched at the pirates,
Rarely he missed them, many he wounded,
Shot them on shield, or sheer through the breast-plate;
While he could wield his weapon in battle.
Still Edward the long held out at the front;
Brave and defiant, he boasted aloud
That he would not yield a hair's breadth of ground,
Nor turn his back where his better lay dead.
He broke through the shield-wall, breasted the foe,
Worthily paid the pirate warriors
For the life of his lord ere he laid him down.
Near him Æthelric, noble comrade,
Brother of Sibryht, brave and untiring,
Mightily fought, and many another;
Hacked the hollow shields, holding their own.
Bucklers were broken, the breast-plate sang
Its gruesome song. The sword of Offa
Went home to the hilt in the heart of a Viking.
But Offa himself soon had to pay for it,
The kinsman of Gadd succumbed in the fight.
Yet ere he fell, he fulfilled his pledge,
The promise he gave to his gracious lord,
That both should ride to their burg together,
Home to their friends, or fall in the battle,
Killed in conflict and covered with wounds;
He lay by his lord, a loyal thane.
Mid clash of shields the shipmen came on,

Maddened by battle. Full many a lance
Home was thrust to the heart of the doomed.
Then sallied forth Wistan, Wigelin's son;
Three of the pirates he pierced in the throng,
Ere he fell, by his friends, on the field of slaughter.
Bitter the battle-rush, bravely struggled
Heroes in armor, while all around them
The wounded dropped and the dead lay thick.
Oswold and Eadwold all the while
Their kinsmen and comrades encouraged bravely,
Both of the brothers bade their friends
Never to weaken or weary in battle,
But keep up their sword-play, keen to the end.
Up spake Byrhtwold, brandished his ash-spear,
—He was a tried and true old hero,—
Lifted his shield and loudly called to them:
"Heart must be keener, courage the hardier,
Bolder our mood as our band diminisheth.
Here lies in his blood our leader and comrade,
The brave on the beach. Bitter shall rue it
Who turns his back on the battle-field now.
Here I stay; I am stricken and old;
My life is done; I shall lay me down
Close by my lord and comrade dear."

[Six more lines and the MS. breaks off. There cannot have been much left. The battle is over. The words of old Byrhtwold make a fitting close for these renderings of Old English verse.]

⎍⎍⎍⎍⎍⎍⎍⎍⎍⎍⎍⎍⎍⎍⎍⎍⎍⎍⎍⎍⎍

14. The obligations of vassals, according to Fulbert of Chartres

The following letter, written in 1020, is one of the first and most complete statements of the duties a vassal owed his lord. The author is the bishop of Chartres, Fulbert, an accomplished writer and one of the first representatives of the intellectual renaissance of the West. The translation is taken from *A Source Book of Medieval History*, ed. F. A. Ogg (New York: American Book Company, 1907), pp. 220–21.

To William, most illustrious duke of the Aquitanians, Bishop Fulbert, the favor of his prayers:

Requested to write something regarding the character of fealty, I have set down briefly for you, on the authority of the books, the following things. He who takes the oath of fealty to his lord ought always to keep in mind these six things: what is harmless, safe, honorable, useful, easy, and practicable. *Harmless*, which means that he ought not to injure his lord in his body; *safe*, that he should not injure him by betraying his confidence or the defenses upon which he depends for security; *honorable*, that he should not injure him in his justice, or in other matters that relate to his honor; *useful*, that he should not injure him in his property; *easy*, that he should not make difficult that which his lord can do easily; and *practicable*, that he should not make impossible for the lord that which is possible.

However, while it is proper that the faithful vassal avoid these injuries, it is not for doing this alone that he deserves his holding: for it is not enough to refrain from wrongdoing, unless that which is good is done also. It remains, therefore, that in the same six things referred to above he should faithfully advise and aid his lord, if he wishes to be regarded as worthy of his benefice and to be safe concerning the fealty which he has sworn.

The lord also ought to act toward his faithful vassal in the same manner in all these things. And if he fails to do this, he will be rightfully regarded as guilty of bad faith, just as the former, if he should be found shirking, or willing to shirk, his obligations would be perfidious and perjured.

I should have written to you at greater length had I not been busy with many other matters, including the rebuilding of our city and church, which were recently completely destroyed by a terrible fire. Though for a time we could not think of anything but this disaster, yet now, by the hope of God's comfort, and of yours also, we breathe more freely again.

⎍⎍⎍⎍⎍⎍⎍⎍⎍⎍⎍⎍⎍⎍⎍⎍⎍⎍⎍⎍⎍⎍⎍⎍

15. Homage, described by Galbert of Bruges

The following text, referring to the year 1127, is our earliest description of the act of homage performed in conjunction with the granting of a fief. It therefore marks, in the estimate of most historians, the emergence of the mature feudal system. The document, translated by D. Herlihy, is taken from Galbert de Bruges, *Histoire du meurtre de Charles le Bon comte de Flandre (1127–1128)*, ed. H. Pirenne (Collection de textes pour servir à l'étude et à l'enseignement de l'histoire, 10; Paris, 1891), p. 89. A complete English translation of this important source is available in *The Murder of Charles the Good Count of Flanders*, trans. J. B. Ross (Records of Civilization, 61; New York: Columbia University Press, 1960).

56. On Thursday, the seventh of the ides of April [April 7, 1127], acts of homage were again made to the count, which were brought to a conclusion through this method of giving faith and assurance. First, they performed homage in this fashion: the count inquired if [the prospective vassal] wished completely to become his man. He replied, "I do wish it," and with his hands joined and covered by the hands of the count, the two were united by a kiss. Second, he who had done the homage gave faith to the representative of the count in these words: "I promise in my faith that I shall henceforth be faithful to Count William, and I shall fully observe the homage owed him against all men, in good faith and without deceit." Third, he took an oath on the relics of saints. Then the count, with the rod which he had in his hand, gave investiture to all those who by this promise had given assurance and due homage to the count, and had taken the oath.

16. An oath of vassalage, from the *Liber feudorum maior*

The lands of southern Europe, probably because of the continuing influence of Roman tradition, maintained the practice of preserving a record in writing of important transactions, including acts of homage, investiture, and feudal oaths. Even though feudal practices never dominated southern society quite as completely as that of the north, the records of the south still possess a special interest. One of the richest collections of such records is the *Liber feudorum maior*, which included charters largely concerning Catalonia and the county of Barcelona. The following oath gives a good indication of the obligations characteristically assumed by vassals. Note the prominence of women in the charter, typical of the regions where the tradition of courtly love takes its origins. For the construction of the castle of Tarrega involved in this oath, see Document 35. The source, translated by D. Herlihy, is the *Liber feudorum maior: Cartulario real que se conserva en el Archivo de la Corona de Aragón*, ed. F. M. Rosell (Barcelona, 1945-47).

No. 172, 1058

I, Richard Altemir, the son of Lady Ermengardis, swear that from this hour forward I will be faithful to you, the lord Count Raymond, son of the Countess Sancia, and Lady Almodis, countess, the daughter of the Countess Amelia, without fraud or evil deceit or any deception, and I, the said Richard, from this hour forward will deprive you, the said Count Raymond and Countess Almodis, neither of your life nor of your members which are attached to your bodies, nor of the city which is called Barcelona, nor of the county which is called Barcelona, nor of the episcopate of the Holy Cross and of St. Eulalia, nor of those fortresses or castles which are in the said county or episcopate, nor of those bastions and hills, cultivated or uncultivated, which are in the said county or episcopate, nor of that city which is called Gerona, nor of that county which is called Gerona, nor of that episcopate of St. Mary of Gerona, nor of the fortresses or castles, bastions, or hills, cultivated or uncultivated, which are in the said county or episcopate or of that castle which is called Cardona with its boundaries and appurtenances, nor of those castles, Camarasa or Cubelles, with their boundaries and appurtenances nor of those castles Estopina, Cannelles, with their boundaries and appurtenances and likewise for that castle of Ribagorza with its boundaries and appurtenances, likewise of those rents of Spain which today by agreement are given you or will later be given you, also of the castle which is called Cleran and that which is called Tarmarito with its boundaries and appurtenances, also that castle which is called Cervera with its boundaries and appurtenances.

And I, the said Richard, shall not refuse to you authority over the castle which is called Tarrega, nor over that which pertains to the said castle. But I shall give to you as many times as you ask it of me, personally or through your messengers or messenger without deceiving you, as long as you are alive, and after your death, similarly the same authority over the same castle of Tarrega with its appurtenances, without deceit to your son to whom you, Countess Almodis, may bestow the said castle of Tarrega orally or by testament. And I, the said Richard, will not take from you, Count Raymond and Countess Almodis, all the above-named things, nor shall I have them taken from you, neither I nor man nor men, woman or women, through my advice or not through my advice, or through my plan. And I, the said Richard, shall make the castellan or the castellans whom I send in the said castle of Tarrega through your counsel to swear to you fidelity at your will. And if one of you shall die, I shall similarly attend to everything which is said above, for the other who remains alive. And I, the said Richard, shall help to maintain and preserve all the above things and to defend them for you, the said count and countess, against all men and women, one or many, who might take, or might wish to take, from you, the said count and countess, all the above things or all the things written below, concerning which you, the said count and countess, or one of you, might warn me through the name or in the name of this oath through you yourselves or through your messengers, and that messenger or message shall at once be respected here. And I, the said Richard, shall not forbid that your warning be seen, and I shall offer help without deceit. As it is written above, I will respect and attend to it without deceiving you, excepting whatever you, Count Raymond and Countess Almodis, or one of you, may absolve me of, in your own gracious spirit, without coercion, with two or three of your men as witnesses who with you will also absolve me when you absolve me, the same Richard. Through God and these holy [relics].

17. Multiple vassalage, in the *Liber feudorum maior*

In the second feudal age, as the lines of dependency extended to form networks, a problem common to the whole of feudal Europe was the conflicts which arose when a vassal was obligated to the service of two or more lords. The usual decision was that he was to choose one of them as his "liege lord," and the term will be encountered in several subsequent documents in this anthology. But the problem and confusion created by conflicting loyalties are well illustrated from this Catalonian charter, concerning the vassalage of two brothers and their efforts to satisfy all their lords. The source again is the *Liber feudorum maior*, and the translation is by D. Herlihy.

No. 349, January 18, 1115

This is the agreement made between the lord Raymond Berenguer, the count of Barcelona, and Countess Dulcia; and Arnau Pere and Bernat Pere, brothers, concerning the castle which is called Papiol and the possession of that castle. First, the said count and countess commend to the said brothers the said castle, so that they may have it and hold it in their service and they will help them to hold and defend the said castle and its possession against all men or women who might wish to take away or diminish or make war upon the said castle and its possession or to take away anything from the said possession. But the said count and countess retain authority over the said castle. As many times as they might ask it for themselves personally or through a messenger, the brothers will not refuse to recognize and hear the message. The count and countess retain in the said possession and territory of the castle a fourth part of all rents and service or profits of justice which may come or ought to come from within the said boundaries and possessions. And the three parts which remain, they give to the brothers in fief. The count and countess retain for their ownership in the said castle that tower with its portal standing before the tower, which is opposite the river of Llobregat. The count and countess may make of it a house underneath the fortress. For reason of the said castle, the possession of which the said count and countess give to them in fief, the brothers named above promise to the said count and countess that they will be their liege and loyal vassals against all men or women, as was said above, in right faith without deceit. Also, the said brothers promise to the said count and countess that they will be their vassals in life and body and in their members and also in their landed possessions which today they have or may later acquire with the aid of God. They will help the said count and countess to hold, to defend and make war, excepting against Jordan, their lord, and Raymond Mironi. And against these men, the brothers agree that one of them should be the liege and loyal vassal of the said count and countess, both them and their successors who may hold Barcelona. In return for that which the above count and countess hold in the said castle and possession, the brothers named above agree that they will be their vassals without any deceit or evil design, both for the above castle and the possession of the castle, as well as for their other possessions wherever they may be. The mark of Count Raymond. The mark of Countess Dulcia; done on the fifteenth of the kalends of February in the seventh year of King Louis. The mark of Berenguer William. The mark of Bernat Pere. The mark of Berenguer the seneschal. The mark of Carbonell. The mark of Solomon, chaplain and judge. Raymond Oligarius, levite, who wrote this with letters in the ninth line, on the day and the year stated above.

I I. *The Fief*

⎿⎿⎾⎿

18. A Merovingian precarial grant

The following document is another example of a model charter from the Merovingian period of Frankish history (see Document 10). It represents a *precarium*, sometimes *precaria*, equivalent to a benefice, by which a church alienated the use of a property while retaining a distant right of ownership over it. This sort of conditional and nonhereditary land grant is considered to be the direct ancestor of the fief. The model charter, translated by D. Herlihy, comes from *Formulae merovingici et karolini aevi*, ed. Zeumer, p. 139.

Formulae turonenses
No. 7. A precarial grant

To the venerable Lord N., rector of the church N., and all the congregation residing there, I, N.: At my request you have willingly granted and ordered that your estate, located in the district of N., in the neighborhood of N., in the place named N., with all improvements pertaining or relating to it, should be given to me in usufructuary tenure. You have done this with the stipulation that I may not from this time forward licitly sell or donate or in any way alienate it. Rather, under your authority as long as you are willing, I should hold it and have the use of it. For this I promise to pay to you every year at the feast of Saint N. so much silver. After my death, the property named above, with whatever relates or pertains to it, with all the things placed upon it, as they should be found at my death, wholly and without diminution, without the intervention of a conveyance or consignment by judges or a request from my heirs, should pass into your right and ownership or that of the agents of the said church. If it should happen that I or any of my heirs or any person should dare to raise any complaint or petition or denunciation against this precarial grant, let him not obtain what he seeks. Rather, let him pay 100 *solidi* to the person against whom he may have brought the complaint. Although the property should be held by me for many years, this precarial grant should not prejudice your rights, but they should remain firm. Let this contract remain for all time inviolate, as if it had been renewed every five years.

19. The *Precarium* by order of the king

Legal historians have traditionally considered that the critical link between the benefice, as an exclusively ecclesiastical form of land tenure, and the true fief was the *precarium verbo regis*, or precarial grant, made by a church but at the king's command. Charles Martel (Frankish ruler, 714–741) seems to have instituted this practice, and the massive secularizations of church property which resulted from it raised a storm of protest from churchmen. In the following capitulary, Charlemagne attempted to satisfy both the Church and the knights: on lands so granted he imposed higher dues, which were to be given to the deprived churches. The words in parentheses represent slightly later glosses and additions to the original text. The source is *Capitularia*, ed. A. Boretius, Vol. I, p. 47; translated by D. Herlihy.

No. 20, 793

14. The possessions of the churches (which until now laymen have held in benefice by order of the king) should remain in their possession, unless the king should order that they be returned to the churches. (If) up to the present a tithe and a ninth have been paid (to the church), they should continue to pay it, and (moreover) one *solidus* should be given in addition (to the churches) for every fifty households, one-half *solidus* for every thirty, and one *tremisse* [one-third *solidus*] for every twenty. (Those who up to the present have paid a different rent should continue to pay it as before.) And if up to the present (nothing) has been paid, and the possession belongs to a church, it should assume a rent; where the possessions have not paid a rent, let a rent be prescribed for them.

A distinction should be made between precarial grants made by order of the lord king and those which (bishops, abbots, and abbesses by their own will and judgment) have made. (They may, whenever they see fit, receive back the possessions which they gave out in benefice in the name of the church, to assure that every man should faithfully and firmly serve in God's cause and God's honor.)

⎍⎍⎍⎍⎍⎍⎍⎍⎍⎍⎍⎍⎍⎍⎍⎍⎍⎍⎍⎍⎍⎍⎍

20. A benefice given by Charles the Bald

The following charter (dated 876) by the Carolingian king Charles II (the Bald) illustrates a precarial grant involving only laymen but similar in its terms to the ecclesiastical benefice. It is interesting to note that the same property later appears in a document as an allodial holding. Those who granted such benefices clearly had difficulty in maintaining their rights over them for an extended period. The charter, translated by D. Herlihy, is found in *Recueil des actes de Charles II le Chauve roi de France*, eds. A. Giry, M. Prou, F. Lot, C. Brunel, and G. Tessier, Vol. II (Paris, 1952), No. 411, July 17, 876.

In the name of the holy and undivided Trinity. Charles by the mercy of Almighty God august emperor. If we give our assent to the just and reasonable petitions of our faithful subjects, we familiarize them with the works of our imperial majesty, and from this we make them more faithful and more devoted in the service of our majesty. Therefore let it be known to all the faithful of the holy Church of God and to our own, present and to come, that one of our faithful subjects, by name of Hildebertus, has approached our throne and has beseeched our serenity that through this command of our authority we grant to him for all the days of his life and to his son after him, in right of usufruct and benefice [*usufructuario et jure beneficiario*], certain estates which are both of them called Cavaliacus, in the county of Limoges. Giving assent to his prayers for reason of his meritorious service, we have ordered this charter to be written, through which we grant to him the estates already mentioned, in all their entirety, with lands, vineyards, forests, meadows, pastures, and with the men living upon them, so that, without causing any damage through exchanges or diminishing or lessening the land, he for all the days of his life and his son after him, as we have said, may hold and possess them in right of benefice and usufruct. And in order that this command of our authority may obtain, in the name of God, fuller and firmer vigor of strength . . . [conclusion omitted].

Audacher the notary in place of Gazlinus recognizes [validates] this act.

Done of the sixteenth kalends of August, the thirty-seventh year of the reign of Charles most glorious emperor in France, and the sixth year in succession to Lothair, the first year of his reign as emperor. Done at Ponthion in the palace of the emperor. In the name of God, happily. Amen.

ЛЛЛЛЛЛЛЛЛЛЛЛЛЛЛЛЛЛЛЛЛЛ

21. The capitulary of Quierzy-sur-Oise

The following capitulary of the Carolingian emperor Charles the Bald was promulgated on the eve of his departure for a campaign in Italy in 877. Apparently to maintain the morale of his forces, Charles declared that the sons of the counts who accompanied him would be given assurance of succeeding their fathers who might die in their absence. The capitulary has a double importance. It shows that offices too were considered to be fiefs, and that fiefs, barring unusual circumstances, were being passed on from father to son. This translation by D. Herlihy of portions of two chapters of the capitulary is based on the text in the *Capitularia*, ed. A. Boretius, Vol. II, p. 358.

No. 281, June 14, 877

9. If a count whose son is with us should die, our son should with our other faithful men appoint, from among those who were his most intimate friends and closest neighbors, someone who shall watch over this county, with the servants of the county and of the bishop, until the news shall have reached us. If, however, the deceased count should leave a son of tender years, this adminis-

trator, with the servants of the county and the bishop in whose diocese he may be, should look after the same county until the news comes to our attention.

If he had no sons, our son, together with our other faithful men, should designate a person who, with the servants of the county and with the bishop in whose diocese he may be, should look after the same county until the news comes to our attention.

If he has no sons, our son, together with our other faithful men, should designate a person who, with the servants of the county and with the bishop, shall administer the county until our decision is made known. Let no one become angered for the reason that we may give the county to a person of our own choice rather than to him who has administered it. The same procedure should be followed in relation to our vassals. We wish and we expressly order that the bishops, as well as the abbots and the counts, and equally our other faithful men, should observe the same procedures in regard to their own vassals. . . .

10. If any of our faithful men, after our death, should wish to renounce the world, leaving a son or a close relative able to perform meritorious service to the commonwealth, he should be allowed to convey to him his offices [*honores*]. If he should wish to live peacefully on his allodial holdings, no one should presume to oppose him, or demand anything from him, saving only that he come to the defense of the fatherland.

22. The constitution of Emperor Conrad II concerning the fiefs of Italy

The following edict, promulgated by the German emperor Conrad II while besieging the city of Milan in 1037, is one of the most important surviving records illustrating the juridical character of the fief and the rights of vassals. Conrad was apparently angered at the attempt of the great prelates of the Church and of others to seize the fiefs of the knights. To prevent further losses, which undermined the strength of his own army, Conrad declared unambiguously that fiefs were heritable within the male line of the vassal. In cases of dispute, knights could lose their holdings only by the judgment of their own peers. The constitution not only confirmed the heritability of fiefs within the empire; it also represents the earliest statement of the right of tenants to be judged by their own peers. The charter, translated by D. Herlihy in its entirety, is found in the *Constitutiones,* ed. L. Weiland (Monumenta Germaniae Historica, Legum Sectio IV; Hanover, 1893), Vol. I, p. 90. The *valvassor* in this contract seems to have been a wealthier knight, perhaps a mesne tenant.

In the name of the holy and undivided Trinity. Conrad, by the grace of God, august emperor of the Romans.

1. We wish that all the faithful of the holy Church of God and our own, both present and to come, know that in order to reconcile the hearts of lords and vassals, so that they may faithfully serve us with loyalty and devotion, we order and firmly establish that no vassal of the bishops, abbots, abbesses, margraves, counts, or any lord, who now holds or once held, and has unjustly lost up to the present, a fief from our public lands or from the properties of the church, that none of them, both from among our great *valvassores* or their vassals, should lose his fief without certain and proved guilt, unless in accordance with the law of our predecessors and the judgment of his own peers.

2. If a dispute should arise between lords and vassals, even though the peers should judge that the vassal ought to lose his fief, if he should protest that this was done unjustly or out of hatred, he should retain his fief until such time that his lord and the accused, with his peers, come before us, and the case should be justly settled. If, however, the peers of the accused fail to support the lord's judgment, the accused should retain his fief, until he with his lord and his peers shall have come before us. The lord or the accused, who has decided to appear before us, should notify him with whom he is disputing six weeks before he begins his journey. This procedure should also be followed in matters involving the great *valvassores.*

3. In regard to the petty vassals in the realm, their cases should be settled either before their lords or before our legate.

4. We also command that when a vassal, great or petty, should die, his son shall receive his fief. If he has no son, but is survived by a grandson born of male issue, the grandson should in equal manner

have the fief, while respecting the customs of the great *valvassores* in giving horses and arms to their lords. If he does not have a grandson born from male issue and if he should have a legitimate brother from the side of his father, and if that brother, after offending the lord, is willing to make amends and become his vassal, he should have the fief which was his father's.

5. Moreover, we absolutely forbid that any lord should dare to exchange a fief held by his vassals, or to give it in fief or lease it without their permission. No one should dare deprive them unjustly of those properties which they have held, whether by right of property or by order [of their lords] or by legal lease or through precarial grant.

6. *Fodrum* [fodder or fodder tax] from the castles, which our predecessors had, we wish also for ourselves. But we do not in any way demand more than what has been customary.

7. If anyone should violate this order, he should pay 100 pounds of gold, one-half to our treasury and one-half to him who suffered the damage.

The mark of the Lord Conrad, most serene and august emperor of the Romans. Cadolus the chancellor confirms the act, in place of Herman the archchancellor. Given the fifth of the kalends of June, the fifth indiction, the year of the Lord's Incarnation 1037, the year of the Lord King Conrad the thirteenth, of his holding the office of emperor the eleventh. Done while besieging Milan, happily. Amen.

⎿⎾⎿⎾⎿⎾⎿⎾⎿⎾⎿⎾⎿⎾⎿⎾⎿⎾⎿⎾⎿⎾⎿⎾⎿⎾⎿⎾⎿⎾⎿⎾⎿⎾⎿⎾

23. The granting of a fief, from the *Liber feudorum maior*

The following grant of a fief by the count of Barcelona is typical of hundreds that have survived from the twelfth century in the documents of southern Europe. The source is the *Liber feudorum maior*, 1154, and the translation is by D. Herlihy.

No. 244, October 4, 1154

In the name of the Holy Trinity, I, Raymond, by the grace of God, count of Barcelona, prince of the kingdom of Aragon, and marquis of Tortosa, give to you, my vassal Bonefacio de la Volta, the castle of Flix in fief along with its seigneurial rights and with its pledges and with the town and its borders and with all its appurtenances, in such a fashion that you and your descendants may have the said castle through me and through my successors in fief in return for fidelity and service to me and to all my posterity forever. And you will return to me the authority over the said castle, whether in anger or in peace, rightly or wrongly, as often as I may ask it of you, personally or through my messenger or messengers. You will guard carefully and keep the said castle without deceit, and you will serve me for it in my land, within the boundaries, that is, of Barcelona, Tortosa, and Spain. I also retain for myself a third part of all the revenues which come from it; two parts I give to you. I firmly grant and concede to you and to your descendants as a fief under the above conditions without any fraud the said castle with all its appurtenances and with all pledges and profits of justice and customary payments.

For this concession described above, I, the said Bonefacio, promise you, my lord, the said Raymond, that I shall be yours without deceit, that I shall be faithful as a vassal ought to be to his lord to whom he commends himself with his own hands, and that I shall follow faithfully in your interest all the above without any fraud. The mark of Count Raymond. This is done on the third nones of October in the year of the Incarnation of our Lord Jesus Christ 1154. The mark of William of Castelvell. The mark of Arvert, his brother. The mark of William of St. Martin. The mark of Berenguer of Torroja. The mark of Arnau of Lercio. The mark of William Obiloto. The mark of Poncio, the scribe who wrote this.

I I I. *Justice and Lordship*

⊔⎍⎍⎍⎍⎍⎍⎍⎍⎍⎍⎍⎍⎍⎍⎍⎍⎍⎍⎍⎍⎍⎍⎍⎍⎍⎍⎍⎍⎍⎍⊔

24. Selections from the Salic law

The law of the Salian Franks was redacted in its earliest version, called the *Pactus legis salicae*, probably under the reign of Clovis, about 500. The following selections illustrate some of the principal characteristics of Germanic justice, which left to the family the chief responsibility for avenging wrongs but sought to regulate the vendetta through setting the monetary fines which could be demanded. The fines varied according to the degree of injury and the dignity of the person. The following translation is taken from *A Source Book in Mediaeval History*, eds. O. J. Thatcher and E. N. McNeal (New York: Charles Scribner's Sons, 1905), pp. 17–18. The phrase "send him to the third hand" in Section XLVII seems to mean that the person should have the property given to a third party until the case was settled. The Carbonaria mentioned is the Ardennes forest.

I. Legal summons
1. If anyone is summoned to the court and does not come, he shall pay 600 denarii, which make 15 solidi.
3. When anyone summons another to court, he shall go with witnesses to the house of that person, and if he is not present the summoner shall serve notice on his wife or his family that he is legally summoned.

XVII. Wounds
1. If anyone is convicted of trying to kill another, even though he fails, he shall pay 2,500 denarii, which make 63 (62½) solidi.
2. If anyone is convicted of shooting a poisoned arrow at another,

even though he misses him, he shall pay 2,500 denarii, which make 63 solidi.

3. If anyone wounds another in the head, so that the brain appears and the three bones which lie above the brain are uncovered, he shall pay 1,200 denarii, which make 30 solidi.

4. If anyone wounds another between the ribs or in the abdomen, so that the wound can be seen and extends to the vitals, he shall pay 1,200 denarii, which make 30 solidi, besides 5 solidi for the healing.

5. If anyone wounds another so that the blood falls to the ground, he shall pay 600 denarii, which make 15 solidi.

6. If a freeman strikes another freeman with a club, so that the blood does not flow, he shall pay 120 denarii, which make 3 solidi, for each blow, up to three.

7. If the blood does flow, he shall pay as much for each blow as if he had wounded him with a sword.

8. If anyone strikes another with the closed fist, he shall pay 360 denarii, which make 9 solidi; that is, 3 solidi for each blow up to three.

9. If anyone is convicted of trying to rob another on the highroad, even though he fails, he shall pay 2,500 denarii, which make 63 solidi.

XXIX. *Injuries*

1. If anyone destroys the hand or the foot of another, or cuts out his eye, or cuts off his nose, he shall pay 4,000 denarii, which make 100 solidi.

2. If the injured hand hangs loose and useless, he shall pay 2,500 denarii, which make 63 (62½) solidi.

3. If anyone cuts off the thumb or the great toe of another, he shall pay 2,000 denarii, which make 50 solidi.

4. If the thumb or the toe hangs useless, he shall pay 1,200 denarii, which make 30 solidi.

5. If he cuts off the second finger, by which the bowstring is drawn, he shall pay 1,400 denarii, which make 35 solidi.

6. If he cuts off the rest of the fingers (that is, the other three) at one blow, he shall pay 50 solidi.

7. If he cuts off two of them, he shall pay 35 solidi.

8. If he cuts off one of them, he shall pay 30 solidi.

XLI. Manslaughter

1. If anyone is convicted of killing a free Frank or a barbarian living by the Salic law, he shall pay 8,000 denarii, which make 200 solidi.

2. If he has put the body in a well, or under water, or has covered it with branches or other things for the purpose of hiding it, he shall pay 24,000 denarii, which make 600 solidi.

3. If anyone kills a man in the king's trust, or a free woman, he shall pay 24,000 denarii, which make 600 solidi.

4. If he kills a Roman who was a table-companion of the king, he shall pay 12,000 denarii, which make 300 solidi.

6. If the slain man was a Roman landowner, and not a table-companion of the king, he who slew him shall pay 4,000 denarii, which make 100 solidi.

7. If anyone kills a Roman *tributarius*, he shall pay 63 solidi.

XLV. The Man Who Removes from One Village to Another

1. If anyone desires to enter a village with the consent of one or more of the inhabitants of that village, and a single one objects, he shall not be allowed to settle there.

3. But if anyone settles in another village and remains there twelve months without any one of the inhabitants objecting, he shall be allowed to remain in peace like his neighbors.

XLVII. The Tracing of Stolen Goods

If one has recognized a slave, or a horse, or an ox, or anything of his own in the possession of another, he is to send him to the third hand. And he in whose hands the thing was recognized is to swear [to his own innocence]; and if both parties [*i.e.,* the rightful owner and the man in whose possession it was found] dwell on this side of the Loire and the Carbonaria, a term of forty days shall be set within which all are to be summoned who have had any part in the affair, who have sold or exchanged or perhaps given in payment the article. That is, each one is to summon the man from whom he got it. And if anyone of these has been summoned and legal hindrance has not kept him away, and he does not come within the appointed term, then the one who had dealings with this delinquent is to bring three witnesses to the fact that he had summoned him and three more to the fact that he had obtained the property from him legally and in good faith; if he does this he is clear of suspicion of theft. But he who would not come and against whom the witnesses have borne testimony, shall be held to be the thief of the man who recognized his own, and he [the thief] shall return the price to the man who dealt with him and shall pay the lawful compensation to the man who recognized his own. All these things are to be done in that court to which he is answerable in whose hands the stolen thing was first recognized and with whom the process started. But if he in whose hands it was recognized dwells beyond the Loire or the Carbonaria the time allowed shall be eighty days.

25. Judgment by hot water

In the courts of the early Middle Ages, guilt or innocence was established by three principal methods: compurgation, the ordeal, and the judicial duel. In the duel, the two contending parties would fight in the presence of the court, on the assumption that God would aid the innocent to emerge victorious. The parties could also appoint champions to fight in their name—a practice which caused many to doubt that God's help was always so decisive (Document 26). By compurgation, the accused marshaled oath-helpers, who would attest not to the facts of the case but to the good reputation which the suspected person held in the community. Judgment by ordeal (cognate with modern German *Urteil*, judgment) remained an integral part of medieval judicial procedure, in spite of some protests, until the thirteenth century. Essentially, it was designed to enlist God's aid in judging guilt on the assumption that God would not allow the innocent to suffer. There were several varieties of ordeals, but three of them seem to have been most common. The ordeal by hot water required that the suspected person immerse his hand in boiling water; if his hand later appeared uninjured, he was considered innocent. In ordeal by cold water, the suspect was thrown into a stream; if the water received him (that is, if he sank), he was regarded as innocent. In the ordeal by iron, the suspect was forced to walk barefoot over hot iron rods; his feet were then inspected for signs of severe burns, a sure indication of guilt. These ordeals were conducted with awesome solemnity, which probably cowed many guilty persons—and perhaps some innocent as well—into a confession. The following two examples of judgment by hot water come from twelfth-century manuscripts but reflect the manner in which the ordeal was conducted over centuries. The suggestion in the first selection that Charlemagne devised the procedure is without historical foundation. These sources, translated by D. Herlihy, are taken from the Ordines iudiciorum Dei, *Formulae merovingici et karolini aevi*, ed. Zeumer, pp. 608–13.

The envious Romans, covetous for the treasure of St. Peter, once took out the eyes and the tongue of Pope Leo. He barely escaped from their hands, and he came to Emperor Charles in order to be rescued from his enemies. The emperor subsequently restored him to Rome and returned him to his palace; but he was able to recover the treasure mentioned above only through this judgment. Blessed Eugene, and Leo and the above-mentioned Emperor Charles, devised this procedure so that the bishops and abbots and counts might firmly abide by it and have confidence in it, because the men who discovered it and approved of it were holy.

If anyone is examined concerning theft, sexual offenses, adultery, or any similar thing, and he refuses to confess to the magistrate, the lord, or the representative of the lord, the following procedure should be observed. The priest should go to the church and should don the sacred vestments, except the chasuble; he should bear in the left hand the holy Gospel with the chrism and the relics of the saints, together with the chalice and the paten. The people should await with the thief or the one implicated in the crime on the porch of the church. The priest should address the people while they are standing at the entrance of the church:

"Behold, brothers, the office of the Christian religion. Behold the law, in which are the hope and remission of sins; here is the anointment with chrism, here the consecration of the body and blood of the Lord. Beware, lest you deprive yourselves of the inheritance and the share of so much beatitude, by involving yourselves in the crime of another. As it is written: 'Not only those who do it but also those who give their consent to the guilty are worthy of death.'"

Then, turning to the criminal, he should say to him and to the people: "I adjure both you and all here standing, through the

Father, the Son, and the Holy Spirit, by the dread Day of Judgment, by the mystery of baptism, by the veneration of all the
saints, that if you are guilty of such an act, or did it, or know about
it or authorized it, or with a knowledge of their guilt aided the
perpetrators, that you should not enter the church or mingle with
the Christian community if you refuse to confess the admitted deed
before you are examined in public trial."

Then he should mark a place in the porch of the church, where
the fire can be applied to the suspended cauldron, in which the
water may be heated to boil. First, though, the spot is to be
sprinkled with holy water, for fear of diabolical deceptions. When
these things are done, the priest should begin the introit: "You are
just, O Lord, and your judgment is right . . ." (Psalm 118.137).

After the celebration of the Mass, the priest together with the
people should go while the Gospel, holy cross, incense container,
and relics of the saints are carried before him, intoning a litany and
the seven penitential psalms, to bless the water, with the words:
"God, just Judge, strong and patient, Who art the Author of peace
and the Lover of justice, and judge equity, look upon our plea and
direct our judgment, because You are just, and Your judgments are
right, Who viewest the earth and causest it to tremble. And, O
God, bless this water boiling with fire . . . through the same
[Christ our Lord . . .].

"All powerful, eternal God, Who lookest into the secrets of the
hearts, we pray You in supplication that if this man is guilty of
the above crimes or if he should have a hardened heart, puffed up by
the devil, and he should dare to put his hand into this boiling water,
may Your most just truth deign to declare it, that Your power may
be made manifest in his body, so that his soul may be saved through
penance and confession. And if by any poisons or herbs prepared
by diabolical art he should refuse to confess his sins, may Your
right hand deign to dispel them. Through Your only begotten Son,
our Lord Jesus Christ, Who with You . . .

"I bless you, creature of water, boiling by fire, in the name of
the Father, the Son, and the Holy Spirit, from Whom all things
proceed, and I adjure you in the name of Him Who commanded
you to wash the whole earth from four rivers and produced you
from a stone and changed you into wine, that neither the snares of
the devil nor the wickedness of men be able to divorce you from
the truth, but that you may punish the guilty and absolve the

innocent man without injury. Through Whom and to Whom all secret things lie open, and Who sent you through the flood over the entire earth, in order to destroy sinners, and Who will come again to judge the living and the dead, and the world by fire. Amen.

"Almighty God, we humbly beseech You for examination of this act, which now we perform among ourselves here, that wickedness should not prevail over justice, but that falsity should be subject to truth. And if anyone should seek to cover or obstruct this present examination through any magic or through herbs of the earth, deign to prevent it, most just Judge, by Your holy right hand.

"Almighty eternal God, Who, ever the just Judge, determine Your judgments with unchangeable disposition, O clement [Lord], in this Your judgment at the invocation of Your holy name, declare what the intention of the faithful implores by Your most just examination, through Christ our Lord . . ."

Then the cauldron or the pot should be perfumed and incensed by the smoke of myrrh both inside and outside and around it, and this prayer should be said:

"God, Who has hidden several great mysteries in the substance of water, propitiously hear our prayers and pour the power of Your blessing into this element prepared by many purifications, so that this creature, serving Your mysteries, may receive the effect of divine grace to uncover diabolical and human lies and refute their pretenses and claims and to destroy their many wiles. Let all the snares of the hidden enemy depart, so that the truth sought through the invocation of Your holy name, by Your judgment may be made clear, concerning these things which we seek, ignorant as we are of both divine knowledge and another's heart. And therefore we ask that the innocent not be condemned unjustly, nor the guilty be allowed to deceive us seeking the truth, by You, Who are true Light, for Whom nothing remains in darkness, for You illuminate our darknesses. You, Whom secret things do not elude, show us and reveal to us by Your power, as You have knowledge of secrets. Give to us who believe in You a manifest knowledge of the truth."

Then the hand is washed by soap, and there should be an admonishment directed to the pot or cauldron before the hand is placed in it: "I adjure you, cauldron, through the Father and the

Son and the Holy Spirit, and through the holy Resurrection, and
through the dread judgment of God and through the evangelists,
that if this man is guilty of this thing, whether in deed or in agreement, the waters will shake and you, pot, will swing. Through
[Christ our Lord . . .]."

Then the hand is placed in the water, and afterward [it is
bandaged and sealed].

Here begins the blessing or the exorcism of hot water, in
which the hand is to be judged.

If you wish to submit men to the proof of judgment by hot
water, first have them enter with all humility into church. When
they have prostrated themselves in prayer, the priest should say
these prayers:

First prayer: "Help, O Lord, those who seek Your mercy and
give forgiveness to those who admit their guilt. Spare those who
beseech You so that we, who are punished by our just merits, may
be saved by Your mercy. Through [Christ our Lord . . .]."

Second prayer: "We ask, Almighty God, that You consider the
tears of Your afflicted people and that You turn away the wrath of
Your indignation so that we who admit the guilt of our infirmity
may be liberated by Your consolation. Through [Christ our Lord
. . .]."

Third prayer: "God, Who sees that we lack all strength, guard
us within and without so that we may be protected from all
adversities in body and cleaned from wicked thoughts in the mind.
Through [Christ our Lord . . .]."

When these prayers are said, the priest should arise and in the
presence of these men sing the Mass and have them offer themselves at the Mass. When they come to communion, before they
communicate, the priest should admonish them and say: "I adjure
you, men, through the Father and Son and the Holy Spirit, and
through Christianity, which you have received, and through the
only begotten Son of God, whom you believe to be the Redeemer,
and through the Holy Trinity, and through the holy Gospel, and
through the relics which are contained in this holy church, that
you do not presume in any fashion to come to this holy communion or that you communicate by receiving, if you have committed such or such an act, or agreed to it, or know any true
information about it, or know who did it."

If, however, they remain silent and make no statement concerning the deed, the priest should go to the altar and communicate in the accustomed manner, and afterward he should distribute communion to them. When they have received communion before the altar, the priest should say: "May this body and blood of our Lord Jesus Christ be for you a proof today."

When the Mass is finished, the priest should go to the appointed place where the examination is to take place. He should bear with him the book of the Gospels and the cross and should sing a short litany. And when he has finished the litany, he should exorcise and bless the water, before it is boiled, with these words:

"I exorcise thee, creature water . . ."

Prayer: "Lord Jesus Christ, Who are a just Judge, strong, patient, and so merciful . . .

"We unworthy persons, Almighty God . . ."

Also another exorcism: "You, creature water, I adjure through the living God, through the holy God, Who in the beginning separated you from the dry; I adjure you through the living God, Who brought you forth from the font of paradise and ordered you to go forth in four streams and commanded you to wet the whole earth; I adjure you through Him Who by His power turned you into wine in Cana of Galilee, Who walked upon you with His holy feet, Who imposed upon you the name of Silone (John 9.7); I adjure you through God Who in you cleansed Naaman the Syrian of his leprosy (4 Kings 5.10–14), saying, 'Holy water, blessed water, water who washes those soiled and cleanses sins'; I adjure you through the living God, that you show yourself to be clear and do not hold in you any spirit but that you be made an exorcised font to chase away and remove and confound every lie and to search out and prove all truth; so that he, who places his hand in you, if he possess truth and justice, may receive no injury from you. And if he lies, may his hand appear seared by fire, so that all men may know the power of our Lord Jesus Christ, Who shall come with the Holy Spirit to judge the living and the dead and the world by fire. Amen."

After this let him remove his vestments, and let him dress him, or them, with clean vestments of the church, that is, with the robe of the exorcist or of the deacon. And he should make them, or him, kiss the Gospel and the cross of Christ and should sprinkle them with this water. And he should give this blessed water to all those who are about to enter upon this judgment, and they should drink it. When he distributes it, he should say to each of them: "This water I give you for a proof today." Then wood should be placed under the cauldron, and the priest should say these prayers, when the water begins to heat:

"In the name of the Holy Trinity. God, just Judge, strong and patient, Who art the clement and merciful Author and Creator and Judge of equity, judge now, Who has commanded that right judgment be made and Who looks forth over the earth and causes it to tremble. You, Almighty God, Who through the coming of Your only begotten Son, our Lord Jesus Christ, have redeemed the world, Who through His passion have aided and saved the human race, make holy this boiling water. Who at the time of Nebuchadrezzar, king of Babylon, through Your angel saved and brought forth uninjured three children, that is Sidrach, Misach and Abednago, from the oven of fire and the burning furnace, grant that if anyone innocent of guilt of this sort, or of cause or reputation of homicide, adultery, or theft, should place his hand in this water, he should remove it whole and unharmed. You, Who also freed the three above-mentioned children and Susanna from false accusation, thus, Almighty God, if he is guilty and, with the devil inflating his callous heart, he places his hand in this created element of boiling water, Your truth may declare it, and it may be made manifest in his body, and his soul may be saved through penance. And if he is guilty of this crime, and through any witchcraft or through herbs or diabolical incantations has sought to hide this guilt of his sin, or believes he can scorn or violate Your justice, by Your magnificent right hand drive out this evil and reveal the entire truth. Through You, most clement Father, Who lives and reigns in the unblemished Trinity. Through all things . . ."

Another: "Let us pray. God, Who freed blessed Susanna from false accusation; God, Who freed blessed Thecla from the theaters; God, Who freed blessed Daniel from the lion's den and three children from the fiery hot furnace, free the innocent and indicate the perpetrators. Through our Lord."

And the one who places his hand in the water at this examination, let him say the Lord's prayer and sign himself with the sign of the cross, and quickly the boiling water should be placed next to the fire, and the judge should place in the water a stone of such a size as is the usual manner. And then he who is entering upon the examination or judgment should lift it out in the name of the Lord. Afterward, with great diligence his hand should be bound and the bandage sealed with the seal of the judge until three days later, when it should be viewed and considered by suitable men.

26. Thoughts on the judicial duel, by Frederick II Hohenstaufen

In the following imperial law, contained in the Constitutions of Melfi (1231), Frederick II comments on and restricts the use of trial by combat in his kingdom of Sicily and southern Italy. Note the emphasis on nature and reason in the law, which is characteristic of European thought in the twelfth and thirteenth centuries. The source is *Historia diplomatica Friderici secundi*, ed. J.-L.-A. Huillard-Bréholles (Paris, 1854), Vol. IV, Pt. 1, pp. 105–6. The translation is by D. Herlihy.

The *monomachia*, called in the vulgar tongue the duel, we wish never again to be used among the people of our kingdom, with only a few exceptions. For the duel cannot be called a true proof; rather, it should be considered a kind of divination, which is contrary to nature, deviates from the common law, and is in discord with reason and equity. Hardly ever can two fighters be found so equal that one is not stronger than the other, or does not have the advantage over the other in some respect, whether by greater energy or more powerful force or at least by mental qualities. From the benefit of this practice we exclude those who are accused of having murdered a person stealthily, by poison or any similar fashion. Also, in such cases, we do not allow the procedure to begin with trial by combat. We order that first the parties should proceed by ordinary proofs, whatever may be available. Finally, after the court has made a careful investigation, if the crime cannot be fully proved through other proofs or through an inquest, then only, after all the above has been fulfilled, the case should be submitted to trial by combat. We wish that the responsible judge should examine all facts, so that he may investigate carefully and

diligently what the inquest may have proved. If he finds, as has
been said, that the case has not been proved, let him grant permission to offer battle to the accuser, without any prejudice to the case
of the accuser deriving from what he has done. If, however, the
accuser first offers to prove his case through witnesses, and if he
fails in the proof, then since there is no reason for proof by inquest
or combat, the accused who is not proved guilty but is assumed
innocent should be absolved. This law we wish to be common
among all, both Franks [i.e., those living by Frankish law] and
Lombards, and in all cases. For we have sufficiently provided in
other ways for the knights and nobles of our kingdom concerning
the competitive manners of proof and for others also who were
able to offer battle, as is more clearly stated in our new constitution. Also, we except the crime of treason, for which, as is noted in
the chapters written farther on, we reserve trial by combat. Do not
wonder that we subject those suspected of treason, or secret
murder, and poisoners to trial by combat; it is not so much for
judgment as for deterrence. It is not that our serenity considers a
certain action to be just in some cases and unjust in others. Rather,
we wish that the punishment of those killers who have not feared
secretly and stealthily to take human life, which only divine power
can create, may serve as an example. We have further declared those
persons who have not feared to plot against the security of our
person, through whom security is given to all others, to be outside
the limits of mercy.

27. Justice for the poor, from the *Life of St. Remi*

The customary law of the early Middle Ages conceded certain traditional rights even to serfs. They were not, for example, to be deprived
of their lands and farms, nor were extraordinary dues to be imposed
upon them. But what chance had the poor to maintain such rights
within a society so greatly dominated by the powerful? The following
two incidents from the *Life of St. Remi*, written by the Carolingian
bishop and scholar Hincmar of Rheims (d. 882), are examples of the
kinds of material historians must work with in answering this difficult

question. From one point of view, the incidents suggest that the poor were helpless before the oppression of the powerful, since they could hope only for divine intervention. On the other hand, the incidents suggest that the moral and ethical sense of the age strongly supported the poor in their rights, for the man who sought to drive them from their homes was visited with death. The strength of this moral sense cannot be entirely discounted. The source, translated by D. Herlihy, is taken from the Vita Remigii episcopi remensis auctore Hincmaro, *Passiones Vitaeque sanctorum aevi merovingici et antiquiorum aliquot,* ed. Bruno Krusch (Monumenta Germaniae Historica, Scriptores rerum merovingicarum; Hanover, 1896), Vol. II, p. 322.

In our age a peasant of the village of the episcopate of Rheims which is called Plumbea-fontana lived next to the royal estate which is named Rozoy [-sur-Serre], but he was not able to use his land peacefully either for harvest or for grazing because of the harassment of the residents on the royal estates. He frequently sought justice from the royal officials, but he was not able to obtain it. Then he took for himself some beneficial counsel. He cooked loaves and meat and he placed beer into jars, as much as he was able. All these things he placed into a container which is called in the vernacular a *benna*, and he placed it upon a cart. Hitching up his oxen, he hurried with a candle in his hand to the basilica of St. Remi. When he arrived, he pleasantly surprised the poor with the bread, meat, and beer; he placed a candle at the sepulcher of the saint and beseeched him for help against the men of the royal estate who were harassing him. He also gathered the dust from the floor of the church, as much as he was able, tied it in cloth, and placed it in the same container. He placed a shroud above it, as is usually put upon the corpse of a dead person. With his cart he returned home. Persons he met on the way inquired what he was bringing in the cart, and he responded that he was bringing St. Remi. They all wondered at his words and deed, and thought that he had lost his mind. However, arriving with the cart into his field, he found there herdsmen from the estate of Rozoy feeding animals of different kinds. He called on St. Remi to help him against his oppressors. The bulls and the cows began with the loudest bellows to attack one another with their horns, and the he-goats to attack the she-goats with their horns, the pigs to fight with the pigs, the rams with the ewes, and the herdsmen dealt each other blows with sticks and arms. As the riot grew greater, both the screaming herdsmen and the animals according to their type began to flee toward Rozoy with the loudest noise and racket, as if a huge multitude of pursuers were beating them with sticks. The men of the royal estate, when they saw and heard these things, were struck with a great terror and believed that they had no more than an hour to live. Thus reprehended for their arrogance, they abandoned the harassment of this poor man of St. Remi, and thereafter the poor man held his belongings in peace and without disturbance. And since he lived near the Serre River in a muddy place, he put up with a great bother in his dwelling from snakes. Taking the dust, which he had brought with him from the floor of the church of St. Remi, he sprinkled it throughout his house, and thereafter a snake did not appear in those places where the dust had been scattered. By the evidence of the miracles, we can accept as certainly proved that if, firm in the faith, we ask from the heart the help of St. Remi, we shall be freed from the attacks of the angels of Satan, who as a serpent deceived the mother of the human race in addressing her; and by the merit and intercession of St. Remi we shall be freed from the wicked deeds of bad men.

Truly [St. Remi], this holy follower of the Lord, did not punish all things, so that his patience might be revealed, nor did he forgive all things, so that his providence might be shown. Although he does not in our times take vengeance so frequently against wicked men, nevertheless he has not desisted completely from the punishment of the presumptuous. Recently, a certain man named Blitgarius purchased from Bernardus, the custodian [of the church], a certain farm from the endowment of the church in the village of Thenailles. From it he drove out with blows the servants of St. Remi, and they called upon St. Remi to help them. This same Blitgarius answered them in derision, "Now let us see how St. Remi shall help you. You see how he comes to your assistance." And in the midst of these words he groaned with the loudest groan and swelled up to unbelievable proportions. Thus, all of a sudden, he gasped and was dead.

Having heard these things, with the fear of divine retribution in us, we should carefully avoid blasphemy against God and His saints, taking care, lest we treat cruelly the servants of the Church. . . . Although in our times miracles worked through His servant may not be so many or so venerable, still we may be certain that the continuing help of his intercessions will not be withdrawn from his city or from us his citizens, as we read of Jeremias, "This is a lover of his brethren and of the people of Israel: this is he that prayeth much for the people and for all the holy city of Jerusalem" (2 Machabees 15.14).

28. A Merovingian charter of immunity

One characteristic of feudal society was the multiplication of jurisdictions among a great number of petty lords. The exact origins of what is traditionally called "private" justice remain obscure, but one practice which contributed to it was the immunities or exceptions granted to churches, and perhaps to laymen, by the Merovingian and early Carolingian rulers. Most immunities did not exactly exempt the church from obligations to the government, but they left such activities as tax collecting, judging, and military recruitment to its own officials. The following model charter of immunity dates from the late seventh century; translated by D. Herlihy, it is taken from the *Formulae merovingici et karolini aevi*, ed. Zeumer, p. 43.

The formulas of Marculf

3. ROMAN IMMUNITY

We believe that we shall erect the greatest monument to our reign if with friendly counsel we confer fitting favors on ecclesiastical institutions and, with the protection of the Lord, confirm their lasting character. Therefore, may your diligence be informed that, at the request of the apostolic Lord N., bishop of the city of N., we have publicly granted, in return for eternal compensation, the following favor. No public judge should presume to enter, to sit in judgment, or to demand taxes at any time from any part of the estates and churches of the lord [bishop N.], which he is known to possess in these times, whether by our grant or that of another, or which divine piety may subsequently place under the ownership of this holy place. The holy bishop and his successors should be able to exercise this right in the name of the Lord under the full title of immunity. We therefore determine that neither you nor your officials nor your successors nor any public judicial authority at any time should presume to enter into the estates of this church given by the generosity of the king or of private persons, wherever they may be found in our realm, in order to hold a court. Nor should you presume to collect taxes from anything whatsoever, neither a house tax nor hospitality payments nor pledges. But whatever the treasury had hitherto been able to expect, whether from the free or the unfree and other persons who live within the fields or borders or on the lands of the said church should by our grant be used by its officers for the illumination of the said church for our future salvation. What we have granted in full devotion in the name of the Lord and for the salvation of our own soul and that of our descendants, let not the royal sublimity or the savage greed of any judges attempt to break. In order that the present document with the help of God may remain inviolate, both in present and future times, we decree that it be confirmed below with the signature of our hand.

29. A charter of immunity from Charles the Bald

The following charter granted by the Carolingian king Charles II to the monastery of St. Germain of Auxerre is typical of many such Carolingian immunities. Note the reference to the merchants attached to the monastery of St. Germain. The charter, translated by D. Herlihy, is found in the *Recueil des actes de Charles II le Chauve roi de France,* ed. A. Giry *et al.*

No. 214, September 11, 859

In the name of the holy and undivided Trinity. Charles by the grace of God king. When in the love of divine worship we favor the just and reasonable petitions of the servants of God, we do not doubt that we become strengthened by heavenly grace. Therefore,

be it known to all the faithful, present and to come, of the holy
church of God, that Hugo, our very dear abbot of the monastery
of St.-Germain d'Auxerre, and our kinsman brought to our attention an authoritative charter of immunity of our lord father Louis,
most serene Augustus, in which is related how in the tradition of
his ancestors he received the said monastery, for the love of
Almighty God and the peace of the brothers residing there, under
the fullest protection and defense of immunity. The said Abbot
Hugo and the monks of the same monastery have requested the
favor of a confirmation, asking that we, in the tradition of our
father, receive the same monastery with the congregation there
serving God, and with all possessions justly appertaining to the said
monastery, under our defense and the protection of immunity.
Their request, for divine love and the peace of the said monks, we
have willingly accepted and we hold under the fullest defense that
congregation with all possessions justly and reasonably belonging
to the same monastery, so that under our protection they may
quietly live, as is contained in the command of our lord father. No
bishop of this diocese or any other episcopal minister may presume
to exercise there any lordship [*dominium*] nor remove anything
from the possessions of the same monastery or turn it to his use or
diminish it or take it away. And no public judge or any official
with judicial authority or any of our faithful should dare enter in
our days or in days to come upon the possessions now subject to or
later to be subject to the same monastery in order to hear cases or
to collect fodder or tribute, or the house tax or hospitality payments, or to take guarantors or constrain the men of the same
monastery, whether free or unfree, living upon the land of the said
monastery. But it should be allowed to the said abbot and his
successors to possess the property of the said monastery in peaceful
order under the defense of immunity. Whatever the royal treasury
may demand from the lands we give wholly to the same monastery, so that it may be of profit and assistance for all time to the
monks serving God there in performing their office. Similarly also,
they showed to our serenity the authoritative charter of our lord
father, in which was related how the same most pious augustus
conceded to the same monastery the entire toll from the merchants
of the monks or from their men who served the same house of
God, or from that which men bear on their backs, whether they
come on their estates or upon their lands within or without and

transact business. The entire toll through the same authoritative charter he conceded to the same monastery. We have willingly acceded to their request, and through this charter we order and command that the same monks or their merchants or their men who are known to serve the said house of God, as the command of our lord father states, should not be forced to pay any toll in the towns or in the markets or in the villages or estates or ports or gates or within the monastery or in the estates or territories or other places subject to them. And in order that this charter of our authority and immunity may be the firmer and be the better preserved in times to come, we have ordered it to be sealed below with the impression of our ring.

Done on the third of the ides of September, the seventh indiction, the twentieth year of Charles, most glorious king. Done at Mardun in the monastery. In the name of God, happily. Amen.

30. The coronation of Charles the Bald

In spite of the proliferation of jurisdictions and the weakness of the central government in the first feudal age, the person of the king retained among the many lords a special distinction. In preserving, or even inspiring, this notion of royal dignity, the Church played a critical role. While expecting the king to act in the ecclesiastical interests, the Church exalted his position by stressing his sacred character and by comparing him with the great kings of the past. The following liturgical *ordo* describes the coronation of Charles the Bald on September 9, 869, and gives a good idea of the Christian and ecclesiastical notions of the sacred character and responsibilities of kingship. The text, translated by D. Herlihy, is from the Ordo coronationis Karoli II in regno Hlotharii II factae, *Capitularia*, ed. A. Boretius, Vol. II, pp. 456–58.

Blessings said over king Charles before Mass at the altar
of St. Stephen
(Adventius bishop of Metz:) O God, You Who care for Your people with indulgence and rule them with love, give to this Your

servant the spirit of wisdom, to whom You have given the exercise of discipline, so that devoted to You with all his heart he may remain always suitable for the government of the kingdom and, persevering in good works, he may with Your guidance attain the eternal kingdom. Through the Lord, etc.

(Hatto of Verdun:) Give, we beseech You, O Lord, to this Your servant the gift of Your grace, so that with Your help, following Your commandments, he may receive the consolation of present and future life. Through the Lord, etc.

(Arnulf of Toul:) Have favor, we beseech You, O Lord, upon our days under the governance of this Your servant, so that with Your help both our own security and Christian devotion may be well administered. Through the Lord, etc.

(Franco of Tongern:) Grant, we beseech You, Lord, to this Your servant health of mind and body, so that adhering to good works he may always be worthy to be defended by Your power. Through the Lord, etc.

(Hincmar of Laudun:) May this Your servant, O Lord, receive Your blessing, so that safe in body and mind he may always show to You a fitting submission and may always find the favors of Your mercy. Through the Lord, etc.

(Odo of Beauvais:) Preserve, we beseech You, O Lord, this Your servant, and purify him mercifully with the abundance of Your blessings, so that he may always abound with Your knowledge and gifts.

(The blessing of Archbishop Hincmar:) May the almighty Lord stretch forth the right hand of His blessing, and may He pour over you the gift of His mercy; may He surround you by a happy wall in the custody of His perfection, through the interceding merits of holy Mary and all the saints. Amen.

May He forgive you all the evil which you have committed, and grant to you grace and mercy which you humbly ask from Him; may He free you from all adversities and from all the snares of visible and invisible enemies. Amen.

May He place His good angels, always and everywhere, to go before you, to accompany you, and to follow you, for your protection; may He by His power free you from sin or the sword or the risk of all perils. Amen.

May He turn your enemies toward the kindness of peace and love, and make you gracious and lovable to those who hate you.

May He visit with saving confusion those persistent in persecuting you. May an eternal sanctification flower above you. Amen.

(At the following words, "May the Lord crown you," Hincmar the archbishop anointed him with chrism on his right ear and on his forehead, as far as the left ear, and on his head.)

May the Lord crown you with the crown of glory in His mercy and compassion, and may He anoint you in the rule of the kingdom by the oil of the grace of His Holy Spirit, with which He anointed priests, kings, prophets, and martyrs, who through faith conquered kingdoms and worked justice and attained His promises. May you too by the grace of God be rendered worthy of those same promises, until you may enjoy their companionship in the heavenly kingdom. Amen.

May He always make you victorious and triumphant over visible and invisible enemies. May He pour continuously into your heart the fear and equally the love of His holy name. And, granting you peace in your days, may He lead you with the palm of victory to the eternal kingdom. Amen.

May He, Who wished to set you as king over His people, grant that you be happy in this present world and the partaker of eternal happiness. Amen.

May He allow you happily to govern by His dispensation and your administration for a long time the clergy and people, whom with His aid He wished to be subject to your authority. May they, therefore, be obedient to the divine commands, avoid all opposition, rejoice in all good things, and be subject to your office in faithful love. May they enjoy in this present world the tranquillity of peace, and merit to possess with you the inheritance of the eternal citizens. Amen. May He deign to grant this.

(At the words, "May the Lord crown you," the bishops set the crown on his head.)

May the Lord crown you with the crown of glory and justice, so that with right faith and the abundant fruit of good works you may attain the crown of the eternal kingdom, through His generosity, to Whom belongs the kingdom and the power for ever and ever.

(At the words, "May the Lord give you the will," they give him the palm and scepter.)

May the Lord give you the will and the power to do as He commands, so that going forward in the rule of the kingdom according to His will together with the palm of continuing victory you may attain the palm of eternal glory, by the grace of our Lord Jesus Christ, who lives . . .

(Prayers at Mass:) Grant, Almighty God, that the venerable celebration of the feast of Your blessed martyr Gorgonius may increase in us devotion and salvation. Through the Lord . . .

We beseech, Almighty God, that Your servant, who in Your mercy has received the reins of the kingdom, may receive from You also increase of virtue, by which suitably adorned, he may graciously avoid monstrous vices and reach You, Who are the way, the truth, and the life, Who lives and reigns with God.

(At the offertory:) Behold, O Lord, the gifts of Your people offered at the feast of Your saints, so that the profession of Your truth may profit us for salvation. Through the Lord . . .

Make holy, we beseech You, O Lord, these gifts we have offered, so that they may become for us the body and blood of Your only begotten Son, and may benefit our king Charles in obtaining salvation of soul and body through Your generosity. Through the same . . .

(After communion:) May the communion received of Your mysteries, O Lord, save us and confirm us in the light of Your truth. Through the Lord . . .

May this saving communion, O Lord, protect Your servant from all adversities, so that he may obtain the tranquillity of ecclesiastical peace and after the course of these days he may attain the everlasting inheritance. Through the Lord . . .

31. Fiefs, feuds, and justice in *Raoul of Cambrai*

Historians today have a fairly good understanding of the juridical character of the institutions of early feudalism, but their knowledge of the manner in which these institutions functioned in fact and in life is much more limited. One precious insight into the character of early feudal society is provided by the French *chansons de geste*, or heroic epics. These poems have survived in abundant numbers from the twelfth and thirteenth centuries, and although of course they represent imaginative literature, they reveal much which the works of the epoch, consciously designed as chronicles or histories, do not show. Because they are products of an oral tradition, they also depict practices much older than the period in which they were put into writing. They can be used, in other words, with appropriate prudence, to project for us a rich picture of early feudal society.

One of the best of these epics, from a historical point of view, is the anonymous *Raoul of Cambrai*, which has been preserved in a single manuscript from the thirteenth century. It is very nearly a poem without a hero, as its realistic depiction of life leaves us with almost no one to admire. Like the great masterpiece of the genre, the *Song of Roland*, it is founded upon a historical event, mentioned by the French chronicler Flodoard in 943. In that year, a certain Rodulfus tried to seize the lands of the deceased Herbert, count of Vermandois, and was killed by his sons. From this spare incident, the poet has elaborated a full and rich story of greed, betrayal and fidelity, war and reconciliation.

The historical interest of the poem rests principally on the conflicts it describes within the society of early feudalism. Did the obligations of a vassal toward his family supersede his obligations toward his lord? Did the claims of a family upon the fief of a deceased vassal supersede the lord's eminent domain over it? Did obligation to a family, or to a lord, prevail over duties to a king? The institutions of early feudalism, as we have mentioned, were founded primarily upon ethical obligations, and these obligations inevitably came into conflict with older values. The confusion of conflicting ethics and laws is forcefully depicted in *Raoul of Cambrai*. Moreover, the battle scenes and the trial by combat near the end of the poem add interest to this remarkably vivid picture of feudal society.

There is a rather inadequate English translation by Jessie Crosland, *Raoul of Cambrai: An Old French Epic* (London, 1926). The following translation, comprising about half of the poem, is by David and Patricia Herlihy; the text may be found in *Raoul de Cambrai: Chanson de geste*, eds. P. Meyer and A. Longnon (Société des Anciens Textes Français, 17; Paris, 1882).

[*1. The Origins of the Conflict*]

I

Hear a song of joy and cheer!
Many and most of you have heard
Of this great family of barons so steeped in valor.

Other troubadors have sung to you
New songs; but they neglect this flower.
This concerns Raoul; he held Cambrai.
He was called Taillefer for his pride.
He had one son who was a good fighter,
Called also Raoul, who had much strength.
Against Herbert's sons he made heavy attack;
But young Bernier then dealt him a painful death.

2

This is a song you must hear.
If you keep your peace, you can hear sing
Of Guerri the Red and of Lady Aalais,
And of Raoul, lord of Cambrai.
His godfather was the bishop of Beauvais.
Against Herbert's sons he raised much strife,
As you shall hear in this song.

3

This Raoul Taillefer of whom I spoke
Was very brave with valorous heart.
He so served the emperor of France
That the emperor gave him a great reward.
He gave him in fief the land of Cambrai
And a lovely wife, no fairer was seen.
All rejoiced, kinsmen and friends.
The wedding was such as you may have heard
At the court of the strong King Louis.
Thereafter, he lived till his hair grew gray,
And when God pleased, he left the world.
The gentle Lady Aalais of complexion fair
Showed such grief as was not seen before.
The barons buried him;
The abbey of St. Geri received him into its earth.
By this baron of whom I have spoken here,
The lady was with child, to tell you the truth.

4

They have buried the valiant knight,
Taillefer, of whom I have told you.

The gentle lady with gentle heart remained
Great with his child.
She carried the child as long as God appointed.
When he was born, much joy filled
The people of the land, the knights and sergeants.
They too had joy, as I know full well,
Whose hearts he later made grim and sad.
The lady of valiant heart took the child
And wrapped him in a costly cloth;
She called two knights without delay;
Some call the first Thiebaut,
I know for sure Acelin was the other.
"Barons," she said, "in God's name, come here.
Go as fast as you can, straight to Beauvais."

5

Lady Aalais had no weak heart.
She laid her son in costly purple.
Then she called two barons of noble birth.
"Straight to Beauvais you should go at dawn
For me, to Bishop Gui, my cousin."
They departed and wasted no time.
They took no rest till they reached Beauvais.
They found the bishop in his palace of marble.
He was the brother of Geoffroy of Lavardin.

6

Both knights go up to the palace;
They carry the infant whom they cherish so much.
They find the bishop who is worthy of praise.
They salute him well with impeccable courtesy.
"May God, Who will judge all things,
Save you and help you, righteous bishop.
This from Lady Aalais of complexion fair,
Wife of Knight Raoul Taillefer.
Dead is the count, there is naught to be done;
But from him the lady has an heir.
With love she has him sent to you,
Lest from his kin he be estranged."
The bishop listens; he blesses himself,

He gives thanks to God, Who guards all things;
"Noble countess, may God give you counsel!
This affair can brook no delay."
He made ready the baptismal font at the abbey,
And oil and chrism to anoint the child,
And he vested himself for his office.

7

The gentle bishop came to the abbey,
He baptized the child who was so well formed.
And for his father, the Marquis Taillefer,
He gave him the name Raoul de Cambrai.
The gentle bishop made no delay;
Well did he dress him as befits a noble.
And the nurse, who was very fair of face,
Was dressed in sable and ermine.
All those came who had heard about him.
On the morrow when they took leave,
All returned home; also there was Guerri the Red.
At the christening there was neither joy nor laughter.
The infant was both loved and cherished,
And by his nurse most gently reared.
Years, months, and days then passed,
More than three years, so the record relates.

8

Lady Aalais had no weak heart.
Now you shall hear of the pain and the strife
Of the great war which ne'er had an ending.
The king of France had a noble young man:
The French called him Gibouin of Mans.
He served the king with his good steel sword;
In many wars he made many an orphan;
He deserved much from our king of noble line
And richly, as champions do.
For his service he wanted full reward.
Those from beyond the Rhine advised
That he be given possession of Cambrai.
Aalais held it who had swayed many a heart,
From the family of Geoffroy of Lavardin.

If God does not halt it, Who from water made wine,
The fief will be given and the affair concluded
For which many noble men shall fall in sudden death.

9

Our emperor heard the barons speak;
The gentle men said in one accord
That he should give as a bride Aalais
Of complexion fair to the baron of Mans, who served him well.
The king agreed and earned reproach.
He invested him with the glove, for which he was thanked,
For which his shoe was kissed.
Then said the king of France:
"Gibouin, brother, you ought well to thank me;
I have given to you a very great fief.
But with this agreement I wish to convey it:
The infant Raoul I do not want bereft.
He is still young. Think to keep him well
Until he can carry arms.
He shall hold Cambrai; no one can deny it to him,
But of other land I shall give to you."
Gibouin replied, "I do not wish to refuse,
But make sure that I marry the lady."
What a fool he was when he dared think this,
For it would cause many a brave man to fall.
The gentle lady of complexion fair
Would not take him though they hack off her limbs.

10

King Louis made that day the greatest blunder,
Who deprived his nephew of his heritage.
And Gibouin did great outrage
When he wished another's lands for his baronage.
For this he would die a shameful death.
Our emperor has spoken to his herald:
"Go at once, saddle the Arabian steed.
Take the news to my sister with the fair countenance.
Go direct to Cambrai, her rich heritage.
She should take as her husband the knight of Mans,
Gibouin, who has so much courage

(Such a knight is not found 'twixt here and Carthage).
All the land is due him in marriage.
Come to my court without any delay.
Let her retinue come with her,
And I shall send for most of my court.
But if she fails me, through arrogance,
I will seize the land, her inheritance.
She shall live from her dowry,
For of no other land shall she take lordly dues."
The messenger took his leave and departed.
He mounted his saddled steed
And leaves Paris; straight to Cambrai he goes;
By the great gate he entered the city.
He went to the great abbey of St. Geri
And found the lady in the square;
Many a knight she had in her company.
The messenger reined his horse and dismounted;
In the king's name he saluted the lady:
"May God, Who made the world
And commands all things in heaven and earth,
Save the countess and those she loves—
This from the king who protects us!"
"May God the Creator guard you too, brother!
Tell me the wishes of the king, conceal nothing."
"In God's name, lady, I shall tell you:
The king, who has so much power, tells you
That he will give you to Baron Gibouin;
Believe me, the king commands it."
Lady Aalais falls to the earth;
Tears fell from her eyes and she heaved a great sigh.
She summons her counselors.
"O God," she says, "this is a wicked command."

[Two pages are missing, the twelfth and thirteenth stanzas.]

14

"Just emperor," said Baron Guerri,
"Do you wish by this to disinherit
One who can neither ride nor walk?
By the faith which I bear you,

Rather you shall see a thousand knights fall,
Before the knight of Mans can boast of this at court.
Just emperor, I cannot conceal from you
That if he should be ever found at Cambrai,
He can be sure of losing his head.
And you, foolish king, deserve reprimand;
The child is your nephew, you should never have thought
To grant his large land to another."
The king replied: "Let all this be;
The gift is made, I cannot revoke it."
Guerri departed; he would not stay longer;
Evil would come of the leave that he took!
At the foot of the stairs the good steeds were waiting,
And the barons thought to mount them.
Guerri commenced to shout in a loud voice:
"Now make ready, you bachelor knights,
Who wish to endure pains.
For by Him who let Himself suffer,
I would rather have all my limbs hacked off
Than fail my nephew as long as I live."
Guerri the Red was filled with great anger.
Back to Cambrai he thought to return.
He dismounted in the square;
Dame Aalais saw her vassal come back,
And spoke to him as you shall hear:
"Sire Guerri, you must not deceive me,
Will you let me know the truth?"
"Lady," he said, "I do not wish to lie.
Your heritage the king has taken away
For Gibouin, may God curse him!
Take him for your husband, for only thus can you reconcile
Louis, who has France in his power."
"God!" said the lady. "Of grief could I die!
I would rather be burned in a fire
Than he should force a greyhound to lie with a mean watchdog.
God will give me food for my infant
Until he can bear these arms."
Guerri replied, "Lady, good for you to have dared to say it.
In your great need, I cannot leave you."

16

Guerri, valiant in spirit, speaks:
"Lady Aalais, by God the Redeemer,
I shall not fail you as long as I live.
Where is my nephew? Bring him forward."
Two young knights arose
And brought the child forward to the square.
He had three years, as I know for sure;
He was dressed in shining silk, and he wore a shift of fine red
   cloth.
No one had ever seen a lovelier child.
Guerri now takes him in his arms.
"Child," he says, "you are not very large,
And the knight of Mans has wicked designs on you.
He wishes to deprive you of your inheritance."
"Uncle," said the child; "let him have it;
I shall get it back if only I live so long
That I may carry arms upon my steed."
"Truly," said Guerri, "you shall not lose a clod of it,
Till there shall die twenty thousand warriors."
The valiant knights ask for water
And sit themselves at table.

17

Lady Aalais and the vassal Guerri
And the barons seat themselves at table.
The seneschals were interspersed;
Each was well taught how to serve.
After dinner the lady of complexion fair
Gave to the barons much sable and ermine.
The rich Guerri the Red makes his departure.
He kisses the lady and then he departs.
To Arras he goes directly, very provoked.
Then there pass many days and years.
There was no din or discord in this land.
When Raoul of Cambrai had fifteen years,
To the admiration of all, he was courteous and gentle;
His vassals and his nobles loved him strongly.
Lady Aalais, honored for her gentle heart,

Saw her child grow large and heavy and handsome.
Fifteen years were finished and passed.
A gentle man there was in this kingdom;
He bore the name Ybert; he was fiercely proud.
He had one son; he was called Bernier
As a baby at his baptism.
The child grew much and was of great goodness,
He was tall and strong when he passed fifteen years.
Count Raoul held him in great love.
Lady Aalais by her kindness
Had raised him from an early age.
Raoul took him to the city of Paris
And acquainted him with the assembly of richest barons.
He served Raoul with wine and claret.
It would have been better, know this for a truth,
For him to have his head hacked from his body,
For he would kill Raoul, sadly and shamefully, in the end.

18

Count Raoul of handsome face
To the admiration of all held Bernier dear.
This was the son of Ybert of Ribemont.
No land contained a fairer youth,
Nor any more skilled at the shield or spear,
Nor of greater wisdom and prudence at the royal court,
Although they called him a bastard.
Raoul of handsome face loved him;
He willingly made him his squire,
But found in him a strange companion.
Dame Aalais saw her son grow up,
Saw that he could wield arms.
She spoke to him as you may hear:
"Gather your people and summon them here
If you wish to see them at Cambrai.
We shall well see who hesitates to serve."
Raoul calls them and tells them his pleasure:
"You should not fail me in my need."

[Gap in the manuscript, probably 58 verses; Raoul asks to be knighted by Emperor Louis.]

22

Our emperor has dubbed the child;
He summons his seneschals.
"Bring me arms for this I command you."

    .   .   .   .

The emperor of valiant heart says,
"Good nephew Raoul, I see you strong and great.
I thank God, Father Almighty."

23

Our emperor much loved the young man.
He gave him a helmet, once a Saracen's,
Whom Roland had killed at the river Rhine.
He placed it over the hood of the double-thick hauberk.
Then he said: "Nephew,
Here is a helmet, once a Saracen's;
No strong arm can dent it a bit.
May He give you faith Who from water made wine
And sat at the wedding of St. Arcedeclin."
Raoul replied, "I take this for this purpose:
Your enemies will have in me a dangerous neighbor.
Evening and morning they shall have no peace."
And that helmet had a nose protector of pure gold;
And it bore a jewel in the middle;
By it on darkest night one could see the road.

24

The emperor girded him with a strong and hard sword.
The pommel and hilt were of gold,
And it was forged in a dark valley;
The one who gave it all his care was named Gallant.
Apart from Durendel, which was the choicest of swords,
Of all others this was deemed the best.
No arm in this world could stand against it.
Such were the arms, I say, which suited his measure.
Handsome was Raoul and of a gentle frame.
If within him there were a little restraint,
No lord ever had a better vassal.
But his excess caused a grievous incident;
An unrestrained man must suffer much sorrow.

[After his knighting, and for reason of service to Emperor Louis, Raoul was rewarded with a grant of lands held by the sons of Herbert; these sons happened also to be the uncles of his best friend, Bernier. Raoul set forth to conquer the land and, against the advice of his mother, began to besiege the town of Origny. Bernier was still in his service, but distraught that his duties as a vassal forced him to make war against the members of his own family.]

[*II. The Siege of Origny*]

59

Raoul takes leave of Cambrai;
He departs from his mother, Aalais, of complexion fair,
And passes through the Arrouaise, which is his land.
Together with him rides Guerri the Red.
Both are well armed on their excellent steeds.
They advance into the Vermandois.
They seize the herds; many a man they make prisoner;
They scorch the earth, and the farms are destroyed.
Bernier was gloomy and pensive;
When he saw the land of his father and his friends
So razed, he almost went mad.
Where the others went, Bernier lagged behind,
And was slow to don his arms.

60

Count Raoul calls Manecier,
Droon the count, and his brother Gautier.
"Take quickly your arms without delay;
Let four hundred of you each upon his charger
Ride to Origny before the fall of night.
Pitch my tent in the middle of the church.
In its porches let my beasts of burden be tied.
Beneath the vaults prepare my food.
On the crosses of gold let my falcons rest.
Before the altar have ready for me
A rich bed where I wish to sleep.
I wish to lean on the crucifix,
And my squires shall possess the nuns.
I wish to destroy and ruin the place,

Since the sons of Herbert hold it so dear."
And they responded, "We must do it all."
Quickly they go to prepare themselves.
The noble warriors mount their horses.
Not a one of them lacks a steel sword,
Shield, lance, and a good double hauberk.
Toward Origny they draw nearer.
The bells ring from the church tower;
They think of God the just Father;
Even the most foolish felt compelled to pray.
They no longer wished to ravish the holy place.
Outside on the meadows they pitch their tents,
The night long they lay until dawn appeared.
Then they carefully made preparations,
As if they intended to remain the entire year.

61

Near Origny there was a lovely and pleasant grove,
Where the valiant knights passed the night
Until on the morrow the dawn appeared.
Raoul came there when matins were sounding;
He rebuked his men:
"Sons of bitches, mean, dirty curs,
You are very much the scheming swine
Who have failed to obey my command!"
"Pardon, fair sire, by God the Redeemer,
We are neither Jews nor tyrants
Who could destroy the holy relics."

62

Count Raoul was extremely abusive.
"Sons of bitches," he said, out of control,
"I commanded that within the abbey be stretched
My linen tents and gold pommels,
By whose order was it placed outside?"
"Truly," said Guerri, "you go too far;
you have only recently been knighted.
If you give offense to God, you soon shall be finished.
This place is honored by noble men.
The holy relics ought not to be violated.

For lovely is the grass and fresh on the meadows
And the river banks are fair
Where your vanguard and your men can lie,
Where they will not be surprised or ambushed."
Raoul replied, "Just as you request,
So shall I allow, since it is your wish."
On the green grass they placed their carpets,
Raoul lay down and took counsel.
He brought ten knights with him.
They gave advice from which evil emerged.

63

Raoul cried, "Knights to arms;
Let's go at once to attack Origny!
I shall never hold dear one who lags behind."
The barons mount: they did not dare to disobey.
Together they were more than four thousand.
Toward Origny they began to advance;
They attacked the fortress and began to hurl their lances.
Those within defended themselves skillfully.
Raoul's men press closer; they go to level the trees before the
    town.
The nuns come forth from the abbey,
The gentle ladies, each one has her psalter,
And they do service to God.
Marcent was there, the mother of Bernier;
"Mercy, Raoul, by the just God!
Gravely would you sin if you permit our destruction;
Although easily we might be destroyed."

64

Marcent was the name of Bernier's mother;
She held a book dating from Solomon's age,
And said a prayer to God.
She grasped Raoul by his shining hauberk.
"Sire," she said, "by God and by His name,
Where is Bernier, gentle son of a baron?
I have not seen him since I nursed him as a babe."
"In the name of God, lady, he's in the master tent,

Where he plays with his many good fellows;
No knight is his equal as far as Rome.
He made me make war against Herbert's sons,
And said that he did not care in the slightest
If I left them stripped to naught save a button."
"God," said the lady, "he has the heart of a felon!
They are his uncles, as everyone knows;
If they lose their possessions, evil will come to him."

65

"Sire Raoul, is it worth nothing to pray
That you withdraw a little distance?
We are nuns, by the s[aints] of Bavaria;
We hold neither lance nor banner,
And by us no one has been laid on a bier."
"Truly," said Raoul, "you are an inveigler.
But I will have nothing to do with a cheap whore
Who has moved from hand to hand, sold for a farthing,
A harlot shared by everyone.
To Count Herbert you also sold your favors;
Your flesh was never very expensive
If anyone wanted it, by the Lord St. Peter;
It's very easy to deny your request."
"God!" said the lady, "I hear fierce words,
I hear myself abused in a strange manner.
I was never passed from hand to hand, sold for a farthing.
One noble person had his way with me.
I had one son of whom I am still proud.
Please God, do not refuse my plea.
Who serves God well shall see His face."

66

"Sire Raoul," said the mother of Bernier,
"We do not know how to manage arms;
Easily you could destroy and ruin us.
Neither shield nor lance shall you see us raise
To defend our bodies; I hide nothing from you.
All our livelihood and all our support
We derive from this altar.

And in this town we make our home.
Noble men hold this place so dear
That they send us silver and purest gold.
Grant us peace for the altar and for the church,
And go rest yourself on our meadows.
By our expense, sire, if you wish to accept it,
We will feed you and your knights.
Your squires shall have rations,
Fodder, oats, and plenty to eat."
Raoul replied, "By the body of St. Richier,
For your love as you have beseeched me,
You shall have the peace, no matter whom it annoys."
And the lady said, "This deserves thanks."
Raoul departs on his charger.
Bernier, who did much to be praised, came there
To see his mother, Marcent, with the fair face.
To speak with her he had very great need.

67

Raoul departs and goes without delay.
Bernier comes dressed in rich cloth
To see his mother, and dismounts from his charger.
She kisses him and takes him in her arms,
Three times she embraces him; she was not at all abashed.
"Fair son," she said, "you have taken arms;
Blessed be the count from whom you have them so young;
Blessed be yourself since you have earned them.
But one thing you cannot conceal from me.
The possession of your father, why do you invade it?
He has no other heirs, you cannot lose it;
By your bravery and by your wisdom you shall have it."
Bernier replied, "By the body of St. Thomas,
I would not do it for the lordship of Baghdad.
Raoul, my lord, is more evil than Judas.
He is my lord; horses he gives me and robes,
Arms and cloths of Baghdad.
I would not do it for the lordship of Damascus,
Until you said, 'Bernier, you do rightly.'"
"Son," said the mother, "by my faith you do rightly.
Serve your lord; God will reward you."

68

In Origny, the great and prosperous town,
The sons of Herbert hold the place most dear,
So that they have enclosed it with a palisade.
But to defend the city, it was not worth a farthing.
There was a marvelous and spacious meadow
Around Origny where one could joust.
The lowlands belonged to the abbey's nuns;
Their cattle grazed from which they drew profit;
Under the heavens no man dared injure them.
Count Raoul there pitched his tent;
All the poles were of silver and purest gold;
Four hundred men could lodge there.
From the army there departed three worthless persons.
From there to the town they did not spare the spurs,
Riches they robbed there; they wished to leave nothing.
But the booty became a burden.
Ten men gave them pursuit; each carried a crowbar;
Two of them died through their great burden;
The third escaped through flight on his horse;
From there to the tents he didn't pause;
He dismounted on the sand
And went to kiss the foot of his just lord;
While begging for mercy, he began to cry;
In a loud voice he commenced to appeal:
"May God never help your body
If you do not take vengeance on the townsmen,
Who are so rich and proud and haughty.
To them neither you nor anyone is worth a farthing.
Thus, they say they will shave your head.
If they can take you or capture you,
All the gold of Montpellier will not ransom you.
I have seen my brother killed and cut up,
And my nephew dead and murdered.
They would have killed me, by the body of St. Richier,
When I took to flight upon this steed."
Raoul heard this, his temperament changed;
He cried aloud, "Forward, noble knights!

I wish to shatter Origny to bits.
Since they have started war against me,
If God aids me, they will pay dearly for it!"
When the knights hear this, they don their armor
Instantly, since they dare not disobey.
There are ten thousand, I have heard it reported.
Toward Origny they begin to gallop.
They cross the moats to better attack it.
They cut the palisades with their steel axes,
Under their feet they trample them down;
They cross the moats beside the fishpond
And do not tarry from there to the walls.
The townsmen had only frustration that day
When they saw that the palisades offered no help.

69

The townsmen see that the palisades are lost;
Even the bravest are much depressed.
They resort to the walled fortifications;
Down they rain stones and many sharp stakes;
Of Raoul's men there are many dispatched.
Within the town not a man remains
Who has not come to the walls for defense,
Who has not sworn by God and his own strength
That if they find Raoul, evil finds him too.
Well they defend themselves, men hairless and hirsute.
Raoul observes them, his heart was wrathful.
He swears to God and his own strength
That if a man escapes, and is not hanged,
He would value his valor not worth a fig.
Aloud he cries, "Barons, put it to flame,"
And they did as they had understood,
Since for booty they had willingly come.
Poorly has Raoul the agreement maintained
Which was between him and the abbess.
This day he rendered them an evil service;
They burned the town, there nothing remained.
Young Bernier from this had great sorrow
When he saw there Origny so ravished.

70

Count Raoul had a heart most enraged
Against the treacherous townsmen.
He swore by God and his own compassion
That not for the archbishop of Rheims would he desist
From burning them all before night should fall.
He called for fire; his men responded.
The rooms are ablaze, the beams collapse.
The barrels explode; their bands are ruptured.
Fires consume the children, sadly and sinfully.
Count Raoul has foully destroyed them.
The day before, he promised Marcent
That the nuns would lose not a folded napkin;
Today he burns them, so greatly was he angered!
They flee to the abbey, but it avails them naught.
They still would have suffered in flight or fight.

71

In Origny, the great and prosperous town,
The sons of Herbert hold the place most dear.
Marcent they placed there, who was Bernier's mother,
With a hundred nuns to beseech the Lord God.
Count Raoul, with spirit so proud,
Has made fire run through the streets.
The houses are burned, the beams collapse.
The wines explode, the cellars run red.
The bacons burn, the fats feed the fire,
The bells fan the flames.
The great belfrey and the towers are ablaze.
The tapestries fall down from their places.
Between the two walls a great furnace rages.
The nuns are aflame, the heat there is too great.
All one hundred burn in the greatest torment.
Marcent is in flames, the mother of Bernier,
And Clamados, the daughter of Duke Renier;
In the midst of the fire, they can but lie down.
From pity weep the bravest knights.
When Bernier saw the ruin,
So much sorrow he had, his mind overturned.

Oh, that you could have seen how he gripped his shield!
With drawn sword he came to the church,
Through the doors he saw the racing flame.
From a distance over which a lance could be thrown,
No man could draw closer to the fire.
Bernier sees by the side of a rich marble,
He sees his mother recumbent, lying;
He sees the face of her, recumbent, lying;
On her breast he sees her psalter burning.
Then the boy said, "There is much folly here.
Never shall the master have help.
O sweet mother, you kissed me yesterday!
In me you have a very bad heir.
I can neither help you nor aid you.
May God, Who must judge the world, take your soul.
O Raoul, felon, God must punish you!
I wish to do you homage no more.
If now I cannot avenge this shame,
I hold myself not worth a farthing."
Such grief remained that he dropped his sword;
Three times he fainted on the neck of his charger.
He went for counsel to Guerri the Red;
But his advice could not aid him.

[Bernier, embittered by Raoul's ruthless sack of Origny, defies
him. The two quarrel bitterly, and Raoul strikes him on the head.
In spite of subsequent apologies, Bernier deserts him to join his
uncles' army. The forces clash, and in the melee, Raoul slices off
the left hand of Ernaut, one of Bernier's uncles. After a bloody
battle, the two antagonists meet in single combat.]

153

Bernier was a very good knight,
Strong and brave and a noble warrior.
With his clear voice he began to shout,
"Uncle Ernaut, you need not be frightened,
For I shall go speak to my lord."
He leaned on the neck of his charger;
In a loud voice he started to shout,
"O Sire Raoul, son of a noble mother,

You made me a knight, this I cannot deny.
But dearly you have made me pay for it since
You have killed so many of our brave warriors.
My mother you burned in Origny's church,
And you struck me a blow on the head.
You offered me justice, this I cannot deny.
In compensation I might have had many a charger.
One hundred good steeds were offered me,
And a hundred mules and a hundred rich palfreys,
And a hundred shields and a hundred double hauberks.
But angry was I when I saw my blood spilling.
To my friends I went to take counsel.
Now the brave knights advised me
If now you renew this offer, I cannot refuse it,
And I shall forgive you everything by St. Richier.
If my uncles can make peace with you,
This battle I would let pass.
You or no one could make complaint,
All our lands I would place in your power;
You would not lack a branch or a tree.
Forget the dead, there is nothing to be done.
O Sire Raoul, by the just God,
Take pity; let us make peace.
It is not right to pursue this dead man farther.
He who has lost a hand has nothing but wrath in him."
Raoul listened; his spirit grew hot.
He stretched himself so that his stirrups bent;
Beneath him buckled his steed.
"Bastard," he called, "you know how to plead;
But flattery avails you naught.
You shall not leave here with your head in one piece."
"Truly," said Bernier, "I have good cause for anger.
Now I will not humble myself."

154

When Bernier sees that the fighting Raoul
Cares not a whit for his plea,
With force he spurs his steed beneath him;
And Raoul, spurring too, comes against him.
They trade great blows on the shields before them;

Beneath the buckles the shields both split.
Bernier, who had so much right, struck him;
The good spear and the affixed flag
He thrust in his body, and he could not go forward.
Raoul hit him with such a great blow,
That his shield and hauberk were not worth a glove.
He should have killed him, believe one who knows,
But God and justice so much aided Bernier
That the iron only grazed his side.
Then Bernier made his turn in anger
And struck Raoul in his shining helmet,
That flowers and jewels went crashing down.
It cut the hood of the good hauberk;
Into the brain he made the sword plunge.
Barons, by God, who could continue this lay,
Since death is near and the man is at his end?
For on his feet he can scarcely stand,
The leader falls down from his horse.
The sons of Herbert rejoice and are glad.
There are those who rejoice who later found sadness,
As you shall hear, if I sing that long.

155

Count Raoul attempts to regain his feet.
With great effort he draws his steel sword.
Oh, that you could have seen him wield his blade!
But he cannot find his mark or use his sword;
Down to earth he lets his arm fall;
Into the meadow the steel blade cuts;
With the great test of effort, he finally frees it.
His beautiful mouth begins to contort,
His sparkling eye begins to dull.
He called on God, Who holds all in His rule:
"Glorious Father, Who can judge all things,
How I see now my body grow feeble!
Under the sky there was no man who, if I struck him yesterday,
After my blow could have arisen.
Evil I see my grant of earth;
This land or other land cannot help me now.
Help me, sweet lady of heaven!"

Bernier heard him, his temperament changed.
Beneath his helmet he began to weep.
In a loud voice he started to cry:
"O Sire Raoul, son of a noble mother,
You made me a knight, this I cannot deny.
But dearly have you made me pay for it since.
My mother you burned within a church,
And my own head you struck.
You offered me justice, this I cannot deny;
More vengeance I do not wish to have."
Count Ernaut began to cry,
"Let this dead man pay for my hand!"
"Truly," said Bernier, "I cannot forbid it;
But he is dead and you have no right to touch him."
Ernaut responded, "I have right to be angry."
In a leftward turn he maneuvered his steed;
His right hand held his steel blade,
And he struck Raoul: he wished not to spare him;
Through his helmet he wished to break.
The great jewel he made fall to the earth;
He cut through the hood of his double hauberk,
And the blade bloodied his brain.
This still was not enough, and again he took the steel blade;
In the heart he made it plunge to the hilt;
The soul of the noble knight departed.
May God receive it, if for this one may pray.

156

Bernier cried out, "St. Quentin and Douai!
Dead is Raoul, lord of Cambrai.
Ernaut and Bernier have killed him, I know it well."
Count Ernaut spurred his bay steed.
Bernier swears by the body of St. Nicholas:
"It pains me that I have killed Raoul,
May God help me, but I did it by my right."
And Guerri, on a great bay steed,
Found his nephew and was greatly distressed.
He mourned for him as I shall tell you.
"Fair nephew," said he, "I have great sorrow for you,
I shall never love the one who has killed you.

With him peace or concord or truce I shall never make
Until that hour when they are all dead.
I shall destroy them all, hanged on the gallows.
Lady Aalais, what sorrow I shall tell you!
Never shall I dare to speak to you."

157

And Guerri, as he galloped along,
Found his nephew lying on the sand.
The noble man still grasped his sword in his hand;
He gripped it so hard between hilt and pommel
That only with great effort could they take it from him;
On his chest was his shield with its lion emblem.
Guerri collapsed on the breast of the baron.
"Fair nephew," he said, "this is an evil deed.
I see here the work of the bastard Bernier,
Whom you knighted in the palace at Paris.
He has killed you for a wicked cause;
But by him who suffered the passion,
If I do not rip from him the liver and the lung,
I will never hold myself to be a valiant knight."

158

Guerri the Red sees his men die,
The last agony and death of his nephew,
And his brain lying over his eyes.
From that grief he almost lost his senses.
"Fair nephew," he said, "I do not know what will happen.
By that Lord Who deigned to suffer,
Those who have taken you from me
Shall never have peace if I can allow it.
I shall destroy them and shame them,
Or soon drive them from the earth.
Now I ask for a truce if I can attain it,
So that I can bury you in the earth."

159

Great sorrow held Guerri the Red of Arras.
He called Perron: "Come forward, friend,
And Hardouin and Berart of Senlis,

Ride forward to my enemies,
And make truce as I request it,
Until my nephew is buried in the earth."
And they responded: "Willingly, at once."
They spur their horses, their shields covering their eyes.
It did not take long to find the sons of Herbert.
They found them seated upon their prize steeds;
They were rejoicing greatly at the death of Raoul.
They also had joy who later would be grieved.
Now the messengers began to speak
With these words, their shields still on their necks:
"You are wrong, by the body of St. Denis;
Count Raoul was of high nobility,
His uncles were our King Louis
And the good vassal Guerri of Arras.
Those who make joy, healthy and whole and well,
Shall later be dismembered and killed.
Guerri the bold and the brave asks you
Respite and truce by the body of St. Denis
Until his nephew shall be buried in the earth."
"We shall grant it," said Ybert of the white beard,
"Even if you ask that it last till Judgment Day."

160

They agreed to the truce before the bells knelled noon.
On the field they walked, turning over the dead.
One found a father or a son,
A nephew, an uncle, or a kinsman.
You may well believe his heart had great sorrow
As Guerri went in search of his own dead kin.
He now forgot both his dead sons
On account of his nephew Raoul the fighter.
He looked before him; he saw John in bloody death.
In all of France there was no knight as tall.
Raoul had killed him, this most of you know.
Guerri saw him and quickly approached.
Both him and Raoul he took now.
With his cutting sword, he opens both their bodies.
He removed the hearts as we read in the records;
On a shield of fine shining gold

He placed them down to see their appearance.
One was as small as a child's,
But Raoul's heart, as most of you know,
Was as large, in my knowledge,
As that of a bull which pulls a plow.
Guerri viewed it; from grief he came weeping.
In tears he called on the knights:
"Noble comrades, in God's name, come forward.
See in Raoul the hardy fighter,
What a heart he had compared to this giant's!
You have pledged me, noble and valiant knights,
Force and aid for all my life.
See my enemies before us.
They have killed the one whom I loved so much.
If I do not avenge it, mark me a scoundrel.
Pierre of Artois, rush to them now;
Renounce the truce which I want no more to maintain."
And they responded, "All at your command."
To Herbert's sons they galloped.
He cried loudly in the hearing of all:
"Guerri tells you, by the body of St. Amant,
Take back your truce; know it for sure,
That if he has his way, none of you shall escape death."
When they heard these things, they were much depressed;
From the battle they were tired,
And their steeds were exhausted and restless.
Back to Guerri came the messenger.
And the Red put all his men in battle array.
Before evening there shall be a thousand sorrows.

[IV. Vengeance, Reconciliation, War]

[The battle is rejoined, and Bernier and Guerri meet in single combat, but no decision is reached. Guerri leaves the battlefield with one hundred and forty men surviving out of ten thousand. He renews his oath to have vengeance from Bernier. Bernier and the sons of Herbert have only three hundred men left out of eleven thousand. Raoul's young nephew, Gautier, similarly swears to avenge his uncle. Several years pass, and after further combat, the emperor attempts to restore peace among his barons by summoning them all to his court on Pentecost.]

222

Our emperor has assembled his vassals,
At thirty thousand their number that day was reckoned.
In the morning they heard Mass,
And afterward they went up into the tiled hall.
The seneschal passed among the tables;
In his right hand he held a stripped branch.
And he cried with a very loud voice:
"Listen, lords, noble and honored men,
This word the king has commanded.
He who causes disturbance here,
Before the evening shall lose his head."
Guerri heard these words and his color changed.
He looked at Bernier with his hand on his sword,
But Gautier pushed it back in the sheath.
"Uncle," he said, "it is proven folly,
As the outcome shows, for a man to undertake something
Of which he has shame and his people are condemned.
See that the affair is tempered.
Disgrace comes to those without restraint,
Until such time as amends can be taken."

223

Great was the revel in the rich palace;
At the high tables sat the knights.
The seneschal has much to learn.
Together he placed Bernier and Gautier,
Guerri the Red and Ybert the warrior,
Wedon of Roie and Louis of the haughty mien,
And the lame Ernaut, who did nothing but rage.
Now these noble warriors are all together.
Guerri sees them and his temperament changed.
In his hand he holds a great steel knife.
He wished that day to throw it at Bernier.
But Gautier would not let him touch him.
"Uncle," he said, "you ought justly be blamed.
You are invited here to a free meal.
You have indeed a great disgrace to amend
If you provoke everyone to mortal combat."

Guerri was served a dish of rich venison,
With the largest bone of the animal's rump.
Guerri saw it and showed no more restraint.
With it he struck Bernier's temple.
From the skin to the bone, he forced it through the flesh.
All his face he made wet with blood.
Bernier saw it and wrath seized him.
The valiant knights had seen it,
Since they had sat down to eat.
He jumped from the table and would have paid him a blow
In the neck and would have spared nothing,
But would have sent him sprawling on the table.
Gautier jumped up to aid his uncle.
By the hair he seized Bernier.
Count Ybert began to rise.
Louis seized an apple bough,
Wedon of Roie ran to his steel sword.
Guerri the Red seized a large crowbar,
And Gautier a big steel knife.
On both sides the baron knights began the assault.
This melee would have cost very much
Had not the sergeants and the dispensers rushed up.
They began to drag the barons from the table
And brought them to the king who rules all France.
The king said, "Who started this?"
"Guerri the Red," said many a knight.
"He was the first to start it."

224

The king said, "Noble knights and barons,
Who first began this strife?"
"Guerri the Red, by the body of St. Simon,
First began it with Bernier."
Then the king swore by the knight St. James:
"I shall have justice according to my decree."
Guerri replied proudly:
"Just emperor, a wicked deed has been done here.
May God help me, you are not worth a button.
How could I have looked at that traitor

Who treacherously killed my nephew?
He was your sister's son, as all know for a fact."
"Truly," said Bernier, "you speak treason.
Raoul I defied in his own tent.
But by the apostle whom pilgrims seek at Rome,
Never in battle shall you lack an opponent.
Certainly, you shall have so many mounted men
Who before evening will count you as a fool."
Guerri heard him; the man had such joy.
He desired him more than a hawk does a lark.

225

Guerri, full of great anger, spoke.
"Just emperor, I cannot lie to you.
All the world will hold you in hate,
Since you are able to look upon him
Who dispatched your nephew's soul from his body.
I wonder how you can refrain
From having him torn limb from limb
Or hanged on the gallows or made to die shamefully."
The king replied, "One cannot agree.
If a noble man summons another to service,
He may not shame or dishonor him.
Nonetheless, by the martyr St. Paul,
If this man cannot defend and maintain himself,
His destruction will surely follow."
Bernier heard him, and he began to grow wrathful.
"My lords," he said, "try to injure me;
All of you can come to the battle."

226

The boy Gautier sprang straight to his feet.
He spoke loudly in the hearing of all.
"Just emperor, hear my thought.
I shall combat with my sharp sword
Bernier, the lying bastard.
I shall beat him and make him remorseful,
And have him confess in the hearing of all
That he killed Raoul, my valiant uncle,
Feloniously, as most of you know."

Guerri replied, "That's enough, you scoundrel.
You are too young, and you still have the mind of a child.
If anyone should tap you on the nose with a single glove,
So that a drop of blood appeared,
You would break into tears, I know for a fact.
But my muscles are strong and hard and resilient,
And I have a brave warrior heart.
When someone strikes me with his sharp lance,
I take vengeance at once with my noble blade.
Against this bastard I wish to take the field.
If before evening I do not make him repent,
Woe betide the king if I am not made to answer for it."
Then said Gautier of the dauntless spirit,
"I would not want for the lordship of Milan
That another than myself should take up the blade."
"Truly," said Bernier, "I grant it.
Before the sun sets in the evening
I shall give you so much battle
That not for another living man will you want to continue."

227

"Just emperor," said the experienced Bernier,
"This battle I shall well assume,
With this understanding, as you shall hear me say.
If the truth is not as you have heard me tell it,
May God, Who was nailed on the cross, not permit
That I return whole and secure."
"Truly," said the king, "I will guarantee it for you,
But nonetheless you must give me hostages."
Bernier replied, "Let it be as you command."
His father was included among them.
Gautier took no delay,
To his lodging he went at once.
He donned the hauberk and tied his helmet.
He girded his sword at his left side;
He leaped on the horse without use of the stirrups,
Then hung his shield on his left side.
The good lance he did not forget,
With the pennon affixed with three golden nails.
Bernier too armed himself well,

With richly burnished arms.
Our emperor acted wisely.

228

In two boats he has them taken across the Seine.
Gautier the noble baron is across;
Also Bernier, who has done many praiseworthy things.
Holy relics the king had carried there,
And had a green cloth placed upon the grass.
Who then saw the cloth shaken by the breeze,
And the relics moving and tumbling,
With great wonder would remember it.

229

The young Gautier rose to his feet.
"Barons," he said, "be quiet and listen.
By all the saints whom you see here,
And by all the others by whom God is beseeched,
Bernier has done perjury.
Presently, he will be remorseful and beaten."
Bernier replied, "If it please God, you lie."
And Gautier is mounted on his steed,
And Bernier mounted his own, which had been led to him.
Gautier was young, newly made a knight,
But he attacked Bernier like a seasoned man.
On his shield he struck such blows
That it was broken and shattered beneath the buckle.
And the hauberk was broken and torn.
Between the ribs the sword blade passed.
So hard did the admirable Gautier press him
That he knocked him down in the midst of the meadow.
And Gautier rode past him,
Crying aloud, "Bastard, you will never recover."
"Truly," said Bernier, "you are not long for this world.
A man overthrown is not always one beaten."
[Stanza 230 is missing.]

231

Bernier had a heavy and angered heart
When he found himself unsaddled and on his feet.

He drew his sword and grasped his lance.
He went to his horse, which he saw was ready.
He mounted it by the golden stirrup.
Within the scabbard he placed his blade.
He spurred the steed and brandished the lance,
And struck Gautier on his quartered shield.
Beneath the buckle he pierced and broke it.
And slashed and rent the hauberk.
He wetted his lance in Gautier's left side.
He rode past him, leaving the blade behind.
He looked toward Guerri and taunted him:
"Vile old man, I see you are downcast;
You will not see the sun set
Before you lose the company of your nephew."
Gautier heard him and cried aloud:
"Vile bastard, have you lost your senses?
Before this evening I shall have justice from you.
Never shall you hold a half-foot of land."
He charges on his steed with his blade drawn forth
And strikes Bernier without sparing,
A wondrous blow on his shining helmet.
He breaks it and cuts it above the band;
The fine hood gave him little help,
For the blade removed a half-foot of flesh.
It cut off his ear and badly wounded him.
"In truth," said Bernier, "you have sorely bloodied me."

232

"God!" said Bernier. "True Father, what shall I do,
When on my right I have lost my ear?
If I do not take vengeance, I shall never be happy."
He raised his lance, as I know well,
And struck Gautier and gave him an awesome wound.
Of the blood of the body a stream gushed forth.
"Truly," said Bernier, "I have struck you.
You will never see again the domains of Cambrai."
"Truly," said Gautier, "never shall I eat
Until the hour that I hold your heart in my hand.
I know for a fact that before night I shall kill you.
You already sorely miss your ear,
And I see the earth covered with your blood."

Bernier replied, "Well shall I take vengeance."
Said Ernaut of Douai, "My nephew shall prevail."
"Son of a bastard," said Guerri of Chimai,
"If I see you there, I will punish you.
Without your left hand you resemble the jay
Who sits on the tree which I willingly shoot.
The arrow carries off a foot and leaves the leg.
If I see you there, I will hurt you."
And Ybert replied, "Do not expect to;
As long as I have life and strength.
With my steel blade I'll make you such music,
Which will never cheer your spirits.
You will never again see the fortress of St. Nicholas."
"Truly," said Guerri, "I shall treat you
As I did your brother Herbert, whom I disemboweled
Near Origny, where I met him.
Or by the neck I'll take you to the gallows."

233

The battle is marvelous and great;
Never did two men fight so fiercely.
Each held his good Bavarian blade;
Each gave back the other's blows.
Their shields were not worth a tinker's damn,
For not even the buckles remained entire.
The hauberks split in front and in back;
Each strove to cut the other's living flesh,
The face of each glowed with blood;
Their blood gushed past their stirrups.
Not for much longer can both continue;
It's a miracle that they are not both on their biers.
Now Geoffroy of Roche Anglière goes back to the palace.
"Just emperor," said the baron, "by St. Peter,
Your men are by no means cowards.
Each of the champions has a strong arm;
They exchange blows on front and rear."

234

Great was the uproar in the rich palace.
The two on the field have no thought of restraint.
In Gautier he has a very good knight,

Large and strong, every inch the fighter.
Against Bernier he is eager to press.
Great blows he delivers on his quartered shield,
But Bernier cannot entirely escape.
Down to the left the steel blade fell,
And cut the flesh on the shoulder.
From there to the bone he drove in the sword;
A half-foot of flesh he hacked to the earth.
If the noble steel blade had not swerved aside,
It would have cut him through to his breeches.
Through the mouth he made the blood spill;
All swooning he knocked him down on the grass.
"Truly," said Bernier, "you wish to destroy me."
Gautier replied, "I do it to punish you.
Thus must a traitor pay
Who has wrongly killed his just lord."
Bernier said, "You lie, Gautier.
You are wrong and shall pay for it dearly.
Of sorrow shall I die if I cannot have vengeance."
Oh, that you could have watched him grasp his shield,
Seize and grip his good sword,
And double and triple his efforts.
When Gautier saw him coming so eagerly,
With great wonder he looked to his own defenses.
Bernier did not wish to spare him.
He dealt him a mighty blow on the pure gold helmet
Which he split by nearly an eighth.
If now the blade did not swerve toward the left side,
Right through to the shoulders it would have cut.
Gautier saw it and had nothing but anger;
He rushed upon him like a man gone wild.
Then both the good warriors would surely have died,
Neither could have rescued himself.
Guerri saw this and wrath again ruled him.
He sounded his shrill horn.
His men responded, they dared not disobey.
He kneeled toward the abbey tower.
On the saints he swore, while many knights watched,
That if he saw Gautier punished to death,
Bernier would have his members cut off.
Ybert heard him; wrath ruled him too;

He summons his men and draws them up for battle.
He swears to the Lord, Who rules all things,
That if he sees Bernier dead or ruined,
He will make Gautier suffer miserably;
All the gold of Montpellier will not protect him,
Nor will Louis, who has France in his sway.
When he will come to do the deed,
If they should meet them with lowered lances,
Gautier could be sure to lose his head.
Geoffroy and Manecier rose to their feet
And went to tell these words to the king.
The king replied, "By the body of St. Richier,
Separate the two; do not allow them to touch each other further."
More than fifty men rushed along the causeway.
Along the Seine they came, racing on the bank.
They separated the two without delay.
Much did it pain them, as I have heard reported,
For still they wished to do battle.
But if they had let them fight longer,
Neither one could have recovered.
Their wounds were great; they did not cease to bleed.
The doctors came and bandaged the warriors,
And fanned them to cool their bodies.
Then they bore them and lay them down in the palace;
Two rich beds were prepared.
But the emperor did something foolish.
So close did the two warriors lie
That they could see each other stirring and reclining.
To Gautier the king first came.
Courteously he began to address him:
"Will you survive? Tell me the truth."
"Yes, surely, sire, I cannot deceive you."
"God," said the king, "I owe you thanks.
I would have you make peace with Bernier."
Gautier heard him; wrath seized him once more.
Loudly he shouted:
"Just emperor, may God curse you!
You were the one who started this war,
Killed and cut up Raoul, my uncle.
By that God Who judges all things,
You shall never see me make peace,

Rather I would dissect all his limbs."
Bernier said, "Now I hear a fool talking.
Now I must not drink or eat.
You shall never see the month of February."

235

Our emperor turned from Gautier.
To Bernier he went directly.
Courteously he spoke to him:
"Sire Bernier, noble and renowned knight,
Will you survive? Tell me the truth."
"Yes, truly, sire, but I am gravely wounded."
"God," said the king, "may you be praised.
Do not misjudge me, I wish to live until
You should be reconciled with Gautier.
But he is so proud and excessive
That he will have nothing of it, for the gold of ten cities."
Bernier said, "Sire, you will not see otherwise.
Gautier is young and newly knighted;
He thinks he can well do whatever he wants.
But by Him Who was hanged on the cross,
It will never happen for all my life
That I shall know remorse or defeat."
Gautier heard him and was much incensed.
"Vile bastard, how excessive you are!
My uncle you killed, who was brave and wise,
Your rightful lord; you are proved a traitor.
Marvelous how you deny it so long.
You've come out of this badly with the loss of your ear,
Which by the Seine lies on the field."
Bernier replied, "You are very wrong.
I gave you a blow, as you well know;
You were almost broken in your left side.
This weighs upon me and I grieve for it.
You do a great sin when you do not make peace."
Gautier heard him, but he took no pity.

236

"Sire Gautier!" said the noble Bernier,
"For the love of God, Who was put on the cross,

Will this war last forever?
God forgave His death to Longinus [who thrust his spear into his
    side].
Accept compensation, excellent and noble knight.
I shall at once give you such justice as you may desire.
I shall surrender to you my land and my country,
I shall go with you to Cambrai.
I shall serve you, this I say in pledge.
I ask only to have two poor horses;
Never shall I wear either ermine or sable.
From my squire I shall beg
For water to drink and for rye bread to eat.
For as long as you wish I will be so punished
Until the hour that pity enters your heart.
Otherwise take your sword and now kill me."
Then both Gautier and Guerri cried,
"Vile bastard, how you have fallen!
By that God Who was placed on the cross,
Your amends will never be accepted.
Rather shall you die, by the body of St. Denis."
"All rests with God," said the noble Bernier.
"I cannot die before God's chosen time."
Into the city comes the sister of Louis.
When she entered the streets of Paris,
On all sides she heard the cries
Concerning the two vassals who had injured each other.
The lady heard it; her heart was saddened.
One might have given her all the wealth of St. Denis,
And she would have shown neither joy nor pleasure,
So much she wished to know what had happened to her friend.
She dismounted from her Arabian horse,
Then mounted the steps of the vaulted palace.
She entered the hall before King Louis,
Together with twenty excellent knights.

237

Lady Aalais, worthy of praise, descended
From her mount without delay.
Up the palace steps she began to mount;
She had with her many a valiant knight.

To meet her came her dearest friends,
Guerri the Red and many another prince,
And the emperor who has France in his power.
He saluted her graciously without delay;
After he had embraced and kissed her,
The gentle lady pushed him back.
"Away with you, king, may you have troubles;
You are not worthy to rule a kingdom.
If I were a man, before the sun sets,
I would show with a sword of steel
That you are wrongly king;
Well could I declare it,
Since you allow at your table to eat
The one who has cut off your nephew's limbs."
She looks ahead and sees Gautier lying there.
From grief she swoons at once.
All her valiant knights hold her erect.
And Gautier began to shout,
"Noble company, take courage and pride.
Tell my aunt what I did to Bernier.
Never in his life will he do service to a man.
I've taken his ear with my steel lance."
The lady heard him and stretched her hands toward the sky:
"Dear Sire God, I owe You thanks."
On the other side she sees Bernier lying,
She ran toward him and seized a crowbar.
Surely she would have killed him without further ado,
But the barons did not allow her to touch him.
And Bernier slipped out of his bed
Gracefully without further delay.
He ran to embrace the legs of Lady Aalais,
And sweetly to kiss her shoe;
"Gentle countess, I wish no further delay.
You reared me, I cannot deny it,
And you gave me to eat and to drink.
Alas, Gautier, by the just God,
If now you do not wish to make peace for Jesus' sake,
See here my sword; from me you can take vengeance,
For I do not wish to fight you further."
Lady Aalais began to weep;

She no longer insisted on cutting his members
When she saw Bernier so humble himself.

238

Great was the movement in the furnished hall.
The youth Bernier with the brave countenance
Bound his head with a bandage of silk.
He wore only breeches and he had no shirt.
On his face he lay, holding his burnished sword;
Before the king he prayed Gautier for mercy:
"Mercy, Gautier, in the name of God, Mary's Son,
Who raised the dead man in Bethany
And received death to give us life.
I pray you, sire, let this folly pass;
This folly should not last all our days.
Either now kill me or grant me life."
Gautier heard him and his complexion grew black.
His loud words shook the hall:
"By God, bastard, thus it shall never end.
Either you shall hang or die at duel,
If you do not flee to Apulia or to Hungary."
To Gautier the court turned.
Their loud cry filled the hall.
"Sire Gautier, you are full of pride.
When he speaks to you, strength nearly fails him;
But he still has a thousand men in his service;
They will not fail him at the risk of their lives."
Bernier responded, avoiding foolish words:
"Mercy, lords, by God the Son of Mary.
If God grant it, Who rules all things,
That my prayer will be favorably received,
Before night this war will be ended."

239

Bernier lay in the vaulted palace,
With his face down he held the sharpened blade.
From St. Germain there comes the abbot,
Precious relics he brings in quantity,
Of St. Denis and St. Honoré.
In a loud voice which all could hear,

"Barons," he said, "hear my will.
You know well by holy charity,
That the Lord God so full of goodness
Had His holy body tortured and pained
On the holy cross on that infamous Friday.
Longinus was there by the blessed body
And struck the left side.
For a long time he had not use of his eyes,
But he rubbed his eyes and perceived the light.
He cried for mercy, with good will,
And our Lord at once pardoned him.
Sire Gautier, by the God of majesty,
This war has lasted too long.
Bernier offers you amends in good will;
If you do not accept it, you will be condemned for it."
The gentle abbot was steadfast.
He called by name on Count Ybert,
Wedon of Roie, Louis the hardened,
And the wise Ernaut of Douai,
Who had his left hand cut from his body
In the battle fought near the meadow of Origny.
"Barons," he said, "now hear my thought.
Each of you take his good sharpened blade,
Let them be so given to your enemies
That if it pleases God, you will be reconciled,
Through that agreement which you shall now hear.
May all your sins be pardoned you
To the same measure that at the Judgment Day their sins are
     pardoned."
"Truly," said Ybert, "this should not be rejected."
They knelt down in the sight of all the barons.
In good will they cried for forgiveness.
But Gautier did not cast them a glance.
The abbot saw this and nearly lost his mind.

240

The abbot, who was very learned, cried out:
"What are you doing, Guerri the Red of Arras?
Bid them rise, noble and gentle knight."
And Gautier cried loudly:

"You bid them rise, lady, by your mercy,
By the Lord God, Who has never lied.
I say that he will never be my friend
Until he be cut up and killed."
Guerri heard him and laughed aloud:
"Fair nephew," he said, "you are greatly prized.
You have much spirit against your enemies.
The caitiff Bernier will never recover."
The abbot heard him and his face grew dark:
"Sire Guerri, you have gray hair,
You do not know the day of your judgment.
If you do not make peace, may St. Denis hear me,
Never will your soul have paradise."

241

The people stirred noisily in the palace.
Before Gautier, Bernier was humbly prostrate.
Before Guerri, the skilled Ybert
And Louis his brother together lay.
Wedon of Roie prayed quietly,
He and Ernaut of Douai of gentle body.
And Bernier cried aloud:
"O Sire Gautier, by the almighty God,
Our five swords are here given to you.
We shall never recover them.
Now by God may your anger pardon us,
Or take the sword and make quick vengeance."
Through the palace seven hundred voices were raised:
"O Gautier, in the name of God, Who knows all things,
For the love of God, noble man, bid them rise."
"God," said Gautier, "I do it sorrowfully."
He quickly and gracefully raised them;
Then they embraced as friends and kinsmen.
The king turned away; he was full of anger,
For he regretted this agreement.
Guerri the Red arose at once.
He went to the window and cried out in a loud voice:
"Brother Bernier, in the name of God, come forward.
This king is a felon; I hold him to be a rascal.
He started this war, as many know.

By the body of St. Amant,
Let us make war on him, noble and valiant knight."
"Truly," said Bernier, "I consent and agree.
I would not fail you for anything living."
Ybert with the mustache spoke:
"All Vermandois, the strong and large land,
I abandon to you to do as you wish.
And against you I will not take a clod of earth
From my land worth a farthing.
This only I regret, by the body of St. Amant,
That this war has lasted so long."
Guerri replied, "It cannot be otherwise.
From now on we shall be as close kinsmen."

242

Great was the movement in the rich palace.
There were Aalais and Ybert, proud of visage,
Guerri the Red and the courteous Gautier,
Count Ernaut of Douai, the warrior,
And Louis and Wedon and Bernier.
Now all the counts go together to eat.
The king of France felt nothing but anger.
He summoned the barons to come and speak with him.
This they do, as they dared not disobey.
Before reaching the palace they did not tarry.
To the king they went and leaned against the table;
He called Ybert, the brave warrior:
"Ybert," he said, "I have held you very dear.
After your death, by the just God,
I wish to give Vermandois to one of my nobles."
Ybert replied: "Sire, you cannot do it.
I gave it the other day to Bernier."
"What, you devil!" said the king of haughty mien,
"Has then a bastard a right to claim a fief?"
Ybert answered and felt nothing but wrath:
"Just emperor, by the just God,
You do a great wrong insulting your vassal.
I too was your vassal this morning,
But I can no longer bear you homage,
If you do not do justice and pledge me the land."

"Truly," said the king, "you vaunt yourself too much.
Never from the land shall you have a farthing.
I've already given it to Gilemer of Ponthieu."
Bernier said: "Sire, you can plead in vain,
Since by Him Who rules all things,
He shall never have from you help or protection
Until I shall have hacked away all his limbs."
The king answered, "Shut up, you rotter and villain!
Miserable bastard, do you want to fight with me?
Soon I shall have you thrown on a dung heap."
Bernier heard this, and wrath came upon him.
In anger he drew his sword of steel
And cried aloud: "What are you doing, Gautier?
Now all your men must aid me."
And Guerri said: "I must not fail you,
Nor shall I fail you for the gold of Montpellier.
This coward king one ought well to ruin,
For he made us begin this war
And caused my nephew to be slain and quartered."
You should have seen how they drew their swords.
Guerri the Red brandished his aloft,
And the king's men trembled and ran.
Many more than seven they overpowered,
Not even the emperor kept his skin intact,
For Bernier went to stab him.
Inside his cuirass he slipped the blade,
So that he made him fall to the earth.

243

The king was saddened and dismayed.
Gautier rose to his feet.
"Just emperor," he says, "you have done a great wrong.
I am your nephew, you ought not to have disinherited me."
The king replied: "Scoundrel, let me be.
By Him Who was hanged upon the cross
Everyone will in the end be disinherited."
Gautier replied, "Since you deny your faith to me,
From now on, beware of my body."
To the lodgings soon a messenger arrived.
He cried aloud: "Noble knights, mount your horses.

Our barons have come to blows in the palace."
When they heard this, all of them speedily mounted.
In a short hour, one thousand of them were armed
And were rushing toward the palace.

244

Great was the movement in the vaulted hall.
Guerri spoke with a brave look:
"Just emperor, it is right that I tell you this.
This war you caused by your stupidity.
Raoul you invested with another man's fief.
You swore to him before the barons
That you would never fail him as long as he lived.
Everyone knows what this guarantee was worth.
Near Origny, close to the abbey, he was killed.
But by Him to Whom all men pray,
Still your entire host has not been summoned."
The king replied, "Old traitor, may God curse you!
Whatever happens, you shall never have Arras.
Within a month you will be deprived of your fief.
If I find you there, by God, Son of Mary,
At the great gate which is built there,
I shall hang you in the sight of my barons."
Guerri listened, and now he defies him:
"Watch out for my burnished sword!
Bernier, my brother, now I have need of help."
Bernier answered with a hardy countenance:
"I will not cease to attend you."
And the court dispersed amid much strife.

245

Guerri the Red descended the stairs.
At the foot he found one thousand armed knights.
Bernier cried out to them:
"Noble knights, think to do well.
Our squires are already armed.
Quickly sack this town.
All that you seize will be yours."
They responded: "Let it be as you command."
They cried for fire, and the town was at once put to the torch,

And it was at once lit up;
Through the streets of the city fire raced,
Up to the palace of which you have heard,
From the great bridge where the ships anchored
To the small bridge which is so renowned.
That day from all its riches there did not remain
Enough to burden a single peasant.

246

They burned the city in their great anger.
Guerri and Bernier quickly departed,
And Gautier quietly left.
They had no wish to stay in the city.
To Pierrefont they came directly,
And they rode all the dark night.
To San Quentin they went quickly.
All the people of the country made secure their houses
Because of the great war soon to break out.
The king held as a great offense
That in the city they have done him such injury.
In bad temper he swears by the body of St. Peter
That neither castle nor fortress will protect them,
Nor kinship nor bonds of vassalage,
Until he takes of them all great punishment.

247

They arrived at San Quentin in the Vermandois.
"Sire Gautier," says the courteous Bernier,
"Guerri my lord will go to Artois,
And you will go at once to Cambrai.
I am still wearied from my wounds,
And you yourself will not be whole for months.
I know full well that the king has great hate for us.
He will make war against us if he can in Vermandois.
He will come against us with terrible strength.
Summon all the men that you can.
Guerri the brave and the courteous will call his men.
And I am very close to Laon;
Very often I shall raise havoc within it.
Neither barricade nor stronghold nor defense

Will restrain my good Viennese blade."
At these words all departed.
Guerri the Red went to Artois,
And Lady Aalais to her land in Cambrai.

248

Directly to Arras went Guerri the Red,
And Gautier returned to Cambrai,
And Aalais was there with complexion fair.
They summoned their men and their best friends.
Guerri the Red did likewise,
For Bernier is certain of war.
The king swears by God, Who was placed on the cross,
That he would not stop for all the gold of Senlis
Until he should have vengeance from the bastard
Who burned and sacked his fortress
And robbed the city of Paris,
And did great shame to the country—
Bernier, Gautier, and Guerri the Red of Arras.
If he does not have their land within fifteen days,
And has not taken Vermandois by force,
He will not consider himself worth two farthings.
He summoned his scribes and addressed them:
"Write my letters as I shall tell you.
I wish to summon at once my best friends,
And my barons and those whom I have reared,
So that for my shame vengeance may be taken.
Neither castles nor forts will protect them.
I shall drag them forth; I am in great haste."
The scribes responded, "All shall be as you wish."
Gautier, Guerri, and the courteous Bernier
Came to St. Quentin in Vermandois.
They stayed there a great part of the month,
For from their wounds they were still weary.
With them they had two good doctors.
When they were cured, they departed at once.
Guerri the Red went to Artois
And with him went the courteous Bernier.
Lady Aalais to her lands in Cambrai
Has gone; she takes Gautier with her.

[This ends the first part of the poem; there exists a continuation, written later and in a much different spirit, largely concerned with the romantic adventures of Bernier.]

32. Lords, vassals, and tenants in the Norman *Summa de legibus*

In the thirteenth century, lawyers nearly everywhere in Europe were drawing up codifications of feudal customs and seeking to establish logical consistency among them. It is only at this epoch that we can speak of a feudal system, and even then we must acknowledge that it is many systems, not just one, with which we are dealing. One of the codifications which excellently illustrates the thirteenth century's spirit of system is the *Summa de legibus* of Normany, substantially redacted by an unknown lawyer before 1258 but subject to numerous later additions and revisions. At this time the king of France was also duke of Normandy. Note the interpretation, implicit to the code, that all land derives ultimately from the duke, and that liege homage is owed by all vassals to him. The duke thus stands at the apex of a pyramid of feudal ties in regard to both personal obligations and property rights, and this is characteristic of the second feudal age. The following selections, translated by D. Herlihy, are taken from the *Coutumiers de Normandie*, ed. E.-J. Tardif, Tome II: *La Summa de legibus Normannie in curia laicali* (Rouen and Paris, 1896). The tenure by parage mentioned refers to the practice, common in France, of younger persons' holding their lands from an older relative, who was in turn responsible before the lord for the services owed by his entire kin and the property held from him. Mills with banal rights attached were those which had a legal monopoly of milling within a certain area.

11. On the duke

1. The duke of Normandy or the prince is the one who holds the lordship [*principatum*] over the entire duchy. This dignity the lord king of France holds together with the other honors to which, with the aid of the Lord, he has been raised. From this it pertains to him to preserve the peace of the land, to correct the people by the rod of justice, and by the measure of equity to end private disputes.

Therefore, he should through the justiciars subject to him see to it
that the people under his authority rejoice in the rule of justice and
the tranquillity of peace. He should search out, capture, and keep
in strong prisons, until they have received the wages of their
crimes, robbers, thieves, arsonists, murderers, the violent deflow-
erers of virgins, rapers of women, committers of mayhem and
other public disturbers, and others held in public infamy, who may
cause damage to life or limb.

12. Concerning liege homage

1. The duke of Normandy ought to have liege homage or the
loyalty of all the men of his entire province. From this they are
bound to him against all men, who may live or die, to offer the
assistance of their own body in counsel and in aid, and to show
themselves to him inoffensive in all things, and in nothing to take
the side of his adversaries.
2. He also is obligated to rule, protect, defend, and treat them
according to the rights, customs, and laws of the land.

13. On fealty

1. All those living in the province are bound to do and to maintain
fealty to the duke. For this they are bound to show themselves
inoffensive and faithful to him in all things, and not to procure
anything against his interests, nor to give counsel or aid to his
manifest enemies. Whoever may be discovered to have violated this
by evident cause should be reputed notorious traitors of the prince,
and all their possessions shall forever remain to the prince, if for
this they are convicted and condemned. For all men in Normandy
are bound to observe fealty to the prince. Therefore, no one ought
to receive homage or fealty from anyone else unless reserving
higher fealty to the prince. This is also to be explicitly stated in
receiving their fealty.
2. Between other lords and their vassals, faith ought so to be maintained that neither one of them ought to call for corporal violence
or for violent blows against the person of another party. If any of
them should be accused of this in court and convicted, he is bound
altogether to lose his fief for violating the faith he was obligated to
observe.
3. If this act should be discovered in a lord, homage should revert
to his superior and dues should no longer be given, excepting what
is owed the prince.

4. If, however, a vassal should be shown guilty of this, he shall be deprived of his land and right, which shall remain to the lord. It is of course understood that they will be clearly convicted of this in court, as the custom of Normandy requires.

22 bis. Concerning the army

1. Service in the army is to be done with arms for the benefit of the prince as it has been customary in fiefs and in towns. This service is for forty days in defense of the land and for the prince's need, when he sets forth in any expedition; those who hold fiefs or live in towns delegated for this service ought to and are bound to perform it. For all knight's fees [fiefs of a knight] instituted for the service of the duchy must fulfill this service; counties and baronies also, as well as all towns having a commune.

2. Knight's fees in the counties and baronies which were not established for the service of the duchy do not owe service in the army, but only to the lords to whom they are subjected, excepting, however, the general levy of the prince [*retrobanium*], to which all who are capable of bearing arms are bound to come without any excuse.

3. The general levy is said to occur when the duke of Normandy, in order to repel an attack of the enemy in any expedition, goes through Normandy and orders that all who are capable of wielding arms should arm themselves for his help, no matter in what sort of arms they may be found, in order to repel the enemy. However, after forty days are completed in the service of the prince, if the need of the prince should demand it, they shall remain in his service at the expense of the prince, as reason should require.

4. No one who owes this service may by any manner excuse himself from service in the army of the prince, unless by the evident impairment of his own body, and then he is bound to send a substitute who can perform for him the service which he owes.

5. At times the name of military aid is given to that monetary payment which the prince of Normandy allows his barons and knights to collect from their [subvassals] who hold from them a knight's fee or from their tenants on a knight's fee, if his barons and knights have served more than forty days. And they were not otherwise able to demand from their tenants a greater aid than that which was conceded to them by the prince of the Normans.

6. Concerning the fiefs which pertain to the duchy, if anyone should deny that any land or fief is of this sort, inquiry ought to be

made through the prince or his bailiffs concerning the truth of the matter without any exception; since the service of these fiefs belongs to the duke, in any diminution of a fief not providing due service the duke may suffer damage. If it is decided that it is a knight's fee, the one holding it is bound to do that service to the prince according to the size of his possession. And this is to be understood not only concerning the fiefs of the prince, but also the fiefs of the barons which pertain to the duchy.

7. It is to be noted also that the barons hold certain fiefs assigned to the service of the duke; they were established before these baronies were granted. These types of fiefs must fulfill service with the barons; whoever does this service fulfills it at the prince's will.

8. The barons ought not to have from the other fiefs, which were not established for the service of the duchy, more than the aid conceded by the prince, as has been said. If perchance they have fiefs so constituted so that one or two, three, or four or more of them ought to provide the service of a single knight for the duke, each of them according to its size should perform and pay a portion of the service, as the barons and the knights may assign to them. Nevertheless, each of them shall be bound to relief and aid for the service of their lords. For although fiefs of this sort are considered as a single unit in regard to the duke's service, nonetheless they are many in relation to the homage owed their lord, and each of them in this respect retains the dignity of a single fief.

9. From all this it is evident that not without reason at the time of English rule it was customary in Normandy that all men holding a knight's fee were bound to possess a horse and armor and that, when they reached the age of twenty-one, they were bound to be enlisted among the knights, so that they would be found ready and prepared at the command of the prince or of their lords.

26. On tenures

1. Concerning tenures the following is to be done.

The tenure is the manner by which tenements are held from their lords.

2. Certain tenures are held through homage, others through parage, others through burgage, and others through alms.

3. Fiefs held through homage are those in which the observance of faith between the lord and his vassal is expressly promised, reserving the higher faith due to the duke of Normandy. This is received

from the lord with his hands outstretched and the hands of the one making the homage placed between them; this is explained more fully in the following chapter.

4. Fiefs are held through parage when a brother or a relative receives a part of the inheritances of his ancestors, which he holds from an older relative. The older relative is in turn responsible for all the individual obligations which the portions of the fief require and which are due to its principal lords. This is made clear below.

5. By burgage are held allods and tenures established in cities which have the customs of burgesses.

6. In alms are held lands given in charity to churches.

7. Besides these, in different parts of Normandy exist fiefs held by bordage, when a cottage is given to anyone for the performance of servile labors and mean services. This holding cannot be sold or given or pledged by the one who received it in inheritance under this sort of tenure, and he does not do homage.

8. There are also held certain free tenements without homage or parage in lay fief. This situation results from an agreement made between certain persons. For example, if a person holds a fief paying twenty shillings a year, and gives half of it to a third party, that third party holds it from him and not from [the lord who] holds homage over it. The third party shall perform no homage as the total fief is considered to be held by a single homage from the lord. This kind of tenure is called voluntary, since it results from the wishes of the ones giving and receiving it and not from the necessity of inheritance.

9. It is also to be noted that certain tenures are of monetary payments, as when someone holds a rent assigned to him while the land remains to the one who holds it.

Certain tenures are of land, such as when one holds of another the fief of the land of another.

Certain tenures are of an office, such as when one holds a certain office from another, for example, holding a warren or a privilege in forests, in markets, or in other places, or holding a sergeancy, or a fine or anything else, which are held from the lords without the possession of lands.

27. On homage

1. Now homage is to be considered. Homage is the promise of keeping faith, offering no obstruction in just and necessary things

but rather providing counsel and aid. It is performed by extending and joining the hands and placing them within the hands of the one receiving homage, with these words: "I become your vassal to bear for you faith against all others, reserving only the fealty owed to the duke of Normandy."

2. It is to be noted that a certain type of homage concerns a fief, another type faith and service, and another type the preservation of the peace.

3. Homage concerning a fief is performed in the manner described above.

4. Homage concerning faith and service is performed when one person receives another as his vassal who is to keep faith to him and to give him service of his own body, to fight for him if necessary, and to do other service of this sort. And if, in return for this, he gives him a pension, this shall not pass on to his heirs unless it is explicitly stated by a condition made between them. Also, if the one serving should perchance succumb while fighting for the other, the pension shall revert to the lord. It is to be understood that he shall hold for his entire life that fief which was conferred upon him by his lord, for whom, upon entering a fight, he succumbed on the field.

And this type of homage is done in the manner described above, with, however, these added words: "Reserving faith to all my other lords."

5. A homage is also sometimes performed for preserving the peace; it is called homage of payment [*paga*], because it was performed as a pledge of peace between certain persons, such as when one person pursues another for any criminal act and peace is agreed on between them, so that the one who prosecuted does homage to the other for conserving that peace. This sort of homage is received as a pledge agreed upon.

And this type of homage is performed in the manner described above with, however, these words stated and heard: "Saving the faith of all my other lords and especially for preserving the peace."

6. In homage it is also implied that the vassal be a guarantor to the lords. For the vassal is bound to provide security for his lord in any court if he should be prosecuted for personal injury and shall appear before a justice at the assigned time. He should extend to the lord a sum equal to the rent he owes him for one year, from his movables, pledges to be paid, debts, and loans.

7. The lord has the right of judgment over all the fiefs which are held from him, whether they are held indirectly or directly.

For certain fiefs are held directly of the lords, as are those which a man holds from his lord, with no other person between them.

Those fiefs are held indirectly when some person comes between the lord and the tenant. And by this manner, all descendants hold fiefs through an older relative, and all tenants hold fiefs under a vassal who is bound by homage to the lord.

8. No one can do justice upon the fief of another unless it is held from him.

9. It should also be noted that no one may sell or pledge the land which he holds of the lord through homage without the special consent of the lord. In regard to a third part or less, many have been accustomed to sell or pledge land, since enough land remained for them in fief through which they were able to fulfill and pay fully to their lords all rights, services, jurisdictions, and offices.

28. On tenure by parage

1. Tenure by parage occurs when the one holding and the one from whom the property is held happen to be equals, by reason of relationship, in the portions of the inheritance deriving from their ancestors. And by this manner those born later hold from those born before up to the sixth degree of kinship; in that degree they are obligated to do fealty to the one born earlier; in the seventh degree of kinship he shall be held to do homage and to hold by homage what was formerly held by parage.

2. The one born earlier may exercise justice over those born later for the dues and services which pertain to the lord of the fief. He cannot exercise justice for other reasons, saving only in three cases, that is, for injury caused to his person or to his first-born or to his wife.

29. On tenure by burgage

1. Concerning tenures by burgage it is to be understood that they can be sold and purchased, just as movable property, without the consent of the lord, and the fees from them ought to be paid according to the custom of the towns.

2. It is also to be noted that the sales of these tenures cannot be revoked by heirs or relatives.

3. It is also to be noted that widows have a half of the sales of this sort of tenure made in their lifetime by their husbands, [which they may claim] from the heirs of their husbands after their husbands' death.

4. Note also that sisters in holdings of this type receive an equal portion with brothers.

5. Note also that holdings of this sort do not provide the usual reliefs or aids in Normandy.

6. Many things held by burgage tenure are also held through homage; this, however, is not done by the customs of the towns, but through an agreement among their possessors. And although the agreement among them ought to be observed, nonetheless, as far as pertains to others, it ought to be considered as tenure by burgage, and it shall retain all the conditions of burgage tenure unless an express condition made in the contract was clearly opposed.

30. Concerning tenure by alms

1. Those who hold lands given in full charity to God and those serving God are said to hold by alms. In this situation the donors retain nothing whatsoever for themselves or their heirs, unless only a right of patronage, and [the recipients] hold from them by alms as from patrons.

2. No one may grant from any land which does not belong to him. Therefore, it is to be noted that neither the duke nor the baron nor anyone, if his men should grant from the lands which they hold from him, may for this reason suffer any injury and, in spite of the grant, the lord shall exercise justice in the lands granted and shall claim his rights.

And it is also to be noted that since the duke has justice and rights of his lordship in the lands of all his subjects, he alone can make the alms free or pure [*frankalmoign*].

3. Many lands have been granted which are held by the peasants possessing them as a lay fief and not by alms; that which laymen hold in them as their own retains the condition of a lay fief. But when peasants are known to hold lands which were given in alms, those things are alms and are to be held in the manner of alms.

4. That which in the manner of alms or as alms has been possessed peacefully without interruption for a space of thirty years is clearly subject to the jurisdiction of the ecclesiastical court. And if

a dispute arises concerning this, it ought to be settled in the court of the duke by an inquisition. For since the jurisdiction of fiefs is known to pertain to the duke of Normandy, disputes arising over them, concerning their manner of tenure, ought to be settled in the duke's court.

32. Concerning reliefs

1. After the above, it is to be noted that the lords of fiefs ought to have reliefs for the lands which are held from them in homage at the passing or the death of those from whom they have the homage.
2. However, men in Normandy may retire in two ways: they may enter religion and renounce all worldly possessions, in which case the inheritance passes to their heirs, and relief and a new homage issues from the heir; or they give the fief to others, retaining nothing in it, whether by a sale or something of the sort, in which case relief and new homage follows. Therefore, it is clear that relief is implicit in homage. For wherever relief is paid, it is necessary that there should also be homage. But the opposite need not be true. For there are many fiefs in various parts of Normandy such as immunities, franchises, and many other offices, which are not subjected to relief; although they require homage, nevertheless they do not pay relief.
3. It is to be known that in fiefs through the whole of Normandy relief is generally defined: in knight's fiefs, fifteen pounds; in baronies, one hundred pounds; and in acres of land under cultivation, the relief is twelve pennies per acre. It is, however, to be understood that a household pays a relief of three shillings, and by this, it frees the first acre of the entire tenement even if there is not a full acre.
4. It is to be known that in various parts of Normandy according to the various customs of taking relief in them, lands which publicly are not subject to cultivation are subject to a variety of reliefs. These lands are to pay relief according to the various traditions observed since antiquity, such as in mills and ovens which are held of themselves without any tenements.

However, mills which have banal rights attached, if they are held of themselves without any fief, customarily pay sixty shillings in relief. If, however, the mills are held together with a knight's fief, to which a sergeancy or a *vavassoria* or other free fiefs pertain, in

the payment of the fief's relief, the relief of the mill is also satisfied.
5. Other possessions preserve other customs concerning relief, such as forests and wooded land which have never been subjected to cultivation; many of these in various parts of Normandy customarily pay relief in union with other holdings.
6. Concerning wooded lands which in Normandy are called dead lands, relief in many places is paid at the rate of six pennies per acre.
7. It is to be noted that at the death of the person who holds in homage from a lord, relief is paid by the heir who succeeds him; and with his passing, in making new homage for the same, the fief is released by the lord.
8. Aid in relief is owed when the lord dies and the heir of this same lord who held the fief secures its release from the chief lord. The aid given ought to be one-half of the value of the relief of the fief held. Therefore, it is to be generally known that all fiefs which owe relief also owe aid in relief at the death of the lord of those tenants. This aid is due to the heirs of the lords, and thus they help them and are bound to help them in releasing their fief from the superior lord.
9. Therefore, it should be noted that certain fiefs are held directly from the prince, and others indirectly. The former are those which are called tenancies-in-chief, such as counties and baronies, and knight's fiefs and free sergeancies and other fiefs which are held in chief and are not subjected to any knight's fief.

To the lords of this sort of fief are owed the three principal aids of Normandy.

Fiefs held indirectly are those which descend from the tenancies-in-chief and are subjected to them, such as servile *vavassorie*, which are held in return for carrying services or for a male horse, and other fiefs which are held according to acres from the chief lord.
10. It is to be noted that for the voluntary retirement of the lord, unless it should be done for the profession of religion, through which he is unable to return to any earthly possession, aid in relief is not owed. Thus, aid is not required when one sells his land or grants it to his son or to an heir, who then does homage to the chief lord and pays relief. The vassals of the fief shall not be bound to pay aid in fief for this, since their lord is not retiring forever, even though to the world he is reputed entirely dead.

33. Concerning the chief aids

1. After the above, now the chief aids of Normandy are to be considered. They are called the chief aids because they are to be rendered to the chief lords.

2. The chief aids of Normandy are three: the first when the first-born son of the lord is elevated to the order of knighthood; the second, when the first-born daughter of the lord is to be married; the third, when the body of the lord is to be ransomed from prison when he is captured in a war of the duke of Normandy.

3. Aids of this sort are in certain fiefs equal to one-half the relief. And in other fiefs, to a third part of the relief.

Vavassorie in some fiefs are accustomed to pay ten shillings in aid. For since a diversity of aids is accustomed to follow a diversity of lords, the customs preserved since antiquity concerning the payment of aids are scrupulously to be observed.

4. It is to be known that if any tenancy-in-chief should be distributed into portions among relatives, each of the sharers in his portion ought to be considered as chief lord and ought to receive payment of the chief aids.

5. It is also to be noted that subtenants are not bound to pay aid to the chief lord, but they are bound to help the intermediate lord to pay his aid to the chief lord. And such aid is called subaid [*subauxilium*] and ought to be one-half the chief aid.

33. Law, custom, and justice, according to Philippe de Beaumanoir

Another of the important codifications of the thirteenth century was the *Coutumes de Beauvaisis*, or, more precisely, the customs of the count of Clermont in the Beauvaisis, in northwest France, substantially written between 1280 and 1283. The uniqueness of the collection is that its author, Philippe de Remi, sire de Beaumanoir, offered an extensive commentary on the customs he was treating, and thus made of his collection a work which was studied by practicing lawyers for the extent of the *ancien régime* and retains great interest for historians today. Philippe de Beaumanoir apparently had no formal legal training but had gained much experience in the administration of the county, and besides his legal interests, he was a poet of some accomplishment. In the following selections, the author states his reasons for redacting customs, hitherto preserved orally, into writing, and discourses on the nature of high and low justice, custom, and usage. The translation, by D. Herlihy, is based on the text in Philippe de Beaumanoir, *Coutumes de Beauvaisis: Texte critique publié avec une introduction, un glossaire et une table analytique*, ed. A. Salmon (Paris, 1899–1900).

Here begins the books of the customs and the usages of Beauvaisis.

Here is the prologue.

1. The great hope which we have for help from Him by Whom all things are made and without Whom nothing could have been made—that is, the Father and the Son and the Holy Spirit, three very holy and very precious beings comprising one sole God in Trinity—gives us the desire to place our spirit and our understanding in study and in thought, to compose a book by which those who wish to live in peace will be briefly instructed how they may defend themselves from those who wrongly and for unjust reason may assault them in court, and how they may know the law of torts used and practiced in the county of Clermont in the Beauvaisis. And since we are from that district and we have undertaken to respect and make respected the rights and the customs of the said county, by the will of the preeminent and very noble Robert, son of the king of France, count of Clermont, we should have a greater will to compile the customs of the said district rather than of any other. Let us consider three principal reasons which should move us to this.

2. The first reason is that God commanded us that we should love our neighbor as ourselves. The inhabitants of this district are our neighbors by reason of proximity and birth, and are thereby related to us. It seems to us very profitable if our labor by the help of God can offer them this book, in which they can learn to attain their rights and to eschew wrong.

3. The second reason is that we can accomplish, with the help of God, something which may please our lord the count and those of

his council, since, if God pleases, by this book he can learn how he ought to keep and enforce the customs of his land of the county of Clermont so that his vassals and the humble people can live in peace under him. By this instruction, dishonest and deceiving men will be recognized in their deceptions and in their treachery be thrown back by the law and by the count's justice.

4. The third reason is that we ought to have a better memory of that which we have seen practiced and judged since our infancy in our district rather than in another district, of which we have not learned the customs or the usages.

5. We do not, of course, expect to have in ourselves the intelligence by which we might complete this book and this undertaking. But often many men have begun good works and did not have the intelligence to finish them; still, God, Who knew their hearts and their intentions, granted them His grace, so that they easily finished that which seemed to them so difficult at the start. And in Holy Scripture He said: "Begin, and I will finish."

6. In the confidence that He will finish and that we can acquire His good will for the trouble and the work which we invest in it, we have begun to write. We intend to base a large part of this book upon the judgments made in our time in the said county of Clermont; and partially upon the clear usages and the clear customs practiced and followed peacefully here for a long time; partially, too, in dubious cases in the said county, upon the judgments made in neighboring jurisdictions [*chasteleries*]; and partially upon the law which is common to the entire kingdom of France. If anyone wishes to know who it was who commenced this book, we do not want to name ourselves before the end of the work, if God grants that we bring it to an end. For sometimes good wines are rejected when the region is named where they grew, for the reason that one does not believe that such lands could produce a good wine. We also fear that if our name were known too early, our work would be valued little because of the little intelligence that is within us.

7. But since we see that the customs of regions are respected and prevail over the ancient laws, we, and others too, believe that all the customs which are followed could well and profitably be written and registered. They may thus be maintained without alteration from this time forward. Since memories are fallible, and the lives of persons are short, that which is not written is soon forgotten. Moreover, it also appears that customs are so diverse that

one cannot find in the kingdom of France two jurisdictions [*chasteleries*] which in every case follow the same customs. Therefore, one should not cease to learn and to retain the customs of the land in which one is resident, since one can learn and retain these more easily than others, and equally, in many cases, they may be consistent in many jurisdictions.

8. One who has need of accomplishing what he cannot accomplish without the aid of the king of France, and is so undeserving toward the king that he fears rejection if he seeks it without help, willingly seeks the aid and the benevolence of those of his council to aid him in his petition to the king. So also it is more necessary without comparison that we call to our aid the men and the women who are in the company of the King of paradise, in order to aid us to petition the Lord of heaven and of earth. Let us call upon the blessed Virgin Mary, who better and more insistently may petition her Son than anyone else, and then all the men and the women saints together and singly. In this prayer we have confidence that God will help us in this work and in all our other works. Let us commence now our book in the manner which follows.

Here ceases the prologue of this book.

Chapter 24

Here begins the twenty-fourth chapter of this book which teaches what custom is and what usage is, and which usages are valid and which are not.

682. Since all pleas are conducted according to custom, and since this book generally speaks according to the customs of the county of Clermont, we shall say in this chapter briefly what is custom, and what ought to be held as custom, even though we have already spoken in other chapters specifically concerning what is suitable in the cases of which we have spoken. Let us also speak of usages and what usage is valid and what is not, and of the difference which exists between usage and custom.

683. Custom is recognized by one of two ways. The first is when it is universal in the entire county and upheld for such a long time that it can be recalled by a person without argument, as, for example, when a certain person admits a debt and is ordered to pay it within seven days and seven nights, or a nobleman within fifteen days. This custom is so clear that I have never seen it questioned. The second way by which custom can be recognized and main-

tained is when an argument occurs concerning it and one of the parties wishes to take advantage of the custom and is supported by court decision. For example, this situation frequently occurs in instances of the division among heirs and in other disputes. By these two ways custom can be recognized. These customs the count is obligated to respect and to have his subjects respect, so that none violate them. And if the count himself wishes to violate them or to allow that they be violated, the king ought not to permit it, for he is obligated to respect the customs of his kingdom and to have them respected.

684. The difference between custom and usage is that all customs are to be maintained, but there are usages of such a nature that if someone wishes to plead against them and go to a court decision, the usage may prove to be of no value. Now let us see which usages are valid and which are not.

685. The usage of a year and a day of peaceful possession suffices to establish seisin [legal possession], as, for example, when someone has worked land—or a vineyard or other real estate—and peacefully has taken its fruit for one year and a day. If another comes who would prohibit him, the lord ought to remove the prohibition, if he is requested, and to maintain him in his seisin until such time as he loses the ownership of the real estate in a full trial.

686. The second type of usage concerns the peaceful tenure of a piece of property for ten years in the view and with the knowledge of those who then would wish to prohibit this. Such types of usage are valid in acquiring ownership and seisin of the property. But one should show with the usage a sufficient cause by which the property was acquired, such as purchase, gift, legacy, forfeit, or inheritance. Also, he should show that the property is held from the lord by some rent which is due him.

687. The third type of usage is peaceful tenure for thirty years, since he who can say that he has held a possession for thirty years is not obligated to show the cause by which he acquired it. And thus his tenure is valid without any other reason being advanced, except that which is held as a dowry or for life or for leasehold or as a pledge. . . .

688. Now let us see which usages are not valid. When the lord sees any of his subjects holding property for which he pays to no one a quitrent, rents, or dues, the lord may lay hands upon it and hold it as his own property, since no one according to our custom may

hold allods; an allod is land which is held without the holder's making payment to anyone. And if the count perceives before any of his subjects that such allods are held in his county, he may seize them as his own and is not obligated to return them or to answer for them to any of his subjects, for the reason that he is lord in his own right of all that which he finds held as an allod. If any of his subjects has laid hands upon it, he ought not to retain it unless he proves that this was from his fief or from that which ought to have been held from him, which he found concealed or taken from him. If he cannot prove it, the allod should remain for the count, nor can he who held it as an allod aid himself by long usage. And therefore, I well recommend to those who hold in such a manner that before the count lays hands upon their belongings, they go to make homage to the count or to render some payment at the pleasure of the said count. And in this case, if they so act, they ought not to lose their holdings, but rather they ought to possess them with the count's good will, since they have clarified those things which their ancestors held improperly.

689. My lord Pierre de Tiverny complained against the town of Les Hayes that the said town, wrongly and without reason, sent its beasts to graze in his meadows, in which he held all justice and lordship. Since the townspeople did not pay quitrent or rent or dues for this usage, he asked that they be prohibited from this practice and that it be stated to them in law that they had no right to do this. To this the townsmen responded that they had followed this practice and had maintained it for as long a time as memory of man could recall, and that this their practice had been well known to the said Lord Pierre. For this reason they asked that they be allowed peacefully to do as they had done for a long time. On this point they went to court.

690. The vassals of Creil, after they had taken all their delays, and after they had consulted in many places, pronounced in judgment that the said town of Les Hayes had no right of use in the meadows of my lord Pierre mentioned above. The long usages which they had put forward were worth nothing to them, since they did not render quitrent, rent, or dues for the said usage. From this judgment, it may be seen that no usage which damages another is valid against the lord of the place where the usage is maintained if there is not rendered to the lord, or to the count, rent, quitrents, or dues. . . .

692. No usage which is used against the general custom of the land is worth anything unless it is granted and confirmed by the sovereign or unless there is rendered to the sovereign some of his rights, that is to say, quitrent, rent, or payments. . . .

Chapter 58

Here commences the fifty-eighth chapter of this book which speaks of high and low justice, and of the cases which appertain to one and to the other, and how it is necessary that each works its own justice.

1641. We said in the chapter which speaks of the jurisdictions which the count of Clermont possesses over his men that all the men of the county of Clermont who hold in fief have in their fief high and low justice. So also do those churches which have been held in free possession for a long time without paying dues to anyone. Nonetheless, there are many districts in which some persons hold high justice and other persons have low justice, and even in the Beauvaisis this can happen by sale or by exchange or by grant of the lord, so that one person can have in a certain place high justice and another person low justice. Therefore, we may well briefly describe what is high justice and what is low justice, so that each may use that justice which appertains to him.

1642. One should know that every case of crime, no matter what it be, for which the one who is seized and convicted for it may and should lose his life appertains to high justice, excepting robbery. For although it may be that the thief loses his life for his robbery, nonetheless, robbery is not a case of high justice. But every other foul case is, such as murder, treason, homicide, forcible rape, destruction of goods by fire or by robbing them at night, and every case which involves wage of battle, and counterfeiting and all acts of consent or of instigation thereto. All such deeds belong to high justice. Thus, when any such cases occur, the cognizance and the justice belongs to him to whom high justice ought to belong. And the cognizance of thefts and of all other crimes in which there is no risk of capital punishment belongs to him to whom low justice belongs. The justice which should be done in the above-mentioned cases and of many others which we do not here mention is elucidated in the chapter which speaks of crimes, and so there is no reason that we speak of them further.

1643. As we have described which cases of crime ought to be

judged by him who has high justice, so also there are certain profits which ought to be his by reason of high justice, as, for example, all the possessions of those who are convicted for any of the above-mentioned cases. But it is to be understood those possessions should be in the territory of the one holding high justice. Everyone who has high justice in his land may take whatever possessions are found in his territory which belong to such malefactors.

1644. Property which is found, and wrecks which have no claimants, and that which comes from bastards to the lord for the reason that they have no family, and that which comes from foreigners when without family no one advances a claim—all these things ought to go to the lord who has the high justice and nothing to him who has the low unless he gain it by long custom, or because it was given to him by privilege. This is the situation in many places where the lords have granted to certain churches all such profits while retaining high justice in that which they gave.

1645. He who has high justice cannot forbid to him who has low justice that he or his sergeant go armed to maintain that which appertains to low justice. Nor can he who has low justice forbid to him who has high that he or his sergeant go [armed] to maintain that which appertains to high justice, since it is licit for each to maintain his right without doing wrong to the other.

1646. It often happens that confused cases occur, concerning which it cannot immediately be known whether the case belongs to high justice or to low, as happens when a heated fight occurs among persons. In those fights, wounds may be inflicted so that it cannot be immediately known if the injured persons will recover from the wounds or will die. And since there is doubt, if the malefactors who inflicted the wounds are taken, they should be put in the prison of him who has the high justice for forty days. Within that period, those who are going to die from wounds should be dead. And if the wounded person recovers, he who has the high justice should return the prisoners to him who has low, to profit from the damages according to the crime. If the wounded person should die from the wound inflicted on him, punishment for the crime belongs to him who has high justice.

1647. Truces broken and peace agreements violated are clearly cases of high justice; therefore, truces ought to be established and peace agreements made upon request by those who have high justice and not by those who have low. And since those who have only low justice cannot force persons to conclude a truce or enter a peace agreement, therefore they ought not to have cognizance of infractions which may occur. . . .

1649. When someone is suspected of any of the major cases of crime mentioned above, whether by presumption or accusation, flight or nonappearance at the court sessions, all the things which ought to be done for his condemnation or acquittal should be done by him who has high justice in the judgment of his court. Nor can he who has low justice forbid that his property be seized or that he be arrested or that he be summoned to justice or that he be banished after he shall have been summoned as custom warrants. But if the accused or the suspect can clear himself, he should be released and should be restored to that status in which he was before. Nevertheless, if he should have suffered some damage for the seizures which were done to him for the suspicion of the misdeed, or because he was put in prison, his lord who has high justice over him for what was done in the process is not bound to compensate him for his damages. . . .

1653. The jurisdictions of several lords are intertwined and mixed one with the others. Those who are responsible to maintain their jurisdictions cannot at times do this unless they pass within the jurisdiction of another. We have noted several times above that some lords wish to disturb the sergeants of other lords, so that they do not pass within their jurisdiction carrying arms, whether bows or arrows or swords or hatchets or axes, or other prohibited arms. But since it behooves that those who undertake to preserve justice be armed so that they can apprehend those who act against justice, and because they cannot easily go without passing on another's land, we have made an ordinance and have enforced it in our custom of Clermont and in our time in such a manner that if it is suitable for one to pass in arms through another's jurisdiction, he may carry his arms in the manner which follows. That is to say, if he wishes to carry bow and arrows, he should carry the bow unstrung and the arrows in his hand or in a quiver; and if he wishes to carry a sword, he should carry it sheathed or in his coat and not in view, and if he wishes to carry a hatchet or ax, he should carry it under his saddle or lowered to the ground until such time as he emerges from the other's jurisdiction. . . .

1662. The count and all those who hold in barony possess the right over their vassals, by reason of the sovereign, by which, if they have need of the castle of their vassals, for their war or to place their prisoners or their garrisons or to keep them or for the common profit of the land, they may take them. Nonetheless, they must take them in such a manner for the above-stated reason that they do no injury to their vassals, as, for example, if they pretend that they take them for any of the reasons stated above, and this was not the truth. For if the count should say, "I have taken it to aid me in my war," and he had no war, then it would appear that he did it in order to harm his vassal. Also, if he should take it to place his prisoners and allows them to stay there a long time when he could easily make amends (if, for example, he could easily remove them from there and take them to his own prison), in such cases he would harm his vassal. Also, if he pretends that he has a certain need and he has hated or made threats against him to whom the castle belongs or if he did it so that he could do villainy with his wife or daughter or another woman who would be in his guard— in all these cases he does injury. As soon as he does this harm and does not wish to desist at the request of his vassal, if the vassal denounces it to the king, the king ought to allow a full hearing between the lord and his vassal in this case. He ought immediately to learn the reason for which the lord has seized the fortress of his vassal; and if he sees that he has seized it for reasonable cause or for his lawful need, he should allow it; if not, he ought to take it and return it to his vassal, prohibit the lord from harming it in any manner, and order him not to take it again unless it be for clear and obvious need.

1663. If he who holds in barony takes the castle of his man for his need, this should not be at the expense of his vassal. For if he places garrisons, this ought to be at his own cost, and if he has prisoners there, he should have them guarded at his own [expense]. And if he damages the castle in any way, he should repair it at his own expense. And if he improves it in order to make it stronger or more elegant for his own needs, his vassal is not obligated to return anything, since it was not done by him, even though he benefits from it.

Part Three

The Feudal Principality

Introduction

From the eleventh century on, many princes in the European West—counts, dukes, and kings—show a new effort, energy, and success in strengthening their own authority and reorganizing their principalities. In this work of reconstruction, part of much broader changes then occurring in European life, feudal institutions were central. Vassalage and the fief, to be sure, had developed spontaneously, largely without a consciously imposed design or direction, within a milieu dominated by disorders. But they remained deeply rooted in the consciousness and behavior of the people, and they offered these self-conscious rulers a means of redefining and more rigorously enforcing the obligations which, they now insisted, their subjects owed. Feudal institutions, in one sense the products of the disintegration of the state, thus became the instruments by which the state was strengthened.

Political reconstruction

The Carolingian rulers, in their desperate and futile efforts to hold together and defend their vast territories, made, as we have seen (Document 12), some use of feudal institutions. For example, they sought to stabilize society by insisting that each freeman find himself a lord, and that lords make sure that their vassals acted in the emperor's interest. But the Carolingian state made no systematic use of feudal practices, and it did not at all events survive the invasions and the civil strife of the late ninth and tenth centuries.

This disintegration of the empire affected the institutions of local administration as well as those of the central government. The Carolingians had relied on an administration based on counties, under an appointed official, the count or viscount, and under them on a division called most commonly the *vicaria*. This was administered by a "vicar" of the count. From the tenth century, at different times in different parts of Europe, there becomes evident in the sources a new kind of local administrative unit, with a new sort of lord set over it. This was the castle and its territory, and the lord who ruled it was the castellan. It was once thought that the great spate of castle building in Europe was a direct reaction to the Viking invasions. Today, historians are not so sure, as the castles seem to have multiplied most rapidly at a time when the momentum of the invasions had already considerably ebbed. Some castles were built on the authorization, even with the financial aid, of the count or king (Document 35), but many others were constructed by no one's permission or fiat. The masters of castles, as they built and ruled, imposed dues and rents upon the surrounding population; these dues were called in hundreds of charters, by those opposed to them, *malae consuetudines*, "bad customs."

The castles and the men who made and controlled them came by the early eleventh century to dominate large areas of the European countryside. The castellans were a tumultuous group, constantly feuding with the counts above them, with neighboring religious institutions, or with one another. The exact social origins of this class of castellans are not precisely known. Most historians have considered them to be self-made men who with force and energy benefited from the opportunities which weak government and much chaos offered. Recent research is, however, at least suggesting a frequent link between castellans and the great families of the region prominent since the Carolingian epoch. Self-made or not, the castellans brought with them a new administrative unit and new problems for those higher lords committed to constructing a more ordered society.

Against this background from ca. 1050 the greater lords began undertaking not so much to destroy the castles as to superimpose order and loyalty upon their masters and to integrate their territories into a stable principality. One great force in this effort to give a larger structure to these moving atoms of feudal society was the Church. The rise of the castellans had paralleled, and in some measure caused, acute disorders in the administration of the Church and the morality of its clergy. These tough warriors had scant respect for either Church lands or Church institutions. They dominated their local churches and monasteries, imposed their own candidates on important offices, and ruthlessly pillaged the ecclesiastical endowment. Amid chaos and impoverishment, the morale and morality of many clerics sank, and vices such as simony (the buying or selling of ecclesiastical offices or services) and clerical concubinage ran rampant among them. The sad plight of the Church seemed to call into jeopardy the salvation of men, and the way was paved for a powerful reaction.

Reaction came in what is usually called the Gregorian reform, named for its greatest leader, Pope Gregory VII (1073–1085). The reformers took as their supreme goal the *libertas ecclesiae*, the freeing of the Church from the domination of the local lay magnates and eventually, daringly, from the tutelage of the emperor. The same men were prime movers in efforts to restrict warfare, which we shall subsequently consider: the Peace of God and the Truce of God (Document 48). Further, they were the great propagandists for the Crusades to the East, which might relieve Europe of its dangerous and disruptive surplus of warriors. As Bernard of Clairvaux was to say in effect (Document 49), the Crusades made holy in the East those men who at home were recognized murderers.

Princes too, from the same period, nearly always with the support of the Church, aimed at imposing discipline upon the castellans, thus to construct ordered and cohesive states. This work of political reorganization progressed most rapidly in the lands between the Loire River and the Rhine, where a number of effectively governed and administered principalities grew up in the eleventh century—the counties of Flanders and Anjou, the duchies of Normandy and Champagne, the royal Ile-de-France. This spirit of rebuilding and some of the institutions which implemented it were exported through Norman pilgrims to southern Italy beginning in the early eleventh century, through Norman conquerors to England in 1066, and through Norman crusaders to the Levant from 1095. In all these principalities, the common policy of princes was to insist that all freemen recognize them as their liege or chief lords, and that all lands be considered fiefs held from them, in return for loyalty and service. The bad subject was also a bad vassal, violating the heavy moral obligations which vassalage imposed, and liable to lose his lands as a fief in forfeit.

Of this remarkable work of state building, one of the best examples is offered by Norman and Angevin England. Historians have, to be sure, long debated whether the Normans truly brought feudalism to England with the Conquest of 1066. Recent research has stressed the debt which Norman England owed to its Anglo-Saxon past. The Normans left virtually intact the institutions of local administration based on the shire and the sheriff, and kept even such national institutions as the Danegeld and the *fyrd* (general levy of freemen). Historians have traditionally stressed the importance of knight service as the cornerstone of Norman feudalism, which implied a tie between tenure and service and imposed quotas of knights upon the great baronies. But there seem to have been some Anglo-Saxon precedents even for this, and some historians question whether, in the twelfth century, mercenaries were not already more important than feudal levies in the English armies.

Certainly, William the Conqueror (king, 1066–1087) brought no grand design for the reform of England. He was fundamentally a pragmatist, adopting or adapting what suited his needs. On the other hand, it would be naïve to discount the Norman contribution to the growth of a strong English monarchy and government. Acting with the freedom of a conqueror, William imposed a new aristocracy on England. He rigorously insisted upon his own rights and defined those rights by feudal concepts. Through the Salisbury Oath, he claimed from all freeholders recognition as their supreme lord. Perhaps the greatest achievement of his reign was the redaction in 1086 of the Domesday Book (Document 37), which was designed to show the king what lands he held and what his barons owed him. William's high sense of his own rights and prerogatives has left historians with an administrative miracle, which punctiliously surveys the lands and population of the realm. Nothing on the continent approaches it in comprehensiveness, and even in England itself, no document of comparable quality exists for the entire length of the Middle Ages, and indeed for some centuries beyond.

Next to, and perhaps surpassing, William in the making of the medieval English constitution was Henry II Angevin, called also

Plantagenet (1154–1189), although some of his reforms had been anticipated by his grandfather Henry I (1100–1135). Henry II's administrative accomplishments were twofold. Under him, the institutions of central administration, based on the *curia regis*, or royal court, grew more specialized and more effective. We have in fact the beginnings of a true bureaucracy, staffed by highly skilled and committed men. Then too, on the local level, Henry succeeded in making the royal courts, royal justice, and royal power available and evident even to the humblest freemen.

The history of central administration in any medieval kingdom is largely the history of the transformations of the *curia regis*, the king's own court. The English court technically included all the king's great vassals, and on certain plenary and solemn sessions held through the year many of these magnates were in attendance. But between these plenary sessions, a small or restricted *curia* carried on the work of administration; it included the chief officials of the palace, and actually anyone whom the king invited to attend. From Henry II's time, the meetings of the small *curia* assumed specialized forms, according to the business to be transacted. We are in fact witnessing the emergence of distinct bureaus of central government, although they were long in severing ties with the parent body. The first specialized bureau to appear was the Exchequer; although it included a subordinate accounting office, the Exchequer was primarily a court which heard cases dealing with royal finance. Another specialized bureau was the Court of the King's Bench, which is clearly recognizable as a separate court only after Henry's death; it dealt primarily with cases, both civil and criminal, in which the king or his officials were principals. The Court of Common Pleas, which concerned itself exclusively with civil litigation between private persons, was the third principal specialization of the *curia regis*. All these branches employed many of the same persons, and it is impossible to date when precisely they became independent of their parent body. But they do illustrate the progress of specialization and also the professionalization of the central administration. Government was slowly but unmistakably becoming a matter for experts, trained for their tasks, committed to them, and substantially contributing to the growth of royal government.

Perhaps still more remarkable are Henry's reforms touching on local administration. Here the central figure was the "justice in eyre" (*in itinere*, "on the journey"), who roamed on fixed circuits at regular intervals through England and carried with him the full authority of the king's court. The itinerant justice had several duties to perform. He investigated and punished crimes committed in the shire. His chief tool was the inquest, in which he impounded a body of good and honest men and asked them what they knew about violent crime in the neighborhoods since his last visitation. This jury was the ancestor of our modern grand jury, or jury of presentment. If the good men identified a crime and expressed suspicion concerning its perpetrator, the suspect would be obligated to show his guilt or innocence through the traditional forms of ordeal. Only in the thirteenth century, after the Fourth Lateran Council (1215) had forbidden clerics to participate in ordeals, did the small or petty jury replace the ordeals as the common means for establishing or deciding guilt or innocence. The justice in eyre also offered his services in the settlement of civil disputes, i.e., those cases, involving no violence, between private persons. Litigants who believed that their case was particularly strong could purchase a writ which effectively brought the dispute from the baronial into the royal court. The advantage of royal over baronial justice was that cases in the baronial court were usually settled by combat; the royal court relied not on the duel but on the inquest, that is, a jury of sworn witnesses. Litigants with a good case preferred the memory of neighbors to the muscle of a champion, and willingly purchased the appropriate writ. The king made no direct effort to suppress the baronial courts and baronial justice, but he did place on sale a brand of justice which deprived them of much of their business. Finally, the justice in eyre investigated the behavior of the sheriff in office; he was, in every sense of the word, the eyes and the ears of the king and a critical link in binding the central government to that of the locality or county.

In this age too, the accumulated decisions of the wandering justices formed and defined a body of legal custom "common" to the whole of England. Legally and administratively, the twelfth century, which witnessed the birth of the still-living common law, must be considered one of the great formative ages for English and American institutions.

On the continent too, this was a period of administrative consolidation. In France, the Capetian Louis VI ("the Fat," 1108–1137), through war and legal action, reduced the castellans of his own demesne to subservience and left his successors a firm base of power in the Ile-de-France. Louis' work was continued especially by his grandson Philip II Augustus (1180–1223), the "Increaser," according to the contemporary misinterpretation of the name. He merited the title primarily through his acquisition of the rich province of Normandy, which he won from the incompetent John of England. His seizure of Normandy provides an excellent example of feudal concepts in the service of princes. John, to forestall a dangerous marriage alliance between the two leading baronial families of northern Aquitaine, had abducted the bride-to-be and married her himself. The baronial families appealed against John to Philip Augustus, their common suzerain. Philip summoned John to court. When the English king failed to appear, he declared him a contumacious vassal and his fiefs held of the French crown forfeit. Arms, of course, were still needed to support this decision, but the incident nevertheless shows how a strong monarch could turn essentially feudal concepts to his benefit.

The royal administration in France grew more slowly than in England; it was, after all, a much larger country, and the king had so much more difficulty in making his presence and power felt throughout the land. The official primarily responsible for the royal interests on the local level, roughly equivalent to the English sheriff, was the *prévôt*. From Philip's reign we hear of *baillis* (later in the south called seneschals), who had responsibility for a particular circuit of territory and seem to resemble, and were perhaps modeled after, the English justices in eyre. Later, under St. Louis (1226–1270), still other wandering inspectors, called the *enquêteurs*, were appointed in the crown's constant battle to maintain a close supervision over its distant officials. The beginnings of specialization are also evident in the royal court, although again the pace is slower than in England. In the early thirteenth century, a special accounting office and fiscal court, the Chambre de Comptes, developed. Under St. Louis, the Parlement de Paris—not really a parliament in the English sense but a supreme court—gained a separate existence and assumed a prominent role in French political life which it maintained for the duration of the *ancien régime*. France, however, never witnessed the high measure of centralization characteristic of England in the same period. In the thirteenth century, France could probably best be described as a confederation of feudal principalities, the chiefs of which were bound together by a common vassalage to the king.

In the Holy Roman Empire, Frederick I Barbarossa (1152–
1190), of the house of Hohenstaufen, made similar efforts to build
an effective central government but faced particularly formidable
obstacles. Frederick seems to have envisioned building a kind of
imperial Ile-de-France based on his native duchy of Swabia on the
upper Rhine, neighboring Burgundy, which he acquired by marriage, and Italy, which he hoped to subdue. As the theoretical basis
for his authority, Frederick effectively enlisted both concepts of
Roman law, familiar especially to his Italian subjects, and the
newer feudal institutions. At a diet held at Roncaglia in Italy
(1158), he appropriated to himself the sovereign rights (regalia)
which Roman law allotted to the emperor. His greatest success
came with his victory over Henry the Lion, the powerful duke of
Saxony. Henry had refused to accompany Frederick on an Italian
campaign in 1176. Upon his return, Frederick summoned him to
trial, condemned him for disloyalty, and confiscated his Saxon
lands. The incident has many similarities with King John's loss of
Normandy.

In spite of this impressive victory, neither Frederick nor his successors proved able to build the same sort of feudal monarchy
which was growing up in the western kingdoms. Probably the
chief reason for the imperial failure was the enormous extent and
great cultural diversity characteristic of the imperial lands. Partially too, unlike the kings of the West, the emperors failed to win
the support of the Church and the towns, especially in Italy. The
two had combined to defeat Frederick at Legnano in 1176, and
forced him to accept the unfavorable Peace of Constance in 1183.
They remained adamantly opposed to imperial efforts to build a
strong state in Italy, which seemed to threaten their own jealously
guarded freedom. The medieval emperors, perhaps because they
were too much swayed by the dream of a universal empire, attempted too much, and made few permanent advances toward
achieving a centralized state. The chief beneficiaries of governmental growth in the second feudal age were the princes and, in
Italy, the city-states.

The thirteenth century
In the assessment of most scholars, medieval civilization in the
thirteenth century enjoyed its greatest measure of success. It is also
the age in which feudal government seems to have functioned

tolerably well, in the sense of maintaining adequate levels of internal order and international peace.

If the twelfth century had been the great age of growth in royal authority, the thirteenth was primarily a period of constitutional consolidation. It witnessed, for example, numerous codifications of feudal customs, which brought a new clarity and consistency to feudal institutions. The Assizes of the Latin Kingdom of Jerusalem, the Constitutions of Melfi of Frederick II Hohenstaufen (Document 44), the Establishments of St. Louis (inaccurately named, as they were not an official code issued by that king, but a private collection of regional customs), the "Seven Parts" (*Siete Partidas*) of Alfonse the Wise of Castile—these are examples of the spirit of system which permeated thirteenth-century legal thought. Law shares that same emphasis upon logic and order which is so remarkably apparent in the great Gothic cathedrals and the *Summae* of the scholastic philosophers.

Statesmen and lawyers of the thirteenth century were active not only in codifying custom and law but in fixing the procedures of government. The period was in fact one of the most important in the development of Western constitutionalism, in the sense of government by defined and recognized procedures. Again, England enjoys a particular prominence in the growth of constitutionalism. The great expansion of royal authority under the Norman and Angevin kings had raised the question as to what, if any, limits could be placed on the *vis et voluntas*, the power and will of the king. The issue came to a head under the reign of that great mismanager, King John. Alarmed at his arbitrary, expensive, and above all unsuccessful policies, the great barons and the Church combined to force the Magna Carta from him in 1215 (Document 43). This "Great Charter" concentrates on defining and protecting the rights of the high aristocracy, the Church, and the barons, and clearly reflects the interests of the classes which demanded it. But that hardly reduces its historical importance and interest. It did affirm that royal power ought not to be arbitrarily exercised but should follow fixed and known procedures. Moreover, in making important decisions, the king should not act alone but should consult the community of his realm, which for those who inspired the Magna Carta primarily meant the barons and the Church.

The Great Charter itself did not provide a workable means of implementing these principles in an institutional sense. But over the course of the thirteenth century a new sort of institution developed, of consummate interest in the history of Western constitutionalism—the representative assembly. A constitutional mechanism unknown in the ancient world, the representative assembly for the first time enabled men living at a distance from the capital or court to take an active role in the affairs of government. Representation was in fact based on two older principles, familiar to Roman law but never before combined in this fashion: the idea of incorporation and the idea of agency. An electoral unit, a shire or borough, could be considered to form a moral or fictional person with a single will; it could appoint an agent to represent its interests. The agent, sitting in Parliament, thus expressed the will of his constituents and bound them by his vote. These conceptions of incorporation and agency are still implied in the modern machinery of representation (see Document 47).

It is not possible to describe even briefly the complex origins and growth of parliamentary or representative institutions in the thirteenth century, even in the single nation of England. One should not of course exaggerate the power which these early Parliaments exercised, or pretend that they possessed a democratic character. Parliament was more truly an expression of royal authority than a limitation upon it. The king wanted consent to taxation not because his people forced him to do so but because it facilitated the collection of the moneys. Edward I, for example, did not allow representatives to come to Parliament; he *commanded* that they appear and bring with them "full and sufficient power" to bind their constituencies. Edward found real administrative advantages in following the dictum of Justinian: "What affects all, by all should be approved" (Document 47).

England was not alone in the growth of parliamentary assemblies. In the thirteenth century, assemblies of estates came to meet frequently if irregularly in all the lands of Europe, although few of them were truly representative. The English Parliament was particularly precocious partially because the land was small and culturally homogeneous; the estates of the clergy, barons, and commoners could develop a sense of unity and common interests. Then, too, Parliament was favored by the very strength of the king who summoned it. Paradoxically, the English Parliament was to be a chief beneficiary of the strong traditions of central government established in England in the twelfth century.

Conclusions

Historians and others have sometimes considered that the feudal system was, primarily, a lack of system, that it was equivalent with a weak central government and a disordered society. This interpretation has doubtlessly some truth in it. The nature of feudal government excluded all possibility of a true absolutism. The basic institution of vassalage, when used to define the rights and relationship of ruler and ruled, retained a notion of contract and preserved the idea that the vassal—or subject—had rights which he could maintain even against his suzerain.

The essence then of feudal government seems to have been this: it was founded upon a kind of partnership in the exercise of power. The king was no autocrat; the poor communications of the epoch, the financial and military resources available to him, would not, in all events, have allowed him to maintain a monopoly of power. Rather, he shared jurisdiction and authority with numerous privileged persons and institutions—not only his great vassals but the clergy, the towns, important guilds such as the universities, or military orders such as the Templars. The balance between the king and his junior partners in government could of course vary in different areas and different times; but the principle that power should be shared and decisions based on consultation among those who held it remained central to feudal government.

Considered under one aspect, this partnership in government could be a source of weakness and disorder. As a renowned English constitutional historian of the nineteenth century, Bishop William Stubbs, remarked, feudalism would have been almost an ideal form of government if men were archangels, that is, if all those who exercised authority used it responsibly and maintained fidelity to the king. But men were not archangels, and moral pressure was not always strong enough to assure the loyalty of the vassals and the stability and cohesiveness of the realm. On the other hand, in comparison with the fragile government of the Carolingians, and in particular with the chaos of the tenth century, feudalism, far from being synonymous with weakness, was a major step toward a more stable political life. And in stressing so strongly that government should follow known procedures, and that "what affects all, by all should be approved," it did leave a heritage which has since remained an integral and influential part of the Western constitutional tradition.

RECOMMENDED READINGS

G. Barraclough, *Origins of Modern Germany* (Oxford: Blackwell, 1962).

S. B. Chrimes, *English Constitutional History* (4th ed.; New York: Oxford University Press, 1967).

———, *An Introduction to the Administrative History of Mediaeval England* (Oxford: Blackwell, 1952).

Robert Fawtier, *The Capetian Kings of France: Monarchy and Nation, 987–1328* (New York: St. Martin's Press, 1962).

C. Warren Hollister, *The Impact of the Norman Conquest* (New York: Wiley, 1969).

Sidney Painter, *The Rise of the Feudal Monarchies* (Ithaca: Cornell University Press, 1965).

C. E. Petit-Dutaillis, *The Feudal Monarchy in France and England from the Tenth to the Thirteenth Century* (New York: Barnes and Noble, 1964).

H. G. Richardson and G. O. Sayles, *The Governance of Mediaeval England from the Conquest to Magna Carta* (Edinburgh: University Press, 1963).

34. On the Governance of the Palace, by Hincmar of Rheims

It is not too much to say that the following tract stands close to the beginnings of the administrative histories of all west European states. It is the earliest surviving essay devoted not to theories of government but to the actual administration of a kingdom. It was written in 882 by Hincmar of Rheims, a renowned scholar who had himself been deeply involved in imperial affairs. Hincmar intended it for the instruction of the young King Carloman, son of Louis III. In the first eleven sections of the essay, the author stresses the responsibilities of the king toward the Church and enlarges upon the acts of a council held at St. Macre, at Fismes, on April 2, 881, which had likewise instructed kings on their duties. The first third of the work thus illustrates the ecclesiastical conceptions of kingship in the late-Carolingian epoch. From Section 12 on, Hincmar substantially incorporates into his treatise an earlier work written by a contemporary of Charlemagne, Adalhardus of Corbie. The second part of the treatise, by far the more interesting from the standpoint of administrative history, describes the central administration of the Carolingian empire at about the year 814. The Latin text, translated here in its entirety by D. Herlihy, may be found in Hincmarus De ordine palatii, *Capitularia*, ed. A. Boretius, Vol. II, pp. 515–30.

The admonition of Hincmar, archbishop of Rheims,
to the bishops and to King Carloman, arranged in chapters.
Hincmar, bishop and servant of the people of God.

1. You have called upon my feeble powers, good and holy men, who are younger than am I in count of years and duration of holy orders. I was present at the deliberations concerning the Church and palace, when the realm flourished in size and unity, and I then heard the counsels and the wisdom both of those who ruled the holy Church in sanctity and justice and of those who felicitously in these past times presided over the strength of the empire. By their instruction I learned the customs of our ancestors. Moreover, after the death of the lord emperor Louis, I stayed in the service of those who sought for peace among his sons, who were at that time our kings. I worked for this as my puny strength allowed, in frequent journeys, addresses, and writings. You ask now that I should describe for the instruction of this young man, our new king, as well as for the restoration of the honor and the peace of the Church and the kingdom, the governance of the Church and the administration of the royal household within the sacred palace, as I heard of it and saw it. Thus, in his inexperience our king may advance in learning, and in governing the kingdom, he may please God, rule happily in this world, and from the present kingdom attain an eternal one. For we know by experience that a new vase once filled with savor and smell retains it for a long time. Just as a wise man has said: "Once a new jug is imbued with a smell it holds it for long" (Horace *Epist.* I, 2, 69).

We have also read how Alexander in his youth had a tutor by the name of Leonidas, who was known for his loose morals and disorderly behavior. These faults the young boy absorbed from him like bad milk. Thus, in adulthood, the wise and brave king blamed himself and sought to mend his ways, but as the story relates, although he conquered all kingdoms, in this he was unable to conquer himself.

2. Therefore, the lord king should understand to what office he has been elevated, and he should pay close heed to the admonition and the warning of the King of kings, Who says to him as to other rulers: "And now, O ye kings, understand: receive instruction, ye who judge the earth. Serve ye the Lord with fear and rejoice unto him with trembling. Embrace discipline: lest at any time the Lord be angry, and you perish from the just way" (Psalm 2.10–12). As we have read that many who have ignored this admonition and warning have perished, so we read that it has happened even in our own days. He should also listen carefully to Holy Scripture which commands him, "Love justice, ye who are the judges of the earth. Think of the Lord in goodness and seek Him in simplicity of heart. For wisdom will not enter into a malicious soul, nor dwell in a body subject to sins" (Wisdom 1.1–4).

3. In response to the duty placed upon me and to your good and reasonable request, I therefore undertake the task you have set for me. I rely neither on my intelligence nor on my style but, as I said above, on the tradition of our ancestors, recalling the words of the Lord to the prophet: "And thou shalt hear the word out of my mouth and shalt tell it them from me" (Ezekiel 3.17). From Me, he says, and not from you, because, as He says, "He that speaketh of himself seeketh his own glory" (John 7.18). Holy Scripture imposes upon every official in every order and profession the obligation that he understand all that he says. If he understands the origin of the office which he occupies, he will want even more solicitously to render an accounting for the "talent" of the administration entrusted to him (cf. Matthew 18.23). We shall all stand before the tribunal of Christ, so that each of us will relate what we did in the flesh, both good and evil. May the king not hear from the just judge what the Lord, as told in the Gospel, said to the bad and lazy servant. Rather may he hear: "Well done, good and faithful servant, because thou hast been faithful over a few things, I will place thee over many things. Enter thou into the joy of thy lord" (Matthew 25.21).

4. We read in the Holy Scripture, in the Old Testament, that David, who was at once king and prophet, and who prefigures our Lord Jesus Christ, Who alone could have become both king and prophet, established two orders among the priests: that is, the supreme pontiffs and the priests in lower orders, who now fulfill the office of priesthood. He made this provision in order that when any of the pontiffs departed this life, whoever among the priests was considered the best should succeed him. And in the New Testament, our Lord Jesus Christ from the multitude of his disciples, as we read in the Gospel, chose twelve whom he named apostles. The place of these apostles the bishops hold in the Church, as both Holy Scripture and the Catholic doctors demonstrate. He also designated seventy-two others who under the twelve apostles prefigure priests, that is, ministers of the second rank. Thus, when bishops die, according to the sacred canon inspired by the Spirit of God and consecrated by the reverent observance of the entire world, persons from among these priests of second or of lower rank are elevated to the height of supreme priesthood in place of the departed bishops. This, Holy Scripture, in the Acts of the Apostles, clearly illustrates. Thus Peter, after the death of Judas, who was counted among the apostles and had received the apostolic commission, addressed his brethren: "Wherefore," he said, "it is fitting that he be among these men who have accompanied us all the time that the Lord Jesus came in and went out among us" (Acts 1.21). The divine election singled out Matthias, who was counted with the eleven apostles.

5. And in the holy Book of Kings, we read that the chief of the priests anointed the kings to their office by holy unction. They set the crown signifying victory on the kings' heads and placed the book of the laws in their hands. Thus, they might know how to rule themselves, correct the wicked, and direct the good along the path of righteousness. As the blessed Pope Gelasius proved from Holy Scripture to the Emperor Anastasius, and as was stated in the acts of the council recently held at the tomb of St. Macra, there are two powers by which this world is principally ruled. Certain things are specifically given to the rule of one or the other. These are the sacred authority of the priests and royal power. Just as the names of the two orders are different, so also are the duties which the offices impose on those persons who hold them. Therefore, each

should diligently pay heed in his order and his profession to the name by which it is known, and strenuously seek that in his office he act consistently with its name. First of all, as the blessed Cyprian said, the bishop should inquire after the meaning of the name of the office, the dignity of which he holds. "Bishop," a Greek name, means "watchman." The responsibility of a watchman, and what is required of him, were revealed by the Lord himself when, in the person of the prophet Ezekiel, he announced to the bishop the purpose of his office in these words: "I have made thee a watchman to the house of Israel" (Ezekiel 33.7). By his office the watchman incessantly proclaims by word and example to the people committed to him how they ought to live. Thus it is written concerning Christ, who commands that we follow, that is, imitate him: "These things Jesus began to do and to teach" (Acts 1.1). The watchman ought, therefore, to pay close attention to the life and the morals of those committed to him. After he has observed, he should try, if he can, to correct them by word and deed, and if he cannot, he ought to drive away, according to the evangelical rule, the perpetrators of iniquities.

6. The king ought to maintain within himself the dignity of his own name. For the name "king" intellectually signifies that he should fulfill the office of "corrector" for all his subjects. But how can he who does not correct his own morals be able to correct others when they are wicked? It is by the justice of the king that the throne is exalted, and by truth that the governments of people are strengthened. What the justice of the king is, the same blessed Cyprian abundantly showed in his treatise "Concerning the Twelve Abuses of the World" in regard to the ninth abuse.

7. The sacerdotal order possesses, to be sure, divinely promulgated laws indicating how a man may arrive at the height of government, that is, the episcopal office; how he who justly attains it ought to live; how he who lives well should teach; how he who teaches well ought to recognize his own weakness daily by much meditation; how he ought to rule the ministers placed under him; finally, with what pure intention he ought to confer the sacred ecclesiastical orders and with what discretion he ought to bind and loose his subjects. These same laws say concerning their own nature: "To no priest is it permitted to be ignorant of the canons or to do anything against those rules which the Fathers established." For there is no less guilt in violating holy tradition than in injuring the

Lord Himself. Since this is the case, as the sacred authority demonstrates, schism and heresy are related. In other words, the schismatic offends no less when by the denial of the holy rules he contemptuously separates himself from the unity of the holy Church, which is the body of Christ, than does the heretic, who holds wrong opinions concerning God, the Head of the Church.

8. We have already said concerning the ecclesiastic laws that "to no priest is it permitted to be ignorant of the canons or to do anything against those rules which the Fathers established." Thus, it is ordained by sacred laws that no one may licitly remain ignorant of the laws or scorn what has been established. When it is said that no one may licitly remain ignorant of the laws or scorn what has been established, no person in any particular secular status is exempt; all are bound by this sentence. For the kings and the ministers of the commonwealth have made laws, which those acting in the various provinces ought to apply. The rulers have established the capitularies of the Christian kings, their ancestors, which, with the general consent of their subjects, they have ordered to be lawfully maintained. Concerning these laws blessed Augustine says: "Although men may exercise a judgment concerning these things at the time they were enacted, nonetheless, once they are established and confirmed, it is not allowed to judges to judge concerning them, but only according to them."

9. It is even less permissible for a king than for anyone else, no matter what his station, to act contemptuously against the divine laws. Therefore, the prince of the land ought strenuously to provide and secure that God be not offended in those persons who chiefly maintain the Christian religion and who keep others from offending. The king by divine judgment has received ecclesiastical property to defend and protect. Therefore, men should be elevated to the episcopal office with his consent, by the election of the clergy and people, and with the approval of the bishops of the province, without any intervention of money. For the Lord says in the Gospel: "He that entereth not by the door into the sheepfold but climbeth up another way, the same is a thief and a robber" (John 10.1). In every respect, without obstinacy, he should honor the ecclesiastical laws, if he does not wish to offend the King of kings. The bishops and the king thus ought to make sure that a bishop is chosen by consideration of nothing save God alone, that is, not for reason of any gift or any human favor or kinship or

friendship or temporal service or any consideration which is opposed to truth or to divine authority. So also the king, as St. Augustine has shown, should take care lest by gifts or the praises of some scoundrel he is wheedled or deceived by flattery. Nor, out of any consideration of blood relationship or of carnal affection, should he spare those who act wickedly against God, the holy Church, or the commonwealth. The spirit of God said through David the prophet: "Have I not hated them, O Lord, that hated thee: and pined away because of thy enemies. I have hated them with a perfect hatred: and they are become enemies to me" (Psalm 138.21–22). To hate the enemies of God with a perfect hatred is to love the purpose of their creation but to condemn what they do, to repress the morals of the wicked and thus to contribute to their salvation.

10. The king ought to appoint such counts and, under them, judges who hate greed and love justice. The counts and justices should conduct their administration in the same manner and appoint similar officials under them. Whoever, in every order and profession, is set in a position of power and is called a lord ought to possess the virtue of command with the assistance and help of God, as St. Cyprian demonstrates in his tract "Concerning the Twelve Abuses of the World" in regard to the sixth abuse. "It profits nothing to have the authority of commanding, if the lord himself does not have the strength of virtue. But this strength of virtue does not require external might, although this also is necessary to secular lords, but rather inner spiritual power. It ought to be practiced along with good morals. For often the power of commanding is lost by weakness of spirit. Three things are necessary for those who rule: fear, obedience, and love. For unless the lord is equally loved and feared, his commands will avail little. Through favors and friendliness, let him seek to be loved, and through just punishments, not for injury to himself but for violations of the law of God, let him strive to be feared. Moreover, because many are dependent on him, he himself should adhere closely to God, Who established him in his position of leadership and Who, so to speak, fortified him to bear the burdens of many persons. For a peg, unless it is very strong and attached to something stronger than itself, quickly falls with everything hung upon it. Thus also the prince, unless he tenaciously adheres to his Creator, will quickly perish and all that he supports." Let a lord also know that, as he has

been made first among men in leadership, so he will earn for himself in the future world unremitting punishment unless upon this present earth he corrects the sinners placed under him.

11. The acts of the council held at the tomb of St. Macra which we have mentioned—salubrious, if they are respected and followed—contain briefly arranged by chapter the decrees of the Fathers of the Church made in accordance with Holy Scripture, and the laws of the Christian kings, which concern the honor and the vigor of the holy Church and her rulers, and those things which are relevant to the strength and maintenance of the king and kingdom, and likewise the administration of the royal household. Nonetheless, the Samaritan (that is, the true guardian of the human race) gave two pennies (that is, the Old and the New Testaments) to the innkeeper (that is, the pontifical order), to whose care he committed the wounded man. He told him, "Whatsoever thou shalt spend over and above, I, at my return, will repay thee" (Luke 11.35). In like manner, I shall seek to add what follows to the above acts, as if in additional payment beyond what has already been given in this book.

12. In my youth I knew Adalhardus, an old and wise man, a relative of the emperor Charles the Great, and abbot of the monastery of Corbie, who was first among the emperor's chief councilors. I read and I copied his work "On the Governance of the Palace." Among other things, it mentioned that the government of the entire kingdom rested chiefly on two principal divisions, excepting, of course, the eternal and ubiquitous judgment of Almighty God. The first division, he said, assured the constant and unfailing rule and governance of the king's palace. The second by zealous attention assured the government of the entire realm, in its various aspects.

13. In that which concerns the first division, the palace of the king was organized in the following fashion, to the honor of the entire government. Excepting the king and the queen with their most noble family, the palace at all times was ruled both in spiritual and in secular or material things through these officers. First, there was the *apocrisiarius*, the one responsible for ecclesiastical affairs. This office took its origins from the time when Emperor Constantine the Great became a Christian. He wished to give testimony of his love and respect for the saints Peter and Paul, through whose teaching and ministry he had come to obtain the grace of the

sacrament of baptism. He therefore by edict granted his capital, that is, the city of Rome, to Pope Silvester. He built his capital in that other city, adding his name to what was formerly called Byzantium. Thus, officers of both the see of Rome and the other principal sees from that time served continuously in the palace, holding the charge of ecclesiastical affairs.

14. The Apostolic See exercised this office sometimes through bishops and sometimes through deacons. St. Gregory, when he was in the deaconate, held this office. The other principal sees similarly filled the office with deacons, as the sacred canons required. In these cisalpine regions, St. Remi by his preaching converted Clovis to Christianity and on the vigil of Holy Easter baptized him together with three thousand Franks. Afterward, under succeeding kings, holy bishops left their sees at suitable times, stayed at the palace, and assumed this office. From the time of Pepin and Charles, this office was given at times to priests and at times to bishops, but by royal authority and with the consent of the bishops, priests filled it more frequently than bishops. For bishops are required to exercise a continuing supervision over their flocks and to guard them by example and word. According to the holy canons, they may not remain absent from their people for long.

15. According to the regulations promulgated from the sacred canons by St. Gregory, bishops may not pointlessly stay in attendance at the praetorial palace, which today is more usually called the royal palace. They would thus incur condemnation, in acting against the canons entrusted to them at their ordination, and would lose their ecclesiastical office. Let us now give examples of both licit and illicit practice. At the time of Pepin and Charles, the priest Fuldradus filled this office with the consent of the bishops; at the time of Charles, the bishops Engelramnus and Hildiboldus; at the time of Louis, the priest Hilduinus and, after him, Fulco, also a priest; finally, the bishop Drogo.

16. The *apocrisiarius*, whom we today call the chaplain or the guardian of the palace, had under his supervision and direction all the clergy of the palace. Associated with him was the archchancellor, who formerly was called a *secretis*. Under him were wise, intelligent, and faithful men, who were to record in writing the imperial commands without excessive desire for payment and would faithfully keep the royal secrets. Under these officers, the sacred palace was administered through these officials: the cham-

berlain, the count of the palace, the seneschal, the wine steward, the constable, the master of lodgings [*mansionarius*], four chief hunters, and one falconer.

17. Under them or associated with them were other officials, such as the porter, keeper of the purse, dispenser, and keeper of the utensils. Also some of these latter had subordinates or deacons, or others associated with them, such as wardens of the forest [*bersarii*], keepers of the kennels, hunters of beavers, and others in addition. Although each of these had a function in the palace according to his specialty, nonetheless, it was not upon them that the strength of the entire realm was dependent. Rather, as is stated below, the strength of the realm rested upon the other officers, in regard to the matters both great and small which occurred daily, whenever they were gathered at the palace. The great officers themselves were not equally useful, because of the diversity of their charges, their competence, and circumstances. Nevertheless, as has been stated, none of them was able to or wished to remove himself from the service of the king, in the interest of preserving true faith to the king and to the realm. Concerning these persons and their offices, much could be said; you have here at least the principal things.

18. First of all, according to the type or the importance of the office, the minister was to be chosen from among those of noble mind and body, stable, intelligent, discreet, and sober. Moreover, since by the grace of God the realm is formed by many regions, if it was possible, care was taken to select these officials from different regions, whether they were chosen for the first or second rank or for any level. Access to the palace was thereby facilitated for all subjects, since they recognized that members of their own families or inhabitants of their own region had a place in the palace.

19. Since we have briefly discussed how the officials mentioned above were selected and appointed, now it is necessary to turn to the rank of the same ministers and their functions, that is, how their offices were carried out. Each of these officials of whom we have spoken held chief authority over his office. He was responsible to no one and acted for no one, unless it was for the king alone or, in some instances, for the queen and for the king's glorious family. Still, in matters which were not part of their responsibility or which concerned other persons, all of them did not have equal access to the king, but each was content with his own measure of

functions and authority. When or where reason required it, they sought the help of another. At the highest rank, there were two officials. One was the *apocrisiarius,* whom we call the chaplain or the custodian of the palace. He had the constant supervision over all ecclesiastical matters and all ministers of the Church. The other was the count of the palace, who had the care of all secular matters and decisions. Thus, neither clerics nor laymen needed to disturb the king unless they had the approval of these two. The officers would determine if the matter ought to be brought before the king. If the matter was secret and it was proper that the king be informed of it before anyone else, these officers arranged to give the interested party an opportunity for speaking. They would inform the king in advance so that he could receive the statement according to the status of the person, whether with honor or patience or also pity.

20. The *apocrisiarius* had supervision over everything which concerned the practices or the constitution of the Church. He considered disputes relative to the canonical or monastic life, and questions of every sort regarding ecclesiastical affairs which reached the palace. He saw to it that only those external issues were brought to the king which without him could not be adequately settled. Further, he had responsibility over those things which especially concerned the honor or the services of the Church within the palace. Moreover, whoever in the entire palace sought any spiritual consolation or advice found it without fail with him, as necessity required. If he discerned that anyone who did not request help of him still had need of it, he strove to rescue him from wicked thoughts and works and to turn him to the way of salvation, according to the station of the person. Other spiritual problems which had to be settled or anticipated and which arose among those who lived continuously in the palace or among visitors—it would be lengthy to enumerate them—whether regarding God or the world, pertained especially to his supervision. We do not mean to say that no one else, either of the palace or a visitor from outside, illuminated in wisdom and true devotion by the grace of God, contributed nothing in this regard. But it was the firm custom that no one did what was to be done without the participation, or at least the agreement, of the *apocrisiarius,* lest someone should by chance bring useless or unworthy matters before the king.

21. The count of the palace, among his other nearly innumerable

duties, held chief responsibility for the just and reasonable settlement of all disputes which, although arising elsewhere, were brought to the palace for equitable decision. In the interest of equity, he also reversed bad judgments. By this he earned favor among all—with God for reason of his justice and among men for his observance of the laws. If a case was presented which the secular laws had not anticipated in their decrees or for which pagan custom demanded a crueler punishment than Christian rectitude or holy authority allowed, this was brought to the consideration of the king. Together with those conversant in both sacred and profane law, who feared the statutes of God more than those of human making, the king would make a decision which, if possible, would respect both laws. If this was not possible, the secular law would properly be suppressed and the justice of God respected.

22. The good management of the palace, and especially the royal dignity, as well as the gifts given annually to the officers (excepting, however, the food and water for the horses) pertained especially to the queen, and under her to the chamberlain. According to the circumstances, they always took care at an appropriate time to prepare for future events, lest something should be lacking at the time it was needed. The gifts given to the various legations were under the chamberlain's supervision, unless the matter was one which, by the king's command, was appropriate for the queen to handle together with the chamberlain. They gave attention to these and to similar things for this purpose, in order that the king, insofar as it could be accomplished reasonably and appropriately, might be freed of all concern for the household or the palace. Thus, continuously placing his hope in Almighty God, he could keep his mind ever intent on the governance and preservation of the state of the entire realm.

23. To three officers—the seneschal, the wine steward, and the constable—each according to the function and importance of his office, fell this responsibility: By common agreement and according to their separate duties, they were not to be remiss in informing all local officials, as soon as possible, concerning the times, places, and seasons of the king's arrival, and the duration of his stay, so that they could collect and prepare what was needed. Otherwise, if the local officials learned of this too late and performed their duties at an impropitious time or with excessive haste, the royal party by such negligence might have been unnecessarily inconvenienced.

Although these responsibilities fell upon both the wine steward and the constable, nevertheless the seneschal was chiefly concerned with them, since all other matters except water or fodder for the horses were his responsibility. The master of lodgings shared these duties with them. As his name indicates, his office had the supervision over, and the chief responsibility for informing, the local officials mentioned above and those known as "receivers" [susceptores], so that they would know at a suitable time, well in advance, when and in what place the king would arrive among them, in order that they might prepare the lodgings. Otherwise, if they learned too late, they would either sin through making excessive demands from their own dependents or, because of an unworthy reception, which occurred in spite of their wishes, they would still offend the king, not by will but by performance.

24. Similarly, the four hunters and the fifth falconer, with the same unanimity, according to the season, had to arrange that those things which pertained to the spheres of their respective ministries were considered at an appropriate time and not too late. They had to determine how many hunters were to be kept at the palace at various times, when all should be present or all dismissed, and how many should be sent, in accordance with the usual custom, to be supported for a time outside the palace. They also at an appropriate time assigned men to designated places for the purpose equally of carrying on the hunt and nourishing themselves. Both the one duty and the other, that is, within the palace and outside, were to be done with moderation and prudence, so that what was profitable would be accomplished and what was not profitable would be omitted. In these offices, it is not possible easily to determine the appropriate number of men or of dogs or of falcons. Therefore, in their judgment rested the decision of determining how many and of what sort these men and animals should be.

25. In all these arrangements the purpose was that officials of sufficient number and type to take care especially of these and other needs and functions should never be missing from the palace. First of all, although these major officials or some of the minor ones might leave the palace for general, special, or private matters, nonetheless at all times the palace was to be adorned with worthy councilors and never deprived of them. Without a suitable number of such officials, it could not function reasonably and appropri-

ately. Furthermore, legations of any sort which came to see the king or to submit to him might be appropriately received. Finally, a first councilor might provide just advice; a second the consolation of pity and kindness; and the language of a third might offer a correction to dishonesty or imprudence. From every part of the entire realm, anyone desolate, impoverished, oppressed by debts, overwhelmed by unjust accusations, or in similar situations which would be too long to enumerate, but especially widows and orphans, of both great men and small, each according to his need or situation, were always to have access to the mercy and the pity of the senior officers. Through one of the councilors, each person might hope to gain the pious ears of the prince.

26. Similarly, there were those who deserved reward for lengthy service, and arrangements were made that none of these needy persons was left entirely destitute. They were to be brought to the attention of the prince not by pleading with him directly but by calling upon the faith and duty of those officers mentioned above. This was to be done for them, first, because the officers would please God with their justice and mercy. Second, the officers would assure among those remaining in the royal service a most steadfast fidelity and constancy in faithfully fulfilling their duties. Finally, they would make joyous and happy even those who lived at great distances within the borders of the realm. And if any of these officers or councilors died, a suitable and competent person was found to replace him.

27. In order that the large numbers which always had to be present in the palace might be maintained without fail, they were divided into three classes. In the first class were found those servants who were without special responsibilities. The kindness and concern of the senior officers provided them with food or clothing or gold or silver, sometimes too with horses or other gifts, both on particular occasions, as time, reason, and propriety allowed them, and also at regular intervals, which was the more usual custom. Thus, these servants never lacked support, and they always held even closer to their hearts the royal service, because the chief officers rivaled one another by daily inviting now some servants, and then others, to their houses. There the chief officers sought to establish close relations with them, not by feeding their hungry stomachs but by sentiments of friendship and love, accord-

ing to their ability. Because of the officers' zeal in this regard, rarely was there found a servant who remained one week without receiving from anyone an invitation.

28. The second class consisted of those young men in the various offices who, closely following their master, both honored him and were honored by him. Each of them, according to circumstances, might gain encouragement in his post by the observation of and conversation with the lord. The third class consisted of those young servants or vassals [*pueris vel vasallis*], whom both the greater and lesser officials zealously sought to have, to the extent that they were able to manage them and support them without sin, that is, without plunder or robbery. In these classes we have mentioned, even apart from those who were always coming to and going from the palace, there was this satisfaction. Their numbers were always adequate for any need which at times might unexpectedly occur. Finally, as we mentioned above, the greater part of them, because of the favors to them already described, always remained cheerful, quick to smile, and intellectually alert.

29. This is the second division, by which the status of the entire realm was maintained, as much as pertained to human reason, always and everywhere excepting the judgment of the omnipotent God. At that time the custom was followed that no more than two general assemblies were to be held each year. The first assembly determined the status of the entire realm for the remainder of the year. No turn of events, saving only the greatest crisis which struck the entire realm at once, could change what had been established. All the important men, both clerics and laymen, attended this general assembly. The important men came to participate in the deliberations, and those of lower station were present in order to hear the decisions and occasionally also to deliberate concerning them, and to confirm them not out of coercion but by their own understanding and agreement. Moreover, all classes were present in order to provide gifts [to the king].

30. The other assembly was held with the important men only and the principal councilors. This assembly began the consideration of the affairs of the coming year. It deliberated over some matters which seemed likely to occur and which called for consideration and action, or over the events of the past year which might require decision or further attention. For example, if the margraves in some part of the realm had made treaties lasting a certain time, what

should be done immediately after the period of the treaties had expired? Should they be renewed or terminated? If war or peace involving certain areas was imminent, and if attacks had to be launched or withstood here and there in some regions, peace was to be established in other areas, as reason might then demand. These same men held council and determined well in advance what the actions or the policy of acting in the future was to be. Once the decision was reached, it was to be kept in silence and to remain thoroughly unknown to all others until the second general assembly, just as if the decision had been discussed by no one. Thus, if perchance a decision had been reached concerning affairs within or without the realm, and certain persons in their foreknowledge might wish to overturn it or to render it fruitless, or through any other ruse obstruct its execution, they were in no way capable of doing this. In such instances, in the second general assembly, whether to satisfy the remaining important persons or to placate or to arouse the spirits of the people, the decision was taken again, with new deliberations and with the consent of the participants, just as if nothing had been settled earlier concerning it. Thus, with the participation of the important persons and under the leadership of God, the policy would be carried. At the end of the first year, the ordinances for the second were to be enacted in the manner described above.

31. Insofar as was possible, councilors, both clerical and lay, were chosen from those who, each according to his character and office, showed a fear of God. They were also to have such fidelity that, with the exception of eternal life, they valued nothing more than the king and the realm, neither friends nor enemies, nor relatives, nor those who offered gifts, nor flatterers, nor those who made threats. They were to be wise, not in a misleading or deceptive fashion, nor according to the wisdom exclusively of this world, which is an enemy to God, but they were to be learned in that wisdom and intelligence which might enable them not only to repress those who placed their hopes in the human trickery mentioned above but to confound them entirely in their own just and right wisdom. Those councilors agreed among themselves and with the king that whatever they had discussed in confidence, whether it concerned the state of the realm or any particular person, ought not to be mentioned by any of them to a servant or to any other individual, without their consent, not for one day or two days or

more or a year but forever. For it frequently happens in these
matters that in order to advance or preserve the general good, the
discussion sometimes touches upon a particular person, who when
learning of it is either greatly disturbed or, what is more serious,
falls into despair or, worst of all, turns to treason. The knowledge
thus renders useless for all profit a person who perhaps could have
done countless services; he would not, however, have been the least
upset if he had known nothing concerning the discussion. What
may happen concerning a single man may also occur concerning
two or a hundred or a greater number or an entire family or even a
whole province, if great precaution is not taken.

32. The *apocrisiarius*, that is, the chaplain or the guardian of the
palace, and the chamberlain were always present at the councils,
and they therefore were chosen with the greatest care or, once
chosen, were so instructed that they could participate with profit.
If a person was found among the other officials who manifested
such qualities that by learning and later by giving advice he might
sooner or later replace the great officers mentioned above, he was
ordered to be present at all the deliberations and to concentrate
with the greatest attention upon what was done, keeping to himself
what was told him, learning what he did not know, and preserving
what was ordained and established. Thus, if by chance an event
occurred either within the realm or beyond its borders, or something unforeseen was announced, for which no plans had been
made, rarely was it necessary that the matter be treated in the
general assembly; moreover, time might not allow that the great
men be summoned. Then the palatine officials, by the mercy of
God, relying on their close acquaintance both with public councils
and with similar discussions, answers, and consultations within the
household, might act with dispatch, in accordance with the nature
of the affair or the time. They might either fully determine what
ought to be done or at least settle how the affair might be post-
poned or held in suspense without any loss for a determined period.
These things regard the major affairs.

33. Concerning minor affairs or those which especially concerned
the palace—not, as we have said, regarding the realm in general but
touching especially those particular persons who were attached to
the palace—the lord king was clearly to arrange with the palatine
officials that no loss would be suffered or, if loss had occurred or
was imminent, it might be lessened, entirely extinguished, and

eradicated. If, however, the case was one which demanded speed, but which might by some means and without sin or prejudice be held in suspense until the general assembly, they were to advise on the means of suspending it, in a manner similar to that used in important matters. Imitating the wisdom of the great men, they were in the meantime to give recommendations which would be pleasing to God and beneficial to the realm. The policy of the great men when they were summoned to the palace was directed toward this especially, that they would not deliberate concerning special or private cases, no matter what they were or who were the persons involved, nor did they hear appeals in contests which were brought concerning facts or law, but they first settled with the mercy of God those things which pertained to the general welfare or the state of the king and the realm. When this was finished, they then considered whatever had been reserved for them, upon orders of the king, which the count of the palace or the other officials in whose competence the cases fell could not themselves settle without the aid of their careful consideration.

34. Whether in one or the other of the general assemblies mentioned above, lest it appear that they were summoned needlessly, the important persons and the senior advisers of the realm were given by royal authority, for their discussion and consideration, the decisions which the king through the inspiration of God had made, and the information which he had learned from every quarter since their last meeting. These documents were titled and arranged in chapters. Having received the chapters, the great men deliberated sometimes one day, sometimes two, three, or more days, according to the importance of the affair. With the aid of messengers chosen from the servants of the palace mentioned above, they proposed questions to the king and received responses on all matters which seemed appropriate to them. However, no stranger joined them until the individual matters, concerning which a decision had been made, were related to the king and placed under his sacred eyes and until all had agreed with whatever he chose to do in the wisdom given him by God. This then is the way in which one, or two, or any number of the chapters were handled until, by the mercy of God, all questions which the times had posed were settled.

35. Meanwhile, while these things were being done in the absence of the king, he himself was occupied with the remaining throng,

receiving presents, greeting important persons, chatting with those rarely seen, sympathizing with the aged, rejoicing with the young, and engaging in similar activities, in regard to both spiritual and temporal affairs. Nevertheless, as often as those withdrawn in council wished it, the king would go to them and remain with them for as long as they desired. They then in all friendliness told him how they had found individual matters; they frankly related what they had discussed on one side and the other, in disagreement or argument or friendly rivalry. It should also be noted that if the weather was pleasant, the assembly was held out of doors. If it was held indoors, different places were designated where the important persons could gather in sufficient number and could hold their meetings, separate from the remaining throng; other, less important persons were then unable to participate in the deliberations. In either case, however, the meeting place of the great men was divided into two sections. In the first, all the bishops, abbots, and more exalted clerics could meet without any lay participation. Similarly, the counts and the princes of comparable rank could honorably gather in the morning apart from the other throng, for the time needed, in either the presence or the absence of the king. Thus the great men in the accustomed manner were summoned, the clerics to their own designated hall, the laymen to their own hall, both of which were suitably furnished with seats. When the great men were separated from the others, they had the power of deciding when they should sit together and when separately, as the nature of the case dictated, whether it concerned spiritual or secular or mixed issues. So also it was in their discretion to summon outsiders, as for example, when they wished provisions or when they wanted to pose questions. Once answers were received, those summoned would depart. This is what happened when those matters which the king wished to have considered were presented to them.

36. The second interest of the king was to interview persons coming from all parts of the realm, to learn if they brought with them information worthy of consideration. Not only was this allowed, but it was also strictly enjoined upon the participants. Before coming, each was to inquire with the greatest diligence into both internal and external affairs. Each was to collect information concerning any relevant matter not only from his own people but from strangers and from both friends and enemies, with no atten-

tion paid or close consideration given to the type of person from whom the information was gained. If the people in any part, region, or corner of the realm appeared agitated, he was to learn the cause of the disturbance, and also if the people were grumbling or the sound of any other upset was echoing, or if similar events were happening which might require the attention of the general assembly. Concerning foreign affairs, he was to make inquiry whether any subjugated people was rebelling or a rebellious people had surrendered or a people not yet conquered seemed to be preparing an attack against the realm or if any other similar occurrence had taken place. He was especially to discover in all matters which presented a certain danger what were the causes for these or other disturbances.

37. In devoted obedience to your request I have offered to you these remarks concerning the governance of the palace and the rule of the kingdom, for the instruction of our king and his ministers and officers of the realm. As I learned them from the writings and words of my elders, and as I myself personally observed them in my youth, I have given them as a supplement to those stipulations collected from the decrees of our ancestors and offered to King Louis, recently deceased. It shall be your responsibility to find the persons who, through their moral stature and high qualities, may restore those institutions which now have decayed. I know that no one is now alive of those whom I saw serving as officers of the palace and of the realm in the days of the lord emperor Louis. However, I do know that sons were born to replace these fathers from their own families, although I am unfamiliar with their morality and their qualities. May they seek not to be deficient in morals, virtue, wisdom, and the liberal arts, as their years and the times may allow. Thus they may deservedly fill the places and positions of their fathers. In assuming those places let them prudently take care, lest, as St. Gregory says, those placed at the pinnacle of honor should be corrupted by the close touch of glory, just as Saul, a humble man before his elevation to a post of honor, later deserved reprimand because of his swollen pride.

⎍⎍⎍⎍⎍⎍⎍⎍⎍⎍⎍⎍⎍⎍⎍⎍⎍⎍⎍⎍⎍⎍⎍⎍⎍⎍ʅ

35. A castle in Spain

Beginning in the late tenth century, a proliferation of castle building occurred across Europe, and the presence of these fortifications profoundly affected local administration. Many such castles were technically "adulterine," in the sense that they were unauthorized by higher lords, but many others were promoted by counts and dukes to strengthen particular parts of their territories. In the following charter, the count and countess of Barcelona arrange for the construction of a castle at Tarrega. Note the prominent use of money in the transaction, which is characteristic of the more developed economy of the European south. The act of homage which the castellan in return gave to the count and countess is given above in Document 16. The source is the *Liber feudorum maoir*, Vol. I, pp. 180–81; the translation is by D. Herlihy.

No. 171, February 5, 1058

In the name of Christ. This is the agreement which was made between Raymond, count of Barcelona, and Almodis, the countess, and Richard Altemir from the same castle of Tarrega. The said count and countess commend to the said Richard the castle of Tarrega. And they give to him in fief the boundaries and appurtenances of the said castle of Tarrega. They give to him for his services as castellan in the same castle every year forty ounces of the gold of Barcelona counted out in the coins known as *mancusi*. Of the said forty ounces, one-half should be given every year at the feast of St. Peter, and the other half at the feast of St. Michael. And the same count and countess, for the work of construction in Tarrega, give to the same Richard, together with what they have already given him and will give to him, one hundred ounces of the gold of Barcelona, counted out in *mancusi*.

The same Richard, in return for the above, agrees with the same count and countess that he will enlarge the tower which now has been undertaken in the castle of Tarrega until it has a height of one hundred palms. And the said Richard will construct in the same castle another tower of stone and mortar of one hundred palms in height and another one hundred in width. Moreover, the said Richard agrees to make there another two bulwarks, each of them fifty palms in height and fifty in width. And among the same towers and bulwarks the same Richard will make excellent walls of stone and mortar, as are suitable there. Also, the said Richard agrees with the said count and countess that he will garrison in the same castle of Tarrega ten excellent knights who will remain there.

Moreover, the said count and countess and Richard agree among themselves that from this time forward, to the extent that the rents from the land of the said castle of Tarrega increase for the support of the said knights who stay there, by so much should the said forty ounces be diminished.

Also, the said Richard agrees with the said count and countess that he will remain in their homage and in their fealty and that he will swear to them fealty and that he will be their helper in holding and defending all their possessions against all men and women in direct faith without deceit. Also, the said Richard agrees with the said count and countess that when they send their army to the said Richard, Richard or his son will go in the said army with the ten knights. And the said Richard agrees with the said count and countess that the said construction of the said castle of Tarrega will be finished on the first Christmas day coming after two years, and he will have established the said ten knights before the next feast of St. Michael. Also, the said Richard agrees with the said count and countess that he will swear to them that he will not deny authority over the said castle of Tarrega, neither to them nor to the son or sons to whom they may bestow the said castle, but he will give that authority to them. And the castellans, which the said Richard will place in the said castle, will be the vassals of the count and countess and they will swear to them what the said Richard will swear to them concerning the said castle. And all this will be done without deceit. This agreement was made on the nones of February in the twenty-seventh year of the reign of King Henry. Raymond the count. Almodis the countess. The mark of Richard Altemir. The mark of Arnall Mironi. The mark of Berenguer Ermenir. The mark of Raymond Ermenir.

ⅬⅬⅬⅬⅬⅬⅬⅬⅬⅬⅬⅬⅬⅬⅬⅬⅬⅬⅬⅬⅬⅬⅬⅬ

36. A castle in the Lyonnais

The following charters from the abbey of Savigny near Lyons in France illustrate the construction of a castle done in defiance of the lord of the area, the abbey itself. The "cemetery" referred to consisted of the consecrated land surrounding a church. The source is the *Cartulaire de l'abbaye de Savigny suivi du petit cartulaire de l'abbaye d'Ainay*, ed. A. Bernard (Paris, 1853), pp. 475–83. The order of the charters has been changed in the translation, which was made by D. Herlihy.

No. 904, ca. *1121*

The church of Savigny once had a certain parishioner by the name of Itier de Bully, who on his deathbed gave a certain cemetery, which he held unjustly, and a certain part of his patrimony to the monks of the said abbey in perpetuity. Also his sons who died after him gave their own portions of their paternal inheritance to the same monks. It happened, however, that afterward, Stephen de Varennes took to wife a daughter of the deceased Itier. He did homage to the abbot and swore fealty. But wishing to obtain the entire inheritance of the father of his wife, he began to harass the abbey. Then the Abbot Ponce, desiring peace, granted three-quarters of the inheritance given to him to Stephen over the opposition of the monks. However, Stephen, ungrateful for such a favor, forced the steward [*villicus*] whom the abbot had placed in charge of his fourth part to swear to him fealty, and he himself seized that fourth part.

Moreover, the same Stephen made a fortification out of a certain house which his father had built for the protection of his sheep near the abbey, at a distance of one league, and within the possession of the abbey. He enclosed it with a mound and a moat, fortified it with wooden towers and stockades, and began to force the serfs of the abbey by threats and tortures to do service to him. Distraught by these injuries, Abbot Ponce admonished his vassal Stephen that he should come to trial; for long he contemptuously refused. Upon the counsel of his friends, however, he gave hostages. The day of the trial was set in the court of the abbot. The constituted judges, after hearing both sides, gave among other things this judgment: Stephen ought to return the fortification to the abbot, who could destroy as much of it as he pleased. In the cemetery mentioned above, between his church and the house, he should allow passage to the chaplains of the church. For a long time Stephen delayed complying with this judgment and did not surrender the fortress to the abbot. But when the abbot started to open a path through the cemetery, as was said, Stephen with an armed band assaulted the monks who were there, hurling at them both projectiles and insulting words. Then, upon leaving, he came to his fortress and threw out the guards of the abbot who were there. He did not cease ravaging the lands of the abbey. Among other ills, he invaded a cell in which six monks were permanently residing. He arrogantly expelled the monks and destroyed their possessions. Finally, as a culmination of the evils, the archbishop interposed himself as a mediator between the parties. He asked for and received hostages from both sides and set a day for the trial. The appointed judges again determined that the fortress should be returned under these terms: the abbot should hold the fortress for the same length of time that Stephen had neglected to hold it in investiture from the abbot. Meanwhile, concerning the other disputes the interested parties should return to trial.

Thus the fortress was once more returned to the abbot, but fraudulently, since the same Stephen with knights and bowmen and his entire family remained in the fortress and by day and night with injurious words and threats incited the men of the abbot to sedition and battle. But the abbot, complaining about the false and damaging investiture to the archbishop, obtained thereby no satisfaction. Seeing therefore that the expenses of guarding the fortification were out of just proportion, with the advice and help of his friends the abbot destroyed it. For this reason, the archbishop, upset beyond measure, excommunicated the abbot and the monks and the churches which pertained to the abbey in his dioceses. He held the hostages, wishing through this to force the abbot to reconstruct that den of thieves.

No. 903, ca. 1121

In the name of the holy and undivided Trinity. Be it known to all men, born and to be born, that Itier de Bully gave to God and St.

Martin of the church of Savigny all his land and his possessions which he was known to have between the Loire and Azergues. This gift he made in the chapter of Savigny, in the presence of the lord Abbot Itier and his monks, with the agreement of his sons, that is, Achard, Hugo, and William. At the death of Achard and Hugo at Jerusalem, William, who remained, upon his deathbed made the same gift and again agreed and in the presence of witnesses confirmed possession to God and to St. Martin of Savigny. Of this grant the witnesses were the lord Girbaldus who was abbot after Abbot Itier, and Girardus the prior and Guido the monk, brother of the same William, Artaldus de Mussy, William of Montfalcon, William Rainerii of Châtillon, and Peter de Bully the chaplain, and many others, who saw and heard it. And since Stephen of Varennes by false subversion has attempted to deprive and take away from the church this gift at the time of the lord Abbot Ponce, who was prepared to do and receive justice, the entire convent of monks serving God at Savigny in regard to Stephen and his heirs who possess the said land and possession, justly given to St. Martin, but unjustly taken from him, ask that Almighty God may deign to do them justice for so great an injury.

No. 900, December 9, 1117 (?)

[Pope] Pascal, bishop, servant of the servants of God, to his beloved sons, the canons of the chapter of Lyons, greetings and apostolic blessing. We have heard the complaint of the brothers of Savigny concerning the castle of Varennes and the hostages extorted from the abbot. We further believe that hostages given for the castle countervene the custom of ecclesiastical courts; the castle near the monastery was rightly destroyed since neither it nor another should have been built to the damage of the monastery, nor is it permissible that it be rebuilt. We therefore command that the hostages are to be returned to the abbot. We dissolve the interdict unjustly placed on the monastery's churches. We decree that the cemetery of Bully, as it was given by the church of Lyons, ought freely and wholly to remain to the monastery. The agreement which was made between the abbot and Stephen of Varennes by the hand of the bishop of Mâcon and Guichard of Beaulieu and Guido of Oingt and Berard, archdeacon of Mâcon, if the same Stephen wishes to observe it, let him in the future entirely desist from attacks on the monastery. Otherwise, as a contumacious person, he should be subjected to canonical punishment. Given at the Lateran the fifth ides of December.

பாபாபாபாபாபாபாபாபாபாபாபாபாபாபார்

37. Documents concerning the Domesday Inquest

Of all European lands, England has preserved the richest series of laws and administrative records illustrating the growth of government in the second feudal age. One of the great documents of the epoch—and indeed of all European history—is the Domesday Book of 1086, which minutely surveyed the entire kingdom. This enabled King William I to gain an excellent idea of the resources of his English possessions and to insist that appropriate services be provided him from his barons. Of the following four documents, the first is the account of the chronicler Robert of Hereford concerning the redaction of the Domesday Book; the second is the Inquest of Ely, a private compilation of the monks of Ely made for their own benefit, but based on the Domesday survey and restating the questions that were asked in its course. The third gives the Domesday survey of Shrewsbury. The fourth is the account of the work given in the *Dialogue concerning the Exchequer*, Chapter 16 (see above, Document 6). The Latin texts of these first three sources are found in *Select Charters and Other Illustrations of English Constitutional History*, ed. William Stubbs (9th ed., rev. by H. W. C. Davis; Oxford: Clarendon Press, 1966), pp. 95, 101. The survey of Shrewsbury is taken from *The Normans in England (1066–1154)*, ed. A. E. Bland (London: G. Bell and Sons, Ltd., 1921), pp. 24–25. The first and fourth translations are by D. Herlihy. The socmen mentioned in the Inquest of Ely were men who held land by the service of attending the lord's court, or soke.

(1) Robert of Hereford
It was the twentieth year of the reign of William, king of the English, when, at his command, in this year, a survey was drawn up of the whole of England. It included the possessions of the individual barons, their fields, houses, their men both slave and free, both those living only in huts and those who possessed houses and fields, plows, horses and other animals, service obligations and

the rent owed by all in this entire land. The inquisitors went in succession, and unknown men were sent to unknown provinces, so that some might criticize the surveys of others, and denounce them as false before the king.

(2) The Inquest of Ely

Here below is written the inquest upon the lands, in what manner the King's barons make enquiry, to wit, by the oath of the sheriff of the shire, and of all the barons and their Frenchmen, and of the whole hundred, of the priest, the reeve, and six villeins of each town. Then how the manor is named; who held it in the time of King Edward; who holds it now; how many hides [farms]; how many ploughs on the demesne, and how many men; how many villeins; how many cotters; how many serfs; how many freemen; how many socmen; how much wood; how much meadow; how many pastures; how many mills; how many fishponds; how much has been added or taken away; how much it was worth altogether; and how much now; how much each freeman or socman there had or has. All this for three periods; to wit, in the time of King Edward; and when King William granted it; and as it is now; and if more can be had therefrom than is had.

(3) The Domesday description of Shrewsbury

In the city of Shrewsbury in the time of King Edward there were 252 houses, and as many burgesses in the same houses, rendering yearly 7l. 16s. 8d. of rent. King Edward had there the customs below written.

If any man wittingly broke the peace of the King given with his own hand, he was made an outlaw. And he who broke the peace of the King given by the sheriff made amends in 100s. and gave as much as he who committed "Forestel" or "Heinfare." These three forfeitures King Edward had in demesne in the whole of England beyond the farms.

When the King lay in this city, twelve men of the city of the better sort served him, keeping watch over him. And when he went hunting there, burgesses of the better sort, having horses, guarded him with arms in like manner. And for beating the woods the sheriff sent thirty-six footmen, so long as the King were there. And for the park of Marsetelie he found thirty-six men by custom for eight days.

When the sheriff wished to go into Wales, he who went not after being summoned by him gave 40*s.* of forfeiture.

A woman in any wise taking a husband gave to the King 20*s.* if she was a widow, 10*s.* if she was a maid, in what wise soever she should take a man.

Any burgess soever whose house should be burned by any chance or hap or by negligence, gave to the King 40*s.* for forfeiture, and to his two nearer neighbours 2*s.* to each.

When a burgess who was on the King's demesne died, the King had 10*s.* by way of relief.

If any burgess broke the term which the sheriff imposed upon him, he made amends in 10*s.* He who shed blood made amends in 40*s.*

When the King went from the city, the sheriff sent to him twenty-four horses as far as Leintwardine, and the King brought them as far as the first manor-house of Staffordshire.

The King had there three moneyers, who, after they had bought their money-dies, on the fifteenth day gave each to the King 20*s.* like other moneyers of the country. And this was done at the change of coinage.

In all, this city rendered 30*l.* a year. The King had two parts, and the sheriff a third.

In the year preceding this survey it rendered 40*l.* to Earl Roger.

This city gelded for a hundred hides in the time of King Edward.

Of these, St. Almund had 2 hides, St. Juliana half a hide, St. Milburga 1 hide, St. Chad a hide and a half, St. Mary 1 virgate, the bishop of Chester 1 hide, Ediet (queen Edith) 3 hides, which Ralph de Mortemer has.

The English burgesses of Shrewsbury say that it is a great burden to them that they render the whole geld as it was rendered in the time of King Edward, although the earl's castle has occupied 51 dwellings, and 50 other dwellings are waste, and 43 French burgesses hold dwellings which gelded in the time of King Edward, and the Earl has himself given to the abbey which he is building there 39 burgesses, who in like manner formerly gelded with the others. In all there are 200 dwellings less seven, which pay no geld.

(4) *Dialogue concerning the Exchequer*, 16

When King William, the renowned conqueror of England, . . . subjected to his authority the farthest reaches of the island and subdued rebellious spirits by terrible examples, he determined to bring the conquered people under written justice and laws. He therefore ordered to be brought before him the laws of the English in their threefold division: that is, Mercian law, Dane law, and Wessex law. Some of these he rejected, and to others he gave his approval. He added to them those Norman laws from overseas which seemed to him most effective in protecting the peace of the kingdom. Finally, lest anything be lacking, as the crowning act of his foresight, he took counsel and commissioned discrete men to go from his side and travel in circuit through the kingdom. They made a diligent survey of the entire land, in forests, pastures, meadows and cultivated fields. In simple language they set down their findings in a book, so that everyone might be content with his own rights and not seek with impunity to encroach upon the rights of others. The survey was divided according to counties, hundreds and hides. The king's name was placed at the head, and then there appeared in order the names of other nobles, his tenants-in-chief, according to the dignity of their status. Numbers were assigned to each name in order; by the numbers one can easily find in the course of the book information which pertains to them. The natives call this book by the metaphor of "Domesday," that is, the "Day of Judgment." For just as the sentence of that strict, dread and final examination cannot be overturned by any skillful cavil, so also, when there occurs in the realm a dispute concerning those things which are recorded there, when the book is consulted, its statement cannot be gainsaid nor rejected with impunity. For this reason we call the survey the "Book of Judgment," not because decisions on various uncertain points may be found in it but because it is impossible to disagree with it, as it will be impossible to disagree with the Last Judgment.

38. Frederick Barbarossa's constitution concerning fiefs

The German emperor Frederick I Barbarossa, another of the great
state-builders of the twelfth century, similarly sought to strengthen his
authority by interpreting the obligations owed him by his subjects in
terms of both Roman conceptions of imperial authority and feudal
notions of lordship. In the following constitution, issued at Roncaglia
in Italy in 1158, Frederick defined the rights and obligations of holders
of fiefs in his empire. The source is the Constitutio de iure feudorum,
Constitutiones et Acta Publica imperatorum et regum, ed. L. Weiland
(Monumenta Germaniae Historica, Legum Sectio IV; Hanover, 1893),
pp. 247–49. The translation is by D. Herlihy.

Frederick, by the grace of God king of the Romans and always
Augustus, to all those subject to his empire.

(1) It behooves our imperial concern so to exercise care over
the commonwealth and to investigate the needs of our subjects, so
that the interests of the realm will continue uninjured and the
status of individual persons may remain unharmed. Therefore,
while according to custom of our predecessors we were sitting in a
general court at Roncaglia for judgment, we received a strong
complaint from the Italian princes, from both the rectors of
churches and other faithful men of the realm, that their tenants
without the permission of their lords had obligated as pledges their
benefices and fiefs which as vassals they held from them, or had
sold them or by some trick had alienated them by lease. Therefore
they were losing the services due, and the honor of the empire and
additional support for our felicitous expedition were very much
diminished.

(2) Therefore, with the counsel of the bishops, dukes, margraves, counts, palatine judges, and other noble men, by this edict
to be valid forever with the mercy of God, we determined that no
one should be allowed to sell the entire fief or any part of it, or to
mortgage it or in any way to alienate it or to give it in alms without

the permission of that higher lord to whom the fief pertains. Emperor Lothar [III], carefully considering the future, promulgated a law prohibiting this.

(3) We, however, considering the larger interests of the realm, quash and reduce to nullity by this present law not only all illicit alienations of this sort which may occur in the future but also those perpetrated in the past, with no limitation of time. For whatever at the beginning was not valid in law ought not to become so with the passage of time. We also oppose the cunning machinations of some who for a money payment, under the form of an investiture which they say is allowed them, sell fiefs and transfer them to others. We absolutely prohibit that this pretense or any other should be plotted in the fraudulent contravention of this constitution. The penalty set by our authority is that both seller and purchaser, who are discovered to have contracted so illegally, should lose the fief, which should be freely returned to the lord. Moreover, the notary who drew up a written instrument concerning this should amid the peril of infamy lose his office and his hand.

(4) Moreover, if anyone older than fourteen inherits a fief and by his carelessness and negligence remains for a year and a day without seeking the investiture of the fief from his proper lord, after the passage of this length of time he should lose the fief and it should revert to the lord.

(5) We also firmly establish both in Italy and in Germany that once a general expedition has been announced, whoever is summoned by his lord to participate in that expedition and rashly neglects to serve a suitable length of time, or refuses to send to his lord an acceptable substitute or does not surrender to his lord one-half the income of his fief for one year, shall lose the fief which he holds from a bishop or another lord, and the lord of the fief shall have full freedom to confiscate it for his own use.

(6) Moreover, duchies, marches, and counties are not henceforth to be divided. Any other fief may be divided, if the co-heirs wish, but with the following conditions: all who hold part of the fief, whether divided or to be divided, shall swear fealty to the lord; no vassal should be compelled to have more than one lord for one fief, and the lord may not transfer the fief to another lord without the consent of his vassals.

(7) Further, if the son of a vassal offends the lord, his father at the request of the lord should bring his son to do satisfaction to the

lord, or force him to leave his household. Otherwise, he shall lose his fief. If the father should want to bring the son in order to do satisfaction, and the son refuses, at the death of the father he shall not inherit the fief, unless he first does satisfaction to the lord. In a like manner, the vassal should act regarding all his own household dependents.

(8) We also command the following. If a vassal should have a rear vassal [a vassal's vassal] from his fief, and if the rear vassal offends the lord of his lord, unless he does this while serving another lord which without fraud he possessed before, he shall lose his fief, and the fief shall return to his lord from whom he held it unless, when requested, he was ready to give satisfaction to the chief lord whom he offended. If the mesne lord, when asked by his lord, does not ask the person who offended the chief lord that he make satisfaction, he shall lose his fief.

(9) In case of controversy between two vassals of the same fief, the lord should have jurisdiction and the controversy should be settled by him. In case of a controversy between a lord and a vassal, it shall be decided by the peers of the lord's court, who are sworn by their oath of fealty.

(10) We also decree that in every oath of fealty the emperor shall be excepted by name.

39. The Assize of Clarendon

One of the great "assizes," or administrative regulations, of Henry II Plantagenet was issued at Clarendon in 1166. It regulated the procedures to be followed by the justices in eyre in regard to criminal cases. The reader should note the use of the sworn inquest or jury in the investigation of crime. The Latin text of the Assize of Clarendon is found in *Select Charters and Other Illustrations of English Constitutional History*, ed. W. Stubbs (9th ed. rev. by H. W. C. Davis; Oxford: Clarendon Press, 1966), pp. 167–73. The following translation is adapted from *Select Documents of English Constitutional History*, eds. G. B. Adams and H. M. Stephens (New York: Macmillan Co., 1914), pp. 14–18.

Here begins the Assize of Clarendon, made by King Henry II
with the assent of the archbishops, bishops, abbots, earls and barons
of all England.

1. In the first place, the aforesaid King Henry, with the consent
of all his barons, for the preservation of the peace and the keeping
of justice, has enacted that inquiry should be made through the
several counties and through the several hundreds, by twelve of the
most legal men of the hundred and by four of the most legal men
of each vill, upon their oath that they will tell the truth, whether
there is in their hundred or in their vill, any man who has been
accused or publicly suspected of himself being a robber, or murderer, or thief, or of being a receiver of robbers, or murderers, or
thieves, since the lord king has been king. And let the justices make
this inquiry before themselves, and the sheriffs before themselves.

2. And let any one who has been found by the oath of the
aforesaid, to have been accused or publicly suspected of having
been a robber, or murderer, or thief, or a receiver of them, since
the lord king has been king, be arrested and go to the ordeal of
water and let him swear that he has not been a robber, or murderer, or thief, or receiver of them since the lord king has been
king, to the value of five shillings, so far as he knows.

3. And if the lord of the man who has been arrested or his
steward or his men shall have claimed him, with a pledge, within
the third day after he has been seized, let him be given up and his
chattels until he himself satisfies the law.

4. And when a robber, or murderer, or thief, or receiver of
them shall have been seized through the above-mentioned oath, if
the justices are not to come very soon into that county where they
have been arrested, let the sheriffs send word to the nearest justice
by some intelligent man that they have arrested such men, and the
justices will send back word to the sheriffs where they wish that
these should be brought before them; and the sheriffs shall bring
them before the justices; and along with these they shall bring
from the hundred and the vill where they have been arrested, two
legal men to carry the record of the county and of the hundred as
to why they were seized, and there before the justice let them satisfy the law.

5. And in the case of those who have been arrested through the
aforesaid oath of this assize, no one shall have court, or judgment,

or chattels, except the lord king in his court before his justices, and the lord king shall have all their chattels. In the case of those, however, who have been arrested, otherwise than through this oath, let it be as it has been accustomed and ought to be.

6. And the sheriffs who have arrested them shall bring such before the justice without any other summons than they have from him. And when robbers, or murderers, or thieves, or receivers of them, who have been arrested through the oath or otherwise, are handed over to the sheriffs they also must receive them immediately without delay.

7. And in the several counties where there are no jails, let such be made in a borough or in some castle of the king, from the money of the king and from his forest, if one shall be near, or from some other neighboring forest, on the view of the servants of the king; in order that in them the sheriffs may be able to detain those who have been seized by the officials who are accustomed to do this or by their servants.

8. And the lord king moreover wills that all should come to the county courts to make this oath, so that no one shall remain behind because of any franchise which he has or court or jurisdiction which he has, but that they should come to the making of this oath.

9. And there is to be no one within a castle or without a castle, or even in the honor of Wallingford, who may forbid the sheriffs to enter into his court or his land for seeing to the frankpledges and that all are under pledges; and let them be sent before the sheriffs under a free pledge.

10. And in cities and boroughs, let no one have men or receive them in his house or in his land or his soc, whom he does not take in hand that he will produce before the justice if they shall be required, or else let them be under a frankpledge.

11. And let there be none in a city or borough or in a castle or without or even in the honor of Wallingford who shall forbid the sheriffs to enter into his land or his jurisdiction to arrest those who have been charged or publicly suspected of being robbers or murderers or thieves or receivers of them, or outlaws, or persons charged concerning the forest; but he requires that they should aid them to capture these.

12. And if any one is captured who has in his possession the fruits of robbery or theft, if he is of bad reputation and has an evil

testimony from the public, and has not a warrant, let him not [retain them]. And if he shall not have been publicly suspected, on account of the possession which he has, let him go to the water.

13. And if any one shall have acknowledged robbery or murder or theft or the reception of them in the presence of legal men or of the hundreds, and afterwards shall wish to deny it, he shall not have [the right].

14. The lord king wills moreover that those who stand trial and shall be absolved by the law, if they are of very bad reputation, and publicly and disgracefully spoken ill of by the testimony of many and legal men, shall abjure the lands of the king, so that within eight days they shall go over the sea, unless the wind shall have detained them; and with the first wind which they shall have afterward they shall go over the sea, and they shall not afterward return into England, except on the permission of the lord king; and then let them be outlawed if they return, and if they return they shall be seized as outlaws.

15. And the lord king forbids any vagabond, that is a wandering or an unknown man, to be sheltered anywhere except in a borough, and even there he shall be sheltered only one night unless he shall be sick there, or his horse, so that he is able to show an evident excuse.

16. And if he shall have been there more than one night, let him be arrested and held until his lord shall come to give securities for him, or until he himself shall have secured pledges; and let him likewise be arrested who has sheltered him.

17. And if any sheriff shall have sent word to any other sheriff that men have fled from his county into another county on account of robbery or murder or theft, or the reception of them, or for outlawry or for a charge concerning the forest of the king, let him arrest them. And even if he knows of himself or through others that such men have fled into his county, let him arrest them and hold them until he shall have secured pledges from them.

18. And let all sheriffs cause a list to be made of all fugitives who have fled from their counties; and let them do this in the presence of their county courts, and they will carry the written names of these before the justices when they come first before these, so that they may be sought through all England, and their chattels may be seized for the use of the king.

19. And the lord king wills that, from the time when the sheriffs have received the summons of the justices in eyre to appear before them with their county courts, they shall gather together their county courts and make inquiry for all who have recently come into their counties since this assize; and that they should send them away with pledges that they will be before the justices, or else keep them in custody until the justices come to them, and then they shall have them before the justices.

20. The lord king moreover prohibits monks and canons and all religious houses from receiving any one of the lesser people as a monk or canon or brother, until it is known of what reputation he is, unless he shall be sick unto death.

21. The lord king moreover forbids any one in all England to receive in his land or his jurisdiction or in a house under him any one of the sect of those renegades who have been excommunicated and branded at Oxford. And if any one shall have received them, he will be at the mercy of the lord king, and the house in which they have been shall be carried outside the village and burned. And each sheriff will take this oath that he will hold this, and will make all his servants swear this, and the stewards of the barons, and all knights and free tenants of the counties.

22. And the lord king wills that this assize shall be held in his kingdom so long as it shall please him.

40. The accounts of the sheriff of Worcester

Of the rich series of English administrative records, one of the most interesting is the pipe rolls, which record the yearly accountings of the sheriffs, made to the Exchequer at Michaelmas (September 29). The oldest surviving pipe roll dates from 1130 (31 Henry I), but the series does not become continuous until the reign of Henry's grandson, Henry II. The accountings were quite complex and detailed undertakings, as the sheriff was responsible for a great variety of revenues. He had to pay the "farm" or rental from the king's demesne in his shire; numerous fines collected in the course of judicial procedures or for violations of the forest law; "purprestures," or fines for encroaching on royal lands; "escheats," or lands coming to the king in default of heirs; dues attached to royal fiefs; amercements made in return for the king's mercies or favors, and many other charges. Moreover the sheriff collected such extraordinary taxes as the Danegeld or the scutage, which royal vassals had to pay if they did not serve personally in the royal host.

In accounting for all these charges, the sheriff was first of all given credit for moneys actually paid to the Treasury. Frequently, he would make some payments earlier in the year at Easter. He would be given a receipt in the form of a notched stick, broken in half, of which he took one part and the Exchequer the other. This is the sense of the word "tallies" (literally, sticks), used in the accounting with the meaning of "payments." He was also credited with all fixed or extraordinary disbursements made at the king's command. If he paid more money to the Treasury than was actually due, the surplus was noted at the end of the accounting; if he was short in his payments, the deficit would be carried over to the accounting of the following year.

For all their complexities, the pipe rolls offer an unexcelled picture of the sources of royal revenue in the twelfth century. Moreover, they provide numerous, vivid insights into the social life of the epoch.

The document is the yearly accounting of the sheriff of Worcester, one of England's midland counties or shires. The year, 1186–87, has a particular interest, as the king was campaigning against Galloway and the sheriff was obligated to collect not only the usual revenues but scutage payments from the royal vassals who were not serving in the army. The reader can thus form a rough judgment as to the importance of scutage in comparison with the king's usual dues. The source, translated by D. Herlihy, is taken from *The Pipe Roll of the Thirty-third Year of King Henry II, A.D. 1186–87* (Publications of the Pipe Roll Society, 37; London, 1915), pp. 215–20. The word "blanch" in regard to money means assayed coins of good silver.

33 Henry II. Worcester

Robert Marmion accounts for 24 shillings blanch of the old farm of Worcester. He has paid the Treasury, and he is quit.

The same concerning the new farm. He has paid in the Treasury 175 pounds, 10 shillings, and 7 pence blanch.

He has spent: in fixed alms, 2 marks to the Knights of the Temple. In fixed payment to the chaplain of Worcester, 30 shillings and 5 pence. To the watchman, 30 shillings and 5 pence. And to the porter, 45 shillings and 7 pence.

In fixed tithes to the monks of Westminster, 8 pounds. To the monks of Cormeilles, 75 shillings. To the monks of Lyre, 30 shillings. To the monks of Gloucester, 20 shillings. And to the cloistered monks of Stoke Prior, 30 shillings and 5 pence.

And in lands given to the abbot of Bordesley, 6 pounds and 3 shillings in Holeweie [in Broadwas]. And to the same, 10 shillings in the fishpond of Martley. And to the same, 24 shillings in Bromsgrove. And to the hunter who captures wolves, 3 shillings.

In payments to 10 knights and 10 foot soldiers for 28 days, whom he sent beyond the sea for the king, 11 pounds, 13 shillings, and 4 pence, according to the writ of the king. And in fixing the drainage at the mansions of the king at Feckenham, 3 shillings and 5 pence.

And he has paid in excess 4 shillings and 2 pence blanch.

CONCERNING PURPRESTURES AND ESCHEATS

The same sheriff accounts for 13 pounds for one hawk and pack horse. He has paid the Treasury, and he is quit.

The same sheriff accounts for 20 pounds of the rents of the forest of Feckenham. He has paid the Treasury, and he is quit.

The same sheriff accounts for 36 shillings in regard to the land which belonged to Fulk of Horseley. He has paid the Treasury, and he is quit.

The same sheriff accounts for 7 shillings in regard to the land which was of Gervase Paynel in Northampton. And for 12 pence in regard to a certain house of Worcester. He has paid the Treasury in two tallies, and he is quit.

The same sheriff accounts for 12 pounds of the farm of Hanley. He has paid the Treasury 10 pounds and 16 shillings. And in fixed tithes to the monks of Lyre, 20 shillings. And to the monks of Malvern, 4 shillings. And he is quit.

The same sheriff accounts for 60 shillings of the rent of the forest of Malvern. He has paid the treasury 55 shillings. And in fixed alms to the monks of Tewkesbury, 5 shillings. And he is quit.

The same sheriff accounts for 20 pounds for the farm of Ederesfeld and Herwich in regard to the members of the same town. He has paid the Treasury 17 pounds. And in regard to the lands given to Simon of Colombes, 60 shillings. And he is quit.

The same sheriff accounts for 6 pounds and 10 shillings of the farm of Bisley. He has paid the Treasury 100 shillings. And in regard to lands given to Simon of Colombes, 30 shillings. And he is quit.

The same sheriff accounts for 27 pounds of the profits of Kidderminster which belonged to Manaseri Biset before the king returned it to his heir. He paid the Treasury, and he is quit.

The same sheriff accounts for 20 shillings of profits from the same town. He has paid the Treasury, and he is quit.

Ulricus and Alardus moneyers account for 105 shillings in amercement. They paid the Treasury 4 shillings, and they owe 100 shillings and 12 pence.

Fulk of Horseley owes 8 pounds and 7 pence amercement. He also owes 9 pounds and 12 shillings from the chattel of fugitives. But he is dead and the king has the income of his land.

The abbot of Westminster owes 20 pounds from the old scutage. But it is a demand in excess, as he says. The bishop of Worcester owes 8 pounds for knights, whom he does not recognize.

Gocelin of Wich accounts for 48 shillings and 4 pence because he took a wife without permission of the king, as she was under the donation of the king. He has paid the Treasury 5 shillings, and he owes 43 shillings and 4 pence.

The same sheriff accounts for 44 pounds, 9 shillings, and 6 pence in respect to the damages, assarts, and pleas of the forest of Worcester. He has paid the Treasury 6 shillings and 8 pence, and he owes 24 pounds, 2 shillings, and 10 pence.

Gilbert of Lanley accounts for 22 shillings and 4 pence for false testimony concerning a robbery. He has paid the Treasury, and he is quit.

William the steward of the prior accounts for 5 shillings in amercement for the outlaw Simon. He has paid the Treasury, and he is quit.

The same sheriff owes 8 pounds, 2 shillings, and 2 pence in respect to the damages, assarts, pleas, and purprestures of the forest of Worcestershire.

The wife of Edricus the moneyer accounts for 5 shillings for the debts of her husband. She has paid the Treasury, and she is quit.

Bonefei the Jew of Worcester owes 1 mark of gold in respect to amercing himself in the presence of the king from the amercement according to the new assize.

CONCERNING THE PLEAS OF GILBERT PIPARD AND
WILLIAM, SON OF STEPHEN, AND THEIR ASSOCIATES

Nicholas of Clifton accounts for 20 pence for unjust disseisin. He has paid the Treasury, and he is quit.

The same sheriff owes 1 mark for the hundred of Pershore, for murder.

CONCERNING THE PLEAS OF THE FOREST THROUGH GALFRIED,
SON OF PETER

Robert of Wich accounts for 46 shillings and 8 pence for dogs against the assize. He has paid the Treasury, and he is quit.

Richard de Puteis owes 2 marks because he represented Richard for Frewin.

Jordan de Ley accounts for 3 shillings and 4 pence for dogs against the assize. He has paid the Treasury, and he is quit.

Ignardus owes 12 pence for damage. The same sheriff owes 4 shillings and 2 pence for damage of the woods of Eckington.

The same sheriff accounts for 3 shillings and 4 pence for damage of the woods of Gravely. And for 12 pence for damage of the woods of Opton. And 2 shillings for damage of the woods of Bredicot. He has paid the Treasury in three tallies, and he is quit.

The same sheriff owes 23 pounds, 15 shillings, and 6 pence for the assarts of Worcester.

Ralph the forester of the abbot of Tewesbury accounts for one-half a mark because he did not have his warrant. He has paid the Treasury, and he is quit.

William Baril owes one-half a mark in amercement for woods sold. William Walensis owes 10 shillings for woods sold. William Niger owes one-half a mark in amercement for the forest. Robert Folet the cleric owes 5 marks for dogs in the forest. Roger the cleric of Cadesley owes one-half a mark for the same. Adam the cleric of Ederesfeld owes one-half a mark for the same.

The abbot of Pershore accounts for 20 shillings for assarts. He has paid the Treasury, and he is quit.

Alexander of Bulebech owes 18 pence for default. Adam Wexman owes 2 shillings for his house which is in the purpresture of the forest; John and Ernwi and Osbert and Hugh owe 3 shillings for purpresture. Alard and Robert of Feckenham owe 12 pence for the same. Richard and Roger of Windsor owe 12 pence for the same.

Turchill, the man of Roger and Alexander and Edricus, accounts for 2 shillings for the same. They have paid the Treasury 12 pence from Turchill. And they owe 12 pence.

CONCERNING THE PLEAS OF GODFRIED DE LUCY AND HUGH BARDULF AND WILLIAM RUFFUS

The same sheriff owes 21 shillings and 2 pence of the hundred of Pershore for murder and for concealment.

CONCERNING GIFTS AND PLEAS OF THE COURT

Simon of Ribbeford accounts for 16 pounds in amercement for the appeal of Ralph of Martley. He has paid in the Treasury 6 pounds, 13 shillings, and 4 pence. And he owes 9 pounds and 6 shillings and 8 pence.

Margaret of Hindlep owes 5 marks for having her part of the fief of half a knight's fief against Alexander of Abetot. But she does not yet have her right.

The abbot of Pershore accounts for 31 pounds and 9 shillings for two disseisins. He has paid in the Treasury 4 pounds, 6 shillings, and 8 pence. And he owes 27 pounds, 2 shillings, and 4 pence.

William of Beauchamp owes 8 pounds, 6 shillings, and 8 pence because he did not have his forester indicted for a forest offense whom his steward pledged.

NEW PLEAS AND NEW AGREEMENTS THROUGH ROBERT MARMION,

Ralph of Lingein accounts for one-half a mark for unjust disseisin. He has paid the Treasury, and he is quit.

NEW PLEAS AND NEW AGREEMENTS THROUGH ROBERT MARMION, RALPH OF ARDEN, AND HUGH PANTULF, AND WILLIAM, SON OF STEPHEN

The same sheriff accounts for 1 mark from the hundred of Evesham for murder. He has paid the Treasury, and he is quit.

CONCERNING THOSE WHO HAVE PAID IN FULL

The same sheriff accounts for 4 pounds, 6 shillings, and 8 pence for small debts of men whose names and the reason for whose debts are in the roll of the justiciars mentioned above, which they have paid the Treasury. They paid it in the Treasury in ten tallies, and he is quit.

The same sheriff accounts for one-half a mark from Aldith of Wrodenhold in amercement. And for one-half mark in frankpledge from Edreth de Mutton for the death of Ern. And for one-half mark in frankpledge from Henry, son of William, for the flight of William. He has paid this to the Treasury in three tallies, and he is quit.

CONCERNING THE PLEAS OF THE FOREST THROUGH ROBERT DE BROC,
WILLIAM OF STANTON, AND ROBERT OF HASELEA

The same sheriff accounts for 1 mark of Robert le Bret for a script badly presented. And for 1 mark from Simon Flavus for the same. And for 1 mark from Fladebrus for the damage of the forest. And for 1 mark of Wichebold for the same. And for 20 shillings from Bredon for a new pond and mill. And for 1 mark from Leg for the same. And for 1 mark of Dieherst for damage of the forest. The total is 100 shillings. He has paid the Treasury in seven tallies, and he is quit.

CONCERNING THOSE WHO HAVE PAID IN FULL, OF WHOM EACH
WAS IN DEBT FOR MORE THAN HALF A MARK

The same sheriff accounts for 6 pounds, 13 shillings, and 4 pence in amercements of men and villages whose names and the reasons for whose debts are in the roll of the justiciars. He has paid the Treasury in twenty tallies, and he is quit.

CONCERNING THOSE WHO HAVE PAID IN FULL IN SMALL THINGS

The same sheriff accounts for 6 pounds, 11 shillings in petty amercements of men and villages for the forfeiture of the forest. He has paid the Treasury, and he is quit.

Richard the Fleming owes 2 shillings for default. Milo Folet owes 20 shillings since although not a forester he distrained men in the forest. Roger, son of Levenod, owes 12 pence for damage of the forest. Pinvin, of the abbey of Westminster, owes one mark for the same. Hugh Mac owes 12 pence for the same. John Panc owes 2 shillings for the same. Forthlton owes one mark for the same.

. . . of Evesham accounts for one-half mark for a false gallon-measure. He has paid the Treasury, and he is quit.

The same sheriff accounts for 26 pounds, 13 shillings, and 11 pence of assarts of Worcester. He has paid the Treasury 7 pounds and 13 shillings. And he owes 19 pounds and 11 pence.

The same sheriff accounts for 27 shillings and 7 pence of the chattels of the outlawed Brian Partriz. And for 8 shillings of the chattels of Robert of Diepedal. And for 2 shillings of the chattel of the outlaw Edred of Muton. He has paid the Treasury in three tallies, and he is quit.

CONCERNING THE SCUTAGE OF THE KNIGHTS OF WORCESTER
WHO DID NOT GO WITH THE KING IN THE ARMY AGAINST GALLOWAY

The bishop of Worcester accounts for 49 pounds and 6 shillings in scutage of his knights. He has paid the Treasury 45 pounds, 6 shillings. And in the given lands which the king holds of the fief of the episcopate, 60 shillings. And in the fief of the count of Gloucester which is in the hands of the king, 20 shillings. And he is quit.

The abbot of Evesham accounts for 4 pounds and 10 shillings for his knights. He has paid the Treasury 4 pounds. He owes 10 shillings. The same accounts for the same debt. He has paid the Treasury, and he is quit.

The abbot of Pershore accounts for 40 shillings in scutage. He has paid the Treasury, and he is quit.

The abbot of Westminster accounts for 15 pounds in scutage for his knights. He has paid the treasury 11 pounds and 10 shillings. And in the desmesne of the king at Stoke which the king holds from the fief of the abbey, 20 shillings. And he owes 50 shillings.

The same sheriff accounts for 30 shillings in scutage for freeholders in the estate of Stoke. He has paid the Treasury, and he is quit.

. . . the sheriff accounts for 110 shillings of the knights of Roger de Toeni in his bailiwick. He has paid the Treasury, and he is quit.

CONCERNING THE TALLAGE OF THE DEMESNE LANDS OF THE
KING AND OF THOSE LANDS WHICH WERE THEN IN THE KING'S
HANDS, THROUGH ROBERT MARMION, RALPH OF ARDEN, AND
WILLIAM, SON OF STEPHEN, AND THEIR ASSOCIATES

The citizens of Worcester account for 20 pounds of their gift. They have paid the Treasury 10 pounds, and they owe 10 pounds.

The men of Hanley account for 20 shillings of the same. They have paid the Treasury 10 shillings, and they owe 10 shillings.

The men of Feckenham account for 43 shillings of the same. They have paid the Treasury 11 shillings and 6 pence, and they owe 31 shillings and 6 pence.

The men of Martley account for 4 marks of the same. They have paid the Treasury 2 marks, and they owe 2 marks.

The men of Suckley account for 4 marks of the same. They have paid the Treasury 2 marks, and they owe 2 marks.

The men of Horseley account for one-half mark of the same. They have paid the Treasury, and they are quit.

The men of Ederesfeld account for 22 shillings of the same. They have paid the Treasury 11 shillings, and they owe 11 shillings.

The men of Bisley account for 10 shillings of the same. They have paid the Treasury 5 shillings, and they owe five.

The men of Bromsgrove account for 8 marks of the same. They have paid the Treasury 4 marks, and they owe 4 marks.

The men of Kidderminster account for 4 pounds of the same. They have paid the Treasury 40 shillings, and they owe 40 shillings.

41. Writs of Henry II Plantagenet

The "writ" was technically an order issued by the king or by his justices. Usually, it was directed to the sheriff and told him to take some action, such as restoring the possession of a disputed land or a right to a particular plaintiff, until such time as the ownership of the land or right could be determined by full trial. Writs were precisely designed for particular cases, and their numbers grew considerably in the twelfth and early thirteenth centuries. The plaintiff had to be certain that he secured the appropriate type of writ for his needs, as otherwise his case would fall. Writs were always purchased from the justice or secured in return for the payment of a fine, and the practice of issuing them therefore added to the royal profits from justice. The first two of the following writs are taken from the chronicle of the monastery of Abingdon; the third is a model writ of the type *Praecipe*, taken from Glanville, "Tract on the Laws and Customs of the Kingdom of England." The translations are taken from *Select Documents*, eds. Adams and Stephens, pp. 7, 28.

Writ concerning lands at Stanton

Henry, king of England, to Hugh of Buckland and William sheriff of Oxfordshire, greeting.

Order on my behalf the men of your counties to declare the whole truth concerning the three virgates of land which Rualcus de Avranches claims, and if they belong to the manor of Stanton which I gave to him, let him have possession; but if not let the abbey of Abingdon have possession.

Witness: Roger the chancellor. By———Basset; at Cambridge.

Writ concerning lands at Caversham

Henry, king of England, to Walter Giffard and Agnes, his mother, greeting.

I order that you render full justice to Faritius, abbot of Abingdon, concerning the land which Ralph of Caversham gave to Abingdon by your permission, and of which the church was seised [had possession].

Witness: Ranulf the chancellor, at Windsor.

The writ Praecipe

The king to the sheriff, greeting.

Command (*Praecipe*) A. that, lawfully and without delay, he restore to B. one hide of land, in such a town from which the said B. complains that the aforesaid A. is keeping him by force, and if he does not do it, summon him by good summoners to be before me or my justices on the morrow after the octave of Easter at such-and-such a place to show cause wherefore he has failed to do it; and have there the summoners and this writ.

Witness: Ranulph de Glanville, at Clarendon.

⎍⎍⎍⎍⎍⎍⎍⎍⎍⎍⎍⎍⎍⎍⎍⎍⎍⎍⎍⎍⎍⎍⎍⎍⎍⎍⎍⎍⎍⎍⎍⎍r

42. Form of proceeding on the judicial visitation in England

In the great growth of royal authority in England under the Norman and Angevin kings, the justices in eyre played a central role; they made the authority of the king's court a reality on the local level, and through their decisions helped elaborate the "common law" of the realm. The justices also exerted a close supervision over the king's rights and over the sheriffs who were responsible for maintaining them. The following document describes the business handled by the justices in their circuit which began in September, 1194. The first paragraph has a special interest, as it describes the election of the grand jury. The "wapentake" is the name used for the hundred, a subdivision of the county, in the part of England know as the Danelaw. The Danelaw was itself the region in the east of England once occupied by the Danes—an experience which long stamped their customs and organizations. The Latin text may be found in *Select Charters*, ed. Stubbs, pp. 251–57. The following translation is taken from *Select Documents*, ed. Adams and Stephens, pp. 29–33.

Form of proceeding in the pleas of the crown
In the first place, four knights are to be chosen from out of the whole county, who, upon their oaths, are to choose two lawful knights of every hundred and wapentake, and these two are to choose upon their oath ten knights of every hundred or wapentake, or, if there shall not be knights sufficient, free and lawful men, in order that these twelve may together make inquisition on each of the following heads in every hundred or wapentake.

Heads of the pleas of the crown
1. Of the pleas of the crown, both new and old, and all those which have not yet been concluded before the justiciaries of our lord the king.

2. Item of all recognizances and all pleas which have been summoned before the justiciaries, by writ of the king or of the chief justice, or which have been sent before them from the supreme court of the king.

3. Item of escheats, what these are now, and what these have been, since the king set out on his expedition to the land of Jerusalem; and what were at that time in the king's hands, and whether they are now in his hands or not; and of all escheats of our lord king, if they have been taken out of his hands, how, and by whom, and into whose hands they have come, and of what kind, and if any person has had any profits from the same, and what, and what was the value thereof, and what is the present value; and if there is any escheat, which belongs to our lord the king, which is not at present in his hands.

4. Item of churches which are in the gift of our lord the king.

5. Item of wardships of children, which belong to our lord the king.

6. Item of marriages of maidens, or of widows, which belong to our lord the king.

7. Item of malefactors, and their harborers and abettors.

8. Item of forgers.

9. Item of murderers of the Jews, who they are, and of the pledges of Jews so slain, their chattels, lands, debts, and writings and who has the same; and how much each person owes them, and what pledges they had, and who holds the same, and how much they are worth, and who has the profits thereof, and what they are; all the pledges and the debts of the Jews so slain are to be seized for the king; and those who were present at the murder of the Jews, who have not made a composition thereon with our lord the king, or with his justiciaries, are to be arrested and are not to be liberated except by our lord the king, or his justiciaries.

10. Item of all aids given for the ransom of our lord the king, how much each person promised, and how much he has paid, and how much is still due from him.

11. Item of the adherents of earl John, and such of them as have made a composition with our lord the king, and such as have not.

12. Item of the chattels of earl John or his adherents, which have not been converted to the use of our lord the king; and how much the sheriffs and their bailiffs have received; and who has given any thing contrary to the ancient customs of the kingdom.

13. Item of all the lands of earl John, of his demesnes, and wards, and escheats, and his gifts, and for what reason the same were given, and all the gifts of earl John are to be seized for our lord the king, except those which have been confirmed by the king.

14. Item of the debts and fines which are due to earl John, and for what causes; and all the same are to be demanded on behalf of our lord the king.

15. Item of usurers, and of the chattels of such of them as are dead.

16. Item of wines sold contrary to the assize, and of false measures for wine as also for other things.

17. Item of such crusaders as have died before setting out for the land of Jerusalem; and who possesses their chattels, and what they are, and how many.

18. Item of grand assizes, which are of lands a hundred shillings in value or less.

19. Item of defaults.

20. Also in every county there are to be three knights chosen, and one clerk, who are to be keepers of the pleas of the crown.

21. And no sheriff is to be justice in his shrievalty, nor yet in any county which he has held since the first coronation of our lord the king.

22. Also all the cities, and boroughs, and demesne lands of our lord the king are to be talliaged.

23. Also, the said justices, together with the bailiffs of William of the Church of Saint Mary, Geoffrey Fitz-Peter, William de Chimelli, William Bruere, Hugh Bardolph, and of the sheriff of each place, are to cause the knights mentioned on the roll to be summoned in their respective counties, to appear at a time and place which they shall signify to them, and to make them swear in their presence that they will use all their lawful endeavors to restore the lands and escheats belonging to our lord the king, and to value the same to the advantage of our lord the king, and not through hatred, favor or regard for any person, to omit so to do. And the said knights before named shall, upon their oath, make choice of twelve lawful knights, or free and lawful men, if knights shall not be found for the purpose, in the different parts of each county on the circuit of the said justices itinerant, as shall seem expedient; who shall, in like manner, make oath that they will use

all their lawful endeavors to restore, and to value and establish the rights of wardship and escheat in those parts, and will give their counsel and assistance to advantage the king therein, as before mentioned. The said jurors shall also, upon oath, choose from free men as many and such as they shall think necessary for the performance of the aforesaid business of our lord the king as to escheats and wardships, in such manner as may be best done for the advantage of our lord the king. It is also to be known, that the said wardships and escheats shall be made good out of the revenues arising therefrom up to the feast of Michaelmas, as also from the revenues at that time due; and, if they shall not suffice, then the deficiency shall be supplied by a toll of our lord the king: it being understood that those who hold the said wardships and escheats to farm shall, at the feast of Saint Michael, answer for the same, and thenceforward for the improvements as well. And as for those who shall hold the said wardships and escheats to farm, our lord the king shall give them warranty for the same from year to year until the termination thereof; so that, although our lord the king should give any of them to any person, the farmer shall still hold his farm till the end of the year, by paying to him to whom our lord the king shall have so given it, the rent which shall be due to the king for the same until the end of the year. The rights of justice of the escheat, however, which he shall have so given shall remain with our lord the king, unless our lord the king shall have given them by name. The farmer, when he shall have given up his farm, is to have all his stock which he shall have placed upon the farm, and all his property over and above the property of the king there, freely and without diminution. They shall also have letters patent of our lord the archbishop, containing the tenor of the charter of our lord the king made relative thereto.

Most diligent enquiry shall also be made what is the rental assessed upon each manor in the demesne, and the value of all other assessments in the said manors, and how many carrucates there are, and how much they are each worth, not estimating them at a fixed value of twenty shillings only, but, according as the land is good or bad, whether the value is likely to increase or decrease. Those persons who shall take these farms shall stock their farms, as already said, according to the above named value from the revenues of the escheats and wardships. Enquiry is also to be made with how many oxen and plough horses each carrucate ought to be stocked; and how many and what amount of stock each manor is able to support and the result thereof is then to be openly and distinctly reduced to writing. The price set upon a bull shall be four shillings, and upon a cow the same, upon a plough-horse the same, upon a sheep with fine wool ten pence, upon a sheep with coarse wool six pence, upon a sow twelve pence, and upon a boar twelve pence; and when the farmers give up their farms they shall be answerable in the aforesaid sums, or in animals payable for the same, at the option of the farmers; and when all the aforesaid stock shall be placed thereon and duly valued, they shall all be enrolled openly and distinctly, and the register thereof shall be deposited in the exchequer. From this assize are to be excepted bishoprics and abbeys, and lands of barons who are nearly of age.

Also let enquiry be made, by the oath of the parties aforesaid, as to all wardships and escheats which are not in the hands of our lord the king, and they are to be taken possession of by our lord the king, and dealt with as other lands and escheats.

24. Heads concerning the Jews.

All debts and pledges of Jews are to be enrolled, as also their lands, houses, rents, and possessions. Any Jew who shall make concealment of any one of these things, shall forfeit to our lord the king his body, as also the thing concealed, and all his possessions and all his chattels; and no Jew shall ever be allowed to recover what he has so concealed. Also, let six or seven places be appointed, at which they shall make their loans, and let two lawful Christians and two lawful Jews and two lawful scribes be appointed, and in their presence, and in that of the clerks of William of the Church of Saint Mary and of William de Chimelli, let such loans be made, and let a deed describing the loan be made, after the manner of an indenture. One part is to remain in the hands of the Jew, sealed with his seal to whom the money is paid, while the other part is to remain in the common chest; on which there are to be three locks; whereof the two Christians are to keep one key, the two Jews another, and the clerks of William of the Church of Saint Mary and of Master William de Chimelli, the third; as also three seals, those who have the keys setting thereon their seals. The clerks also of the two Williams aforesaid are to have a register containing copies of all the deeds, and as the deeds are altered so shall the register be altered. For each deed shall be paid three pence; a moiety thereof by the Jew and a moiety by him to whom the money is lent; of which the two scribes are to have two pence, and the keeper of the register the third: and, for the future, no loan shall be made, no payment made to Jews, no alteration of the deeds, except in presence of the persons aforenamed, or the major part of them, if all shall be unable to be present. The said two Christians also are to have a register of receipts for payments made henceforth to Jews, and the two Jews are to have one, and the keeper of the register one. Also, every Jew shall make oath on his roll [of the Law] that he will cause all his debts, pledges, rents, and all his property and possessions to be enrolled, and that, as above stated, he will not conceal anything; and that, if he shall be able to learn that any one has concealed anything, he will secretly disclose the same to the judges sent to them, and that forgers of deeds and clippers of money, when he shall know of such persons, he will give information against, and detect the same, and the like with regard to the deeds so forged.

25. Also, the inquisition which was to be made relative to the exactions and seizures made by all bailiffs of the king, as well by the justices as by the sheriffs, constables, and foresters and their servants, since the time of the first coronation of our lord king Richard, and why such seizures were made, and by whom; and relative to all the chattels, gifts, and promises made on the occasion of seizure of the lands of earl John and his supporters; and who received the same, and what, and how much, was deferred by command of Hubert, archbishop of Canterbury, the king's chief justice.

43. Magna Carta

Bishop Stubbs, the great nineteenth-century historian, maintained that "the whole of the constitutional history of England is a commentary on this charter." Few historians today believe that, but most still regard it as a major step in the growth of English constitutionalism. The translation here is taken from *Select Documents*, eds. Adams and Stephens, pp. 42–52.

John, by the grace of God, king of England, lord of Ireland, duke of Normandy and Aquitaine, count of Anjou, to the archbishops, bishops, abbots, earls, barons, justiciars, foresters, sheriffs, reeves, servants, and all bailiffs and his faithful people greeting. Know that by the suggestion of God and for the good of our soul and those of all our predecessors and of our heirs, to the honor of God and the exaltation of holy church, and the improvement of our kingdom, by the advice of our venerable fathers Stephen, archbishop of Canterbury, primate of all England and Cardinal of the Holy Roman Church, Henry, archbishop of Dublin, William of London, Peter of Winchester, Joscelyn of Bath and Glastonbury, Hugh of Lincoln, Walter of Worcester, William of Coventry, and Benedict of Rochester, bishops; of Master Pandulf, subdeacon and member of the household of the lord Pope, of Brother Aymeric, master of the Knights of the Temple in England; and of the noblemen William Marshall, earl of Pembroke, William, earl of Salisbury, William, earl Warren, William, earl of Arundel, Alan of Galloway, constable of Scotland, Warren Fitz-Gerald, Peter Fitz-Herbert, Hubert de Burgh, seneschal of Poitou, Hugh de Nevil, Matthew Fitz-Herbert, Thomas Bassett, Alan Bassett, Philip d'Albini, Robert de Ropesle, John Marshall, John Fitz-Hugh, and others of our faithful.

1. In the first place we have granted to God, and by this our present charter confirmed, for us and our heirs forever, that the English church shall be free, and shall hold its rights entire and its liberties uninjured; and we will that it thus be observed; which is shown by this, that the freedom of elections, which is considered to be most important and especially necessary to the English church, we, of our pure and spontaneous will, granted, and by our charter confirmed, before the contest between us and our barons had arisen; and obtained a confirmation of it by the lord Pope Innocent III; which we will observe and which we will shall be observed in good faith by our heirs forever.

We have granted moreover to all free men of our kingdom for us and our heirs forever all the liberties written below, to be had and holden by themselves and their heirs from us and our heirs.

2. If any of our earls or barons, or others holding from us in chief by military service shall have died, and when he has died his heir shall be of full age and owe relief, he shall have his inheritance by the ancient relief; that is to say, the heir or heirs of an earl for

the whole barony of an earl a hundred pounds; the heir or heirs of a baron for a whole barony a hundred pounds; the heir or heirs of a knight, for a whole knight's fee, a hundred shillings at most; and who owes less let him give less according to the ancient custom of fiefs.

3. If moreover the heir of any one of such shall be under age, and shall be in wardship, when he comes of age he shall have his inheritance without relief and without a fine.

4. The custodian of the land of such a minor heir shall not take from the land of the heir any except reasonable products, reasonable customary payments, and reasonable services, and this without destruction or waste of men or of property; and if we shall have committed the custody of the land of any such a one to the sheriff or to any other who is to be responsible to us for its proceeds, and that man shall have caused destruction or waste from his custody we will recover damages from him, and the land shall be committed to two legal and discreet men of that fief, who shall be responsible for its proceeds to us or to him to whom we have assigned them; and if we shall have given or sold to any one the custody of any such land, and he has caused destruction or waste there, he shall lose that custody, and it shall be handed over to two legal and discreet men of that fief who shall be in like manner responsible to us as is said above.

5. The custodian moreover, so long as he shall have the custody of the land, must keep up the houses, parks, warrens, fish ponds, mills, and other things pertaining to the land, from the proceeds of the land itself; and he must return to the heir, when he has come to full age, all his land, furnished with ploughs and implements of husbandry according as the time of wainage requires and as the proceeds of the land are able reasonably to sustain.

6. Heirs shall be married without disparity, so nevertheless that before the marriage is contracted, it shall be announced to the relatives by blood of the heir himself.

7. A widow, after the death of her husband, shall have her marriage portion and her inheritance immediately and without obstruction, nor shall she give anything for her dowry or for her marriage portion, or for her inheritance which inheritance her husband and she held on the day of the death of her husband; and she may remain in the house of her husband for forty days after his death, within which time her dowry shall be assigned to her.

8. No widow shall be compelled to marry so long as she prefers to live without a husband, provided she gives security that she will not marry without our consent, if she holds from us, or without the consent of her lord from whom she holds, if she holds from another.

9. Neither we nor our bailiffs will seize any land or rent, for any debt, so long as the chattels of the debtor are sufficient for the payment of the debt; nor shall the pledges of a debtor be distrained so long as the principal debtor himself has enough for the payment of the debt; and if the principal debtor fails in the payment of the debt, not having the wherewithal to pay it, the pledges shall be responsible for the debt; and if they wish, they shall have the lands and the rents of the debtor until they shall have been satisfied for the debt which they have before paid for him, unless the principal debtor shall have shown himself to be quit in that respect towards those pledges.

10. If any one has taken anything from the Jews, by way of a loan, more or less, and dies before that debt is paid, the debt shall not draw interest so long as the heir is under age, from whomsoever he holds; and if that debt falls into our hands, we will take nothing except the chattel contained in the agreement.

11. And if any one dies leaving a debt owing to the Jews, his wife shall have her dowry, and shall pay nothing of that debt; and if there remain minor children of the dead man, necessaries shall be provided for them corresponding to the holding of the dead man; and from the remainder shall be paid the debt, saving the service of the lords. In the same way debts are to be treated which are owed to others than the Jews.

12. No scutage or aid shall be imposed in our kingdom except by the common council of our kingdom, except for the ransoming of our body, for the making of our oldest son a knight, and for once marrying our oldest daughter, and for these purposes it shall be only a reasonable aid; in the same way it shall be done concerning the aids of the city of London.

13. And the city of London shall have all its ancient liberties and free customs, as well by land as by water. Moreover, we will and grant that all other cities and boroughs and villages and ports shall have all their liberties and free customs.

14. And for holding a common council of the kingdom concerning the assessment of an aid otherwise than in the three cases

mentioned above, or concerning the assessment of a scutage we shall cause to be summoned the archbishops, bishops, abbots; earls, and greater barons by our letters individually; and besides we shall cause to be summoned generally, by our sheriffs and bailiffs all those who hold from us in chief, for a certain day, that is at the end of forty days at least, and for a certain place; and in all the letters of that summons, we will express the cause of the summons, and when the summons has thus been given the business shall proceed on the appointed day, on the advice of those who shall be present, even if not all of those who were summoned have come.

15. We will not grant to any one, moreover, that he shall take an aid from his free men, except for ransoming his body, for making his oldest son a knight, and for once marrying his oldest daughter; and for these purposes only a reasonable aid shall be taken.

16. No one shall be compelled to perform any greater service for a knight's fee, or for any other free tenement than is owed from it.

17. The common pleas shall not follow our court, but shall be held in some certain place.

18. The recognition of *novel disseisin, mort d'ancestor,* and *darrein presentment* shall be held only in their own counties and in this manner: we, or if we are outside of the kingdom our principal justiciar, will send two justiciars through each county four times a year, who with four knights of each county, elected by the county, shall hold in the county, and on the day and in the place of the county court, the aforesaid assizes of the county.

19. And if the aforesaid assizes cannot be held within the day of the county court, a sufficient number of knights and free-holders shall remain from those who were present at the county court on that day to give the judgments, according as the business is more or less.

20. A free man shall not be fined for a small offence, except in proportion to the measure of the offence; and for a great offence he shall be fined in proportion to the magnitude of the offence, saving his freehold; and a merchant in the same way, saving his merchandise; and the villain shall be fined in the same way, saving his wainage, if he shall be at our mercy; and none of the above fines shall be imposed except by the oaths of honest men of the neighborhood.

21. Earls and barons shall only be fined by their peers, and only in proportion to their offence.

22. A clergyman shall be fined, like those before mentioned, only in proportion to his lay holding, and not according to the extent of his ecclesiastical benefice.

23. No vill or man shall be compelled to make bridges over the rivers except those which ought to do it of old and rightfully.

24. No sheriff, constable, coroners, or other bailiffs of ours shall hold pleas of our crown.

25. All counties, hundreds, wapentakes, and trithings shall be at the ancient rents and without any increase, excepting our demesne manors.

26. If any person holding a lay fief from us shall die, and our sheriff or bailiff shall show our letters-patent of our summons concerning a debt which the deceased owed to us, it shall be lawful for our sheriff or bailiff to attach and levy on the chattels of the deceased found on his lay fief, to the value of that debt, in the view of legal men, so nevertheless that nothing be removed thence until the clear debt to us shall be paid; and the remainder shall be left to the executors for the fulfilment of the will of the deceased; and if nothing is owed to us by him, all the chattels shall go to the deceased, saving to his wife and children their reasonable shares.

27. If any free man dies intestate, his chattels shall be distributed by the hands of his near relatives and friends, under the oversight of the church, saving to each one the debts which the deceased owed to him.

28. No constable or other bailiff of ours shall take any one's grain or other chattels, without immediately paying for them in money, unless he is able to obtain a postponement at the good-will of the seller.

29. No constable shall require any knight to give money in place of his ward of a castle if he is willing to furnish that ward in his own person or through another honest man, if he himself is not able to do it for a reasonable cause; and if we shall lead or send him into the army he shall be free from ward in proportion to the amount of time during which he has been in the army through us.

30. No sheriff or bailiff of ours or any one else shall take horses or wagons of any free man for carrying purposes except on the permission of that free man.

31. Neither we nor our bailiffs will take the wood of another man for castles, or for anything else which we are doing, except by the permission of him to whom the wood belongs.

32. We will not hold the lands of those convicted of a felony for more than a year and a day, after which the lands shall be returned to the lords of the fiefs.

33. All the fish-weirs in the Thames and the Medway, and throughout all England shall be done away with, except those on the coast.

34. The writ which is called *præcipe* shall not be given for the future to any one concerning any tenement by which a free man can lose his court.

35. There shall be one measure of wine throughout our whole kingdom, and one measure of ale, and one measure of grain, that is the London quarter, and one width of dyed cloth and of russets and of halbergets, that is two ells within the selvages; of weights, moreover it shall be as of measures.

36. Nothing shall henceforth be given or taken for a writ of inquisition concerning life or limbs, but it shall be given freely and not denied.

37. If any one holds from us by fee farm or by socage or by burgage, and from another he holds land by military service, we will not have the guardianship of the heir or of his land which is of the fief of another, on account of that fee farm, or socage, or burgage; nor will we have the custody of that fee farm, or socage, or burgage, unless that fee farm itself owes military service. We will not have the guardianship of the heir or of the land of any one, which he holds from another by military service on account of any petty serjeanty which he holds from us by the service of paying to us knives or arrows, or things of that kind.

38. No bailiff for the future shall put any one to his law on his simple affirmation, without credible witnesses brought for this purpose.

39. No free man shall be taken or imprisoned or dispossessed, or outlawed, or banished, or in any way destroyed, nor will we go upon him, nor send upon him, except by the legal judgment of his peers or by the law of the land.

40. To no one will we sell, to no one will we deny, or delay right or justice.

41. All merchants shall be safe and secure in going out from England and coming into England and in remaining and going

through England, as well by land as by water, for buying and selling, free from all evil tolls, by the ancient and rightful customs, except in time of war, and if they are of a land at war with us; and if such are found in our land at the beginning of war, they shall be attached without injury to their bodies or goods, until it shall be known from us or from our principal justiciar in what way the merchants of our land are treated who shall be then found in the country which is at war with us; and if ours are safe there, the others shall be safe in our land.

42. It is allowed henceforth to any one to go out from our kingdom, and to return, safely and securely, by land and by water, saving their fidelity to us, except in time of war for some short time, for the common good of the kingdom; excepting persons imprisoned and outlawed according to the law of the realm, and people of a land at war with us, and merchants, of whom it shall be done as is before said.

43. If any one holds from any escheat, as from the honor of Wallingford, or Nottingham, or Boulogne, or Lancaster, or from other escheats which are in our hands and are baronies, and he dies, his heir shall not give any other relief, nor do to us any other service than he would do to the baron, if that barony was in the hands of the baron; and we will hold it in the same way as the baron held it.

44. Men who dwell outside the forest shall not henceforth come before our justiciars of the forest, on common summons, unless they are in a plea of, or pledges for any person or persons who are arrested on account of the forest.

45. We will not make justiciars, constables, sheriffs or bailiffs except of such as know the law of the realm and are well inclined to observe it.

46. All barons who have founded abbeys for which they have charters of kings of England, or ancient tenure, shall have their custody when they have become vacant, as they ought to have.

47. All forests which have been afforested in our time shall be disafforested immediately; and so it shall be concerning river banks which in our time have been fenced in.

48. All the bad customs concerning forests and warrens and concerning foresters and warreners, sheriffs and their servants, river banks and their guardians shall be inquired into immediately in each county by twelve sworn knights of the same county, who shall be elected by the honest men of the same county, and within

forty days after the inquisition has been made, they shall be entirely destroyed by them, never to be restored, provided that we be
first informed of it, or our justiciar, if we are not in England.

49. We will give back immediately all hostages and charters
which have been liberated to us by Englishmen as security for
peace or for faithful service.

50. We will remove absolutely from their bailiwicks the relatives of Gerard de Athyes, so that for the future they shall have no
bailiwick in England; Engelard de Cygony, Andrew, Peter and
Gyon de Chancelles, Gyon de Cygony, Geoffrey de Martin and
his brothers, Philip Mark and his brothers, and Geoffrey his
nephew and their whole retinue.

51. And immediately after the reëstablishment of peace we will
remove from the kingdom all foreign-born soldiers, cross-bow
men, serjeants, and mercenaries who have come with horses and
arms for the injury of the realm.

52. If any one shall have been dispossessed or removed by us
without legal judgment of his peers, from his lands, castles, franchises, or his right we will restore them to him immediately; and if
contention arises about this, then it shall be done according to the
judgment of the twenty-five barons, of whom mention is made
below concerning the security of the peace. Concerning all those
things, however, from which any one has been removed or of
which he has been deprived without legal judgment of his peers by
King Henry our father, or by King Richard our brother, which
we have in our hand, or which others hold, and which it is our
duty to guarantee, we shall have respite till the usual term of
crusaders; excepting those things about which the suit has been
begun or the inquisition made by our writ before our assumption
of the cross; when, however, we shall return from our journey or
if by chance we desist from the journey, we will immediately show
full justice in regard to them.

53. We shall, moreover, have the same respite and in the same
manner about showing justice in regard to the forests which are to
be disafforested or to remain forests, which Henry our father or
Richard our brother made into forests; and concerning the custody
of lands which are in the fief of another, custody of which we have
until now had on account of a fief which any one has held from us
by military service; and concerning the abbeys which have been
founded in fiefs of others than ourselves, in which the lord of the
fee has asserted for himself a right; and when we return or if we

should desist from our journey we will immediately show full justice to those complaining in regard to them.

54. No one shall be seized nor imprisoned on the appeal of a woman concerning the death of any one except her husband.

55. All fines which have been imposed unjustly and against the law of the land, and all penalties imposed unjustly and against the law of the land are altogether excused, or will be on the judgment of the twenty-five barons of whom mention is made below in connection with the security of the peace, or on the judgment of the majority of them, along with the aforesaid Stephen, archbishop of Canterbury, if he is able to be present, and others whom he may wish to call for this purpose along with him. And if he should not be able to be present, nevertheless the business shall go on without him, provided that if any one or more of the aforesaid twenty-five barons are in a similar suit they should be removed as far as this particular judgment goes, and others who shall be chosen and put upon oath, by the remainder of the twenty-five shall be substituted for them for this purpose.

56. If we have dispossessed or removed any Welshmen from their lands, or franchises, or other things, without legal judgment of their peers, in England, or in Wales, they shall be immediately returned to them; and if a dispute shall have arisen over this, then it shall be settled in the borderland by judgment of their peers, concerning holdings of England according to the law of England, concerning holdings of Wales according to the laws of Wales, and concerning holdings of the borderland according to the law of the borderland. The Welsh shall do the same to us and ours.

57. Concerning all those things, however, from which any one of the Welsh shall have been removed or dispossessed without legal judgment of his peers, by King Henry our father, or King Richard our brother, which we hold in our hands, or which others hold, and we are bound to warrant to them, we shall have respite till the usual period of crusaders, those being excepted about which suit was begun or inquisition made by our command before our assumption of the cross. When, however, we shall return or if by chance we shall desist from our journey, we will show full justice to them immediately, according to the laws of the Welsh and the aforesaid parts.

58. We will give back the son of Lewellyn immediately, and all the hostages from Wales and the charters which had been liberated to us as a security for peace.

59. We will act toward Alexander, king of the Scots, concerning the return of his sisters and his hostages, and concerning his franchises and his right, according to the manner in which we shall act toward our other barons of England, unless it ought to be otherwise by the charters which we hold from William his father, formerly king of the Scots, and this shall be by the judgment of his peers in our court.

60. Moreover, all those customs and franchises mentioned above which we have conceded in our kingdom, and which are to be fulfilled, as far as pertains to us, in respect to our men; all men of our kingdom as well clergy as laymen, shall observe as far as pertains to them, in respect to their men.

61. Since, moreover, for the sake of God, and for the improvement of our kingdom, and for the better quieting of the hostility sprung up lately between us and our barons, we have made all these concessions; wishing them to enjoy these in a complete and firm stability forever, we make and concede to them the security described below; that is to say, that they shall elect twenty-five barons of the kingdom, whom they will, who ought with all their power to observe, hold, and cause to be observed, the peace and liberties which we have conceded to them, and by this our present charter confirmed to them; in this manner, that if we or our justiciar, or our bailiffs, or any one of our servants shall have done wrong in any way toward any one, or shall have transgressed any of the articles of peace or security; and the wrong shall have been shown to four barons of the aforesaid twenty-five barons, let those four barons come to us or to our justiciar, if we are out of the kingdom, laying before us the transgression, and let them ask that we cause that transgression to be corrected without delay. And if we shall not have corrected the transgression or, if we shall be out of the kingdom, if our justiciar shall not have corrected it within a period of forty days, counting from the time in which it has been shown to us to our justiciar, if we are out of the kingdom, the aforesaid four barons shall refer the matter to the remainder of the twenty-five barons, and let these twenty-five barons with the whole community of the country distress and injure us in every way they can; that is to say by the seizure of our castles, lands, possessions, and in such other ways as they can until it shall have been corrected according to their judgment, saving our person and that of our queen, and those of our children; and when the correc-

tion has been made, let them devote themselves to us as they did before. And let whoever in the country wishes take an oath that in all the above-mentioned measures he will obey the orders of the aforesaid twenty-five barons, and that he will injure us as far as he is able with them, and we give permission to swear publicly and freely to each one who wishes to swear, and no one will we ever forbid to swear. All those, moreover, in the country who of themselves and their own will are unwilling to take an oath to the twenty-five barons as to distressing and injuring us along with them, we will compel to take the oath by our mandate, as before said. And if any one of the twenty-five barons shall have died or departed from the land or shall in any other way be prevented from taking the above-mentioned action, let the remainder of the aforesaid twenty-five barons choose another in his place, according to their judgment, who shall take an oath in the same way as the others. In all those things, moreover, which are committed to those five and twenty barons to carry out, if perhaps the twenty-five are present, and some disagreement arises among them about something, or if any of them when they have been summoned are not willing or are not able to be present, let that be considered valid and firm which the greater part of those who are present arrange or command, just as if the whole twenty-five had agreed in this; and let the aforesaid twenty-five swear that they will observe faithfully all the things which are said above, and with all their ability cause them to be observed. And we will obtain nothing from any one, either by ourselves or by another by which any of these concessions and liberties shall be revoked or diminished; and if any such thing shall have been obtained, let it be invalid and void, and we will never use it by ourselves or by another.

62. And all ill-will, grudges, and anger sprung up between us and our men, clergy and laymen, from the time of the dispute, we have fully renounced and pardoned to all. Moreover, all transgressions committed on account of this dispute, from Easter in the sixteenth year of our reign till the restoration of peace, we have fully remitted to all, clergy and laymen, and as far as pertains to us, fully pardoned. And moreover we have caused to be made for them testimonial letters-patent of lord Stephen, archbishop of Canterbury, lord Henry, archbishop of Dublin, and of the aforesaid bishops and of Master Pandulf, in respect to that security and the concessions named above.

63. Wherefore we will and firmly command that the Church of England shall be free, and that the men in our kingdom shall have and hold all the aforesaid liberties, rights and concessions, well and peacefully, freely and quietly, fully and completely, for themselves and their heirs, from us and our heirs, in all things and places, forever, as before said. It has been sworn, moreover, as well on our part as on the part of the barons, that all these things spoken of above shall be observed in good faith and without any evil intent. Witness the above named and many others. Given by our hand in the meadow which is called Runnymede, between Windsor and Staines, on the fifteenth day of June, in the seventeenth year of our reign.

44. The growth of royal interests: a law concerning air pollution

The thirteenth century brings with it an abundance of legislation, and some of it possesses a surprisingly modern ring. The following imperial constitution concerning air pollution is taken from the great compilation of laws, the Constitutions of Melfi (1231), redacted under Emperor Frederick II Hohenstaufen and concerned with southern Italy and Sicily. The soaking or "retting" of the hemp which bothered Frederick separated the bast from the woody tissues but resulted in objectionable fumes. The *augustalis* mentioned is a gold coin minted by Frederick. The translation, by D. Herlihy, is based on the Constitutiones regni Siciliae, titulus 48, *Historia diplomatica Friderici secundi,* ed. J.-L.-A. Huillard-Bréholles (Paris, 1854), Vol. IV, Pt. 1, pp. 151–52.

On the conservation of the air

The same Augustus. We are disposed to preserve by our zealous solicitude, insofar as we are able, the salubrious air which divine judgment has provided. We therefore command that henceforth no one be permitted to place linen or hemp for retting in any waters within the distance of one mile from any city or castle, lest from this, as we have learned certainly happens, the quality of the air is corrupted. If anyone does this, he should lose the linen and the hemp which he has immersed and it should be given to the court. We order that the bodies of the dead, not placed in coffins, should be buried to a depth of one-half a rod. If anyone does the contrary, he shall pay our court one augustalis. We further order that those who take the skins of animals should put the carcasses and wastes which create an odor outside the territory [of a city] by a fourth part of a mile, or throw them into the sea or river. If anyone does the contrary, he shall pay to our court one augustalis for dogs and animals which are larger than dogs, and one-half an augustalis for smaller animals.

45. The imperial chancery under Frederick II

Frederick II Hohenstaufen (d. 1250) is credited with establishing in his kingdom of Sicily one of the first of the truly bureaucratic states. All officials served only at the pleasure of the king, and many of them, such as the justiciars who administered the local communities, served for only one year and were subject to a rigorous accounting after their term of office had expired. The following three fragments provide some notion of the organization of the imperial chancery, the central secretariat, which was at the heart of the government. The first fragment is apparently a letter to the local justiciars concerning the publication of imperial edicts and concerning communications with the central government. The following two fragments describe the handling of petitions. One of the results of increased centralization was a flood of petitions from subjects directed to the emperor and his officials. The reader might note the high level of professional training required of the notaries, judges, lawyers, and accountants who were responsible for the operation of the chancery office. The source is *Acta imperii inedita seculi XIII: Urkunden und Briefe zur Geschichte des Kaiserreichs und des Königreichs Sicilien in den Jahren 1198 bis 1273*, ed. E. Winkelmann (Innsbruck, 1880), pp. 733–39. The translation is by D. Herlihy.

[Statute concerning the offices]

1. The form given and devised by the emperor before his deposition concerning the expeditious dispatching of petitions and letters and concerning the organization of the chancery.

We wish that in every province both in the empire and in the realm subject to our dominion, our new constitutions, which we have ordered to be made with considered and deliberate counsel in our court, should henceforth be rigorously observed. We, therefore, order you in strict fidelity that you should henceforth scrupulously observe the form of these new constitutions, which we have included in this present letter, and that you should have them observed inviolably in our court, if you wish to count on our favor. Not even you are exempt from observing the form of the law. When you receive this letter, you should make public the same constitutions in some populous city or locale in your jurisdiction at a solemn session of your court. There, according to the form contained in the same constitution, you should publicly take an oath and should receive an oath from your officials that you will respect everything which pertains to your office in your court. Furthermore, you should appoint from your court an energetic and faithful man, in whom you have full confidence, who will exercise with you the office which Master Philip, cantor of the queen, chaplain, and our faithful servant, exercises with us. Moreover, we wish and we command you that henceforth the messengers which you may send to our court in the future should swear to you that, in coming to our court, they will concern themselves with nothing except the business for which they are sent. They will not exercise any agency in private affairs, under the penalty imposed on those guilty of perjury. You should estimate precisely the cost of their journey through faithful and experienced men before they begin their trip to our court, so that, if a dispute should arise, there would be no reason for doubting the amount of their expenses.

2. In receiving and dispatching petitions, this procedure is to be followed. All petitions, no matter what their content or who their authors, should be given to Master N. He should receive them in the early morning before the office of the chancery. Similarly, in the evening he should appear there once more to receive the petitions which are offered. These are to be read on three days in the week, that is, on Monday, Wednesday, and Friday. If on any of these days consideration is prevented for a just reason, on the following day the consideration which was due the day before will be given. Once the petitions are read they shall be distributed by the same master and consigned to notaries. An answer will be

written on the back of each petition; if a decision of the emperor is required in making the answer, the master will bring it forward in council before the feet of his highness, unless it so intimately involves the emperor or a member of his court that he should relate it to the lord alone. What he will command will be given by him to the notaries, so that they may dispatch the response.

The notaries should handle no business of private persons unless in the form of petitions, which they shall receive in the manner described above. Each of them should be bound by oath to dispatch the petitions within two days, in good faith and without malice or fraud, from the day the petition was received and the charter given by a party, not counting those days in which the court may have been in transit, excepting those involving the court, which they should dispatch as soon as they are received without delay or postponement. Also, all the notaries on every day ought to be present in the chancery to write, unless they are prevented by just cause and with the permission of Master Peter and Master Taddeo. If, however, any of them on any day is not in the chancery without permission or a just reason, he shall be fined for the scribal expenses incurred on that day.

The petitions shall be read by Lord Philip, the imperial chaplain, in the presence of Master Peter and Master Taddeo or either of them, if any of them is prevented by illness or was unavoidably absent. They shall be read in the chamber which shall be above the chancery, with no one else present. If the chamber is not available, they shall be read in a secluded part of the palace.

Also, all the letters which are sent to the lord emperor should be read by Master William de Tocco, who has been appointed to receive all these letters, unless they contain something concerning the secrets of the lord or regarding him in particular, or anyone of the court. These he shall read to the lord himself. Once they are read, he shall distribute them to the notaries to be dispatched by them. The answers to the letters shall be written on the back of each one, and the notaries shall be briefly instructed what to write. All the letters and all the answers will be read again in the presence of those mentioned above and will be sealed with the seal of one of them, as may be fitting. When they are brought to be sealed [finally?] all the seals will be there with which each ought to dispatch his letters.

Letters requested concerning the affairs of private parties shall be read on Tuesday, Thursday, and Saturday and at the evening hour publicly in the chancery, and if anyone appears in opposition, he shall not be denied a copy of his opposing statement. Two judges who on that same day should be sitting to hear cases shall read the letters under the seal of justice and those only which are approved and signed by them shall be sealed, as was said.

The keepers of the seal shall assign the sealed letters to Lord Philip the chaplain, who must make his own mark on every sealed letter and receive an oath from the one to whom the letter is given that he intends to give nothing to anyone of the imperial court. If he has already given something or promised something to such a person, the same Lord Philip should reveal to the lord emperor to whom and how much. He should be strictly bound by an oath scrupulously to observe this ruling.

These documents, which may be approved by the judges of the court, after they have been signed, shall be given to the same lord Philip, to be restored to the person whom they concern. He shall in the above manner receive an oath from each concerning what was given and promised. This is also to be followed in notes, privileges, and patent letters.

Henceforth it will also be observed in appellate judgments and cases that the loser will be obligated to give to the victor the expenses and the profits received from the time the litigation began. In estimating the amount of the profit, the winner should have the option either of proving the estimate or of accepting the oath of the loser with the preceding estimation of the judges.

Also, the oath regarding contempt [of the court's decision] should be observed in cases as is prescribed by law.

Also, if one who delays cannot justify the delay, so that the judge deems it to be evident and manifest contempt, he should exact the penalties prescribed by law.

In writing depositions and copying transcripts of the acts, examinations, or headings, the notaries shall receive no fee. But if someone else should write them who does not have his expenses from the court, he should receive the moderate sum of two pennies for witnesses and one for each heading.

The lawyers attached to the court should swear according to the form of the constitution of their office that they will be content with the fee first promised them. They shall not presume to ask, either tacitly or openly or through any signs, through themselves or through others, payment beyond that which was promised them from the parties involved or their representatives. If they presume to do this, they shall be forever excluded from petitioning in law. But if questions should arise concerning the amount of the fee between the lawyer and his client, it shall be settled by the decision of the judges. If among the judges there should be such disagreement that they cannot reach a decision, the dispute should be settled by him who sits in the court of the master justiciar.

If it should happen that a lawyer is dispatched in the business of the court, the remaining lawyers chosen by the party should handle the cases of the one dispatched on the business of the court for nothing, without receiving any salary for the service during the absence of the said lawyer.

3. The form of oath of the counselors according to the emperor: I, N., swear that I shall accept nothing in hand or in promise through me or through another, when I am at the court or when appointed to a legation outside the court, from anyone who may have business or cases at the court or whom I expect to have them, whether from him in person or from anyone acting in his interest. If I may have accepted something from a person who I later learned was to handle some business or to have some case, then when he is present at the court or handles his business or conducts his case through someone else, I shall be bound at once to return everything except food and drink, which cannot be measured by number and quantity. Also, as quickly as I am able, I shall expedite the business given to me or pertaining to my office. I shall completely and faithfully, according to my ability, observe all things which pertain to the oath of counsel. As far as I am able I will see that other officials also observe them. If I should discern any member of the court receiving anything against the form of his oath, I shall take care to denounce this to the lord emperor as soon as possible.

The judges shall swear to all the above except those things which pertain to the council. They should especially swear that as quickly as they can they will settle litigations and faithfully and with fair judgment determine the fees of the lawyers, if between them and their clients disputes should arise concerning the amount, according to the quality of the persons and the matter. In general they shall swear all things which pertain to the office of judging. They shall swear that they will accept nothing except moderate payment for their services as is contained in the constitution.

The notaries shall swear to all the above except that which pertains to the council and to the office of judge.

The guardians of the seals shall swear to all the above except that which pertains to the council and to the office of the judge.

Master I. of Ydronto shall swear to all the above except what pertains to the council and the office of the judge. He shall also swear that he will not alter or hide any petition touching the lord emperor or any person, but he will faithfully read it and report it, as is incumbent upon his office, barring all hate, favor, price, fear, or love.

Lord Philip the cantor shall swear to all the above except everything which pertains to the council and to the office of judge.

The accountants of the court shall swear not to receive anything, in accordance with the above stipulation, and that in the three days each week stated above they shall receive accounts and dispatch them as quickly as they are able in good faith without fraud. . . .

In the chancery there shall be lodging for the counselors, keepers of the seal, notaries, judges, lawyers, and the notaries of the court of justice.

᠋ᠦᠦᠦᠦᠦᠦᠦᠦᠦᠦᠦᠦᠦᠦᠦᠦᠦ

46. The writ *Circumspecte Agatis*

Edward I (1272–1307) ranks only after Henry II Plantagenet as the greatest lawgiver among the medieval English kings, and his efforts to systematize the law are typical of the monarchs of the thirteenth century. The series known as the Statutes of the Realm, in which the laws of England are still today entered, takes its origins from his reign. In a series of great statutes, he largely defined the land law of England. The following example of Edward's legislative work appears to have been in origin not a statute but a writ, to which other material of uncertain derivation was added. The writ served the purpose of defining the limits of the jurisdiction of the "courts Christian," that is, the courts of the Church. The translation is taken from *Select Documents*, eds. Adams and Stephens, pp. 80–81.

The king to such and such judges, Greeting.

See that ye act circumspectly in the matter touching the bishop of Norwich and his clergy, in not punishing them if they shall hold pleas in the court Christian concerning those things which are merely spiritual, to wit:—concerning corrections which prelates inflict for deadly sin, to wit, for fornication, adultery, and such like, for which, sometimes corporal punishment is inflicted, and sometimes pecuniary, especially if a freeman be convicted of such things.

Item if a prelate impose a penalty for not enclosing a church-yard, leaving the church uncovered or without proper ornament, in which cases no other than a pecuniary fine can be inflicted.

Item if a rector demand the greater or the lesser tithe, provided the fourth part of any church be not demanded.

Item if a rector demand a mortuary in places where a mortuary has been usually given.

Item if a prelate of any church demand a pension from the rector as due to him:—all such demands are to be made in the ecclesiastical court.

Concerning laying violent hands on a clerk, and in case of defamation, it has been granted formerly that pleas thereof may be held in the court Christian, provided money be not demanded; but proceedings may be taken for the correction of the sin; and likewise for breach of faith. In all these cases the ecclesiastical judge has to take cognizance, the king's prohibition notwithstanding, although it be put forward.

Wherefore laymen generally obtain a prohibition for tithes, oblations, mortuaries, redemptions of penances, laying violent hands on a clerk or a lay-brother, and in case of defamation, in which cases proceedings are taken to exact canonical punishment.

The lord the king made answer to these articles, that in tithes, obventions, oblations, and mortuaries, when proceedings are taken, as is aforesaid, there is no place for prohibition. And if a clerk or religious person shall sell for money to any one his tithes stored in the barn, or being elsewhere, and be impleaded in the court Christian, the royal prohibition has place, for by reason of sales, spiritual things are temporal, and then tithes pass into chattels.

Item if dispute arise concerning the right of tithes, having its origin in the right of patronage, and the quantity of these tithes exceeds the fourth part of the church, the king's prohibition has place.

Item if a prelate impose pecuniary penalty on any one for sin, and demand the money, the king's prohibition has place, if the money is exacted before prelates.

Item if any one shall lay violent hands on a clerk, amends must be made for a breach of the peace of the lord the king, before the king, and for excommunication before the bishop; and if corporal penalty be imposed which, if the defendant will, he may redeem by giving money to the prelate or person injured, neither in such cases is there place for prohibition.

In defamations of freemen let the prelates correct, the king's prohibition notwithstanding, although it be tendered.

47. Writs of summons to Parliament

Assemblies of estates grew in importance nearly everywhere in Europe in the thirteenth century, and among them the English Parliament possesses a special interest. The following writs of summons to Parliament, issued under Edward I in 1295, give us an excellent view of the development of representative institutions, as they inform us what the members of Parliament were empowered to do. The reader should note in the summons to the representatives of the counties and boroughs the reference to "full and sufficient power," which the representatives were to be given. They were thus legally competent to bind their constituencies to decisions taken in Parliament. The English Parliament, at the beginning of the thirteenth century, was the plenary assembly of the royal court, but with rather vague functions and powers. By the end of the century, while far from replacing the king at the center of the constitution, it had become at least an authentically representative institution. The translations are taken from *Select Documents*, eds. Adams and Stephens, pp. 82–84.

Summons of the clergy

The King to the venerable father in Christ Robert, by the same grace archbishop of Canterbury, primate of all England, greeting.

As a most just law, established by the careful providence of sacred
princes, exhorts and decrees that what affects all, by all should be
approved, so also, very evidently should common danger be met
by means provided in common. You know sufficiently well, and it
is now, as we believe, divulged through all regions of the world,
how the king of France fraudulently and craftily deprives us of
our land of Gascony, by withholding it unjustly from us. Now,
however, not satisfied with the before-mentioned fraud and injustice, having gathered together for the conquest of our kingdom a
very great fleet, and an abounding multitude of warriors, with
which he has made a hostile attack on our kingdom and the inhabitants of the same kingdom, he now proposes to destroy the English
language altogether from the earth, if his power should correspond
to the detestable proposition of the contemplated injustice, which
God forbid. Because, therefore, darts seen beforehand do less
injury, and your interest especially, as that of the rest of the citizens of the same realm, is concerned in this affair, we command
you, strictly enjoining you in the fidelity and love in which you are
bound to us, that on the Lord's day next after the feast of St.
Martin, in the approaching winter, you be present in person at
Westminster; citing beforehand [præmunientes] the dean and
chapter of your church, the archdeacons and all the clergy of your
diocese, causing the same dean and archdeacons in their own
persons, and the said chapter by one suitable proctor, and the said
clergy by two, to be present along with you, having full and
sufficient power from the same chapter and clergy, to consider,
ordain and provide, along with us and with the rest of the prelates
and principal men and other inhabitants of our kingdom, how the
dangers and threatened evils of this kind are to be met. Witness the
king at Wangham, the thirtieth day of September.

*Identical summons were sent out to the two archbishops and
eighteen bishops, and, with the omission of the last paragraph, to
seventy abbots.*

Summons of the barons

The king to his beloved and faithful relative, Edmund, Earl of
Cornwall, greeting. Because we wish to have a consultation and
meeting with you and with the rest of the principal men of our
kingdom, as to provision for remedies against the dangers which in
these days are threatening our whole kingdom; we command you,

strictly enjoining you in the fidelity and love in which you are bound to us, that on the Lord's day next after the feast of St. Martin, in the approaching winter, you be present in person at Westminster, for considering, ordaining and doing along with us and with the prelates, and the rest of the principal men and other inhabitants of our kingdom, as may be necessary for meeting dangers of this kind.

Witness the king at Canterbury, the first of October.

Similar summons were sent to seven earls and forty-one barons.

Summons of representatives of the counties and boroughs

The king to the sheriff of Northamptonshire. Since we intend to have a consultation and meeting with the earls, barons and other principal men of our kingdom with regard to providing remedies against the dangers which are in these days threatening the same kingdom; and on that account have commanded them to be with us on the Lord's day next after the feast of St. Martin in the approaching winter, at Westminster, to consider, ordain, and do as may be necessary for the avoidance of these dangers; we strictly require you to cause two knights from the aforesaid county, two citizens from each city in the same county, and two burgesses from each borough, of those who are especially discreet and capable of laboring, to be elected without delay, and to cause them to come to us at the aforesaid time and place.

Moreover, the said knights are to have full and sufficient power for themselves and for the community of the aforesaid county, and the said citizens and burgesses for themselves and the communities of the aforesaid cities and boroughs separately, then and there for doing what shall then be ordained according to the common counsel in the premises; so that the aforesaid business shall not remain unfinished in any way for defect of this power. And you shall have there the names of the knights, citizens and burgesses and this writ.

Witness the king at Canterbury on the third day of October.

Identical summons were sent to the sheriffs of each county.

Part Four

Chivalry

Introduction

⎍⎍⎍⎍⎍⎍⎍⎍⎍⎍⎍⎍⎍⎍⎍⎍⎍⎍⎍⎍⎍⎍⎍⎍⎍⎍⎍⎍⎍⎍

Feudal society bequeathed to subsequent generations not only certain distinctive conceptions and institutions of government but also a social ideal concerning the proper behavior of the knight, the warrior, and the man. This was chivalry, which meant in the most literal sense the art of mastering or managing *caballi*, horses. It held out a high image of the perfect warrior which, if rarely achieved and often ignored, still exerted a lasting influence on the manners and morals of the West.

Sources of the chivalric ideal

Probably all societies, and especially those engaged in almost constant warfare, have formed their own images of the hero. The chivalry of the Middle Ages itself inherited and absorbed older traditions of heroism, coming not only from the barbarian but also from the Greco-Roman worlds. Like Beowulf, the paradigm of Germanic heroes, the knight was expected to be a great and courageous fighter, a true master of the arms he wielded. Morally, he was to be undaunted by overwhelming odds against himself and by the certainty of his own death; he was to be selfless, willing to turn his skill and his strength toward the protection of his people, his friends, and all who needed him. He was to make war against the evil forces which harassed and endangered the human race. Tales of the classical and Biblical heroes—Alexander the Great or Judas Maccabeus—similarly, if more remotely, influenced the medieval conception of heroism. The legend of St. George and the dragon (Document 50), for example, bears close similarities with the story of Perseus and the monster in classical mythology.

But if chivalry maintained older traditions of heroism and manliness, it still possessed two unique qualities. The first was the assumption that fighting, even killing, could be a blessed and religiously meritorious act. The second was the conviction that among the virtues decorating the knight should be the art of acting courteously, of conducting himself well, not only on the battlefield but in the drawing room; not only among warriors but among women.

The Church, and especially the reformers of the eleventh century, were primarily responsible for lending to warfare a religious aura. Violence was a major and recognized plague in Western society, and churches and churchmen were among its most frequent victims. To reform the Church required a stabilization and pacification of society. Beginning in the late tenth century, councils in the south of France tried to limit fighting, to restrict it to certain persons and allow it only at certain times. This selective pacifism embraced movements known as the Truce of God and the Peace of God (Document 48).

But even in curtailing fighting, these councils did not attribute positive social and religious value to fighting. The warrior at rest, not in action, merited commendation. In this respect, the Crusades in particular worked a decisive change. In urging the armed men of the West to go to Palestine, Pope Urban II had told them at Clermont in 1095 that death while fighting for the cross would surely bring grace, remission of sins, and heavenly reward from God. "God wills it," the assembled knights shouted in reply; by this they meant that God willed war and death. Probably the best description of the crusading spirit is the book or sermon *In Praise of the New Chivalry*, by Bernard of Clairvaux (Document 49), himself the preacher of the second Crusade. This "hortatory sermon" was written for the Knights Templars, a military-religious order founded in Palestine in the early twelfth century. Bernard argued that the knight who fights and kills for religion commits no evil but rather does good, for his people and himself. If he dies in the battle, he gains heaven; if he kills his opponent, he avenges Christ. Either way, God is pleased.

In the following century, Raymond Lull, a Catalan who had opportunity to observe the behavior of knights at the court of Aragon, wrote one of the best and most popular tracts on the nature of chivalry in the Middle Ages: the *Book on the Order of Chivalry* (Document 51). In it he describes both the expected function of the knight (to do good and repress evil by his sword) and his deserved rewards. For reason of the good purposes for which the knight wields his weapon, he is justified, says Raymond, in a privileged life, in living freely from the bread which the peasants painfully supply him.

The Church profoundly influenced this image of the perfect warrior by limiting warfare and by blessing its use only for what it considered to be socially beneficial purposes. The twelfth century further witnessed, initially in southern France and Spain and then widely through Europe, a rebirth of court life. One of the most salient features of this new court society was the prominence and influence acquired by women. The great ladies of the court became the arbiters of what constituted acceptable social and moral behavior. They set the standards which the "gentle" man (i.e., the one of noble birth) had to follow. Knights were to act politely, as befitted a courtier (see, in this regard, Document 7). They needed skill not only in slaying enemies but in pleasing women, and these combined arts from then on constituted the quintessence of gallantry.

Training

Chivalry, founded upon physical skills and moral qualities, could not be acquired by birth alone, although high birth (as Raymond Lull himself insists) might be prerequisite for it. This noble art demanded training. The twelfth and thirteenth centuries, among their many accomplishments, also effected profound changes in educational institutions. Guilds, for example, closely supervised the training of the young in their particular art and thus secured the transmittal of the skill over generations. The bishop's school and then, from about 1200, the university performed a similar function in regard to the art of teaching. Both guilds and the university (itself fundamentally a guild) determined that the aspirant to the profession should serve an apprenticeship at the feet or in the service of a recognized master. At the end of his apprenticeship, he should give the community of masters some evidence that he had learned his lessons well and was ready to join them as an equal in the practice of the profession.

Training for knighthood shows close parallels to the forms of education which the guilds were establishing in the other arts. The apprentice knight was the squire. The young boy would usually be sent away from home to another castle or court to observe the doings of the knights who were there and to enter the personal service of a master warrior. Like the member of the Germanic *comitatus* many centuries before, he would follow his master into battle, fight for him and under him, learn from him, and hope for his gracious favor. Perhaps in battle itself he might achieve some feat of arms, a *beau geste*, a masterpiece of his profession, which would prove to all that he had learned the art and was ready for admission to the ranks of master warriors. Or he might show his skill less dramatically through time and training under the observance of his elders. Raymond Lull, in the *Book on the Order of Chivalry*, assumes that the master knight will carefully examine the candidates to the order to assure himself that they possess the noble skills and understand the exalted purposes of knighthood.

Having shown by feat of arms or other proof that he was prepared, the squire was admitted to full membership in the order through a ceremony known as dubbing. The master knight delivered a blow to the squire with the flat of the sword. This gesture has strong reminiscences of the Christian sacrament of confirmation, in which the bishop too gives the recipient a blow; the sacrament is to make him a "strong and perfect Christian and a soldier of Jesus Christ." The blow warned the young knight that he should be ready to suffer hurt and harm in the service of chivalry. Dubbing or the accolade took on a quasi-sacramental character and was often accompanied by the formal blessing of the knight's arms. Raymond Lull presents an eloquent and rich description of the symbolic meaning of the arms the knight would carry.

The ceremony of dubbing or the accolade had one important social result. From the twelfth century on, the custom of admitting only the sons of knights to the ranks of knighthood increased. The circle of warriors in the early Middle Ages had been opened to all with the wealth and skill to fight. But from the twelfth century, European society loses its former fluidity. Probably the chief reason for this was the new competition now offered to the warriors by the rich men of the towns. The warriors had traditionally dominated lay society, but now the bourgeoisie, armed with the awesome power of money, challenged their position. In reaction, they tended to place greater emphasis on birth and lineage, and to exclude from their ranks those who could not claim it. Of course, through royal patents or marriages the sons and daughters of the townsmen could gain noble status. But it remains true to say that the hereditary nobility of European society is primarily a product of the twelfth and thirteenth centuries. At the same time, the nobles claimed for themselves in recognition of their function special privileges, which again are well described by Raymond Lull. The estate of nobles thus was defined as a class largely closed to outsiders, and possessing its own juridical status and its own distinct privileges; these would be in large part maintained until the French Revolution.

Chivalry thus had the function of providing to one of the great classes of traditional European society a justification for its privileges and position. For centuries thereafter, the European nobles pretended that God had given them the sword for the repression of evil and the defense of the good. But apart from its close association with a privileged class, chivalry further defined for a larger group of individuals how a gentleman should appear and how he should act in love and war. No doubt the ideal was honored more in the breach than in the observance. But there is also no doubt that the fashioning of this image brought with it a new refinement in the social life of the Western peoples.

RECOMMENDED READINGS

ARTHUR B. FERGUSON, *The Indian Summer of English Chivalry: Studies in the Decline and Transformation of Chivalric Idealism* (New York: Duke University Press, 1960).

SIDNEY PAINTER, *French Chivalry: Chivalric Ideas and Practices in Medieval France* (Ithaca: Cornell University Press, 1964).

———, *Mediaeval Society* (Ithaca: Cornell University Press, 1951).

EDGAR PRESTAGE (ed.), *Chivalry: A Series of Studies to Illustrate Its Historical Significance* (New York: Knopf, 1928).

⎍⎍⎍⎍⎍⎍⎍⎍⎍⎍⎍⎍⎍⎍⎍⎍⎍⎍⎍⎍⎍⎍⎍⎍

48. The peace and truce of God at the Council of Toulouges

Chivalry was founded on the assumption that violence should be used only for socially acceptable purposes. One source of this assumption, and one effort to define what those purposes were, was the movement known as the "Peace of God" and the "Truce of God." From 989, councils in the south of France demanded that certain places and persons be accorded a special "peace" or immunity from violence, and somewhat later, other councils attempted to impose a truce or prohibition of all fighting on certain days. The following acts of a council in 1041 at Toulouges near Perpignan define the essential features of both movements. While it would be difficult to maintain that such enactments altered the habits of warriors, nonetheless they did help develop the consciousness that even professional warriors had responsibilities to the Church and community. The translation is taken from *A Source Book of Mediaeval History*, ed. F. A. Ogg, pp. 229–30.

1. This Peace has been confirmed by the bishops, by the abbots, by the counts and viscounts and the other God-fearing nobles in this bishopric, to the effect that in the future, beginning with this day, no man may commit an act of violence in a church, or in the space which surrounds it and which is covered by its privileges, or in the burying-ground, or in the dwelling-houses which are, or may be, within thirty paces of it.

2. We do not include in this measure the churches which have been, or which shall be, fortified as châteaux, or those in which plunderers and thieves are accustomed to store their ill-gotten booty, or which give them a place of refuge. Nevertheless we desire that such churches be under this protection until complaint of them shall be made to the bishop, or to the chapter. If the bishop or chapter act upon such information and lay hold of the malefactors, and if the latter refuse to give themselves up to the justice of the bishop or chapter, the malefactors and all their possessions shall

not be immune, even within the church. A man who breaks into a church, or into the space within thirty paces around it, must pay a fine for sacrilege, and double this amount to the person wronged.

3. Furthermore, it is forbidden that any one attack the clergy, who do not bear arms, or the monks and religious persons, or do them any wrong; likewise it is forbidden to despoil or pillage the communities of canons, monks, and religious persons, the ecclesiastical lands which are under the protection of the Church, or the clergy, who do not bear arms; and if any one shall do such a thing, let him pay a double composition. . . .

5. Let no one burn or destroy the dwellings of the peasants and the clergy, the dove-cotes and the granaries. Let no man dare to kill, to beat, or to wound a peasant or serf, or the wife of either, or to seize them and carry them off, except for misdemeanors which they may have committed; but it is not forbidden to lay hold of them in order to bring them to justice, and it is allowable to do this even before they shall have been summoned to appear. Let not the raiment of the peasants be stolen; let not their ploughs, or their hoes, or their olive-fields be burned.

6. . . . Let any one who has broken the peace, and has not paid his fines within a fortnight, make amends to him whom he has injured by paying a double amount, which shall go to the bishop and to the count who shall have had charge of the case.

7. The bishops of whom we have spoken have solemnly confirmed the Truce of God, which has been enjoined upon all Christians, from the setting of the sun of the fourth day of the week, that is to say, Wednesday, until the rising of the sun on Monday, the second day. . . . If any one during the Truce shall violate it, let him pay a double composition and subsequently undergo the ordeal of cold water. When any one during the Truce shall kill a man, it has been ordained, with the approval of all Christians, that if the crime was committed intentionally the murderer shall be condemned to perpetual exile, but if it occurred by accident the slayer shall be banished for a period of time to be fixed by the bishops and the canons. If any one during the Truce shall attempt to seize a man or to carry him off from his château, and does not succeed in his purpose, let him pay a fine to the bishop and to the chapter, just as if he had succeeded. It is likewise forbidden during the Truce, in Advent and Lent, to build any château or fortification, unless it was begun a fortnight before the time of the Truce.

It has been ordained also that at all times disputes and suits on the subject of the Peace and Truce of God shall be settled before the bishop and his chapter, and likewise for the peace of the churches which have before been enumerated. When the bishop and the chapter shall have pronounced sentences to recall men to the observance of the Peace and the Truce of God, the sureties and hostages who show themselves hostile to the bishop and the chapter shall be excommunicated by the chapter and the bishop, with their protectors and partisans, as guilty of violating the Peace and the Truce of the Lord; they and their possessions shall be excluded from the Peace and the Truce of the Lord.

49. *In Praise of the New Chivalry* by Bernard of Clairvaux

One of the most influential of all works in shaping the character of chivalry was a sermon written by the great Cistercian abbot and saint Bernard of Clairvaux (d. 1153) for the edification of a new military-religious order, the Knights of the Temple. The Knights had formed their order about 1118, and they initially took as their principal work the protection of pilgrims on the highways to Jerusalem. Their first house was located near the site of the ancient temple of Solomon at Jerusalem, and this gave them their name. In 1128 the Knights asked for papal approval of their order, and the pope in turn requested that a council of French prelates meeting at Troyes provide them a definite rule. The council commissioned Bernard to write the rule, which he accomplished. At an unknown date between 1128 and May, 1136, he also wrote this exhortatory sermon addressed to the master of the order, Hugues de Payns. In it, with considerable rhetorical brilliance, he argued in no uncertain terms that it was right and beneficial for salvation for the Knights to kill in the interest of confounding the infidel and protecting the holy places. The following translation, by D. Herlihy, gives the first five of the work's eleven chapters. In the latter half of the work, Bernard turned to a consideration of the mystical significance of the names of the holy places in Palestine. While frequently ingenious, this part has almost nothing to say on the character of chivalry and the religious justification for violence. The source is

from *S. Bernardi Opera*, Vol. III: *Tractatus et opuscula*, eds. J. Le-
clercq and H. M. Rochais (Rome, 1963), pp. 213-24.

To the Knights of the Temple, a book in praise
of the new chivalry
PROLOGUE

To Hugh, soldier of Christ and master of the chivalry of Christ,
Bernard of Clairvaux, abbot only by name: fight the good fight.

Once, twice, and again a third time, unless I am mistaken, you
have asked me, my dear Hugh, to compose for you and for your
fellow knights a sermon of exhortation, and that I to whom the
lance is not allowed should strike with the pen the tyrannical
enemy. You tell me that it would be of no little help to you if I
should inspire by letters those whom I cannot inspire by arms. To
be sure, for a time I have hesitated, not because your request
seemed contemptible to me but because I feared that my agreement
would be condemned as being facile and hasty. Should I, an inexperienced man, assume that which a better person could better
fulfill? Should this quite necessary task be inadequately accomplished through me? But when I saw that the long delay helped me
not at all, I feared that I should appear unwilling rather than
incapable, and I therefore have done what I was able. Let the
reader decide whether I have done it well. Although this work may
please some or displease others, or prove insufficient, I do not care;
as far as my wisdom allows, I have responded to your wish.

I

TO THE KNIGHTS OF THE TEMPLE, A HORTATIVE SERMON

1. We have heard that a new sort of chivalry has appeared on
earth, and in that region which once He Who came from on high
visited in the flesh. In those places where once in the strength of
His arm He cast out the princes of darkness, from there also He
now exterminates their satellites, their unbelieving sons, scattered
by the arm of His valiant men. Now also He works the redemption
of His people, and again raises for us an army of salvation in the
House of David, His servant. I say that this is a new sort of
chivalry, unknown through the centuries, because it tirelessly
wages an equal and double war, both against flesh and blood and
against the spiritual forces of evil in the other world. To resist

bravely a bodily enemy with bodily force—this I judge to be neither remarkable nor rare. When a strong soul declares war against vice or demons, this too I would not call remarkable, although certainly laudable, since discernibly, the world is filled with monks. However, when a man of both types powerfully girds his sword and nobly distinguishes himself by his cuirass, who would not consider this, which clearly has hitherto been unknown, worthy of all admiration? Surely, it is an intrepid knight, protected on every side, who clothes his body with the armor of iron and his soul with the armor of faith. Thus, supremely protected by arms of both types, he fears neither demon nor man. Nor indeed does he who wishes to die fear death. He whose life is Christ, and for whom death is profit, what should he fear in life or in death? He stands faithfully and willingly for Christ; but he would much prefer disembodiment so as to be with Christ. This is great progress. Go forward, therefore, in confidence, O knights, and with dauntless spirit drive out the enemies of the cross of Christ. Be certain that neither death nor life can divorce you from the love of God, which is in Christ Jesus. In all danger repeat this within yourselves: "Whether we live or whether we die, we are the Lord's" (Romans 14.8). With what happiness they die, martyrs in the battle! Rejoice, brave athlete, if you live and conquer in the Lord. But exult and glory the more, if you should die and be joined to the Lord. Life for you is fertile and victory glorious, but over both is sacred death rightly to be preferred. For if "Blessed are the dead who die in the Lord" (Apocalypse 14.13), how much more blessed are those who die for the Lord?

2. Whether a person dies in bed or in battle, precious without doubt will the death of His saints be in the eyes of the Lord. However, death in battle is so much the more precious, since it is the more glorious. O safe life, when the conscience is pure! O safe life, I say, when death is awaited without fear, looked for with desire, and received with devotion. O truly holy and secure chivalry, and entirely free from that double peril by which the human race has frequently in the past been endangered, when, that is, Christ is not the cause for soldiering. You who fight according to the worldly chivalry: whenever you go forth, you must fear either that you may kill the enemy in his body and yourself in your soul or that you perchance may be killed by him, at once in the body and in the soul. The danger or the victory of the Christian is

determined by the intent of the heart rather than the outcome of the battle. If the cause for which one fights is good, the battle cannot end badly; so also its end shall never be considered good when the cause is not good and the intention which preceded it not just. If it should happen that in desiring to kill another, death should come to you, you shall die a murderer. If you prevail and in your wish to best a man or to take vengeance upon him you by chance kill him, you live a murderer. However, it little profits the dead or the living, the victor or the vanquished, to be a murderer. Unhappy victory by which, in overcoming a man, you succumb to vice and under the rule of anger or of pride you vainly glory in the vanquishing of a man. There is, however, the person who kills a man not out of zeal for vengeance or passion to conquer, but only to save himself. But I would not call even this a good victory, since of the two evils it is a lesser thing to die in body than in spirit. For the soul does not die because the body is killed; but "the soul that sinneth, the same shall die" (Ezekiel 18.4).

II
CONCERNING THE WORLDLY CHIVALRY

3. What, therefore, is the purpose or the fruit of this worldly—I cannot call it a militia but a malice—if the killer sins fatally, and the one killed eternally perishs? To utilize the words of the apostle: "He that ploweth, should plow in hope, and he that thrasheth, in hope to receive fruit" (1 Corinthians 9.10). Therefore, O knights, what astounding error is this, what insupportable madness is here, to fight with such expenses and such efforts for no pay at all, unless it be death or crime? You cover your horses with silk cloths; you place over your cuirasses hangings of I know not what material; you paint your lances, shields, and saddles; you embellish your reins and your spurs with gold, silver, and gems. With such pomp, in shameful furor and thoughtless stupor you hurry to your deaths. Are these the ornaments of soldiers, or rather of women? Will perchance the enemy's sword respect the gold, spare the gems, and be unable to penetrate the silks? Finally, as you yourselves often and certainly have learned by experience, three things are necessary for the warrior: that is, that the knight be strong, energetic, and alert in protecting himself; quick in movement; and swift to strike. You, on the contrary, raise in womanly fashion a coiffure which obstructs the vision. You entangle your own steps by your

long and billowing robes; you bury your delicate and soft hands in ample and flowing sleeves. Above all these things, there is also the fact that the cause for which this perilous service is undertaken is so light and frivolous that it terrorizes the conscience of the armed man. For surely, no other cause raises wars and disputes among you unless it be the irrational movements of anger, or the appetite for empty glory, or the desire for some sort of worldly possession. For these reasons it is safe neither to kill nor to succumb.

III

ON THE NEW CHIVALRY

4. On the other hand, the soldiers of Christ wage the battles of their Lord in safety. They fear not at all the sin of killing an enemy or the peril of their own death, inasmuch as death either inflicted or borne for Christ has no taint of crime and rather merits the greater glory. The one clearly serves Christ; the other brings union with him. Christ freely accepts the death of the enemy in just vengeance and the more freely offers himself to the knight in consolation. I say that the soldier of Christ kills in safety and dies in greater safety. He profits himself when he dies, and he profits Christ when he kills. "For he beareth the sword not in vain. For he is God's minister; and an avenger to execute wrath upon him that doth evil, and one to praise him that doth good" (Romans 13.4). Truly, when he kills a criminal, he commits not homicide but, as I would call it, malicide, and clearly he may be considered the avenger of Christ in those who do wrong, and a defender of the Christians. When, however, he is killed, he is known not to have perished but to have profited. The death that he inflicts is to the benefit of Christ; the death which he receives is to his own benefit. In the death of a pagan, the Christian is glorified because Christ is glorified; in the death of a Christian the generosity of the King is revealed when the knight is taken to his reward. Therefore, the just man will always rejoice when he sees this just vengeance. "If indeed there be fruit to the just: there is indeed a God that judgeth them on earth" (Psalm 57.12). The point is not, of course, that pagans ought to be killed, if by some other means or in some other fashion they could be repressed from their extreme harassment and oppression of the faithful. Now, however, it is better that they be killed than to allow the rod of the sinners to stand over the fate of the just, lest the just also should extend their hands toward iniquity.

5. What is this? If to strike with the sword is altogether wrong for a Christian, why then did the herald of the Lord enjoin soldiers to be content with their wages? Why did he not altogether forbid them service in arms? But if, as is true, it is permissible to all, or at least to those who have been divinely appointed for this and do not profess a higher calling, to whom does it belong more justly than to those by whose strength of arms Sion, the city of our strength, is held for our common protection? They have cast out those who transgress the divine laws; and the just people, the guardians of the truth, may enter her in safety. Let therefore the nations who wish for war be scattered, let those be cut down who disturb us. Let all who do iniquity be extirpated from the city of the Lord—those who sought to rob the Christian peoples of the inestimable riches preserved at Jerusalem, to profane holy places, and to hold in inheritance the sanctuary of the Lord. Let both swords held by the faithful be drawn against the necks of their enemies, in order to destroy all arrogance which extols itself against the science of God which is the Christian faith. "Lest the Gentiles should say: where is their God?" (Psalm 113.2).

6. With their expulsion He may return into His inheritance and His house, of which He said in anger in the Gospel, "Your house shall be left to you desolate" (Matthew 23.38). And through the prophet He thus complained, "I have forsaken my house, I left my inheritance" (Jeremiah 12.7). That prophecy will also be fulfilled: "For the Lord has redeemed his people and has delivered them and they shall come and shall give praise in Mount Sion and they shall rejoice in the good things of the Lord" (*cf.* Jeremiah 31.11–12). Rejoice, Jerusalem, and know the time of your visitation, "Rejoice and give praise together, O ye deserts of Jerusalem, for the Lord has comforted his people: he hath redeemed Jerusalem. The Lord hath prepared his holy arm in the sight of all the gentiles" (Isaiah 52.9–10). You had fallen, O virgin Israel, and there was no one who would raise you. Rise now, lift yourself from the dust, O virgin, captive daughter of Sion. Arise, I say, and stand upright, and behold the joy which comes to you from your God. "Thou shalt no more be called forsaken, and thy land shall no more be called desolate: because the Lord hath been well pleased with thee: and thy land shall be inhabited" (*cf.* Isaiah 62.4). "Lift up thy eyes round about, and see. All these are gathered together: they are come to thee" (Isaiah 49.18). This is the help which comes to you

from the Holy One. Through them now is altogether fulfilled the ancient promise, "I will make thee to be an everlasting glory, a joy unto generation and generation. And thou shalt suck the milk of the gentiles: and thou shalt be nursed with the breast of kings" (Isaiah 60.15). And also, "As one whom the mother caresseth, so I will comfort you: and you shall be comforted in Jerusalem" (Isaiah 66.13). Do you see how frequently the testimony of the ancients approves the new chivalry, and that, "As we have heard so we have seen in the city of the Lord of hosts" (Psalm 47.9)? Of course this literal interpretation, which we have applied from the words of the prophets to our own times, ought not to prejudice spiritual meanings, by which we are led to hope in eternity. Otherwise, that which is seen will erase that which is believed, and an impoverished reality may diminish the riches of hope; the experience of present things would be a loss of things to come. Rather the temporal glory of the earthly city does not diminish the good things of heaven, but adds to them, if only we do not hesitate to consider this city a figure of our mother who is in heaven.

IV
ON THE LIFE OF THE KNIGHTS OF THE TEMPLE

7. But now as a model for, or rather for the confusion of, our knights who fight not surely for God but for the devil, let us briefly discuss the morals and the life of the knights of Christ, how they live, in war and at home, in order that it be evident how much the chivalry of God differs from the chivalry of the world. First of all, discipline is maintained in both war and peace, obedience is never disparaged, since, as Scripture testifies, the undisciplined son shall perish and, "It is like the sin of witchcraft to rebel: and like the crime of idolatry to refuse to obey" (1 Kings 15.23). They go and they come upon the orders of him who is their chief; they don what he gives them, and they have no other clothing or supplies. Both in food and in garments all excess is avoided, and only necessity is considered. They live in common, in a cheerful and sober manner, without wives and without children. And lest they fall short of evangelical perfection, they keep no private possession, but they live as a single community in a single house, eager to preserve unity of spirit in a bond of peace. You would say that in the entire throng there is but a single heart and a single soul. The individual by no means seeks to follow his own will but rather to

obey his commander. At no time do they sit in idleness or wander about in curiosity. But always, when they are not riding forth to war—and rarely are they not—they repair damaged arms or clothing or refurbish what is old, put what is untidy into order, and whatever else the will of the master or communal necessity indicates, lest they fail to earn their bread. Among them there is no distinction of persons; noble deeds, not noble birth, gain respect. They are attentive to one another in honor; they bear one another's burdens, so that they may fulfill the law of Christ. Insolent speech, useless actions, immoderate laughter, even a low grumble or whisper never, when they are noticed, are left unpunished. They detest chess and dice; they abhor hunting and take no pleasure, as is customary, in the silly chase of birds. They detest and abominate actors, magicians, storytellers, immodest songs and plays; these for them are vanities and follies. They cut their hair, knowing that, according to the Apostles, it is shameful for men to grow long hair. Always unkempt, rarely bathed, usually they are shaggy, dirty, dusty, and darkened by their cuirasses and by sunburn.

8. When war is imminent they arm themselves within by faith and without by iron, not by gold, so that armed and not adorned, they may strike fear into the enemy and not incite his avarice. They seek to have strong and swift horses, not colored and bedecked. They plan to fight, not to parade; they seek victory and not glory, fear more than admiration. Then they are not turbulent or impetuous, carried away for slight reasons, but advisedly and with all caution and prudence they arrange themselves and take their positions in the battle line, as was written concerning the fathers [of Israel]. As true Israelites, they go forth calmly to the wars. But when the battle is joined, then at last they put aside all restraint as if they were saying, "Have I not hated them, O Lord, that hated thee: and pine away because of thy enemies?" (Psalm 139.21). They charge their adversaries, they regard the enemy like sheep; although they may be few, they fear neither barbarian savagery nor great numbers. For they know not how to presume on their own powers; they hope for victory only in the power of the Lord of hosts, and in the words of Machabaeus, they believe that, "It is an easy matter for many to be shut up in the hands of a few: and there is no difference in the sight of the God of heaven to deliver with a great multitude or a small company. For the success of war is not in the multitude of the army: but strength cometh from

heaven" (1 Machabaeus 3:18–19). This they have frequently experienced, so that often one man has routed a thousand, and two
men have put ten thousand to flight. Finally, in a marvelous and
singular fashion, they are seen to be meeker than lambs and more
ferocious than lions, so that I nearly hesitate in deciding whether I
should call them monks or knights. Perhaps I should most suitably
call them by both names, since they are lacking in neither the
gentleness of the monk nor the strength of the knight. What is to
be said concerning this, but only that it was done by God and is a
wonder in our eyes? These soldiers God has chosen for Himself;
he has gathered His ministers from the valiant men of Israel, from
the far reaches of the earth. With sword in hand, experienced in
battle, they all vigilantly and faithfully guard the bed of the true
Solomon, that is, the holy sepulcher.

V

CONCERNING THE TEMPLE

9. There is a temple at Jerusalem in which all men live equally. It is
inferior to that ancient and famous temple of Solomon in its structure, but not inferior in its glory. For all the magnificence of
Solomon's temple was contained in corruptible gold and silver, in
dressed stones and a variety of woods. The entire beauty and
pleasing ornament of this temple is the religious piety of those who
inhabit it and their most ordered lives. This older temple was to be
seen for its varied colors; this new one is to be venerated for its
varied virtues and holy actions. For sanctity suits the house of
God, Who is pleased not by polished marbles but by glistening
morals, and loves pure minds more than golden walls. The façade
of this new temple is indeed embellished, but by arms and not by
gems; the walls are covered not by ancient golden crowns but
by shields hung about. The building is everywhere adorned not by
candelabra, incensers, and spice jars, but by harnesses, saddles and
lances. Clearly, all these things demonstrate that the zeal of these
knights for the house of God burns with the self-same fervor as
that of the Leader of the knights, who, violently angered, entered
the temple, drove out the merchants, scattered the coins of the
changers, and overthrew the tables of those selling doves—this he
did by his armed and most holy hand, not by iron but by a corded
whip. For he thought it disgraceful that the house of prayer

should be sullied by merchants of this type. Moved by the example of their King, this devout army, recognizing that it is far more disgraceful and far more insupportable for the holy places to be polluted by infidels than to be infested by merchants, now remain in the holy house with horses and arms. They have driven out all the filthy and lawless madness of infidelity from this and all the other holy places, and night and day they are there occupied in both honest and fruitful office. They zealously honor the temple of God by diligent and sincere services; they devotedly offer continuous sacrifice, not the flesh of animals according to the ancient rite, but truly pacific offerings—fraternal love, devout obedience, willing poverty.

10. These things are done at Jerusalem, and the world is aroused. The islands listen and the peoples hear from afar. From east to west they surge forward like a glorious flowing river of nations and like a forceful flood, giving joy to the city of God. This is what appears most cheering and is accomplished most profitably: among that great multitude of men who converge toward Jerusalem, there are few who are not criminals and sinners, ravishers and the sacrilegious, murderers, perjurers, and adulterers. In their departure a double good is attained and joy too is doubled. Their departure makes their own people happy, and their arrival cheers those to whom they are hastening to help. They aid both groups, not only by protecting the one but also by not oppressing the other. Thus, Egypt rejoices in their departure; Mount Sion is no less gladdened by their protection, and the daughters of Judah rejoice. The first glories in being liberated from their hand; the second rightly glories the more in being liberated by their hand. The first willingly loses its most cruel devastators; the second with joy receives its most faithful defenders. The sweet consolation of the first is the saving desolation of the second. Thus does Christ know how to take vengeance upon his enemies, so that he frequently triumphs the more gloriously and the more powerfully, not only over them but through them. Happily and helpfully, he has begun to turn those who for long were his opponents into his champions. He who once from the persecutor Saul made Paul the preacher now turns an enemy into a knight. Therefore, I do not wonder if indeed the heavenly court, according to the testimony of the Savior, exults the more over one sinner doing penance than over many just men who have no need of penance, since the con-

version of the sinner and the evil man beyond doubt profits as much as his former life had done injury.

11. Hail, therefore, holy city, whom the Most High sanctified as a temple to Himself, so that in you and through you so great a generation might be saved. Hail, city of the great King, out of whom wonders, novel and joyous to the world, have never been lacking almost from the beginning. Hail, mistress of the nations, queen of the provinces, property of the patriarchs, mother of the prophets and apostles, womb of the faith, glory of the Christian people, whom God has allowed from the beginning to be attacked, so that you might be an occasion for bravery among strong men and thus also their salvation. Hail, promised land, who once flowing in milk and honey offered sustenance only to those who dwelled in you; now you hold forth to the entire world the means of salvation. I say that you are a good land, the best land; you received in your most fertile womb a heavenly seed from the treasury of the Father's heart and have brought forth a great harvest in the celestial progeny of martyrs. No less among the other faithful you, a fertile earth, have returned fruit in all the world thirty times, sixty times, and a hundred times more than the sowing. Joyfully satiated and richly filled by the great abundance of your sweetness, those who have seen you everywhere disseminate the memory of your plentiful sweetness and speak of the magnificence of your glory to the ends of the earth. They recount the wonders which occur in you. "Glorious things are said of thee, O city of God" (Psalm 86.3). But now from your abundant delights let us describe a few of them here in praise and glory of your name.

⎍⎍⎍⎍⎍⎍⎍⎍⎍⎍⎍⎍⎍⎍⎍⎍⎍⎍⎍⎍⎍⎍⎍⎍⎍⎍

50. The Legend of St. George, according to Jacobus de Voragine

The great patron of western chivalry, and a model for knights over centuries, was St. George of Cappadocia. According to an uncertain and confused tradition, which has led the Catholic Church today no longer to regard him as a historical figure, he lived and died under the emperor Diocletian (284–305). The story of his battle with the dragon closely resembles the pagan myth concerning the hero Perseus and the maiden Andromeda, and represents an example of the survival of pagan lore under a Christian veneer. Both Gregory of Tours in the sixth century and Bede the Venerable in the eighth mention his cult in the West. Under Edward III, he became patron of England; he was also patron of Portugal and one of the spiritual guardians of Genoa and Venice. The following version of his life, translated by D. Herlihy, is taken from the *Golden Legend* of Jacobus of Voragine (written *ca.* 1255), the most popular collection of hagiographical tales produced in the Middle Ages. The Latin text may be found in Jacobus a Voragine, *Legenda Aurea*, ed. T. Graesse (3d ed.; Vratislav, 1890), pp. 259–64.

Concerning St. George

George, the tribune, born of a family from Cappadocia, came once to the province of Lybia to a city which is called Silena. Near the city, in a swamp similar to the sea, dwelled a poisonous dragon who often turned to flight the people who came against him in arms. Approaching the walls of the city, he killed by his breath many of its inhabitants. Compelled by this, the citizens daily offered to him two sheep in order to cultivate his favor. If no offering was made, he attacked the walls of the city and so poisoned the air that many died. Soon the supply of sheep had almost been exhausted. Because the citizens did not possess large numbers of sheep, they took council, and thereafter every day they offered a sheep together with a human being. The sons and daughters of all the persons were therefore surrendered by lot, and the lot spared no one. When nearly all the sons and daughters had been consumed, the lot fell upon the only daughter of the king, and she was seized and destined for the dragon. Then the saddened king said, "Take gold and silver and half my kingdom, but give me back my daughter, lest she die so cruel a death."

The people answered him in anger, "You, O king, made this edict, and now all our children are dead. Do you wish to save your daughter? Unless you require of your daughter what you have required of others, we shall burn you and your palace."

The king, hearing this, began to weep for his daughter with these words, "Woe is me, my sweetest daughter, what shall I do for you? Or what shall I say? When now shall I see your wedding?"

Turning to the people, he said, "I ask that you give to me a delay of eight days in order that I may mourn for my daughter." The people granted it, but at the end of the eight days they returned in anger and said to him: "Why do you destroy our people for your daughter? Do you not see that we all shall die by the breath of the dragon?"

Then the king saw that he could not save his daughter. He dressed her in royal robes, and embracing her with tears, he said: "Woe is me, my sweetest daughter. I once hoped to nourish the sons born of you in my royal lap. And now you are departing in order to be eaten by the dragon. Woe is me, my sweetest daughter, I had hoped to invite princes to your wedding, to decorate the palace with pearls, to hear drums and organs, and now you depart in order to be eaten by the dragon."

Kissing her, he sent her away with the words, "Would, my daughter, that I could have died before you, rather than to lose you so."

Then she fell at the feet of her father and asked from him his blessing. When her father had blessed her amid tears, she went to the lake.

By chance the blessed George, who was passing by, saw her there weeping and asked her what was the matter. She answered him: "Good young man, quickly mount your horse and flee, lest you too should die equally with me."

George said to her, "Have no fear, daughter, and tell me, what are you asking here in the sight of all the people?"

She said, "I see, good young man, that you have a magnificent heart, but do you wish to die with me? Flee, quickly."

George responded, "I shall not depart before you have informed me what is the matter."

When, therefore, she had told him everything, George said, "Daughter, do not fear, for I shall help you in the name of Christ."

"Good knight," she said, "you must make haste to save yourself lest you perish with me. It is enough that I die alone, for you cannot save me and shall die with me."

As she said these things, behold, the dragon lifted his head from the water. The girl, seized with terror, said, "Flee, good lord, flee quickly!" Then George, mounting his horse and arming himself with the sign of the cross, bravely rode against the dragon coming toward him. Brandishing his lance vigorously and commending himself to God, he gravely wounded the dragon and threw him onto the earth. He said to the girl, "Put your girdle around the neck of the dragon and do not fear, my daughter." When she did this, the dragon followed her like the gentlest puppy.

When, therefore, she led him into the city, the people who saw this began to flee to the mountains and the hills, saying, "Woe to us, for we shall all perish."

Then blessed George restrained them, saying, "Do not fear; it is for this reason that the Lord has sent me to you, so that I might free you from the persecution of the dragon. Only believe in Christ and let each of you be baptized, and I shall kill the dragon."

Then the king and all the people were baptized. Finally, George drew his sword and killed the dragon. He ordered that it be dragged outside of the city. Then four pairs of oxen pulled the dragon forth to a large field. On that day twenty thousand persons were baptized, not counting children and women. The king built a church of marvelous size in honor of the blessed Mary and of blessed George. From its altar a living stream gushed forth; to drink from it cured all the sick people. The king offered immeasurable wealth to blessed George, but he refused it and ordered that it be distributed among the poor. Then George briefly instructed the king concerning the four duties—to take care of the churches of God, to honor the priests, to attend divine services faithfully, and always to remember the poor. Having kissed the king, he left those regions.

In some books it is stated that when the dragon came to eat the girl, George armed himself with the sign of the cross and killed the attacking dragon.

At that time, there reigned Diocletian and Maximian who through the governor Dacian subjected Christians to intense persecution, so much so that in a single month twelve thousand received the crown of martyrdom. Among the great number of those tortured were many Christians who weakened and sacrificed to the idols. When George saw this, he was touched with great sorrow. He distributed his possessions among the poor and, casting aside his knightly garments, put on the clothing of the Christians. He thrust himself into the midst of the tyrants and said, "All the gods of the pagans are devils. The Lord made the heavens."

The angered governor replied, "By what presumption do you dare to call our gods demons? Tell me, who are you and what is your name?"

The saint replied, "My name is George and I come from a noble family of Cappadocia. With the help of Christ, I have come to Palestine. I have abandoned all things so that I might more freely serve the God of heaven."

When the governor was unable to bend George to his will, he ordered that he be fixed to a cross and that his body be torn limb from limb by iron claws. He also ordered that burning torches be applied to his body in such a way as to disembowel him. His wounds were also to be rubbed with salt. That same night, the Lord appeared to George in a great light and comforted him sweetly. By this sweet vision and conversation he was so strengthened that he thought naught of his torments.

When Dacian saw that he could not break George by tortures, he summoned a magician and said to him, "The Christians by their magical arts laugh at tortures and count sacrifices to our gods as nothing." The magician answered, "If I am unable to overcome his spells, I shall willingly lose my head." He therefore mixed poison with wine by means of his magical spells, while invoking the names of his gods. He gave it to George to drink. The man of God made the sign of the cross and drank the potion, without suffering the slightest ill. Again the magician concocted an even stronger potion of poison, which the man of God, making the sign of the cross, once more drank without suffering any harm. The magician, when he saw this, fell at George's feet. In tears he asked forgiveness and requested to become a Christian. The judge at once ordered his head chopped off. The following day he commanded that George be placed on a wheel, set all around with blades sharpened on both sides. But the wheel at once broke and George was found to be entirely uninjured. Then the maddened governor had him thrown into a cauldron with molten lead. But George, after having made the sign of the cross, entered it, and by the power of God began to feel in it as if he were warmed in a bath.

Dacian, seeing this, thought that he would seduce with honeyed words the one whom he was unable to overcome by tortures. He addressed him with these words, "You see, my dear son George, how merciful are our gods, who have so patiently put up with your blasphemies. They are no less ready to favor you, if you are willing to turn to them. Most dear son, do therefore what I ask, and, abandoning your false law, sacrifice to our gods so that you may obtain great honors from them and from me."

Smiling, George answered him, "Why did you not from the beginning persuade me with soft words rather than with torments? Behold, I am ready to do what you wish."

Dacian, fooled by this agreement, was filled with joy. Through a herald he ordered that all the people should gather in order to see George, who had resisted for so long, finally submit and offer sacrifice. The entire town was infused with joy, and when George entered the temple in order to sacrifice to the idols, all gathered there rejoicing. But George knelt down and prayed our Lord to destroy the temple with its idols and allow nothing to be preserved of it, both for His own glory and for the conversion of the people. Immediately, fire descended from heaven and burned up the temple, the idols, and the priests. The earth opened up and swallowed all their remains. St. Ambrose exclaimed concerning this, in his preface, "George, the most faithful knight of Christ, when the profession of Christian belief was hidden in silence, alone among the Christians bravely confessed the Son of God. God's grace gave him such steadfastness that he spurned the commands of tyrannical authority and did not fear the tortures of countless sufferings. O happy and glorious fighter for the Lord! The enticing promise of the earthly kingdom not only did not sway him, but fooling his persecutor, he cast down their false gods into the abyss."

When Dacian heard this, he had George brought before him and said, "What is your wickedness, O most evil of men, that you have committed such a crime?"

St. George said, "Do you not believe that it is so? Come with me and you shall see me sacrifice again."

Dacian answered him, "I see all too well your trickery. You want to destroy me as you did my temple and my gods."

And George answered, "Tell me, unhappy man, how will your gods, who were unable to help themselves, be able to help you?"

The maddened ruler said to Alexandria, his wife, "I am dying, for I am convinced that this man has overcome me."

His wife said to him, "Cruel and murderous tyrant, have I not implored you often not to persecute the Christians? For their God fights for them. Know that I also wish to become a Christian."

The astounded ruler said, "Oh, what sorrow! You also have

been seduced!" Then he had her hanged by the hair and cruelly beaten with whips. While they were beating her, she said to George, "George, light of truth, where do you think I, who have never received baptism, shall go?"

George answered her, "Daughter, have no fear. The blood which you shed shall be considered your baptism and your crown." Then she, praying to the Lord, gave up her spirit. St. Ambrose confirms this in his preface with the words, "The queen of the Persians, condemned by her cruel husband, before she had received the grace of baptism merited the palm of her glorious passion. Therefore, we cannot doubt that the rosy tide of her flowing blood allowed her to enter the locked gates of heaven and to possess the heavenly kingdom."

The following day George was sentenced to be dragged through the entire city. They then cut off his head. Still he prayed to the Lord that whoever might ask George's help might obtain the fulfillment of his request. The divine voice came to him, saying that it would be as he had prayed. After he finished his prayer, he consummated his martyrdom with the loss of his head under Diocletian and Maximian, who began to rule about the year 287. When Dacian returned to his palace from the place where George had been executed, lightning struck and pulverized him together with his ministers.

Gregory of Tours relates that when several persons who were carrying the relics of St. George stayed overnight in a certain oratory, in the morning they were by no means able to move the reliquary until they had left a particle of the relics there.

The history of Antioch relates that when the Christians were besieging Jerusalem, a handsome young man appeared to a certain priest. He announced that he was St. George, the leader of the Christians, and told him that they should carry his relics with them into Jerusalem and he would be with them. When they were besieging Jerusalem and did not dare to mount the scaling ladders against the resistance of the Saracens, blessed George, dressed in white armor and a red cross, appeared to them and guaranteed that if they ascended after him, they would be masters of the city. Inspired by this, they captured the city and massacred the Saracens.

ாாாாாாாாாாாாாாாாாாாாாாாாாாா

51. The *Book on the Order of Chivalry*
by Raymond Lull

Raymond Lull, poet, alchemist, theologian, mystic, and missionary, was born about 1235 at Palma in Majorca and spent his youth at the court of James II of Aragon. In 1266 he underwent a religious conversion and devoted the rest of his long life, until his martyrdom in 1315, to missionary work among the Saracens of North Africa. He learned Arabic and wrote in that language and in his native Catalan an enormous number of works, which one scholar has estimated at 486. Among them was in its Catalan title the *Libre del Orde de Cauayleria*, which Lull wrote probably about 1280, and for which he made use of his own experiences as a young courtier. The work was soon translated into Latin, and French versions of it, as shown by the number of surviving manuscripts, enjoyed a wide popularity. William Caxton translated the work from French into English and printed it about 1484. The English version is longer than the original Catalan because of the inclusion of illustrative materials originally made by the French. But it faithfully preserves the spirit of the original text and shows its continuing strong appeal. Caxton added a final "exhortation to the knights of England," which provides us with a rare example of the original prose and sentiments of the great English printer.

Lull's disquisition owed its remarkable popularity to its comprehensiveness and to the wealth of learning and imagery it contains. It remains still today probably the best single contemporary introduction to the ideals which guided, or were supposed to guide, the chivalry of the Middle Ages.

The following version of the *Book* is based upon Caxton's edition of *ca.* 1484. The present editor has, however, in the interest of easier comprehension, modernized the spellings, simplified many sentences, and paraphrased some of the more difficult passages. He hopes that the text will therefore be more easily understood and that it will preserve at the same time some of the stateliness of Caxton's original translation. Caxton's text has been edited and reprinted in *The Book of the Ordre of chyvalry translated and printed by William Caxton*, ed. Alfred T. P. Byles (Early English Text Society: London, 1926).

Here begins the Table of this present book entitled the Book
of the Order of Chivalry or Knighthood

To the praising and divine glory of God, Who is Lord and sovereign King above and over all things celestial and worldly, we begin this book of the order of chivalry in order to show that just as God the Prince Almighty reigns above the seven planets that run across the heavens and have power and dominion in governing and ordaining the terrestrial and earthly bodies, so ought the kings, princes, and great lords to have power and dominion over the knights. And the knights similarly ought to have power and domination over the common people. And this book contains eight chapters.

The First Chapter says how a knight, who had become a hermit, devised for a squire the rule and order of chivalry.

The Second concerns the origins of chivalry.

The Third concerns the office of chivalry.

The Fourth concerns the examination that ought to be made of the squire when he wishes to enter into the order of chivalry.

The Sixth concerns the meaning of the arms belonging to a knight, all by order.

The Seventh concerns the customs that appertain to a knight.

The Eighth concerns the honor that ought to be done to a knight.

Thus ends the table of the book of chivalry.

Hereafter follows the matter and tenor of this same book.

1. The first chapter tells how a good hermit devised for a
squire the rule and order of chivalry

There was a country in which it happened that a wise knight long had maintained the order of chivalry. By the strength and nobility of his high spirit and wisdom and by risking his body, he had sustained just wars and tournaments, and in many battles had won many noble and glorious victories. Because he saw and thought in his spirit that he might not live long, as one who for a long time had been by course of nature close to his end, he chose for himself a hermitage. For nature failed him with age; and he had no power or manliness to use arms as he was wont to do. Thus he left his inheritances and all his riches to his children, and he made his habitation or dwelling place in a great wood abounding in waters and in great high trees, bearing fruits of diverse types. He fled the world because of the weakness of his body, in which he was fallen by old age, lest he dishonor that which in honorable and adventurous deeds he had a long time honored. The same knight, thinking about death, and remembering the departure from this world into that other, also thought of the redoubtable sentence of our Lord, which he would face at the Day of Judgment.

In one of the parts of the same wood was a fair meadow, in which a tree, well laden and charged with fruit, grew during the time that the knight lived in the forest. Under the same tree was a very fair and clear fountain that watered and moistened all the meadow. Here the knight was accustomed to come every day to pray and adore God Almighty, to Whom he rendered thanksgiving for the honor that He had done to him in this world all the days of his life.

In that time it happened that at the beginning of a great winter a noble and wise king, full of good customs, sent for many nobles, in order to hold a great court. Because this court had great renown, it happened that a squire bestirred himself to go there with the intention that there he should be made a knight. Thus, as he went all alone riding upon his palfrey, it happened that for the exertion that he had sustained from riding, he went to sleep upon his horse. Meanwhile, as he rode so sleeping, his palfrey turned from the right way and entered into the forest, where the knight hermit dwelled. The squire's horse went so far that he came to the fountain at the same time that the knight who dwelled in the wood arrived to do his penance, to pray to God, and to scorn the vanities of this world, just as he was accustomed to do every day. When he saw the squire come, he left his prayers and sat in the meadow in the shadow of a tree and began to read in a little book that he had in his lap. When the palfrey had come to the fountain, it began to drink, and the squire who slept, feeling that his horse had stopped moving, quickly awoke. Then there came to him the knight, who was very old and had a great beard, long hair, and a thin gown, worn and ripped from excessive wear. By the penance that he daily made, it was much discolored and thin, and by the tears which he had shed, his eyes were much wasted, and he had an aspect or countenance of a very holy life. Each of them marveled at the other. For the knight who had been so long in his hermitage had

seen no man since he had left the world; and the squire marveled
much concerning how the knight had come to that place. Then the
squire descended from his palfrey and saluted the knight; the
knight received him courteously, and afterward they sat themselves upon the grass one by the other. Before either of them spoke,
each beheld the other's face.

The knight, who knew that the squire would not speak first in
order to show reverence, spoke first and said: "Fair friend, what is
your spirit or intent, and whither are you going, why have you
come here?" "Sire," said he, "the news is spread through distant
lands that a very wise and noble king has summoned a general
court. There he himself will be made a new knight, and afterward,
he will dub other foreign barons and private persons and will make
them new knights; and therefore I go to this court in order to be
dubbed knight. But when I was asleep from the exertion I have
sustained during the great journeys I have made, my palfrey turned
from the right way and brought me to this place."

When the knight heard knighthood and chivalry spoken of and
remembered the order of the same and that which appertains to a
knight, he heaved a great sigh and fell into great thought, remembering the honor in which chivalry had been long maintained.

While the knight thus thought, the squire asked him why he was
so pensive.

The knight answered him, "Fair son, my thought is of the order
of knighthood or chivalry, and of the greatness in which a knight is
held in maintaining the greatness and the honor of chivalry." Then
the squire prayed the knight that he would describe to him the
order and the manner in which he ought better to honor and keep
it, in high dignity, as it ought to be after the ordinance of God.
"How, son," said the knight, "do you not know what is the rule
and order of knighthood? And I marvel how you dare ask for
chivalry or knighthood before the time that you know the order.
For no knight may love the order nor that which appertains to his
order unless he knows the faults that he commits against the order
of chivalry. Nor ought any knight to make other knights unless he
himself knows the order. For he who makes a knight and cannot
show the order or the custom of chivalry to him is a disorderly
knight."

After the knight said these words to the squire who asked about
chivalry without knowing its meaning, the squire answered and

said to the knight, "Sire, if it be your pleasure, I beseech you that you will describe to me the order of chivalry. For it seems good, I think, that I should learn it because of the great desire that I have for it. According to my power, I shall follow it, if it please you to instruct, show, and teach it to me."

"Friend," said the knight, "the rule and order of chivalry is written in this little book that I hold here in my hand. In it I read and busy myself at times, to the end that it may make me remember or think about the grace and goodness that God has given and done to me in this world, because I honored and maintained with all my power the order of chivalry. For just as chivalry gives to a knight all that appertains to it, in like manner a knight ought to give all his forces in order to honor chivalry."

Then the knight delivered to the squire the little book, and when he had read therein, he understood that among a thousand persons only the knight is chosen worthy to have a more noble office than all the thousand, and he also understood by that little book the rule and order of chivalry. Then he remembered a little, and afterward said, "Ah, sire, blessed be you who have brought me in place and in time that I might have knowledge of chivalry, which I have for a long time desired, without knowing the nobility of the order or the honor in which our Lord God has set all those who are in the order of chivalry."

The knight said, "Fair son, I am an old and feeble man and may not from now on live much longer; and therefore this little book, which is made for the devotion, loyalty, and ordinance that a knight ought to have in holding his order, you shall bear with you to the court where you are going, and show to all those who would be made knights. And when you have been newly dubbed a knight, and have returned to your country, come again to this place, and let me have knowledge about those persons who have been newly made knights and have been obedient to the doctrines of chivalry." Then the knight gave to the squire his blessing, and the squire took leave of him and took the book very devoutly. Then he mounted upon his palfrey and went forth hastily to the court. When he had arrived he presented the book very graciously and politely to the noble king, and furthermore he offered that every noble man who would be in the order of chivalry might have a copy of the said book, to the end that he might see and learn the order of knighthood and chivalry.

2. The second chapter concerns the origins of chivalry
or knighthood

When charity, loyalty, truth, justice, and virtue fail in the world, then cruelty, injury, disloyalty, and falseness begin. And therefore error and trouble came into the world, in which God has created man with the intention that man know, love, fear, serve, and honor Him. At the beginning, when wickedness had come to the world, justice was restored by fear to the honor in which it was wont to be. And therefore all the people were divided into thousands, and of each thousand there was chosen a man most loyal, most strong, and of most noble spirit, and better educated and mannered than all the others. And afterward, they inquired and searched what beast was most suitable, most fair, most courageous, and most strong to sustain exertion, and most able to serve man. And because among all the beasts the people chose the horse and gave him to this same man who was so chosen among a thousand men, that man is named *chevalier*, after the horse, which is called *cheval* in French; and this man is called "knight" in English. Thus to the most noble man was given the most noble beast. It behooved after this that there should be chosen all the arms such as are most noble and suitable to battle and to defend the man from death. And these arms were given and assigned to the knight.

He who would enter into the order of chivalry must think on the noble origins of chivalry. And it behooves him that the nobility of his spirit and his good customs accord with the origins of chivalry. For if it were not so, he should be in opposition to his order and to its beginnings. And therefore it is not a suitable thing that the order of chivalry receive its enemies in honors, nor them who are contrary to its origins. Love and fear are against hate and wickedness. And therefore it behooves that the knight, by nobility of spirit and noble customs and goodness and by the so great and high honor made to him by election, by his horse, and by his arms, be loved and feared by the people, and that by love he restore charity and instruction, and by fear he restore virtue and justice. Inasmuch as a man has more wit and understanding and is of a stronger nature than a woman, so much the more may he be better than the woman. For if he were not more powerful and inclined to be better than the woman, it would follow that goodness and strength of nature were contrary to goodness of spirit and to good works. Furthermore, just as a man by his nature is more prepared to have noble spirit and to be better than the woman, in like manner he is much more inclined to be vicious than a woman. For if it were not thus, he should not be worthy to have greater merit in being good, more than the woman. Take care, squire, who would enter into the order of chivalry, what you shall do. For if you be a knight, you receive honor and the servitude that must be had to the friends of chivalry. For inasmuch as you have a more noble beginning and have more honor, so much the more are you required and bound to be good and agreeable to God and also to the people. And if you be wicked, you are an enemy of chivalry and are contrary to its commandments and honors.

So very high and so very noble is the order of chivalry that it is insufficient that knights be chosen from the most noble persons, or that the most noble beast, and the best and most noble arms, and the best only be given to them. But it behooves the knight, and it must be, that he be made lord of many men. For in dominion is there much nobility, and in servitude equivalent subjection. Therefore, if you are a vile and wicked man, by taking the order of knighthood you do great injury to all your subjects and to your fellows who are good. If you are wicked, for such villainy you deserve to be put under a serf or bondsman. And because of the nobility of knights who are good, it is unseemly and not worthy that you be called a knight.

Election or horse or arms are still not sufficient to the high honor which belongs to a knight, but it behooves that there be given to him a squire and servant who may take heed to his horse. And it behooves also that the common people labor in the lands in order to bring forth fruit and goods, whereof the knight and his beasts have their living, and that the knight rest himself and stay at his abode according to his nobility, disporting himself upon his horse in order to hunt or in other manner, according to how it shall please him, and that he take his ease and delight in things of which his men have pain and travail.

Clerics study in doctrine and science how they may learn to know God and love Him and His works, to the end that by good example they give doctrine to the lay and bestial people to know, love, serve, and do honor to God our glorious Lord. To the end that they may properly do these things, they follow and attend the schools. Just as the clerics, by honest life, by good example, and by science, have received order and office to incline the people to devotion and a good life, in like manner the knights, by nobility of spirit and by force of arms, maintain the order of chivalry and have the same order to the end that they incline the small people by fear, by which the one hesitates to do wrong to the other. The science and the school of the order of chivalry involves the knight's making his son learn to ride in his youth. For if he does not learn in his youth, he shall never learn it in his old age. The son of a knight, in the time that he is squire, should also learn to take care of horses. And it behooves him that he serve and that he be first a subject before he becomes a lord. Otherwise, he would not know the nobility of the dominion when he becomes a knight. Therefore every man who will come to knighthood ought to learn in his youth to carve at the table, to serve, to arm and dub a knight. Just as a man who wants to learn to sew or hew, in order to become a tailor or a carpenter, should have a master who can sew or hew, in like manner it behooves that a noble man who loves the order of chivalry and wants to become a knight have first a master who is a knight. Just as it is unsuitable for a man who wants to learn to sew to study sewing from a carpenter, it is similarly unsuitable for a squire to learn the order and the nobility of chivalry from any man other than a knight. So very high and honored is the order of chivalry that it is not sufficient for a squire just to care for the horse and learn to serve a knight, and to go with him to tournaments and battles. But it is necessary that there be held for him a school of the order of knighthood, and that the science be written in books, and that the art be shown and read in such manner as other sciences are read, and that the sons of knights learn first the science that appertains to the order of chivalry, and that after they are squires they ride through diverse countries with the knights. If there were no error in the clergy and in the knights, there would scarcely be any in other people. For from the clergy the people should learn devotion and love of God. And from the knights they should learn to fear to do wrong, commit treason, and cause strife one against another. Since the clerics have masters and doctrine and go to schools to learn, and since there are so many sciences that they are written and set forth in doctrine, great wrong is done to the order of knighthood because it is not a science written and read in schools as the other sciences. And therefore he who made this book beseeches the noble king and all the noble company of noble knights

who are in this court assembled in the honor of chivalry that it may
be amended of the wrong that is done to it and that satisfaction be
done.

3. Of the office that appertains to a knight

The office of a knight is the end and the beginning, wherefore
began the order of chivalry. If a knight does not use his office, he is
opposed to his order and to the principles of chivalry, as was said
before. Because of such opposition, he is not a true knight, although he bears the name, for such a knight is more vile than the
smith or the carpenter who performs his office as he ought to do
and has learned it.

The office of a knight is to maintain and defend the holy Catholic faith, according to which God the Father sent His Son into the
world to take human flesh in the glorious Virgin our Lady Saint
Mary. And to honor and multiply the faith he suffered in this
world many travails, indignities, and agonizing death. As our Lord
God has chosen the clergy to uphold the holy Catholic faith with
scripture and reason against the wicked and the unbelievers, in like
manner the God of glory has chosen knights in order that by force
of arms they may vanquish the wicked who daily labor to destroy
the holy Church. Such knights God holds for His friends, honored
in this world and in that other, when they keep and uphold the
faith, by which we expect to be saved. The knight who has no
faith and uses no faith and is opposed to those who uphold it
resembles the understanding of a man to whom God has given
reason and who uses the opposite. He who has faith and is opposed
to faith and yet wants to be saved acts against himself. For his will
accords with wickedness, which is contrary to faith and to salvation. By the same wickedness, a man is condemned to unlimited and
lasting torments.

Many there are who have offices which God has given to them
in this world, to the end that by them He should be served and
honored. But the most noble and the most honorable offices that
exist are the offices of the clergy and the knights. And therefore
the greatest friendship that should be in this world ought to be
between the knights and the clergy. Just as clerics are not directed
by their status to be against the order of chivalry, so also knights,
who are bound to love and hold the order of chivalry, do not
support by the order of chivalry those who are opposed to the

clergy. The order is not given to a man so that he love his order only, but he ought to love the other orders. For to love one order and to hate another is not at all to love order. God has given no order which is opposed to another order. The religious person who loves his own order so little that he is enemy of another order does not follow or pursue the rule of the order; even so a knight does not love the office of a knight when he so much loves and praises his own order that he despises and hates another order. For if a knight loved the order of chivalry and destroyed some other order, it would seem that the order would be opposed to God, which cannot be, since He has established order.

So very noble is chivalry that every knight ought to be governor of a great country or land. But there are so many knights that the land may not be sufficient to grant one knight lordship over all things. The emperor ought to be a knight and lord of all the knights. But because the emperor may not by himself govern all knights, it behooves that he have under him kings who are knights, to the end that they aid and help in upholding the order of chivalry. And the kings ought to have under them dukes, earls, viscounts, and other lords. Under the barons ought to be knights, who ought to govern themselves after the ordinance of the barons, who are in the high degree of chivalry named before, in order to show the excellence, dominion, power, and wisdom of our glorious Lord God Who is one only God (in Trinity) and can and may govern all things. Therefore it is not a suitable thing for one knight by himself to govern all the people of this world. For if one knight alone might do so, the dominion, power, and wisdom of God would not be so well manifest. And therefore, in order to govern all the peoples who are in the world, God wills that there be many knights, of whom he is governor only, as it has been said at the beginning. Therefore, kings and princes who make provosts and bailiffs of persons other than knights act against the office of chivalry. For the knight is more worthy to have dominion over the people than any other man, and because of the honor of his office greater honor ought to be granted to him than to any other man who has not so honorable an office. Because of the honor that he receives of his order, he has nobility of heart, and by nobility of spirit he is less inclined to do a villainous act or deed than another man.

The office of a knight is to uphold and defend his worldly or earthly lord, for neither a king nor any high baron has the power to maintain righteousness in his men without aid and help. If any man acts against the commandment of his king or prince, it behooves that the knights aid their lord, who is but a man only as another is. Therefore, the evil knight whose first priority is to help a man who would put down his lord from the dominion that he ought to have over him follows not the office by which he is called a knight.

Justice ought to be upheld and kept by the knights, for just as the judges have the office to judge, in like manner the knights have the office to protect them from violence in exercising the act of justice. If it might be that chivalry and clerical status come together in such a manner that knights should become learned, so that by science they were sufficient to be judges, no office should be so suitable to a judge as chivalry. For he by whom justice is best upheld is more suitable to be a judge than any other.

Knights ought to take chargers to joust and to go to tournaments, to hold open table, and to hunt deer, boars, and other wild beasts, for in doing these things the knights exercise themselves at arms, in order to uphold the order of knighthood. To disdain and to leave that custom for which the knight is most prepared to use his office is only to despise the order. And thus, as all the aforesaid things appertain to a knight in regard to his body, in like manner justice, wisdom, charity, loyalty, truth, humility, strength, hope, quickness, and all other similar virtues appertain to a knight in regard to his soul. Therefore, the knight who uses the things that appertain to the order of chivalry in regard to his body, but has none of these virtues that appertain to chivalry in regard to his soul, is not the friend of the order of knighthood. For if he were to separate the above virtues, saying that they do not appertain to the soul and to the order of chivalry together, it would mean that the body and chivalry were opposed to the soul and these virtues, and that is false.

The office of a knight is to maintain the land, for because of the fear that the common people have of the knights, they labor and cultivate the earth, out of terror lest they be destroyed. And out of fear of the knights they respect the kings, princes, and lords by whom the knights have their power. But the wicked knight who does not aid his earthly lord and natural country against another prince is a knight without office. He is like faith without works and like disbelief which is against the faith. Then if any knight were to follow the office of chivalry in turning himself away and not in aiding his lord, such a knight and his order would do wrong against that knight who fights to the death for justice, in order to uphold and defend his lord. There is no duty, however common, the performance of which is assured. For if that which is done might not be defeated, that would be a thing like to God, Who is not nor may not be defeated or destroyed. Because the office is made and ordained of God and is upheld by them who love the order of chivalry, for this reason the wicked knight who does not love the order of chivalry defeats the knight in himself. However, the earl, king, or prince who defeats in himself the order of chivalry defeats it not only in himself but he defeats it in the knights who are put under him, who, because of the wicked example of their lord, do that which does not appertain to a knight, so that by disloyal flattery they may be loved by the lord. For this reason wicked princes are not only opposed to the order and office of chivalry in their persons, but they are also opposed to chivalry in those who are in submission to them, in whom they defeat the order of chivalry. If to cast a knight out of chivalry is great cruelty and great wickedness, it is a much greater fault to cast many out of chivalry. A noble prince or high baron may have at his court or in his company wicked knights, false men and traitors, who never cease to advise him that he practice wickedness, strife, treasons, and extortions on his true subjects. If the good prince by the strength of his noble spirit and by the great love and loyalty which he has for chivalry surmounts, vanquishes, and destroys them lest in himself he destroy chivalry, such a lord has within himself very great strength of spirit and great nobility. He is a great friend of chivalry when he takes vengeance on such enemies who would take from him and pluck away the good and honor of chivalry and corrupt his noble spirit.

If chivalry existed in strength of body more than in strength of spirit, the order of chivalry would accord more with the body than with the soul. If it were so, the body would be more noble than the soul. But that is openly false. Nobility of spirit cannot be vanquished by man—and when it is in its full strength, it cannot be surmounted by all the men who exist. When a body is easily taken and vanquished by another, it well appears that the spirit of man is stronger and nobler than his body. Sometimes when a knight is in

battle with his lord, for lack of courage he flees from the battle
when his aid is needed; he who dreads the torment or peril of his
body more than that of his spirit, and does not use the office of
chivalry, is neither a servant nor obedient to other honors, but is
against the order of chivalry, which was begun by nobility of
spirit.

If the lesser nobility of spirit suited the order of chivalry better
than greater nobility, sloth of heart and cowardice against bravery
and against strength of spirit would suit chivalry. If such were the
case, sloth and cowardice would be the office of a knight, and
bravery and strength of spirit would degrade the order of chivalry.
Then why is it all the opposite? Therefore a noble knight who
loves chivalry, the less help he has from his fellows, the less he has
of arms and the less to defend, so much the more it behooves him
to force himself to have the office of a knight by bravery of a
strong spirit and of noble appearance against those who are opposed to chivalry. And if he dies in order to uphold chivalry, then
he advances chivalry, in that he has the better loved and served it.
For chivalry abides nowhere so agreeably as it does in nobility
of spirit. No man honors and loves chivalry more than he who
dies in order to love and honor the order of chivalry, nor can any
act contribute to chivalry more than death.

Chivalry and bravery may not be in accord without prudence
and discretion. If foolishness and ignorance were in accord with
chivalry, prudence and discretion would be opposed to the order
of chivalry, and that is an impossible thing. By this it is openly
signified to you, knight, that you have great love for the order of
chivalry, for just as chivalry by nobility of spirit has made you
brave, so that you fear neither peril nor death in order to honor
chivalry, in like manner it behooves that the order of chivalry
make you love wisdom, by which you may love and honor order
against the disorder and failing which are in them who are wont
to pursue and follow the order of chivalry by foolishness and
ignorance and without understanding.

The office of a knight is to maintain and defend women, widows,
orphans, and men diseased and not powerful or strong. For just as
by custom and reason the greatest and most mighty help the feeble
and weak, who have recourse to the great, even so does the order of
chivalry, because it is great, honorable, and mighty. The knight
should succor and aid those who are under him and less mighty and

less honored than he. Therefore, to do wrong and violence to women, widows who have need of aid, and orphans who have need of direction, and to rob and destroy the feeble who have need of strength, and to take away from them what is given to them—these things do not accord with the order of chivalry. This is wickedness, cruelty, and tyranny. The knight who instead of these vices is full of virtues is deign and worthy to have the order of chivalry. Just as God has given eyes to the working man to see to work, even so He has given eyes to a sinner to the end that he mourn his sins; and just as God has given to the knight a heart to the end that he be bold in his nobility, so ought he to have mercy in his heart. His spirit should be inclined to the works of mercy and of pity, that is to say, to help and aid those who all in tears ask of the knights aid and mercy, those who have their hope in the knights. Knights who have no eyes by which they may see the feeble and impotent, nor the heart or mind by which they may recall the needs of pitiful and helpless people, are not worthy to be in the order of chivalry. If chivalry, which is so much an honorable office, were to rob and to destroy poor and helpless people and do wrong to good women, widows who have nothing to defend them, the knight's office then would not be virtuous—it would be vicious.

The office of a knight is to have a castle and horse in order to guard the highways and defend those who work the lands and the earth. And knights ought to have towns and cities in order to hold court for the people and to gather in one place men of many diverse crafts, who are very necessary to the ordinance of this world, to keep and maintain the life of man and of woman.

Furthermore, just as knights in order to maintain their offices are so much praised and lauded that they are lords of towns, castles, cities, and many people, they should understand that if destroying castles, cities, and towns, burning houses, hewing down trees, slaying beasts, and robbing in the highways were the work of knights, such actions would be contrary to the order of chivalry. For if this were the case, chivalry would not be well ordained, for then good ordinance and its contrary should be synonymous, and that cannot be.

The office of a knight also includes searching for thieves, robbers, and other wicked folk in order to have them punished. For just as the ax is made in order to hew and destroy evil trees, the office of a knight is established in order to punish trespassers and delinquents.

Because God and chivalry are in accord, it is inappropriate for false swearing and untruth to be in those who uphold the order of chivalry. If lechery and justice were compatible, chivalry, which accords with justice, would accord with lechery. Therefore, if chivalry and lechery accorded, chastity, which is contrary to lechery, would be against the honor of chivalry. Thus, in maintaining lechery, knights would be honoring and maintaining chivalry. But we know that lechery and justice are opposites, and chivalry is ordained in order to maintain justice.

The knight should be just and totally opposed [to lechery], consistent with the ideals by which the order of knighthood was first established. If justice and humility were incompatible, chivalry, which advocates justice, would be contrary to humility. If a knight is proud, he is in opposition to humility. Therefore, when a knight who maintains chivalry is filled with pride, he corrupts his order, which was begun by justice and humility in order to sustain the humble against the proud. If the situation has changed, those who are now knights would not be in the same order as those first knights. But all knights who are now injurious and proud, full of wickedness, are not worthy of chivalry; they ought to be reputed as naught. Where, in such persons, are humility and justice—what do they do or wherefore do they serve? And if justice and peace were opposites, chivalry, which accords with justice, would be opposed to peace. By such reasoning, those who love wars, thefts, and robberies would be knights, and those who pacify and bring accord to good people and who flee the tribulations and wickedness of the world would be evil and wicked knights.

But the high emperor God, Who sees and comprehends all, knows well that it is contrary and otherwise, for injurious felons are contrary to chivalry and to all honor. I ask you then: Who were the first knights who adapted themselves to justice and peace and pacified by justice, by force, and by strength of arms? Just as in the time in which chivalry began, the office of chivalry is to pacify and reconcile the people by force of arms. The injurious and bellicose knights who now exist [do not] maintain, but rather disrupt, the order of chivalry. There are many ways in which a knight can and should use his office.

But because we have to speak of many things, we continue as quickly as we may. At the request of the very courteous squire, loyal, truthful, and well instructed in all courtesy and honor, which for a long time the rule and order of chivalry has lacked, we have begun this book. For the love of him, and to satisfy his desire and will, we propose briefly to speak in this book in order that shortly he shall be dubbed and made a new knight.

4. Of the examining of the squire who desires to enter into the order of chivalry and knighthood

To examine a squire who desires to enter into the order of chivalry, it is suitable and it behooves him to have an examiner who is a knight and who, second only to God, loves chivalry or knighthood above all things. For some knights love a great number of knights, although they are evil and wicked, more than a small number of good [knights]. Notwithstanding this, chivalry has no regard to the multitude of number but loves only those who are full of nobility of spirit and of good instruction, as was said before. Therefore if the examiner loves a multitude of knights more than the nobility of chivalry, he is not suitable or worthy to be an examiner; but he should be required to be examined and reproved for the wrong that he has done to the high honor of chivalry. First, it behooves him to ask the squire, who desires to be a knight, if he loves and fears God. For without loving and fearing God, no man is worthy to enter into the order of chivalry. And dread makes him fear the faults by which chivalry is dishonored. Should a squire who does not fear God be made a knight, he takes honor in receiving chivalry and receives dishonor inasmuch as he receives knighthood without honoring and fearing God, Whom chivalry honors. Therefore a squire without love and fear of God is not deign or worthy to be a knight, whose function is to destroy and punish wicked men.

Suppose a knight is a robber, wicked, and a traitor. If it be true that thieves and robbers ought to be taken and delivered to death by the knights, then the knight so blemished with wicked conditions should take justice and right of himself and use his office just as he would with others. And if he will not use his office on himself as he would use it on another, it follows that he loves the order of chivalry better when applied to another than to himself. But it is not a suitable or lawful thing that a man slay himself. Therefore a

knight who is a robber and a thief ought to be taken and delivered
to death by other knights. And every knight who sustains and allows a knight to be a robber and thief, in so doing does not use his
office. For if he performed in that manner, he would then act
against his office. Therefore false men and traitors, who are not very
true knights, ought to be destoyed. If you, knight, have any evil or
sore in one of your hands, that sore or pain is nearer to your other
hand than to me or to another man. Thus every knight who may
be a traitor and robber is nearer to you who are a knight than to
me who am no knight nor of your office. The traitor whom you
tolerate is nearer and is such by your failure. And if that same evil
grieves you more than me, wherefore then do you excuse yourself
from punishing such a man who is opposed to chivalry and an
enemy of it? Those who are not knights you reprove or ought to
reprehend for their defaults.

A knight who is a thief does greater theft to the high honor of
chivalry, inasmuch as he takes away the name of a knight without
cause, than does he who takes away or steals money or other
things. For to steal or take away honor is to give evil fame and
repute and to blemish that which is worthy to have praise and
honor. For honor is worth more than gold or silver without any
comparison. First because it is said that it is a lesser failing to steal
money or things other than honor. For if it were the opposite, it
should follow that money and other things should be of more
value than honor. Second, if any traitor who slew his lord or lay
with his wife or betrayed his castle were named a knight, what
name would that man have who dies in the feat of arms to honor
and defend his lord? Third, if a knight who is a traitor be tolerated
for his fault, for what other fault could he then be reproved
and punished, since his lord does not punish him for treason? And
if his lord does not respect the order of chivalry in punishing his
traitor knight, in whom shall he respect it? And if he does not
destroy his traitor, what thing shall he destroy? And every lord
who does not take vengeance on his traitor, wherefore is he a lord
or a man of any power?

The office of a true knight is to accuse a traitor and to fight
against him, and the office of a traitor knight is to betray his calling
and to fight against a true knight. These two offices are well opposed, one against the other. For so very evil is the spirit of a
traitor knight that he may not vanquish and surmount the noble

spirit of a good knight, although sometimes by arrogance he happens to prevail in fighting. The true knight that fights for the right may not be surmounted. For if a knight, a friend of chivalry, were vanquished, that should be a pity and against the honor of chivalry. If to rob and to take away were the office of a knight, to give would be contrary to the order of chivalry. And if to give belongs to any other office, what value is there for a man to maintain this office in order to give? If to give away stolen goods belonged to chivalry, to whom would it belong to return and to restore? If a knight took away from good people that which God has given them and retained it as his possession, how would good men be defended of their right? He knows little and keeps poorly who commends his sheep to the keeping of the wolf and who puts his fair wife in the keeping of a young traitor knight and delivers his strong castle to a covetous knight.

If such a man foolishly delivers his things for keeping, how can he keep well the things of other men? Is there no knight who would gladly keep his wife from a traitor knight? Certainly I believe there is. Also, is there no covetous knight and robber who never likes to steal? Certainly, no such knights who are evil and wicked may be brought again or readmitted into the order of chivalry.

To have a fair and good harness and to know how to take command of his horse is the office of a knight. That is to say, a knight ought to know well how to act as a good master, in order that he may reprove the defaults of those whom he has commissioned to do or make any thing. And if it were the office of a knight to have a harness and no horse, it would seem that that which is and that which is not were the office of a knight. But to be and not to be are contrary things. Therefore a knight without harness cannot be, and ought not be, named a knight.

There is a commandment in our law that no Christian man should be perjured. A false oath ought also to be reproved in the order of chivalry. He who perjures himself is not worthy to be in the order of chivalry.

A squire who has a vile disposition and wishes to be a knight wants to destroy the order that he asks for. Why does he ask for the order which he does not love and which he intends to destroy by his evil nature? And he who, by favor or otherwise, makes a knight of vile disposition, with knowledge that he be such, acts

against his order and burdens his conscience. Seek not nobility of
character in the mouth, for not every mouth says the truth. Nor
should you seek it in honorable clothing, for under many a fair
habit has been vile character full of strife and wickedness. Nor seek
it in the horse, for he cannot answer. Nor seek it in the fair garments or the fair harness, for within fair garments is often a wicked
and a cowardly heart. If you desire to find nobility of character,
ask it of faith, hope, charity, justice, strength, temperance, loyalty,
and other noble virtues. For in them is nobility of character. By
them is defended the heart of a noble knight from wickedness,
from treachery, and from the enemies of chivalry.

A new knight should be of suitable age. A squire who is too
young is not worthy to be a knight because he may not be wise
enough to have learned the things that a squire should know before
he becomes a knight. And if he becomes a knight in his infancy, he
may not remember that which he has promised to the order of
chivalry when need requires that he remember it. If the squire who
desires to be a knight is vile before he becomes a knight, he does
villainy and injury to chivalry, which is maintained by strong men
and fighters and is befouled by cowardly men and those who are
faint of heart, weak, feeble, defeated, and deserters. Just as manliness and moderation abide in the middle of two contrary extremes,
that is, haughtiness and weakness, exactly so a knight ought to be
made a knight and be trained at a suitable age, so that he will remain manly to the end. Otherwise, manliness and chivalry would
be contraries. And if they are contraries in you, a squire who has
negligently put off becoming a knight, why then do you wish to
be in the order of knighthood or chivalry?

If by beauty of fashion, or by a fair, great, and well-adorned
body, or by fair hair, by looks or fastidious grooming, and by
other charms a squire should be dubbed a knight, you may make
knights of villains and of people of little lineage, low and vile.
And if you made them you would dishonor and scorn your own
lineage. You would lessen and cheapen the nobility which God
has given more to man than to woman. By such criteria you might
choose women to be knights, for they often have mirrors in their
hands. In so doing, you would diminish and make low the order
of chivalry, for any vile woman or any villain in heart might be
granted the very high honor of the order of chivalry.

Peerage and chivalry go together. For peerage is nothing but honor anciently recognized, and chivalry is an order that has endured from the time it was begun until the present time. Because peerage and chivalry go together, if you make a knight of someone who is not of the peerage, you cause chivalry to be contrary to peerage. By such reasoning, he whom you make a knight is contrary to peerage and to chivalry. If you want to uphold the order of chivalry, you may not have so much power that you make a man of vile character into a knight. In trees and in beasts nature honors corporal nature, but man has nobility because of the reasonable soul which is present only in the human heart; therefore nature has granted greater virtue to the human body than to the bestial body. In the same fashion, the order of chivalry is more suitable and much more fitting to a gentle heart replenished with all virtues than to a vile man of evil life. If it were otherwise, it would ensue that chivalry agrees with the nature of the body better than to the virtue of the soul, and that is false. For it agrees with the soul better than with the body. Nobility of character belongs to chivalry.

When examining a squire who desires to be a knight, it is appropriate to inquire as to his customs and manners. For evil answers provide occasions to put the wicked knights out of the order of chivalry. It is an unsuitable thing for a squire who is wicked to be made a knight, and for him to enter into the order from which he will have to be expelled because of his wicked deeds and disagreeable customs. For chivalry casts out of its order all the enemies of honor and receives those who have worth and maintain honesty. If it were not so, chivalry might as a result be destroyed in vileness and might not be repaired or restored to nobility. And that is false. Therefore you, knights, who examine the squire are bound to search more strongly for nobility and worthiness in a squire than in any other person.

You, knights, who have the office to examine a squire who desires to enter into the order of chivalry, ought to know for what intention the squire wishes to live or to be honored, whether he does not wish to honor chivalry and those who honor it. And if it appears that for [selfish] cause he seeks to be a knight, know that he is not worthy to be made knight in order to have the order. Just as the intention is false in clerics who by simony are elevated to be prelates, even so an evil squire falsifies and sets his will and intention against the order of chivalry. And if a cleric have simony, it is opposed to his office as prelate. Even so a squire who has false intention in the office of chivalry is against the order of chivalry, whatsoever he does. A squire who desires chivalry ought to know the great charge and the perils that are prepared for those who want to have chivalry and maintain it. A knight ought to fear the blame of the people and his dishonor more than the peril of death. And he ought to bear greater suffering in his spirit than hunger or thirst, heat or cold, may give to his body. Therefore all such perils ought to be shown and told to the squire before ever he be dubbed or made knight.

Chivalry cannot be maintained without a harness which is suitable to a knight, nor without the honorable costs and expenses which appertain to chivalry. For this reason, if a squire who is without harness and has no riches to pay his expenses be made a knight, he might perchance out of need become a robber, thief, traitor, liar, or beguiler or have some other vices which are opposed to chivalry.

A lame man or one who is too tall or too fat or who has any other bad feature of his body, because of which he is unable to perform the office of chivalry, is not suitable to be a knight. For the order of chivalry would not be honest if it received a man to bear arms who was blemished in being deformed and not mighty. So very noble and high is chivalry in its honor that a squire lame of any member, no matter how noble or rich and born of noble lineage, is not deign or worthy to be received into the order of chivalry.

Afterward, the squire who asks for chivalry ought also to be asked if he ever did any falseness or treachery which is against the order of chivalry. For such a deed he may have done and yet thought little of it; however, he is not worthy that chivalry should receive him into its order nor that he be made a fellow of those who maintain the order of chivalry. If a squire has vainglory for what he does, he is not worthy to be a knight. For vainglory is a vice which destroys and brings to naught the merits and rewards of the benefice of chivalry. A squire who is a flatterer does not accord to the order of chivalry, for a man who is a flatterer corrupts his good intention, and by such corruption the nobility that marks the character of a knight is destroyed and corrupted. A squire who is proud, evilly taught, full of villainous words and of villainous character, avaricious, a liar, untrue, slothful, a glutton, a perjurer or one who has any other similar vices does not accord with chivalry. If chivalry might receive those who are against the order, it should follow that in chivalry, order and disorder were one and the same thing. Since chivalry is known for the order of valor, therefore every squire ought to be examined before ever he be made a knight.

5. In what manner a squire ought to be received into the order of chivalry

When a squire first seeks to enter into the order of chivalry, it behooves him that he confess himself of his faults which he has done against God, and he ought to receive chivalry with the understanding that in the same he intends to serve our Lord God Who is glorious. And if he be clean from sin, he ought to receive his Savior. It is suitable to make and dub a knight on the day of some great feast, such as Christmas, Easter, Whitsundaytide, or another solemn day because by the honor of the feast many people assemble in that place where the squire ought to be dubbed knight, and God ought to be adored and prayed that He give to him grace to live well after the order of chivalry. The squire ought to fast the vigil of the same feast in honor of the saint of whom the feast is made that day, and he ought to go to the church to pray to God and ought to stay awake the night and be in his prayers and ought to hear the word of God and concerning the matter of chivalry. If, on the other hand, he hears troubadours and storytellers who speak of rottenness and sin, he will begin to dishonor chivalry.

On the morn after the feast on which he has been dubbed, it behooves him that he have a Mass sung solemnly, and the squire ought to come before the altar and offer to the priest, who holds the place of our Lord to the honor of Whom he must oblige and submit himself, to keep the honor of chivalry with all his power. On that same day a sermon ought to be preached in which are recounted and declared the twelve articles in which the holy Catholic faith is founded, the ten commandments, the seven sacraments of the Holy Church, and the other things which appertain to the faith. The squire ought very diligently to take heed and retain all these things to the end that he keep in his mind the office of chivalry touching the things that appertain to the faith.

The twelve articles are these: to believe in one God only, that is the first. And it behooves to believe that the Father, the Son, and the Holy Ghost are one God only in three Persons without end and without beginning, which make unto the fourth article. To believe that God is Creator and Maker of all things is the fifth. The sixth is to believe that God is Redeemer, that is to say that He has redeemed or bought again the human lineage from the pains of hell to which it was judged by the sin of Adam and Eve, our first father and mother. The seventh is to believe that God gave glory to those who are in heaven. These seven articles appertain to the Deity; the other following appertain to humanity, that the Son of God was born of our Lady Saint Mary. The first of the seven articles appertaining to humanity is to believe that Jesus Christ was conceived of the Holy Ghost, when St. Gabriel the Archangel saluted our Lady. The second and third is to believe that he has been crucified and died to save us. The fourth is to believe that his soul descended into hell to deliver his friends, that is to say, Adam, Abraham, and other prophets who believed in his holy coming. The fifth is to believe that he has been raised from death to life. The sixth is to believe that he has ascended into heaven the day of ascension. The seventh is to believe that Jesus Christ shall come at the Day of Judgment when all shall arise and he shall judge the good and evil and shall give to everyone pain and glory according to what he has deserved in this transitory world. It behooves all good Christian men to believe these articles, which are true witnesses of God and of His works. For without these articles no man may be saved.

The commandments of God which He gave to Moses upon the Mount of Sinai are ten. The first is that you shall adore, love, and serve only one God. You shall not perjure yourself. Make holy and sanctify Sunday. Honor your father and mother. Do not be a homicide or murderer. Do no theft or fornication. Do not bear false witness, nor covet the wife of your neighbor, nor have envy of the goods of your neighbor. To all knights it behooves to know the ten commandments that God has given.

The sacraments of the Holy Church are seven, that is to say, baptism, confirmation, the sacrament of the altar, orders, marriage, penance, and unction. By these seven sacraments we all hope to be saved. A knight is bound by his oath to honor and accomplish these seven sacraments. Therefore every knight should know well his office and the things to which he is bound, since he has received the order of knighthood. All these things said before, and of others that appertain to chivalry, the one who preaches ought to make mention in the presence of the squire, who ought to pray very devotedly that God give to him His grace and His blessing, by which he may be a good knight all the days of his life from then on.

When the preacher has said all that appertains to a knight's office, the prince or baron who will dub the squire a knight must then have in himself the virtue and order of chivalry. For if the knight who makes knights is not virtuous, how may he give that which he has not? Such a knight is in worse condition than are the plants. For the plants have power to give their natures the one to the other. Of beasts and of fowls there is also a similar and like thing. But this the knight cannot do. A knight who is evil and false will in a disorderly way multiply his order. He does wrong and villainy to chivalry. He will do that which is not a suitable thing to do, and he will defeat and blemish that by which he ought to honor chivalry. If a squire learns chivalry from a knight who is filled with such faults, the squire is not aided or maintained by the grace of our Lord, or by virtue, or by chivalry, as much as he would have been if a good and loyal knight had taught him. Such a squire is a fool, and so are all others who from such a knight similarly receive the order of chivalry.

The squire ought to kneel before the altar and lift up to God his bodily and spiritual eyes and raise his hands to heaven. And the knight ought to gird him in a sign of chastity, justice, and charity with his sword. The knight ought to kiss the squire and give him a palm in order that he remember that which he receives and promises and the great charge in which he is obligated and bound and the great honor which he receives by the order of chivalry. Afterward, when the spiritual knight, that is, the priest, and the temporal knight have done that which appertains to their office regarding the making of a new knight, the new knight ought to ride through the town and show himself to the people, in order that all men may know and see that he is newly made a knight, and that he is bound to maintain and to defend the high honor of chivalry. Because of this act, so much the more shall he hesitate to do evil. For in fear of the shame he might receive from the people who know his chivalry, he shall hold back so much the more from doing evil against the order of chivalry.

That same day it behooves him to make a great feast and to give fair gifts and great dinners, to joust and to sport and do other things which appertain to the order of chivalry and to give gifts to kings-at-arms and to heralds, as has been customary since ancient times. The lord who makes a new knight ought to give to the new knight also a present or gift. Also, the new knight ought to give gifts to his lord and to others that same day. For whosoever receives a gift so great as the order of chivalry does not honor his order if he does not give according to his powers. All these things and many others which I will not now recount because of shortness of time appertain to chivalry.

6. Of the significance of the arms of a knight

The garments with which the priest vests himself when he sings the Mass have significance which concords with his office. And the offices of priesthood and of chivalry have great concordance. Therefore, the order of chivalry requires that all the things which are necessary to a knight regarding the use of his office have some significance, for they indicate the nobility of chivalry and of its order.

To a knight is given a sword, which is made in semblance of the cross in order to signify how our Lord God vanquished in the cross the death of the human lineage, to which it was judged for the sin of our first father, Adam; and likewise a knight ought to vanquish and destroy the enemies of the cross by the sword. Chivalry means the maintaining of justice. Therefore is the sword made cutting on both sides, to signify that the knight ought with the sword to maintain chivalry and justice.

To a knight is given a spear in order to signify truth. Truth is a right and even thing. And that truth ought to go before falseness. The iron or head of the spear signifies strength, which truth ought to have over falseness. The pennon signifies that truth shows faith to all and has no dread or fear of falseness or treachery. Truth is sustained by hope and also by other things, which are signified by the spear of the knight.

The hat of steel or iron is given to the knight to signify dread of shame. A knight without dread of shame cannot be obedient to the order of chivalry. Just as dread of shame makes a man ashamed and causes him to cast down his eyes to the earth, likewise the hat of iron forbids a man to look upward on high and makes him look toward the ground and is the middle between high and low things. It covers the head of a man, which is the highest and principal member in the body of a man. Dread of shame also prohibits the knight, who has the most noble and highest office next to the office of cleric, from inclining or bowing himself to villainous and horrible deeds, and prevents nobility of spirit from abandoning him or giving him to strife, wickedness, or any evil instruction.

The hauberk signifies a castle and fortress against vices and faults. Just as a castle and fortress are closed all about, likewise a hauberk is strong and closed on all sides, signifying to a noble knight that he in his spirit ought not to enter into treason or any other vice.

Leggings of iron or leg harnesses are given to a knight in order to keep and hold surely his legs and feet from peril, to signify that a knight with iron ought not to stray, that is, he should understand with the sword, spear, and mace and other arms of iron how to take the malefactors and to punish them.

Spurs are given to a knight to signify diligence and swiftness, in order that with these two things every knight may maintain his order in the high honor which belongs to it. Just as with the spurs he pricks his horse in order to hasten him to run, even so does diligence hasten him to make preparations and to procure the harness and forsee the expenses that are necessary to a knight, to the end that he not be caught unprepared or taken suddenly.

The gorget is given to a knight to signify obedience. For every knight who is not obedient to his lord or to the order of chivalry dishonors his lord and goes out of his order. And just as the gorget surrounds or goes about the neck of a knight in order to defend it from blows and wounds, likewise obedience makes a knight to be within the commandments of his sovereign and within the order of chivalry, to the end that treason, pride, or any other vice does not corrupt the oath that the knight has made to his lord and to chivalry.

The mace is given to the knight to signify strength of spirit. For just as a mace or poleax is strong against all arms and smites on all sides, even so force or strength of character defends a knight from all vices and enforces virtues and good customs, by which knights maintain the order of chivalry in the high honor which is due and appertains to it.

The misericord, or knife with a cross, is given to a knight so that if his other arms fail him he may have recourse to the misericord or dagger. Or if he be so near to his enemy that he cannot wound or smite him with his spear or with his sword, he must come together with him and overcome him, if he can, by the force or strength of his misericord. This weapon which is named misericord shows to a knight that he ought not to trust entirely in his arms or in his strength, but he ought to have so much faith and trust in God, and to join to Him by very good works and by the very hope that he ought to have in Him, that by the help and aid of God he may vanquish his enemies and those who are against the order of chivalry.

The shield is given to the knight to signify the office of a knight. Just as the knight places his shield between himself and his enemies, even so the knight is the mean between the prince and his people. And just as the blow falls upon the shield and saves the knight, even so the knight ought to prepare himself and present his body before his lord when the lord is in peril, hurt, or taken.

Gauntlets are given to a knight to the end that he put his hands therein, in order to be safe and to receive the blows (if it should come about that his other hand armor fails him). As the knight with his gauntlets handles more surely the spear or his sword, and to show the significance of the gauntlets he lifts his hand up on high, even so ought he to lift them up in thanking God for the victory that he has had. The gauntlets also signify that he ought not to lift up his hand in making a false oath, nor handle with his hands any evil or foul or dishonest things.

The saddle in which the knight sits when he rides signifies surety of character, the charge and the great burden of chivalry. For just as the saddle makes a knight sure upon his horse, even so surety or luck, friend of chivalry, aids him. By surety are scorned many cowards, boasters, and many vain appearances which make cowardly men to appear hardy and strong of spirit. And by surety many men are held back in such manner that they dare not pass to the front in that place where noble and strong spirit ought to be and cross the path of a valiant and hardy knight.

The saddle signifies the burden of a knight. For the saddle, as we have said, holds the knight firm and sure upon his horse, so that he cannot fall or move lightly, unless he wants to. And therefore the saddle, which is so great, signifies the burden of chivalry, that the knight ought not in any way move for slight things. If it behooves him to move, he ought to have great, noble, and hardy spirit against his enemy in order to enhance the order of chivalry.

To the knight is given a horse and also a charger in order to signify nobility of spirit. And the reason that he is well horsed and high is that he may be seen from far. And that signifies that he ought to be more ready to do all that which the order of chivalry demands, more than the ordinary man.

To the horse is given a bridle, and the reins of the bridle are given into the hands of the knight, in order that the knight may at his will hold his horse and refrain him. This signifies that a knight ought to refrain his tongue and hold back from speaking foul or false words.

And also it signifies that he ought to refrain his hands, lest he give so much that he become wanting and needy, and in order that he need not beg or demand anything. Neither ought he be too hardy, but in his hardiness he should have reason and temperance. And by the reins is signified to the knight that he ought to be led wherever the order of chivalry will lead him or send him. When it shall be time of necessity to make gifts, his hands must give and spend to the measure that it appertains to his honor. He should be hardy and fear his enemies not at all, for fear weakens strength of spirit. And if a knight does contrary to all these things, his horse keeps the rule of chivalry better than he does.

The knight's horse is given a headpiece to signify that a knight ought to do feats of arms with reason. Just as the head of a horse goes before the knight, even so ought reason to go before all that a knight does. For all works without reason are vices in him. Just as the headpiece keeps and defends the head of the horse, even so reason keeps and defends a knight from blame and from shame.

The horse's armor is provided to keep and defend the horse. And it signifies that a knight ought to keep his goods and his riches in order that they might be sufficient to maintain the office of chivalry. Just as the horse is protected from blows and injuries by his armor, and without it he is in peril of death, even so a knight without temporal goods cannot maintain the honor of chivalry, nor can he be protected from evil perils. Poverty causes a man to think of strife, falsities, and treasons. For this reason, the Scriptures say, "Because of poverty many have failed."

A coat is given to a knight in significance of the great labors that a knight must suffer in order to honor chivalry. Just as the coat is above the other garments of iron and is in the rain and receives blows before the hauberk and other armor, even so is a knight chosen to sustain greater labors than any other man. All the men who are under his nobility and in his guard ought, when they have need, to have recourse to him. The knight ought to defend them according to his power. And the knights ought rather to be taken, hurt, or dead than the men who are in their guard. Because this is so, very great and large [is the burden of] chivalry; therefore are the princes and barons in such great labors in order to keep their lands and their people.

A token or a sign of arms is given to a knight in his shield and in his coat, in order that he be known in the battle, and that he be praised if he be hardy and if he do great and fair feats of arms. And if he be a coward, a false man, a scoundrel, the sign is given to him in order that he be blamed, vituperated, and reproved. The sign is also given to a knight to the end that it be known whether he is a friend or an enemy of chivalry. Wherefore every knight ought to honor his sign, that it be kept from blame, for such blame casts down the knight and puts him out of chivalry.

The banner is given to a king, a prince, a baron, and a knight bannerer, who has under him many knights, to signify that a knight ought to maintain the honor of his lord and of his land. For a knight is loved, praised, and honored by the honorable people of the kingdom of his lord. And if they dishonor their land and their lords' land, such knights are more blamed and shamed than other men. Just as for honor they should be more praised in order that in them there ought to be the honor of a prince and of the knight and of the lord, even so in their dishonor they ought to be more blamed. And by reason of their cowardice, falsehood, or treason kings and princes are more disowned than any other men.

7. Of the customs that appertain to a knight

Because of his nobility of spirit, a knight is chosen to be above all other men who are under him in servitude. Thus, nobility of customs and good rearing appertain to a knight. For nobility of spirit will not grow within the high honor of chivalry without cultivating virtues and good habits. Because this is so, it necessarily behooves to a knight to be replenished of good customs and of good instructions. Every knight ought to know the seven virtues which are the beginning and root of all good customs and are the way and path of the celestial, lasting glory. Of the seven virtues three are theological or divine, and the other four are cardinal. The theological are faith, hope, and charity. The cardinal are justice, prudence, strength, and temperance.

A knight without faith cannot have good customs in him. For by faith a man sees God and His works spiritually and believes invisible things. And by faith a man has hope, charity, and loyalty and is a servant of verity and truth. By default of faith, a man does not believe God to be a man, His works, and the things which are invisible. These a man without faith cannot understand or know. Knights are accustomed to faith; by faith they have gone into the land overseas in pilgrimage. There they proved their strength and chivalry against the enemies of the cross, and they are martyrs if they die. For they fight in order to enhance the holy Catholic faith. Also by faith do knights defend the clerics from wicked men, who by default scorn, rob, and disinherit them as much as they can.

Hope is a virtue which very strongly appertains to the office of a knight. For by the hope that he has in God, he expects to have victory in the battle; because he has more confidence in God than in his body or in his arms, he comes to prevail over his enemies. By hope the character of the knight is strengthened, and weakness and cowardice are vanquished. Hope enables knights to sustain and suffer labors and to be fortunate in the perils in which they often put themselves. Also hope enables them to suffer hunger and thirst in castles, cities, and fortresses, to the guarding of which they are assigned, and to defend themselves and the castle valiantly as much as they can. If there were no hope, a knight could not use his office. And also hope is a principal instrument with which to use the office of a knight, just as the hand of a carpenter is the principal instrument of carpentry.

A knight without charity cannot be without cruelty and evil will. And cruelty and evil will do not accord to the office of chivalry, because charity is an attribute of a knight. If a knight does not have charity for God and for his neighbor, how or in what ways can he possibly love God? And if he has no pity on poor, weak, and diseased men, how can he have mercy on men taken and vanquished who ask for mercy and do not have the power to escape and cannot find the ransom that is demanded of them for their deliverance? If in a knight there is no charity, how can he be in the order of chivalry? Charity is a virtue above other virtues, for it drives out every vice. Charity is a love which every knight ought to have in sufficient quantity to maintain his office, and charity also enables a man to bear lightly the heavy burdens of chivalry. Just as a horse without feet cannot bear the knight, even so a knight cannot without charity sustain the great charge and burden of his order. And by charity may chivalry be honored and enhanced.

If a person without a body were a man, then a man would be an invisible thing. And if he were invisible, he would not be a man or that which he is. In similar fashion, if a man without justice were a knight, justice necessarily would not exist in the form in which it now exists, or chivalry would be a thing diverse from the chivalry as it is now. And how can a knight have the principle of justice and be injurious, wishing that which does not appertain to chivalry to belong to chivalry? For chivalry and justice accord so strongly that without justice, chivalry cannot exist. An injurious knight is an enemy of justice; he defeats and casts himself out of chivalry and out of his noble order, and denies it and despises it.

The virtue of prudence is that by which a man has knowledge of good and evil. By prudence, a man has grace to be a friend of the good and an enemy to the evil. For prudence is a science by which a man has knowledge of the things that are to come by the things present. Prudence exists when by any stratagems and skills a man can eschew bodily and spiritual damages. As knights are ordained in order to put away and destroy evil—for no men put their bodies in so many perils as do knights—what thing is then more necessary to a knight than the virtue of prudence? By the customs of a knight, it is appropriate to arm himself and to fight. But that accords not so much to the office of a knight as does use of reason and understanding and ordered will. Battles are many times won more by skill, by wit, and by industry than by multitudes of people, of horses, or of good arms. For this purpose the valiant knight Judas Machabaeus made a statement to his people when he saw his enemies, who numbered six times more than his men and came in order to fight. "O my brethren," said he, "do not be in doubt that God will help us at this time. For I say to you well that victory lies not in great multitude, for therein is great confusion." By the wit and good prudence of Judas Machabaeus was the battle against his enemies won, and he obtained glorious victory. Because this is so, if you, knight, will train your son to the office of a knight in order to maintain chivalry and its noble order, make him first to train himself and to use reason and understanding. And ensure that with all his power he be a friend to good and an enemy to evil. For by such usages prudence and chivalry come together to honor the order of chivalry.

Strength is a virtue which remains and dwells in noble spirit against the seven deadly sins, because of which men go to hell to suffer and sustain grievous torments without end. These sins are gluttony, lust, avarice, pride, sloth, envy, and wrath. A knight who follows such a way enters not into the house of noble hearts, nor does he make there his abode or habitation.

Gluttony engenders weakness of body as a result of too outrageous drinking and eating. Because of too much drinking, gluttony burdens all the body with fat and engenders sloth and weakness of body which weighs upon the soul. Thus all the vices are contrary to chivalry. Therefore the strong spirit of a noble knight fights against gluttony with the aid of the abstinence, prudence, and temperance which he has.

Lust and chastity fight the one against the other. The arms with which lust makes war on chastity are youth, beauty, much drink and much meat, stylish and elegant clothing, falsehood, treason, injury and contempt of God and of His glory, doubting the pains of hell, which are infinite, and other things similar to it. Chastity and strength war and fight against lust and surmount it by remembrance of His commandments, and by remembrance and good understanding of the goods and glory that God gives to those who love, serve, and honor Him, as well as the evil and the pain prepared for those who despise and believe not in Him. By loving God well, the knight is worthy to be loved, served, and honored. Because chastity wars against lust and vanquishes it with nobility of spirit, whoever will not submit to evil or to foul thoughts will not be brought down or removed from his high honor. A knight is named chevalier because he must fight and war against vices and ought to vanquish and surmount them by force of noble and good character, so if he is a person without strength and has not the heart of a knight or has not the arms with which he ought to fight, then he is no one.

Avarice is a vice which causes a noble spirit to descend and fall down and be subjected to vile and foul things. Because they lack the strength and good character which would defend them against avarice, many are subjected and vanquished. Because of a similar lack, the character of a knight who would be strong and noble is vanquished. Thereby knights become covetous and avaricious. By their covetousness much wrong and wickedness are done, and they are serfs and bondsmen to the goods which God has abandoned and submitted to them. Strength has such a custom that it never aids its enemy or ever helps a man who does not ask for its help and aid. For so very noble and high a thing is strength of character in itself, and so much great honor is due it, that in the face of labors and perils it ought to be summoned and aid ought to be asked of it. When the knight is tempted to incline his character to avarice, which is mother and root of all evils and of treason, then he ought to have recourse and to run to truth, in which he shall never find cowardice or laxness or weakness or default of succor and of aid. For with strength a noble heart may vanquish all vices. You then, covetous knight, why do you not have a strong and noble spirit, like that of the noble character of the powerful King Alexander? Despising avarice and covetousness, he always had his hands stretched forth to give to his knights, so much that by the renown of his generosity those who were soldiers of the avaricious king who made war against him turned and came toward Alexander and confused his covetous enemy, who previously had been their master. And therefore you ought to think to the end that you be not given to villainous works and to foul thoughts by avarice, which does not accord or appertain to chivalry. For if it appertained to it, who should then deny that lechery also appertained to a knight?

Sloth is a vice by which a man is a lover of wickedness and of evil and hates goodness. By this vice, signs of damnation may be known and seen in men better than by any other vice. And by the contrary, by strength, the sign of salvation may be known in a man better than by any other virtue. Therefore whoever will overcome and surmount sloth, him it behooves that in his heart he have strength, by which he vanquishes the nature of the body, which by the sin of Adam is inclined and prepared to do evil. A man who has laziness or sloth has sorrow and anger when he knows that another man does well. And when a man does harm to himself, he who has laziness or sloth is heavy and sorrowful that the man has not more and greater [harm]. Therefore such a man has sorrow both of the good and of the evil of other men. Ire and displeasure give suffering and pain to the body and to the soul. Therefore, knight, if you want to vanquish and surmount that same vice, you ought to pray for strength, that it will arm your character against laziness, remembering that if God does good to any man, it does not necessarily follow that He ought also to do well to you. For He does not give to him all that He has, nor what He might give, nor in so giving does He take anything away from you. And therefore our God has given to us an example in the Gospel of those who labored in the vineyard. He reproved those who had worked from the morning until the evening, because they murmured that the lord of the vineyard gave as much salary and wages to those who had come at evening time as to those who had labored all the day. The lord said that he did the murmuring workers no wrong and that in his favors he might do as he wished.

Pride is the vice of inequality, to be unequal to another and not like it. A proud man will have no peer equal to him; he loves better to be the only one, not like any other. Therefore humility and strength are two virtues which love equality, and in that respect, they are against pride. If you, proud knight, want to vanquish your pride, gather within your character humility and strength. For humility without strength is nothing, nor can it hold against pride. Pride can be vanquished only by humility and strength. When you shall be armed and mounted upon your great horse, you shall perhaps be proud. But when strength and humility make you remember the reason and the intention wherefore you are a knight, you can never be proud. And if you are proud, you shall never have the strength in your character to cast out proud thoughts. But if you be beaten down from your horse in battle, taken and vanquished, you shall not be as proud then as you were before. For strength of body has vanquished and surmounts the pride of your spirit. Thus, if strength of body may vanquish and surmount the pride of your spirit, how is it that nobility is not a corporal thing? Strength and humility, which are spiritual things, are much better able to cast out pride of noble spirit.

Envy is a vice disagreeable to justice, to charity, and to generosity, which appertain to the order of chivalry. When any knight has a slothful heart and is lacking in character, when he cannot sustain or follow the order of chivalry for default of the strength which is not in his character, when he has not in himself the virtues of justice, charity, or of generosity, all that does force, violence, dishonor, and injury to chivalry. For this reason, many a knight is envious of the welfare of others and is slow to get the above-said goods by strength of arms and is full of evil spirit, inclined and ready to take away other men's things that are not his and of which he was never in possession. Therefore, it behooves him to think how he might make strife and falsehood in order to get riches; by such actions the order of chivalry is sometimes dishonored.

Wrath is a disturbance in the spirit and remembrance of a

wicked will. By this trouble and remembrance, it turns the spirit into forgetting or negligence, the understanding into ignorance, and the will into not caring. Because to remember, to understand, and to will are often illuminating, by which a knight may follow the way and the rule of chivalry, who will then cast out of his spirit that which troubles the understanding? In his spirit it behooves him to cultivate strength of character, charity, temperance, and patience, which have domination over wrath; they are rest and alleviation of the labors and passions which wrath gives. The greater a man's wrath, so much the more it behooves that he have strength of character, which will surmount and join with him benevolence, abstinence, charity, patience, and humility. Thus shall wrath be surmounted and evil will, ire, and impatience and the other vices be shortened and bound. When the vices are diminished and the virtues such as justice and wisdom are increased, by the greatness of justice and of wisdom the order of chivalry is the greater. We have said heretofore the manner according to which strength ought to exist in the spirit of a knight against the seven deadly sins. And we shall speak here concerning the virtue of temperance.

Temperance is the virtue which dwells in the middle of two vices; the one vice is sin by too great quantity and the other vice is sin by too little quantity. Therefore, between too much and too little there must be temperance in so reasonable a quantity that it be a virtue. If there were no virtue between the too great and the too little, there should be no mean, and that cannot be. A knight used to good customs and well instructed ought to be temperate in hardiness and bravery, in eating, in drinking, in words and expenses, and other things similar to the same. Without temperance a knight cannot maintain the order of chivalry and he cannot be in the place where virtue dwells.

It ought to be the custom and usage of a knight to hear Mass and the sermon, to adore and pray to God, and to love and fear Him. For by that custom a knight may remember the death and filth of this world and ask of God the celestial glory, and dread and fear the pains of hell. By such a habit he may accustom himself to use virtues and other things which aid in maintaining the order of chivalry. But a knight who does the contrary to this and believes in divinations and in the flying of birds acts against God and has greater faith and hope in the fancies of his head and in the works that the birds do and in the diviner than in God and in His works.

Therefore, such a knight is not agreeable to God, nor does he maintain the order of chivalry. The carpenter and the tailor and other artisans do not have the power to use their offices without the art and the manner which appertains to their offices. Since God has given discretion and reason to a knight in order that he may use his office and can maintain the rule of chivalry, if he then does not do so, he commits wrong and injury to discretion and to reason. A knight who leaves his discretion and that which reason and understanding signify and show, a knight who follows and believes the divinations of those who divine by the flight of birds and say that the bird that flies on the right side signifies contrary to the left side, a knight who thinks and believes such things, casts away the nobility of his spirit; he is like to a fool who uses neither wit nor reason, but does everything by chance. Therefore such a knight is against God; by right and reason he ought to be vanquished and surmounted by his enemy who uses reason and discretion against him and has hope in God. And if it were not thus, it should follow that the diviners—who put faith in the flight of birds and other things without reason—and the order of chivalry agree more than chivalry agrees with God, reason, discretion, hope, faith, and noble character. And that is openly false. Knights, by their false belief, give faith to diviners who say that it is an evil happening to see a woman uncovered in the morning and that a knight cannot make or do a good deed of arms the day that he sees the head of his wife or any other woman bare and uncovered. Also, just as a judge uses his office when he judges according to custom, even so a knight uses his office when he judges according to custom and when he uses reason and discretion, which are the custom of chivalry. Sometimes a judge, who should give sentence according to evidence, gives false judgment based on the flight of birds or the barking of dogs or such other similar things; even so a knight acts against his office if he behaves contrary to that which reason and discretion show to him and give witness, if he bases his judgment on what the birds do by their necessities and the way they go flying in the air at chance. Because this is so, he ought to follow reason and discretion, and act according to the significance which his arms represent, similarly to what we have said before. The things that happen by chance he ought not to take as a necessity or custom [of chivalry].

It is appropriate for a knight to be a lover of the commonweal. For by the communality of the people was chivalry founded and established. And the commonweal is greater and more necessary than individual and special good.

A knight should speak nobly and courteously; he should have a fair harness and be well clad and hold a good household and an honest house. All these things are necessary to honor chivalry. Courtesy and chivalry are in concord together. For villainous and foul works are against the order of chivalry. Familiarity and acquaintance of good people, loyalty and truth, hardiness, generosity, honesty, humility, pity, and other similar things appertain to chivalry. Just as he ought to relate all his nobility to God, even so a knight ought to relate all that from which chivalry may receive honor to those who are in its order. The customs and the good instruction which a knight applies in relation to his horse do not maintain the order of chivalry as much as the good customs and good instructions that he applies to himself and to his children. Chivalry is not only in the horse or in the arms; it is largely in the knight who instructs and teaches his horse well and accustoms himself and his son to good teaching and virtuous works. And so a wicked knight who teaches himself and his son evil instructions and doctrines tries to make of himself and of his sons beasts and of his horse a knight.

8. Of the honor that ought to be done to a knight

God has honored a knight, and all the people honor him, just as is recounted in this book. And chivalry is an honorable office above all offices, orders, and estates of the world, excepting the order of priesthood, which appertains to the holy sacrifice of the altar. The order of chivalry is very necessary to the government of the world, as we have before mentioned. Therefore chivalry, for all these reasons and many others, ought to be honored by the people. If nobility of chivalry is not present in a king or a prince because they lack what they should have and have not either the virtues or the honor that appertain to the order of chivalry, they are not worthy to be kings or princes or lords of countries. For chivalry ought to be honored in them. Knights ought then to be honored by kings and great barons. Just as, by the knights, the high barons are honored above the mean people, even so the kings and the high barons ought to hold the knights above the other people.

Chivalry and privilege accord together. And the privilege and lordship of the king or of the prince accord to the knights. The knight must be free and privileged because the king is his lord. Therefore it behooves that the honor of a king or of a prince or of every baron and lord of a land be in accord with the honor of a knight, in such manner that the king or prince be lord and the knight be honored. It is appropriate to the honor of a knight that he be loved for his bounty and goodness, and that he be feared and dreaded for his strength, and that he be petitioned for his gentleness and friendship, because he is a councilor of the king or of the prince or of any other high baron. Therefore, to despise a baron, because he is of the same nature of which every man is, is to despise all the aforesaid things for which a knight ought to be honored. Every noble baron and high lord who honors a knight and supports him in his court, in his council, and at his table, honors himself; similarly, he who honors him in battle honors himself. The lord who makes a wise knight his messenger or ambassador entrusts his dignity to a noble spirit, and the lord who multiplies honor in a knight who is in his service multiplies honor in himself. The lord who aids and maintains a knight performs his office and enforces his lordship. The lord who is friendly with a knight has friendship with chivalry.

To require folly of the wife of a knight or to incline her to wickedness is not appropriate to the honor of a knight. And the wife of a knight who has children of a serf does not honor the knight but destroys and brings to naught the ancient and noble confraternity and noble lineage of a knight. A knight also who has children of a serf woman does not honor nobility nor chivalry. Because this is so, gentleness and the honor of chivalry accord together in a knight and in a lady by virtue of marriage. And the contrary is the destruction of chivalry.

Since men who are not knights are obliged and bound to honor a knight, much more is a knight obliged and bound to honor his body in being well and nobly clad and in being well horsed and in having a fair, good, and noble harness and in being served and honored by good persons. These advantages he should enjoy more than others. The knight wishes to honor the nobility of his character, for which reason he is in the order of chivalry, and this character is disordered and dishonored when a knight puts foul thoughts, wickedness, and treasons in himself and casts out of his spirit noble thoughts and good meditations, which appertain to the order of chivalry; the knight who dishonors himself and his peer— that is to say, another knight—is not deign or worthy to have honor. If he were worthy, wrong should be done to the knight who holds and maintains the attributes of chivalry in regard to himself and to that other knight. Because chivalry has its dwelling in the noble spirit of a knight, no man can honor or dishonor chivalry more than a knight. Many are the honors and the reverences which ought to be done to a knight. And the greater the knight is, the more he is charged and bound to honor chivalry.

In this book we have spoken shortly enough of the order of chivalry. Therefore we now make here an end, to the honor and praise of God our glorious Lord and of our Lady Saint Mary, who be blessed for ever and ever. Amen.

Here ends the book of the order of chivalry, which book is translated out of French into English at the request of a gentle and noble squire by me, William Caxton, dwelling at Westminster beside London in the best manner that God has allowed me, and according to the copy which the said squire delivered to me. This book is not requisite for every common man to have, but to noble gentlemen who by their virtue intend to come and enter into the noble order of chivalry, which in these late days has not been used according to this book heretofore written but forgotten, and the practice of chivalry not used, honored, or exercised as it has been in ancient times. At that time the noble acts of the knights of England who used chivalry were renowned through the universal world. That is to say, before the Incarnation of Jesus Christ, where were there ever any like to Brenius and Belynus, who from Great Britain, now called England, conquered many realms and lands unto Rome and far beyond? Their noble acts remain in the old histories of the Romans. And since the Incarnation of Our Lord, behold that noble king of Britain, King Arthur, with all the noble knights of the Round Table, whose noble acts and noble chivalry of his knights occupy so many large volumes that it is as a world or as a thing incredible to believe.

O you knights of England, where is the custom and usage of noble chivalry which was used in those days? What do you now but go to the baths and play at dice? And some not well advised do not use honest and good rule, [which is] against all order of knighthood. Leave this and leave that, and read the noble volumes of the Holy Grail of Lancelot, of Galahad, of Tristram, of Perseforest, of Percival, of Gawain, and many more. There shall you see manhood, courtesy, and gentleness. And look in later days at the noble acts since the conquest, as in the days of King Richard

the Lionhearted, Edward the First and the Third and his noble
sons, Sir Robert Knolles, Sir John Hawkwood, Sir John Chandos,
and Sir Walter Manny. Read Froissart. And also behold that
victorious and noble king Harry the Fifth, and the captains under
him, his noble brethren the Earl of Salisbury, Montaigu and many
others whose names shine gloriously by their virtuous nobility and
acts which they did in honor of the order of chivalry. Alas, what
do you do but sleep and take ease, and are all disordered from
chivalry. I would ask a question if I should not displease: How
many knights are there now in England who have the use and the
exercise of a knight, that is to say, that he knows his horse and his
horse him, that is to say, he being ready at a point to have everything that belongs to a knight and a horse that is in accord and
broken after his hand, his armors and harness suitable and fitting,
and so forth, et cetera? I suppose a due search should be made;
there would be many found lacking, the more pity is.

I would it pleased our sovereign lord that twice or thrice in a
year or at the least once he would have the justice of the peace cry,
to the end that every knight should have a horse and harness, and
also the use and craft of a knight. And also to joust one against the
one, or two against two, and the best to have a prize, a diamond or
jewel, such as should please the prince. This should cause gentlemen to resort to the ancient customs of chivalry to great fame and
renown—and also to be always ready to serve their prince when he
calls them or has need. Then let every man who is come of noble
blood and intends to come to the noble order of chivalry read this
little book and do thereafter in keeping the lore and commandments therein contained. And then I doubt not that he shall attain
to the order of chivalry et cetera.

And thus this little book I present to my redoubted natural and
most dread sovereign lord King Richard, king of England and of
France, to the end that he command this book to be had and read
to other young lords, knights, and gentlemen, within this realm,
and that the noble order of chivalry be hereafter better used and
honored than it has been in late days passed. And herein he shall do
a noble and virtuous deed. And I shall pray Almighty God for his
long life and prosperous welfare and that he may have victory over
all his enemies and after this short and transitory life to have everlasting life in heaven, where is joy and bliss, world without end.
Amen.

Index

DOCUMENTARY HISTORY OF WESTERN CIVILIZATION
Edited by Eugene C. Black and Leonard W. Levy

ANCIENT AND MEDIEVAL HISTORY OF THE WEST

Morton Smith: ANCIENT GREECE *

A. H. M. Jones: A HISTORY OF ROME THROUGH THE FIFTH CENTURY
Vol. I: The Republic
Vol. II: The Empire

Deno Geanakoplos: BYZANTINE EMPIRE *

Marshall W. Baldwin: CHRISTIANITY THROUGH THE THIRTEENTH CENTURY

Bernard Lewis: ISLAM TO 1453 *

David Herlihy: HISTORY OF FEUDALISM

William M. Bowsky: RISE OF COMMERCE AND TOWNS *

David Herlihy: MEDIEVAL CULTURE AND SOCIETY

EARLY MODERN HISTORY

Hanna H. Gray: CULTURAL HISTORY OF THE RENAISSANCE *

Florence Edler de Roover: MONEY, BANKING,
AND COMMERCE, THIRTEENTH THROUGH SIXTEENTH CENTURIES *

V. J. Parry: THE OTTOMAN EMPIRE *

Ralph E. Giesey: EVOLUTION OF THE DYNASTIC STATE *

J. H. Parry: THE EUROPEAN RECONNAISSANCE: Selected Documents

Hans J. Hillerbrand: THE PROTESTANT REFORMATION

John C. Olin: THE CATHOLIC COUNTER REFORMATION *

Orest Ranum: THE CENTURY OF LOUIS XIV *

Thomas Hegarty: RUSSIAN HISTORY THROUGH PETER THE GREAT *

Marie Boas Hall: NATURE AND NATURE'S LAWS

Barry E. Supple: HISTORY OF MERCANTILISM *

Geoffrey Symcox: IMPERIALISM, WAR, AND DIPLOMACY, 1550-1763 *

Herbert H. Rowen: THE LOW COUNTRIES *

C. A. Macartney: THE HABSBURG AND HOHENZOLLERN DYNASTIES
IN THE SEVENTEENTH AND EIGHTEENTH CENTURIES

Lester G. Crocker: THE AGE OF ENLIGHTENMENT

Robert and Elborg Forster: EUROPEAN SOCIETY IN THE EIGHTEENTH CENTURY

REVOLUTIONARY EUROPE, 1789-1848

Paul H. Beik: THE FRENCH REVOLUTION *
David L. Dowd: NAPOLEONIC ERA, 1799-1815 *
René Albrecht-Carrié: THE CONCERT OF EUROPE
John B. Halsted: ROMANTICISM
R. Max Hartwell: THE INDUSTRIAL REVOLUTION *
Mack Walker: METTERNICH'S EUROPE
Douglas Johnson: THE ASCENDANT BOURGEOISIE *
John A. Hawgood: THE REVOLUTIONS OF 1848 *

NATIONALISM, LIBERALISM, AND SOCIALISM, 1850-1914

Eugene C. Black: VICTORIAN CULTURE AND SOCIETY
Eugene C. Black: BRITISH POLITICS IN THE NINETEENTH CENTURY
Denis Mack Smith: THE MAKING OF ITALY, 1796-1870
David Thomson: FRANCE: Empire and Republic, 1850-1940
Theodore S. Hamerow: BISMARCK'S MITTELEUROPA *
Eugene O. Golob: THE AGE OF LAISSEZ FAIRE *
Roland N. Stromberg: REALISM, NATURALISM, AND SYMBOLISM:
Modes of Thought and Expression in Europe, 1848-1914
Melvin Kranzberg: SCIENCE AND TECHNOLOGY *
Jesse D. Clarkson: TSARIST RUSSIA: Catherine the Great to Nicholas II *
Philip D. Curtin: IMPERIALISM *
Massimo Salvadori: MODERN SOCIALISM

THE TWENTIETH CENTURY

Jere C. King: THE FIRST WORLD WAR *
S. Clough, T. and C. Moodie: ECONOMIC HISTORY OF EUROPE:
Twentieth Century
W. Warren Wagar: SCIENCE, FAITH, AND MAN:
European Thought Since 1914
Paul A. Gagnon: INTERNATIONALISM AND DIPLOMACY BETWEEN THE WARS, 1919-1939 *
Henry Cord Meyer: WEIMAR AND NAZI GERMANY *
Michal Vyvyan: RUSSIA FROM LENIN TO KHRUSHCHEV *
Charles F. Delzell: MEDITERRANEAN FASCISM, 1919-1945
Donald C. Watt: THE SECOND WORLD WAR *

---

* In preparation

Date Due